DOMESTIC AND COMMERCIAL OIL BURNERS

Installation and Servicing

THIRD EDITION

Charles H. Burkhardt

Executive Vice President, New England Fuel Institute, Inc.
Member, American Society of Heating, Refrigeration and Air Conditioning Engineers

McGraw-Hill Book Company

New York   St. Louis   San Francisco
London   Sydney   Toronto
Mexico   Panama

TO MY WIFE
LILLIAN

DOMESTIC AND COMMERCIAL OIL BURNERS

Library of Congress Catalog Number: 68-31659

07-009039-4

DODO 8 9 8 7 6 5 4 3

PREFACE

The first edition of *Domestic Oil Burners* was published in the spring of 1951. Now, seventeen years later, the third edition has been completed. At the time of the first publication of *Domestic Oil Burners* very few people could have predicted the growth of the oil heating industry in a period of almost two decades. Today more than 11 million oil burners operate daily for a minimum of six months a year to bring comfort to 40 million or more people. In New England alone, with only 6 per cent of the nation's population (11 million people), 2,035,000 oil burners are operating, providing 80 per cent of the population of that area with heat.

The longevity and growth of *Domestic Oil Burners* into its second and third editions, *Domestic and Commercial Oil Burners: Installation and Servicing,* is a mirror that reflects the growth of the industry over this long period of time.

The author wishes to thank those who provided assistance, encouragement, illustrations, and technical data for this third edition, especially Norton D. Saude of Honeywell, Inc. Mr. Saude expended considerable time and energy in providing complete data, information, and illustrations on the new developments in the oil-heating control field that occurred between the publishing of the second edition and the inception of the third.

Thanks and appreciation are also due the following, who provided illustrations and technical material for the third edition:

Fred Williams, White Rodgers Co.
Bert Watling, The Carlin Co.
Ralph Dennis, Boston Machine Co.
Edwin Ely Smith, H. B. Smith Co.
B. L. Soderberg and C. W. Lang, Sundstrand Hydraulics, Division of Sundstrand Corporation
W. J. Wenzell, Heating Division, Sta-Rite Industries
Charles E. Kramb, formerly of Gulf Oil Corporation
Alfred Metzger, Sun-Ray Burner Mfg. Corp.
Harry Shook, formerly of William Wallace Division, Wallace-Murray Corp.

J. E. Sackett, Service Recorder Company, Fuelometer Division

R. B. Plass, Ray Burner Company

R. C. Wright, formerly of Space Conditioning, Inc.

S. Czarnecki, Jr., Eddington Metal Specialty, Engelhard Minerals and Chemicals Corp.

James L. Kelly and Joseph Eubanks, Thermo Dynamics Corp.

Eugene O. Olson, Delavan Mfg. Co.

Harry Potter and Leo F. Pfister, Field Control Division, Conco Engineering Works, Inc.

A. Stamm, PowRmatic, Inc.

William Judd, Stewart Warner Corporation, Heating and Air Conditioning Division

Carlos Morgan, Penn Controls, Inc.

Verne Resek, Industrial Combustion, Inc.

John R. Wiles, Bacharach Instrument Co., Division American Bosch Arma Corp.

Richard Berry, McDonnell & Miller, Inc.

Charles H. Burkhardt

Other Books by the Author

Residential and Commercial Air Conditioning
Oil Burner Installation and Service Technician
Practical Baseboard Heating

CONTENTS

PART ONE

DOMESTIC AND COMMERCIAL OIL BURNERS AND THEIR COMPONENTS

CHAPTER 1

DOMESTIC OIL BURNERS AND THEIR METHODS OF PREPARING FUEL FOR COMBUSTION

Since the dawn of time man has concerned himself with the problem of keeping warm. Men who dwell outside of tropical regions have been forced to this concern by rigorous climate or inclement weather. To some the problem of warmth was coupled with that of survival, and to others it was merely a matter of comfort.

The open fire was man's greatest friend in either case, and from this primitive method of keeping the body protected against the attacks of wintry blasts and low temperature there has been a gradual development in methods of heating. Today, fully automatic central heating is commonplace; it is one of the landmarks of the American high standard of living. More than 11,000,000 American homes utilize oil burners for central heating.

The development of heating devices has accompanied man's utilization of the three different types of fuel: solid fuels, liquid fuels, and gaseous fuels. The large-scale use of liquid and gaseous fuels resulted in the final development of fully automatic residential heating, for with these fuels the problems of residue and ash disposal were completely solved and the need for manual work with home heating systems disappeared.

Central heating as it is known today revolves about what is technically called the *process of combustion.* According to the dictionary, combustion is the union of oxygen with a substance, producing light (flame) and heat. Simply put, it means the process of burning, during which heat is liberated.

The substance being burned is generally referred to as a *fuel,* and in the case of oil burners it is specifically a *liquid fuel.* A liquid fuel as such will not burn. It must be changed to a gas or vapor and mixed with air if it is to support combustion. Some liquid fuels such as gasoline and benzene burn quite readily at ordinary temperatures, for they are highly volatile. This means that they quickly and easily change to a vapor at ordinary temperatures. In truth, such liquid fuels are constantly evaporating from the liquid to the gaseous or vapor state.

The more readily a liquid fuel changes to a vapor, the more easily it will burn and the less complicated will be the mechanism required to prepare it for combustion. If a match is held above a small saucer of kerosene, the fuel will immediately begin to burn, for at room temperature it is evaporating from the liquid to the vapor state. Thus the burners used for kerosene are comparatively simple and are not as complicated as those designed to burn heavier heating oils such as No. 2.

As fuel oil becomes heavier, it is more difficult to get it into the vapor state necessary for it to burn. As a result of this, the oil burner makes its appearance, for it is essentially nothing more than a device to prepare or process the liquid fuel for combustion by facilitating or hastening its change to a vapor that can be easily mixed with air and burned.

A number of specifications determine the grade of a fuel oil. These are mainly the API (American Petroleum Institute) *gravity,* the *viscosity,* and the *flash point.* There are others, too, such as the *pour point, end point,* and *10 and 90 per cent distillation points.*

The flash point, viscosity, and distillation points are very important. The flash point is an indication of the safety with which the oil may be stored, and the viscosity tells how it may be graded or classified for commercial purposes.

Flash point is the temperature at which the fuel oil will momentarily support combustion. At this temperature enough of the volatile parts of the oil will vaporize to support combustion for a moment if ignited. However, the vapors are burned much faster than they are produced and the flame soon goes out. No. 2 fuel oil has a flash point of 110°F minimum and 190°F maximum, which means that the lowest temperature at which it will momentarily burn will be 110°F—a fact that makes it ideal for domestic storage with a minimum of fire hazard.

The temperature of the cellar of a home will normally never reach 110°F, and for this reason there is little chance of the tank of oil representing too great a fire risk.

Viscosity, which is the measure of the flowing quality, can also be defined as a measure of the resistance to flow. Oil with a high viscosity will be very thick and flow very slowly. Oil with a low viscosity will flow very freely. Viscosity is measured in the number of seconds it takes a measured amount of the oil to pass through a certain opening (orifice) at 100°F.

If an oil has a high viscosity, it will require specific treatment (preheating) before it will flow freely enough for the burner to handle it. In view of this, viscosity is important, for a burner is designed to handle oils of a certain flow rate. Thus a burner designed to handle a No. 2 fuel oil with a viscosity of 50 seconds Saybolt Universal (SSU) will not be able to handle one of 100 seconds Saybolt Furol (SSF) viscosity, since the latter oil will be too viscous. From this it can be seen that viscosity is an important factor in (1) determining how an oil burner will be designed and (2) choosing what method it will use to prepare the oil for combustion.

TWO METHODS OF PREPARING FUEL FOR COMBUSTION

Domestic burners usually are confined to the use of oils ranging in grade from No. 1 to No. 4 and employ either one of two methods to prepare the fuel oil for combustion. These are *atomization* (spraying) and *vaporization* (heating).

Atomization or spraying is divided into three types, namely, high-pressure atomization, low-pressure atomization, and centrifugal atomization.

With high-pressure atomization used by high-pressure gun-type burners, the oil pressure is built up to 100 psi by a pump and delivered through an oil line to a specially designed nozzle from which it sprays out into the combustion chamber in a vaporous cloud of tiny globules or droplets.

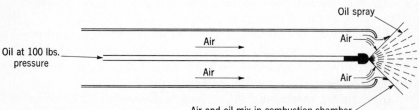

Fig. 1-1 High-pressure gun-type burner, showing method of oil and air delivery.

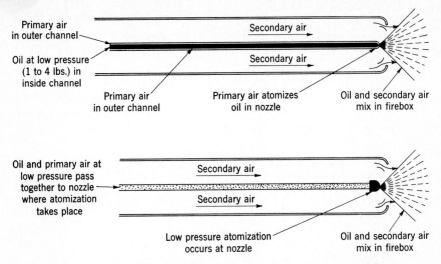

Fig. 1-2 Methods of low-pressure oil atomization and air delivery.

This mist of fine oil droplets is met by a current of air moving down the blast (gun) tube, and the oil and air mix in the combustion chamber after leaving the burner. Ignition is accomplished with an electric spark.

The characteristic parts of the high-pressure gun-type burner which uses the high-pressure method of atomization are the pump and nozzle. Both of these devices are precision-made and do a remarkable job in breaking up the oil fine enough so that it can be united with air and burn properly.

Low-pressure air atomization is also a well-known method that has been used successfully by domestic oil burners to prepare the oil for combustion. This method is peculiar to low-pressure burners. These burners achieve their objective by delivering oil and air to the nozzle at a pressure of from 1 to 15 psi, depending upon the make of the burner. Note from Fig. 1-2 that with these burners the oil and air come in contact with each other before leaving the burner. The air is used to atomize the oil into fine particles, and it leaves the nozzle opening in the form of a mist. (How this is accomplished is explained fully in Chap. 3.)

The other characteristic parts of low-pressure burners are the devices for metering the oil, the rotors that create air and oil pressure, float assemblies that control the rate of oil flow to the nozzle, and the air cushioning chamber.

A point worth mentioning concerning the introduction of combustion air arises at this stage of any discussion of low-pressure burners. The air that contacts the oil *prior* to its leaving the nozzle is referred to as *primary*

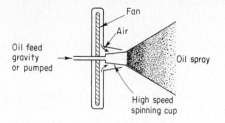

Fig. 1-3 Horizontal rotary with centrifugal atomization.

air. The introduction of air from a blower or fan into the combustion chamber *after* the oil has left the nozzle is referred to as *secondary air.*

Low-pressure gun-type burners are capable of consuming fuels over a wider grade range than most domestic oil burners. They are less sensitive to viscosity changes in the oil. However, the operating efficiencies of both high- and low-pressure burners are good and demonstrate the important fact that proper, thorough mixing of finely divided oil and air is the key to clean combustion.

The third way in which oil is atomized is by use of centrifugal force. The oil is fed to a rapidly rotating cup (3,450 rpm or faster). It then spreads throughout this cup in a fine film and flies off the outer edge at a high rate of speed in a very finely divided state (Fig. 1-3).

Burners that make use of such centrifugal force are of two types from the standpoint of their design: the horizontal rotary type and the vertical rotary type. High-speed motors are required by burners that use this type of atomization exclusively. With centrifugal atomizing burners there is no contact between oil and air until both have left the burner and entered the combustion chamber.

Horizontal rotary burners spin the oil from a cup that fits into the boiler on a horizontal plane, as do the gun types. Vertical rotary centrifugal atomizers (Fig. 1-4) stand vertically within the boiler or furnace, and the flame has the appearance of a giant sunflower. They spin the oil from a cup or from between disks that are rotating at a speed of anywhere from 3,450 to 12,000 rpm. Vertical rotary burners do not use a combus-

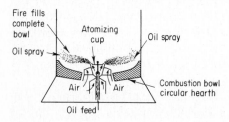

Fig. 1-4 Vertical rotary centrifugal atomizer with sunflower flame (3,450 rpm or faster).

tion chamber because of the manner in which they are installed within the boiler or furnace. Instead they use a circular *hearth*, as shown in Fig. 1-5. The characteristic parts of these burners are their cups and high-speed motors, in addition to float valves or other devices used to maintain a constant flow of oil.

The other method of preparing fuel oil for combustion is *vaporization*, which is achieved by heating the fuel. This is the simpler of the two methods. Pot-type burners and the vertical wall-flame rotary use this method.

A pot-type vaporizing burner is essentially a simple burner in design. It consists of a metal retort or vessel in which the oil is heated and vaporized. The vapors are mixed with air and the combustible mixture burns. The pot is usually kept warm by means of a low oil fire or pilot flame. Upon a call for heat, the flow of oil to the pot is increased, and as a result the flame increases in size. The pot now becomes hotter, thereby increasing the rate of vaporization. Eventually the vapors rise so fast and in such quantity that the fire rises from the pot and burns above it, usually off a distributor head, which channels additional air to the fire. The flame resembles a sunflower when at full fire.

This method of increasing and decreasing the flame size as the heat demand increases or diminishes is called *high-low fire*. Instead of cutting off the oil flow completely, it decreases it to a point at which the fire will just sustain itself and keep the retort warm. The call for heat results in the increased oil flow and consequent expansion of the flame.

Cabinet-type space heaters utilize vaporizing burners but generally use kerosene instead of No. 2 fuel oil and depend upon natural draft. Most vaporizing burners that use No. 2 oil are mechanical-draft burners and may use this forced draft for the small low-fire flame.

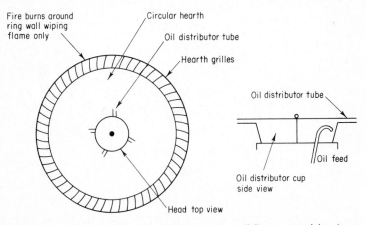

Fig. 1-5 Vertical rotary: wall-flame, vaporizing type.

Vertical rotary burners producing a wall-wiping flame also use this method to prepare the fuel oil for combustion (Fig. 1-5). With this burner the cup rotates at about 1,750 rpm, and the oil is thrown out in tiny droplets from oil-distributor tubes projecting from the cup and travels across the hearth to land on a specially constructed ring.

Situated at opposite sides or on one side of the ring are the two electrodes or the single electrode. The oil ignites at the electrode from the spark thereon, and the circular ring begins to heat. In a short time, the flame burns around the entire ring as it becomes hot enough to vaporize the oil being thrown upon it by the rotating distributor. This flame burns around the inner circumference of the boiler or furnace only, and from this fact gets its characteristic name of "wall-wiping flame." Combustion is complete when the hearth ring is hot; the flame is mostly blue with yellow tongues. This burner is a true vaporizer and uses the centrifugal force of the spinning cup to place the divided oil on the hearth ring where it is heated and vaporized. Like other burners it has a fan for forced draft.

The overall relationship of the two methods of preparing fuel for combustion to domestic oil-burner design is visualized in Fig. 1-6.

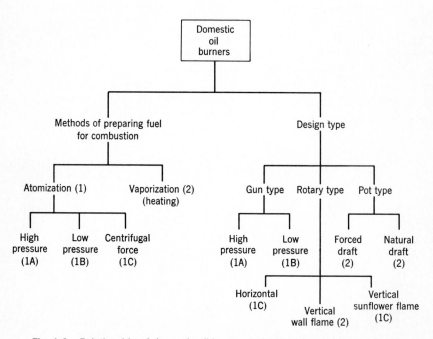

Fig. 1-6   Relationship of domestic oil-burner design types to method of preparing fuel for combustion.

QUESTIONS

1. What is combustion?
2. What must be done to a liquid fuel in order to make it burn?
3. Define viscosity; flash point.
4. What two methods are employed by domestic oil burners to prepare fuel for combustion?
5. Name the different design types of domestic burners.
6. Explain how each of the different design types prepares fuel for combustion.
7. What is meant by primary air; by secondary air?

CHAPTER 2

HIGH-PRESSURE
GUN-TYPE BURNERS

The preceding chapter described the breakdown of the various types of domestic oil burners according to the way they prepared fuel for combustion and the manner in which they delivered the required quantity of air so necessary for combustion. In order to obtain a clearer picture of the mechanical construction and differences of these various burners, they must be examined in the light of the parts of which they are constructed.

PUMPS

The high-pressure gun-type burner is essentially an "assembled" burner. Most parts are standard and are assembled on a specifically designed housing or casting. Because of the standardization and accessibility of the majority of parts used on this type of burner, the service problem is not great. If a mechanic can service one high-pressure gun-type burner, he can fairly well service them all.

Actually, all the pumps used on high-pressure gun-type burners are made by a small number of well-known manufacturers, and the same is true for the other parts (nozzles, transformers, motors, etc.). The standardization of parts has been one of the main reasons for the wide acceptance of this kind of burner, for it does away with complicated maintenance and installation problems.

The two characteristic parts of this type of burner are the pump and the nozzle. Although there are also motors, fans, transformers, and ignition assemblies on other types of burners, the pump and nozzle as they exist on the high-pressure gun-type burner are peculiar to it alone and are not found on any of the other types.

The function of the pump is to pick up the oil and deliver it at a constant operating pressure to the nozzle. It is then the job of the nozzle to break the oil down under this pressured delivery into a multitude of tiny droplets that issue forth as a fine spray. This spray is ignited electrically and begins to burn, receiving the necessary air for combustion from the fan. It is obvious that the pump pressure is a necessary requisite for the nozzle to achieve its purpose.

The main purpose of the pump is to furnish the proper "atomizing" or operating pressure (100 psi). In addition to this, it has other functions to perform. One of these may be, as is the case with an underground tank, to draw the oil up to the burner by creating a suction or vacuum that enables the lifting of the oil to take place. Once the oil is lifted, the pressure function of the pump takes over and delivers the oil to the nozzle. The pump must also furnish the oil in sufficient quantity to provide a surplus over the needs of the nozzle. Thus surplus quantity is taken care of through a bypass system, the function of which will be discussed later.

Today, almost all domestic oil burners are equipped with fuel-pumping *units*. The term "unit" implies that the pump, filter, and pressure regulating valve are all in one housing or unit. The term "pump" as now popularly used is synonymous with "unit" and includes the strainer, the pumping mechanism, and the pressure regulating valve. Pumps, however, may exist alone with special flange mountings that permit the attachment of separate strainers and pressure regulating valves. Suffice it to say that the oil-burner fuel-delivery unit as we know it today is a remarkably ingenious and well-engineered device that functions with excellent control and accuracy over long periods of time with little noise, annonyance, or trouble; and it is responsible to a large degree for the wide popular acceptance of the high-pressure gun-type burner.

The actual pumping mechanism of the fuel unit may be of two kinds: the internal gear pump and the external gear pump (see Figs. 2-1 to 2-3).

These gear-type pumps depend for their successful operation on the close tolerances between the adjacent parts. The gears clear the housing and each other by minute fractions of an inch. The oil flows through a

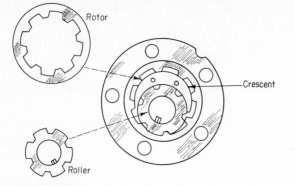

Fig. 2-1 Internal gear pump, showing rotor, roller, and crescent. (*Sundstrand Hydraulics*)

suction port and passes between the teeth of the gears; as the gears mesh, the oil is squeezed out through a discharge port in the housing and passes to the pressure regulating valve.

It is extremely important, because of the close fit of the parts of these pumps, that they remain free of foreign matter in order to prevent wear. For this reason, a filter or fine-mesh strainer always precedes the suction-port opening. This filter catches the dirt and foreign matter in the oil, preventing them from reaching the gears where they can do harm. If for any reason the gears become worn, their pumping ability will be seriously reduced, since oil can then pass between the meshing gears instead of being squeezed out into the discharge port.

A new type of filter, shown in Fig. 2-14, is the rotary filter, which

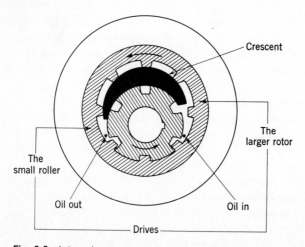

Fig. 2-2 Internal gear pump, showing drive method. The small roller is attached to the shaft. (*Sundstrand Hydraulics*)

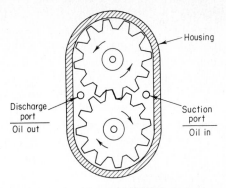

Fig. 2-3 External gear-type pump. Oil passes around between gear teeth and housing and is displaced as gears mesh.

consists of two ring-shaped flat surfaces between which runs a thin rotating member made of razor blade stock. It is driven by the pump shaft.

One of the rings is formed in the outer surface of the cover for the pump gears, its inner diameter being formed by a generally dish-shaped recess connected by a drilling to the pump inlet and its outer diameter described by a groove about 2 mm wide by 1 mm deep turned into the face of the cover plate.

The second ring is on the face of a member called the "cleaner cover." Its inner diameter is also formed by a dish-shaped recess, and its outer diameter by a groove similar to those on the gear cover.

When matched face-to-face, the gear-cover and cleaner-cover recesses form a chamber connected to the pump inlet, with no entrance except through the space between the two ring surfaces.

The cleaner cover has several radially extending ears or lugs provided with holes for attaching screws, one face of the ears coplanar with the ring-shaped face. In this manner a ring-shaped shim or spacer whose inner diameter is greater than the outer diameter of the grooves may be placed between the gear cover and the cleaner cover ears to provide precise spacing.

The rotating cleaner blade is made very slightly thinner than the shim so that it has running clearance between the two ring surfaces. It is made either square or triangular, its corners projecting radially slightly beyond the outside of the ring surfaces and its straight edges inside the inner diameter of the rings.

The outer corners of the spaced ring surfaces are the filtering edges. In the unit, oil is drawn between the two ring surfaces into the chamber, and from there into the gears. Particles of foreign matter which may be in the oil lodge on the filtering edges and are repeatedly dislodged by the corners of the rotating blade. This repeated agitation and mechanical working apparently have the effect of a ball-milling operation, resulting in reducing the foreign particles to such minute sizes that they pass harmlessly through the filter, the pump, and the nozzle.

Although a gear pump may operate constantly for hours, it will remain cool and require no lubrication because the fuel oil passes through it. The fuel oil not only cools the pump but also has enough lubricity in it as it flows through to keep the pump lubricated. The actual lubricity of fuel oil is slight; but, by a constant change of oil as it flows over the gears to the pressure regulating valve and thence to the nozzle, enough lubrication is obtained for the moving parts of the pump.

Besides the gear mechanism, which is the heart of the pump, another important part is the seal through which the driveshaft enters the housing. The seal prevents any air leaking into, and oil leaking from around, the shaft and is usually of a mechanical type. This type of seal can be obtained by having a spring exert tension on two very finely machined disk surfaces. On a seal of this kind there cannot be too much pressure exerted, and for this reason it may be vented to the suction side of the pump or with a two-pipe system to the atmosphere via the return line to the tank. The flexible part of the seal may be held in place by a diaphragm or bellows, and the solid contact is maintained by the tension exerted by the spring (see Figs. 2-4 and 2-5).

It can be seen that the pump itself is comparatively simple and rugged in construction and has only the gears, shaft, and a section of the seal as moving parts.

Today the simple fuel-oil pump with its flanges on which to mount the filter and pressure regulating valve is hardly ever used with domestic oil burners. It has been replaced by the more practical fuel unit which incorporates the pump, the strainer, and the pressure regulating valve in the one housing. This means lower initial cost, easier servicing, and simpler installation.

These fuel units (see Figs. 2-6 to 2-10) comprise two types when classified by their pumping function: the single-stage and two-stage pump. These terms refer to the separation of the suction and pressure functions within the pump. If the same set of gears is used for suction and for pressure delivery of the oil (in other words, if the pump has only one set of pumping gears), it is a *single-stage* pump. If the pump has two sets of gears, one for pulling the oil from the tank and the other for delivering it under pressure to the nozzle, it is a *two-stage* pump (see Figs. 2-6 and 2-10).

The single-stage pump should always be used with a single-line gravity-fed system, that is, with an oil tank which is higher than the burner. This will enable the pump gears to be used entirely for the pressure delivery of oil, and they will be relieved of any suction work because the oil will be delivered to the fuel unit by gravity. The employment of a two-stage pump on a gravity system results in no practical use being

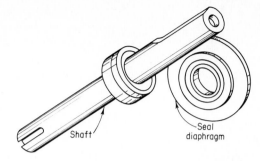

Fig. 2-4 Diaphragm-type seal. *(Sundstrand Hydraulics)*

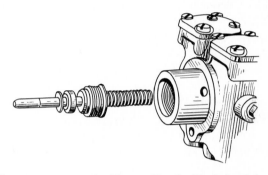

Fig. 2-5 Bellows-type pump seal. *(Heating Div., Sta-Rite Industries)*

Fig. 2-6 Webster 1R single-stage pump. *(Heating Div., Sta-Rite Industries)*

Fig. 2-7   Webster 2R two-stage pump.   (*Heating Div., Sta-Rite Industries*)

made of one set (first stage) of gears since they have no suction function to perform.   They are in truth wasted.

With a two-pipe system (tank below burner level) a two-stage pump should always be used.   The first stage of gears will draw the oil from the tank and deliver it to a tiny reservoir in the pump.   Here the second stage of gears will pick up and deliver it under pressure to the nozzle.   Thus the pressure and suction functions are divided and performed by separate

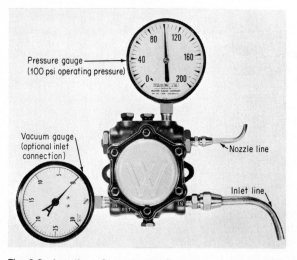

Fig. 2-8   Location of pressure and vacuum gauges on Webster fuel unit.   (*Heating Div., Sta-Rite Industries*)

Fig. 2-9 Sundstrand single-stage fuel unit.

Fig. 2-10 Sundstrand Model H two-stage fuel unit. This is a fast priming unit designed to perform when mounted in any of three recommended positions. A special circuit has been included in this pump for long-line, high-lift applications.

When starting dry, both sets of gears draw on the suction line. Air pumped by both the first- and second-stage gears then is discharged into the return line. Fast priming therefore occurs.

Once prime is established, the first stage continues to discharge to tank. The second stage then builds pressure, causing the regulating valve to bypass excess oil back into the strainer chamber. Consequently, flow through the suction and return lines is greatly reduced, and friction losses are minimized, permitting use of longer- or smaller-diameter lines.

Furthermore, because the first stage has an inlet above that of the second stage, any air drawn into the unit after priming is immediately picked up by the first stage and discharged to tank. Also, the second stage can draw in only solid air-free oil. Thus, there is no air in the oil delivered to the nozzle, and sharp cut-off is assured.

Model H units illustrated in this chapter are designed to be mounted with the valve horizontal, at either top or bottom. Certain model designations of this unit may also be mounted with the valve vertical. Earlier H models that had a designation ending in "1" or "2" were intended only for mounting with the valve underneath.

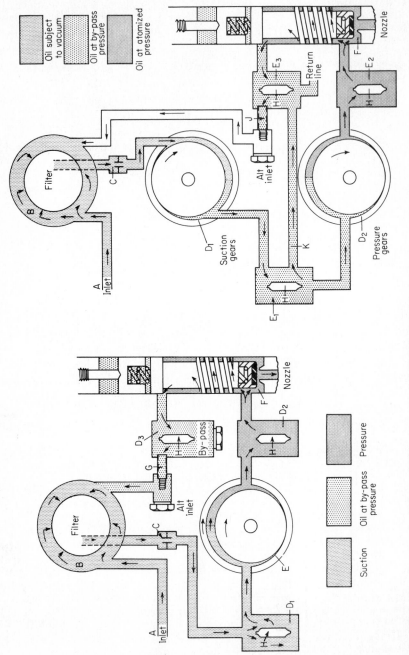

Fig. 2-11 Flow diagrams for Webster 1R (single-stage) and 2R (two-stage) fuel units.

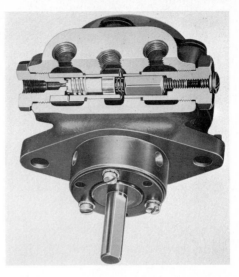

Fig. 2-12 Cutaway view of Webster fuel unit showing piston-type pressure regulating valve. (*Heating Div., Sta-Rite Industries*)

sets of gears. Figures 2-11 and 2-16 show the oil-flow diagram for one- and two-stage pumps. The use of the two-stage pump on a buried tank results in greater pulling power (vacuum), greater capacity, quieter operation, and longer life for the pump. A single-stage pump can do the job on a sunken tank with a two-pipe system, but not with the quietness of operation or efficiency of a two-stage pump. The use of a single-stage

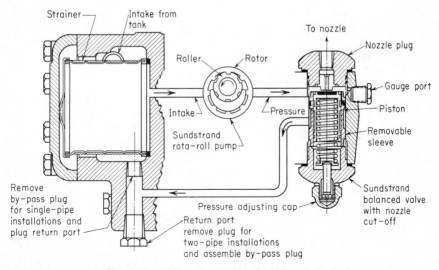

Fig. 2-13 Oil-flow diagram for Sundstrand single-stage pump.

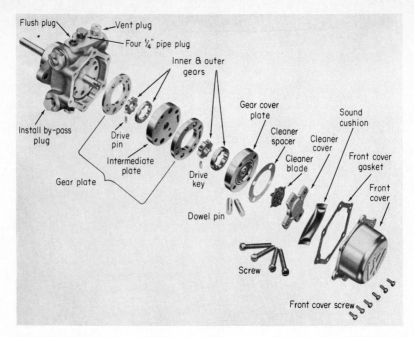

Fig. 2-14 Exploded view of Webster two-stage pump. Note the cleaner blade and the cover. This rotary filter reduces particles of foreign material so small that they pass through the filter, pump, and nozzle. (*Heating Div., Sta-Rite Industries*)

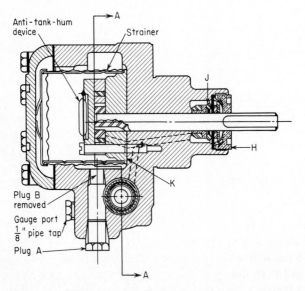

Fig. 2-15 Oil-flow diagram for Sundstrand pump (cross section).

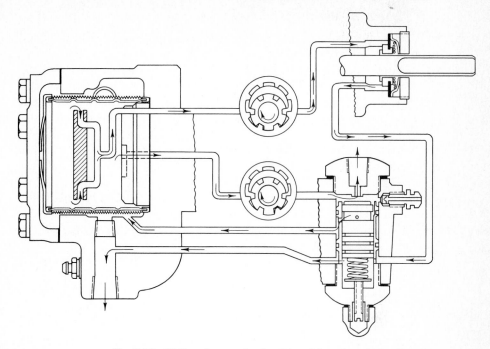

Fig. 2-16   Oil-flow diagram for Sundstrand two-stage fuel unit.

pump where there is any great lift involved can materially shorten the life of the pump.   The best procedure is to use a two-stage pump on all systems that have the tank below the level of the burner.

The use of a two-stage pump, two-pipe system, is an added advantage in the event of air leaks in the suction line or in the event of a dry tank. A *small* leakage of air into the suction line will immediately prevent the delivery of oil in a single-pipe system.   In the case of a two-pipe system the operation will hardly be affected.   The pump on a one-pipe system will have to be vented in the event that the oil tank runs dry, for it will become air-bound.   If oil is delivered, the pump will not be able to operate until the air is released to the atmosphere.   This is not the case with a two-pipe system when the tank runs dry; the pump will vent itself and return the air bubbles by way of the return line to the tank and thus operate normally.   Even with a two-pipe system, it is wise to prime the pump with oil or vent it to the atmosphere through the plug or port provided, in the event there is a considerable distance between tank and burner.   This prevents the gears from rotating for any length of time without fuel oil flowing between them.

PRESSURE REGULATING VALVES

Since the pump shaft is connected directly to the motor shaft by means of a coupling, the fuel unit will always operate at constant speed. This means that, the viscosity of the oil remaining constant, the pump will have a specific output in gallons per hour for a certain pressure. Oil-burner pumps always deliver oil in excess of the burner's need, the nozzle output capacity being much less than the pump output capacity. Since the pump operates at constant speed, its output cannot be controlled by slowing it down. Thus, a different method must be employed to take care of the excess oil as well as to control the pressure at the nozzle, the latter being extremely important.

The device that does this is known as the *pressure regulating valve.* The pressure regulating valve may be an integral part of the pump, as is the case with the fuel unit, or a separate valve mounted on the pump by means of a bracket of flange.

The purpose or function of the pressure regulating valve is three-fold:

1. To allow no oil to reach the nozzle until a minimum operating pressure has been reached; this is usually about 60 to 70 psi. Below

Fig. 2-17   Detroit Lubricator CRC-270 pressure regulating valve.

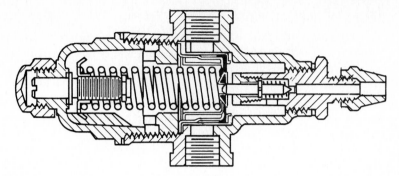

Fig. 2-18 Cross section of a Detroit Lubricator bellows-type pressure regulating valve.

this pressure the nozzle will not atomize oil properly, and it is not efficient or safe to have it entering the combustion chamber. Once the minimum atomizing pressure is reached, the valve opens and allows oil to flow to the nozzle. This leads us to the second function.

2. To maintain a constant operating pressure, usually 100 psi. This is necessary to provide a constant-sized, clean-burning fire, free from noise and pulsations, and to enable the nozzle to furnish a spray fine enough for good combustion.

3. To provide a quick, clean cutoff as the pressure drops when the burner goes off. Also to prevent, by properly sealing off the port to the nozzle, any oil from dripping into the chamber during the OFF cycle. Thus, in the OFF cycle, the valve must prevent afterfire and afterdrip, both of which are highly troublesome conditions.

The pressure regulating valve accomplishes its function in a simple manner. As the burner comes on, there are no openings to release the oil; consequently, the pressure builds up immediately. The valve now moves as the pressure increases and at about 60 psi uncovers the port to the nozzle. The oil now is atomized at the nozzle and ignites. The pump continues to build pressure as the motor comes up to speed and moves the valve, further compressing the spring. As the valve continues to move and the pump capacity becomes greater as normal motor speed is reached, much more oil than the nozzle can deliver is reaching it. The valve now takes care of the excess oil. After lifting a certain distance, it uncovers a bypass port that bypasses the excess oil. As the pressure increases, this bypass port is uncovered even more and opens and closes directly as the pressure increases or decreases. The excess oil is bypassed back to the suction side of the pump, in which case we have an internal bypass (one-pipe system), or it can be returned directly to the tank. In the latter instance, we have an external bypass with a two-pipe system. The valve controls and maintains a constant pressure at the nozzle by

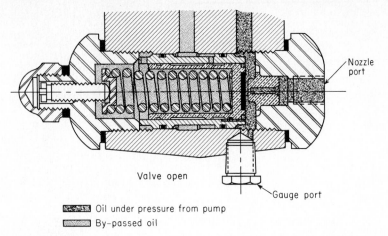

Nozzle port

Valve open

Gauge port

▨▨▨▨ Oil under pressure from pump

▨▨▨▨ By-passed oil

Fig. 2-19 Cross section of a piston-and-spring-type pressure regulating valve. (*Sundstrand Hydraulics*)

opening and closing the bypass port as pressure is increased or decreased. Adjusting the tension of the spring makes it easier or harder for the valve to uncover the bypass port and furnishes a means thereby of setting the pressure at the nozzle at any point desired.

As pressure drops when the motor comes to a stop, the bypass port is first covered completely; and on a further drop (about 20 to 30 psi below

Fig. 2-20 Webster RV-2000 pressure-regulating valve for all fuel oils No. 1 through No. 6. It combines pressure regulation and cutoff functions. It is corrosion-resistant and designed to provide a sharp cutoff.

Fig. 2-21 Webster RV-3000 pressure regulating valve for fuel oils No. 1 through No. 6. This valve provides only the pressure regulating feature, without cutoff.

pressure setting), the nozzle port is covered and the flame is extinguished.

It is very important that the flame be extinguished *instantly* to prevent smoke, soot, and afterdrip of oil. Some pumps employ an electromagnetic (solenoid) valve which instantaneously opens the bypass as soon as the current to the motor is cut off. This provides an immediate loss of pressure and instant extinguishing of the fire. Figures 2-22 and 2-23 show how this is accomplished on single-and two-stage pumps.

This quick cutoff is also accomplished by use of a clutch mechanism (Fig. 2-24) on one type of modern burner. As soon as the motor slows down, the clutch disengages the pump driveshaft and pressure falls off instantly. On the start, the clutch does not engage the driveshaft until the motor is well up to speed, thereby providing a sharp start that helps to eliminate starting pulsations.

Pressure regulating valves are operated mainly by three devices—the piston, the bellows, and the diaphragm—tension being exerted by a spring. The piston and bellows types are the more popular.

It must be remembered that pressure regulating valves are accurate control devices and quickly adjust to rising and falling pressures. These valves should always be adjusted with a pressure gauge. This gauge should be installed at the pressure port opening, and the valve adjusted by inserting a screw driver or Allen key into the slot provided. Pressure of 100 psi is regarded as normal for operating domestic high-pressure gun-type burners.

Fig. 2-22 Webster delayed-opening valve. Elimination of smoky starts and stops is accomplished through the use of the delayed-opening valve. On cold starts this unit delays the delivery of oil to the nozzle, allowing the oil-burner motor to come to full speed and establish suitable draft, assuring complete atomization and the proper amount of air for combustion. On the shutdown, Delaytrol cuts off the fuel supply instantly, extinguishing the flame while the draft fan is still operating at full speed. As a result, sooting of flue passages, nozzle tips, and electrodes is greatly reduced; combustion rumbles, puffback, and flutter on starts and stops are eliminated; all gases are properly exhausted; and combustion is maintained at peak efficiency for heating economy. These factors have become particularly important because of trends to high-velocity combustion heads and restricted flue passages in compact boiler and furnace units.

From the foregoing, we can see that the fuel unit as it is known today is comprised of three distinct parts in one housing, namely, the strainer, the pump, and the pressure regulating valve. The strainer is usually of fine steel mesh located on the suction side to filter the oil before it reaches the gear pumping mechanism. The gear mechanism can be of either the internal or external gear type. The gears deliver the oil to either a piston- or a bellows-type pressure regulating valve which regulates and controls the constant operating pressure and furnishes the quick cutoff necessary to normal operation.

Pumps do not present involved service problems. If the maintenance mechanic is at all in doubt, the pump should be removed and replaced with a new one. Except for cleaning strainers, adjusting pressure, or changing regulating valves or valve parts, there is little that can be done on pumps in the field. If it has a leaky seal, the pump should be replaced. The plate or part of the housing that covers the gears should never be removed. These parts are machined so closely that it is almost impossible to remove and replace them without allowing dirt to enter the

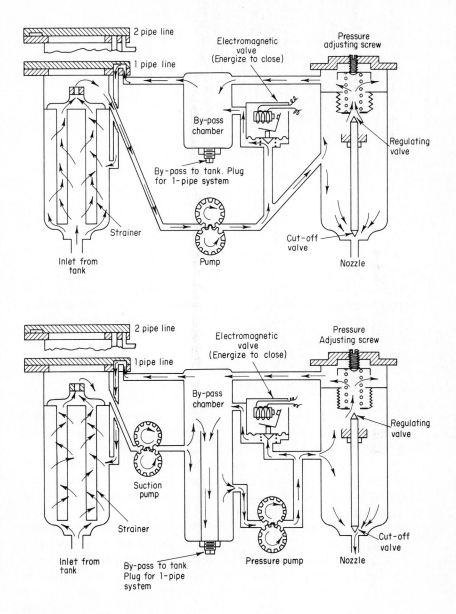

Fig. 2-23 Simple flow diagram, showing solenoid-type bypass opener cutoff, as used on older models of Webster pumps.

Fig. 2-24 Gilbarco clutch assembly used for fast cutoff on larger gph capacity burners.

gear mechanism or distorting the cover plate by unequal bolt tightening. This may cause the gears to bind.

When installing a pump, be sure that it is set properly for an external or internal bypass. When a one-pipe gravity-fed system is used, the excess oil will be bypassed internally through the pump. The internal bypass port plug should then be *out*, and oil will bypass through the pump. When a two-pipe system (external bypass) is used, the bypass port plug will be *in*, and a return line must be connected to the return port to send the excess bypassed oil back to the tank. Some fuel units can be changed over from one- to two-pipe systems by merely reversing the strainer cover plate (see Chap. 26 for service data).

NOZZLES

Once the pump has built the oil pressure up to the point where the valve opens (about 60 or 70 psi), the oil flows through to the nozzle. The pressure conditions are stabilized by the bypass of the valve, and the normal operating pressure (100 psi) is maintained if it is so adjusted. It is now the function of the nozzle to receive the oil at this pressure and convert the pressure into velocity. This is necessary, for we are dependent upon sufficient velocity to obtain proper atomization. The term "atomization" has long been used to describe what the nozzle does to the oil. However, it is far from being technically correct, since the nozzle merely breaks the oil down into a very fine mist or spray by forcing it apart into small droplets and delivering these to the combustion chamber.

The oil is forced along by the pump pressure into the nozzle itself and passes through the small nozzle strainer first. This nozzle strainer is a safeguard against dirt entering the nozzle, where it can easily clog

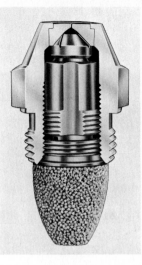

Fig. 2-25 Cutaway view of Delavan oil-burner nozzle.

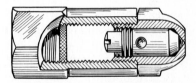

Fig. 2-26 Cutaway view of Monarch nozzle, showing strainer, insert, and tip.

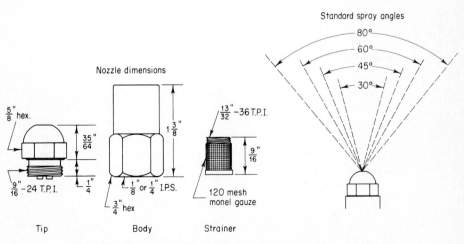

Fig. 2-27 Some nozzle dimensions. (*Monarch Manufacturing Works*)

the small slots in the head of the insert or even the orifice itself. After the oil leaves the strainer, it passes along between the insert outer wall and the inner wall of the adapter and nozzle tip. From there it moves up to the face of the insert stem, or distributor, as it is called, and then through tiny slots into a small chamber (see Figs. 2-25 and 2-33). These slots are the only entrance to the small swirl chamber between the tip of the insert and the nozzle tip. Since these slots are very small, the oil picks up velocity as it passes through them. The oil particles then enter the swirl chamber, which is circular in shape and has a gradually decreasing diameter as it approaches the orifice.

The circular shape of this tiny chamber causes the oil to approach the nozzle opening in a swirling motion, during which time it is constantly increasing in velocity because of the chamber's smaller diameter as it gets closer to the orifice. Moving at this high rotational velocity, it passes through the orifice, getting its forward motion or velocity from the pressure. The pressure of 100 psi under which the oil enters the nozzle from the oil line drops to about 60 psi, more or less, in the swirl chamber. The actual drop in pressure between the oil in the swirl chamber and the oil entering the nozzle adapter at the rear of the nozzle depends upon the design of the nozzle. Smoothness of finish of the internal parts of a nozzle is very important in this respect.

When the oil leaves the orifice, it is whirled away from the center by centrifugal force. It is actually moving in a very thin sheet that reaches rates of speed as high as 40 mph. It now breaks up into tiny droplets, which begin to leave the sheet and travel in straight lines; *they do not whirl or rotate.* In order to make these droplets whirl, there must be whirling streams of air delivered by the burner. Some of these droplets are so small that they are about $\frac{1}{10,000}$ in. in diameter.

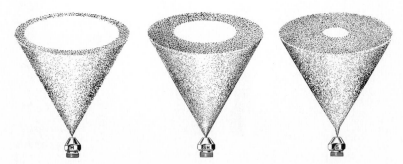

Fig. 2-28 Hollow, semihollow, and solid-spray patterns. (*Engelhard*)

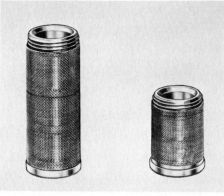

Fig. 2-29   Nozzle strainers.   (*Delavan Manufacturing Co.*)

THREE NOZZLE FUNCTIONS

The nozzle has three basic functions to perform.   These are:

1. *Atomizing*   As just discussed, this process speeds up the vaporization by breaking up the oil into tiny droplets—approximately 55 billion per gallon of oil at a pressure of 100 psi.   The exposed surface of a gallon of oil is thereby expanded to about 690,000 in. of burning surface.   Individual droplet sizes range from 0.002 to 0.010 in.   The smaller droplets are necessary for fast quiet ignition and to establish a flame front close to the burner head.   The larger droplets take longer to burn and help fill the combustion chamber.

2. *Metering*   A nozzle is so designed and dimensioned that it will deliver a fixed amount of atomized fuel to the combustion chamber—within a plus or minus range of 5 per cent of rated capacity.   This means that functional dimensions must be controlled very closely.   It also means that nozzles with many flow rates must be available to

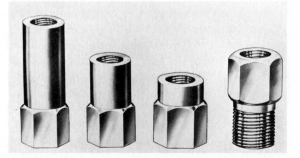

Fig. 2-30   Delavan nozzle adapters (left to right): long, standard, short, male.

Fig. 2-31 Multiple-nozzle adapters; two- and three-nozzle types.

satisfy a wide range of industry needs. Under 5 gph, for example, 21 different flow rates and 6 different spray angles are considered standard.

3. *Patterning* A nozzle is also expected to deliver the atomized fuel to the combustion chamber in a uniform spray pattern and a spray angle best suited to the requirements of a specific burner.

It can be seen from the foregoing that the high-pressure oil-burner nozzle is a precision device and must be handled carefully. The use of metal brushes or surfaces in the cleaning of these nozzles should be avoided, since they will distort or injure the finely machined surfaces. The removal of the insert and the replacing of it should be done with care. It should not be seated with a heavy screw driver, because screwing the insert in too tightly will only damage it or distort the slots and thereby affect its performance (see Chap. 24 for service data). The snug fit of the insert prevents vibration.

Nozzles are usually made of brass or steel, the actual orifice usually being of hard material. This may be stainless steel or hardened steel. The reason for this lies in the fact that the swirl chamber is the part of the nozzle subject to wear owing to the constant whirling of the oil, under pressure, through it. Any soft material at this point would result in excessive wear and consequent increase in the capacity of the nozzle far over its original rating. Even with the use of harder materials for tips, it is wise to replace nozzles at least every year.

High-pressure-type nozzles come in varied sizes from $\frac{1}{2}$ up to 35 gph. Angles of spray vary from 30 to 90 deg, and the spray may be hollow cone or full cone (Fig. 2-28). In the higher gallonage ranges, it is wiser to use two or three smaller nozzles than one large one. This can be accomplished by using a multiple adapter (Fig. 2-31). Such a procedure gives finer atomization and better dispersion, requires less excess air for good combustion, and furnishes cleaner fires.

Any increase in operating pressure will result in an increase in the capacity of the nozzle, as shown in Table 2-1, and correspondingly any decrease in pressure will cause a decrease in capacity. Viscosity has

Table 2-1 Pressure Effect on Nozzle Performance: Flow Rate Chart, gallons per hour (gph)

Decrease pressure (not recommended):		Rated flow at:	Increase pressure:				
60 psi	80 psi	100 psi	120 psi	140 psi	160 psi	200 psi	300 psi
0.39	0.45	0.50	0.55	0.59	0.63	0.70	0.86
0.50	0.58	0.65	0.71	0.77	0.82	0.92	1.12
0.58	0.67	0.75	0.82	0.89	0.95	1.05	1.30
0.66	0.76	0.85	0.93	1.00	1.08	1.20	1.47
0.70	0.81	0.90	0.99	1.07	1.14	1.27	1.56
0.78	0.89	1.00	1.10	1.18	1.27	1.41	1.73
0.85	0.99	1.10	1.21	1.30	1.39	1.55	1.90
0.97	1.12	1.25	1.37	1.48	1.58	1.76	2.16
1.05	1.21	1.35	1.48	1.60	1.71	1.91	2.34
1.16	1.34	1.50	1.64	1.78	1.90	2.12	2.60
1.28	1.48	1.65	1.81	1.95	2.09	2.33	2.86
1.36	1.57	1.75	1.92	2.07	2.22	2.48	3.03
1.55	1.79	2.00	2.19	2.37	2.53	2.82	3.48
1.74	2.01	2.25	2.47	2.66	2.85	3.18	3.90
1.94	2.24	2.50	2.74	2.96	3.16	3.54	4.33
2.33	2.69	3.00	3.29	3.55	3.80	4.25	5.20

Nozzles above 3.0 gph: For flow rates higher than those shown, multiply the rating by the flow of the 1.00-gph nozzle at the desired pressure; e.g., 9.0-gph nozzle at 300 psi = 9.0 × 1.73 = 15.6 gph.

Spray angle: Pressure has no effect on spray angle **measured at the orifice.** If pressure is too low, the spray tends to collapse.

Spray pattern: Reduced pressure (less than 100 psi) produces a pattern approaching solid cone. The fire becomes heavier in the center and longer.

Increased pressure (over 100 psi) produces a more definite hollow cone, especially with cold or high viscosity oil. Fire is shorter and has less tendency to pulsate in most burners.

Droplet size: Higher pressure produces smaller droplet size (finer spray).

somewhat the same effect. As the viscosity increases (within limits), that is, as the oil becomes thicker, the capacity of the nozzle increases (Fig. 2-32). This is not usually realized, and the opposite is often taken for granted. Heavier oil or oil of a higher viscosity will not rotate as rapidly in the swirl chamber, for it has a greater resistance to flow. The lesser velocity results in higher pressure in the swirl chamber. The higher pressure in the swirl chamber causes an increase in the amount of oil flowing through the orifice. In this way viscosity affects nozzle capacity. The average viscosity of domestic fuel oil is from 32 to 38 sec at 100°F. This means that it will take 32 to 38 sec for 60 cc of fuel oil at 100°F to flow through the Saybolt Universal viscosimeter.

To put it another way, if the oil has a lower viscosity, there will be a higher swirl-chamber velocity, resulting in a thinner wall of oil with a lower flow. Conversely, if the oil has a higher viscosity, there will be a lower swirl-chamber velocity, a thicker wall of oil, and consequently higher flow rate.

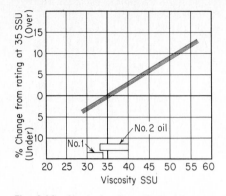

Fig. 2-32   Chart showing effect of increased oil viscosity on nozzle performance.

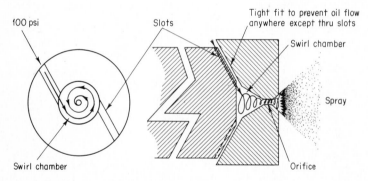

Fig. 2-33   Oil passing through slots into swirl chamber.

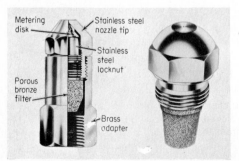

Fig. 2-34   View of Engelhard (left) and Steinen (right) nozzles, showing bronze filters.

Fig. 2-35 Boston Machine porous bronze filter: standard on fractional-gallon sizes; embodies the principle of "depth filtration." It is made of thousands of small bronze balls fused together to a desired shape and thickness. Because of the depth of filtration mass, dirt that might pass through a screen-type strainer will not pass through the thick wall of the porous bronze filter. It is for use on nozzles under 1.00 gph. If such devices were used on larger nozzle sizes, too much material would be filtered out; this could create a need for service by necessitating frequent strainer cleaning.

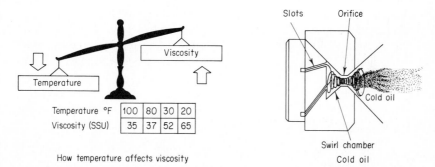

Temperature °F	100	80	30	20
Viscosity (SSU)	35	37	52	65

How temperature affects viscosity

Cold oil

Fig. 2-36 As temperature goes down, viscosity goes up. In other words, as the temperature decreases, the oil thickens and flows less freely. Outside storage tanks are the usual reason for cold oil. As the thickened oil passes into the swirl chamber, its rotational velocity is slowed. This causes a thickening of the walls in the cone of oil as it emerges from the orifice, so the nozzle actually delivers more fuel and larger droplets. As a result, the flame front moves away from the burner head. In severe cases, atomization may be so poor that fuel cannot be ignited. If it is, it often produces a long, narrow, and noisy fire that burns off the back wall of the combustion chamber. (*Delavan Manufacturing Co.*)

Fig. 2-37 A cartridge-type filter installed before the pump or at the tank outlet will materially assist in keeping tiny particles of rust, scale, and dirt away from the pump and nozzle. These filters subject the fuel oil to many successive fine filtrations that remove impurities down to microscopic size. (*Engelhard*)

FANS AND AIR-CONTROL DEVICES

The amount of air necessary to give the oil the oxygen required to make it burn properly and cleanly is furnished by the fan. The oil-burner fan has become completely standardized and is of the multibladed, impeller type shown in Fig. 2-38. This fan is attached directly to the shaft of the motor and is usually held in place by an Allen setscrew. It is important that its many concave blades be clean so that it can deliver the required amount of air. Characteristically, this fan can deliver a large quantity of

Fig. 2-38 Torrington air impeller.

air at relatively low velocity, which makes it very suitable for gun-type burners. Air-quantity control devices can be placed before the fan, in which case the air input is controlled, or on the discharge side of the fan, in which case the output is controlled. New studies show that it may be better to quantitatively control the air before the fan.

Actually about 1,540 cu ft of air is required to burn 1 gal of oil, but because of the mechanical inability of the burner to mix all the air with oil, about 25 to 30 per cent in excess of the 1,540 cu ft is often required. Most burners furnish 2,000 to 2,200 cu ft of air per gallon, and there are some that run as high as 40 per cent in excess air delivery.

Gun-type burners that have to furnish such a large quantity of excess air cannot be efficient and are in need of devices to mix the air and oil more thoroughly. Standardization has proceeded so far with gun-type burners that they are fairly much alike in all respects except that of air delivery and one or two other details. It is air delivery that can set one gun-type burner apart from another and make it more or less wasteful or economical in the use of fuel oil. The less excess air a burner uses, the more efficient it will be. This is more thoroughly explained in Chap. 21.

It is interesting to note how the air delivery also determines the capacity of the burner. Any size nozzle from 1 to 30 gal can be screwed into the nozzle adapter, but what determines the actual amount of oil that can be burned is the quantity of air delivered. True, a larger fan can be used, but this is limited by the burner housing. Thus, the burner housing itself becomes the limiting factor in the capacity of a burner because it in turn limits the size of the fan.

As the air leaves the fan, it moves with comparatively fair velocity through the blast tube, which gives it forward direction. If the air were allowed to approach the oil spray in this fashion, a very inefficient fire would be produced, being unstable and smoky. Devices must be used to give the air further energy, velocity, and direction and thereby create the proper turbulence that will give a thorough mixture of oil and air.

Two conditions are essential for efficient fires as far as air delivery is concerned; these are (1) as little excess air as possible and (2) sufficient turbulence. The greater the turbulence obtained, the less excess air will be needed, for the air that escapes the mixing process will be held to a minimum.

Turbulence is created by the use of a number of devices, the most common of which was the bladed diffuser or stabilizer (which also served as an electrode holder), used in conjunction with an air cone at the mouth of the blast tube (burner gun), as shown in Fig. 2-39. With many older burners the best performance is obtained from this combination when the multibladed stabilizer is as far forward in the blast tube and thus as close to the air cone as possible. The blades of the stabilizer and the air cone

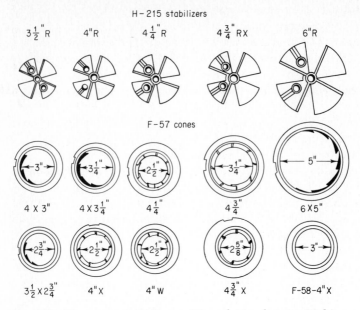

Fig. 2-39 Air cones and stabilizers. (*Monarch Manufacturing Works*)

should face in the same direction. If they do not, the air cone will counter the spin given to the air by the stabilizer, and direction and velocity may be extensively decreased. The mouth of the blast tube should be narrowed where it approaches the spray to increase velocity and force the air into the spray closer to the nozzle. This is very important, since the sooner the mixing commences, the more thorough it will be. The smaller the nozzle, the smaller should be the blast-tube mouth.

More complicated devices to achieve a better mixture of oil and air are now being used and are constantly developed in order to burn catalytic types of oils cleanly. Some of these devices are discussed in the following paragraphs.

Perhaps the best-known air-delivery control device is the Shell combustion head, developed for domestic burners by the Shell Oil Co. This head (Figs. 2-40 and 2-41) consists of a cone equipped with a narrowed orifice at one end, containing an inner and outer secondary air nozzle. The cone is capped at the rear and has an adjustable secondary air-control ring to meter the quantities of air necessary to serve as a vacuum breaker inside the cone, according to the gallonage rate. The air moving down the blast tube meets this cone and is forced to travel between the blast tube and the outside of the cone. Thus being forced through a narrower space, it increases in velocity and travels over the mouth of the cone, between it and the narrowed blast-tube orifice, where it gains in spin, turbulence, and velocity and merges with the oil spray.

Fig. 2-40   Shell combustion head.

This head produces a hollow, conical sunflower flame of high temperature and high carbon dioxide content, indicating that little excess air is required. With a head of this type, the width and height of the chamber are more critical than the length because of the conical shape of the flame. Static pressure within the blast tube should be 0.50 in. of water in order to achieve satisfactory performance. Figure 2-42(a) and (b) gives further details on applications of this device to dual- and single-nozzle burners.

Figure 2-43 shows the application of the same principle. The application here is simpler mechanically and consists of an inner cone that moves back and forth as in the Shell device. This older model Arco air diverter or turbometer forces the air through a narrower space between the diverter and blast tube, causing increased velocity, and over a turbolater (vaned cone), where it gains in turbulence. It penetrates and surrounds the oil spray close to the nozzle, obtaining a fine mixture that produces a sunflower hollow-cone flame with a high carbon dioxide content flue gas. Both the foregoing devices require hollow-cone spray nozzles.

The combustion head shown in Fig. 2-44 is one of the more modern types and was developed as a result of research study about pulsation.

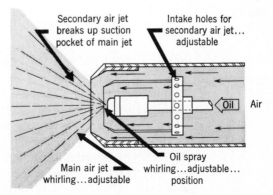

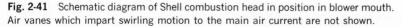

Fig. 2-41   Schematic diagram of Shell combustion head in position in blower mouth. Air vanes which impart swirling motion to the main air current are not shown.

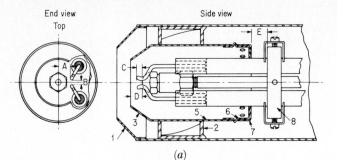

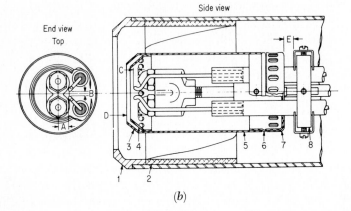

Fig. 2-42 There are two types of later-model Shell heads. The head mixes oil and air in the proper proportions within the combustion head and then distributes it outside the combustion head immediately in front of the burner. (a) Head for single-nozzle oil burners; (b) head for dual-nozzle oil burners.

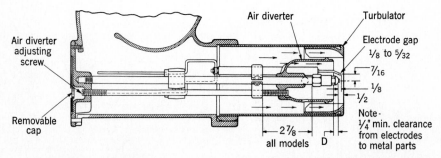

Fig. 2-43 Detail drawing showing old model Arcoflame air diverter (turbometer) and distance dimensions from diverter to nozzle tip. (*American-Standard*)

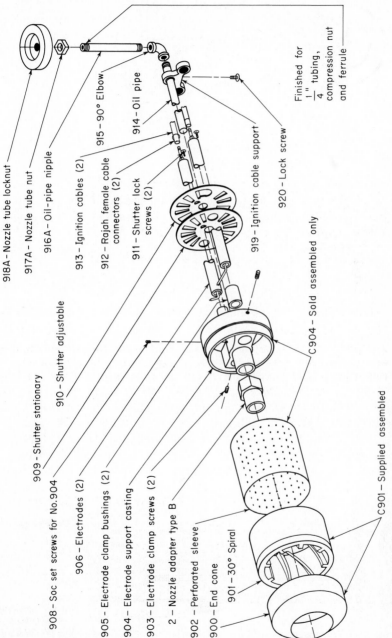

918A - Nozzle tube locknut

917A - Nozzle tube nut

916A - Oil-pipe nipple

915 - 90° Elbow

914 - Oil pipe

913 - Ignition cables (2)

912 - Rajah female cable connectors (2)

911 - Shutter lock screws (2)

910 - Shutter adjustable

909 - Shutter stationary

908 - Soc set screws for No.904

906 - Electrodes (2)

905 - Electrode clamp bushings (2)

904 - Electrode support casting

903 - Electrode clamp screws (2)

2 - Nozzle adapter type B

902 - Perforated sleeve

901 - 30° Spiral

900 - End cone

919 - Ignition cable support

920 - Lock screw

Finished for $\frac{1}{4}$" tubing, compression nut and ferrule

C904 - Sold assembled only

C901 - Supplied assembled

Fig. 2-44 Boston Machine combustion head, exploded view.

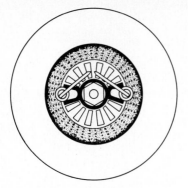

Fig. 2-45 Boston Machine head, front view.

It combines in the single head the ability to obtain two definitely different-shaped flames.   One of these is the so-called "sunflower" flame similar to that produced by static-pressure-type heads.

The other-shaped flame obtainable with this head is called by the manufacturer of this device an "antipulsating" flame.   It is an oval-shaped fire, the oval being flattened and elongated.   An adjustment of the head can produce either flame.

The sunflower flame is obtained when the shutters on the back of the head are closed (see Fig. 2-46).   The air from the fan must pass entirely through the spiral, resulting in an air pattern that produces the sunflower flame.   With this flame, a thorough mixture of oil and air is attained, consequently achieving an increase in combustion efficiency.

The manufacturer of this device considers the sunflower flame to be most desirable, but there are installations in which its performance is not satisfactory.   A lack of draft in the combustion chamber, with resultant pressures, would cause it to increase the tendency to pulsate.   If the chamber is narrow, impingement could result.   The sunflower flame is more sensitive in relation to the noise factor.   Where sound level is a

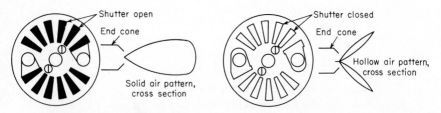

Fig. 2-46 Boston Machine head.   Shutter in open and closed positions, showing solid and hollow air patterns.

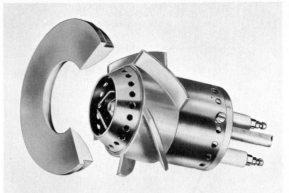

Fig. 2-47 Engelhard combustion head, model HP-53-M. This head has three major segments. (1) The end cone shown detached (left) from the (2) primary air cup and (3) the swirl ring with curved blades which slips over the primary air cup.

The blades give directional velocity and turbulence to the air being pushed through by the fan. The narrower orifice of the end cone results in a further increase in velocity which then achieves a better mixture of oil and air.

concern the antipulsating, flattened, oval-shaped flame would be more desirable.

The antipulsating flame is obtained with this combustion head when the shutters on the back of the head are opened. Now a large percentage of the fan air will pass through the center of the burner head and less through the spiral. This air travels in a straight line from the fan and opposes the tendency of the flame to move or jump back to the nozzle, causing pulsation.

Air patterns charted with instruments show that this head can produce two distinctly different air patterns, each capable of producing a flame to do a specific job.

Another head for use with high-pressure burners is shown in Fig. 2-47. The manufacturer of this head recommends that a delayed oil valve be installed between the nozzle and the pump. This head, when firing at capacities up to and including 1.35 gph, has the adjustment cup moved as far as possible counterclockwise, thereby closing the holes half-way. When firing at capacities from 1.35 to 2 gph, the cup is rotated as far as possible clockwise. This will fully open the holes, allowing a maximum amount of air to pass through into the inside of the cup. Recommended combustion-chamber sizes for this head are shown in Table 2-2.

As noted above, the performance burners can be improved by designing the firing head for specific rates. This is accomplished by matching the air-flow rate, cone shape, and air velocity with the oil-spray pattern.

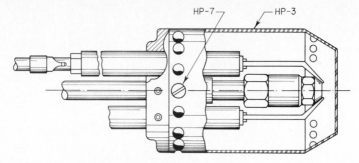

Fig. 2-48 Adjustment of Engelhard combustion head. (1) When firing capacities up to 1.35 gph, loosen two screws HP-7 and rotate the primary air cup HP-3, closing the holes halfway. Tighten both adjustment screws HP-7. (2) When firing capacities from 1.35 to 2.00 gph, loosen adjustment screws HP-7, rotate primary air cup until holes are fully open. Tighten both adjustment screws HP-7.

VISUAL AIR PATTERNS

A glance at Fig. 2-49 shows an advanced visual method of determining the air pattern of a burner. This visualization is accomplished by taking air-pressure readings at one cross-sectional area through the air emerging from the end cone of the oil burner. The readings are obtained from a draft gauge (air-pressure gauge) and are plotted on a special graph. The outer ring of this graph gives the angle embracing the flame area. The vertical radius in the center gives the air pressure and is graduated like a draft gauge with readings from 0.02 to 0.20 in. (water).

The air pattern of the burner shown in Fig. 2-49(a) is that of a sunflower. When the burner produces a flame of this shape, it has a partial vacuum in the center, as no fan air is dispersed down through it. The angle between the outer edges of the flame includes an area of 60 deg. It is easy to see from this pattern that the best type of nozzle for this burner would be a 60-deg, hollow-spray type (see Fig. 2-28).

A burner equipped with a conventional turbulator and end cone produces a quite different spray pattern. Fig. 2-49(b) shows graphically

Table 2-2 Recommended Combustion-chamber Sizes for Engelhard HP-53 Combustion Head and H Series Spray Nozzle

Nozzle size, gph, 80 deg.	0.75	0.85	1.00	1.20	1.35	1.50	1.65	2.00
Firebox width, in.	12	12	12	13	14	15	15	16
Firebox length, in.	9	10	10	11	12	13	13	14
Center line of nozzle to floor, in.	6	6	6	6½	7	7½	7½	8
Draft over fire	0.02	0.02	0.02	0.02	0.02	0.03	0.03	0.03
Btu at bonnet	78,000	89,000	105,000	127,000	144,000	157,000	175,000	210,000
Sq ft hot water	525	595	700	840	945	1,050	1,155	1,400
Sq ft steam	338	383	450	540	608	675	743	900

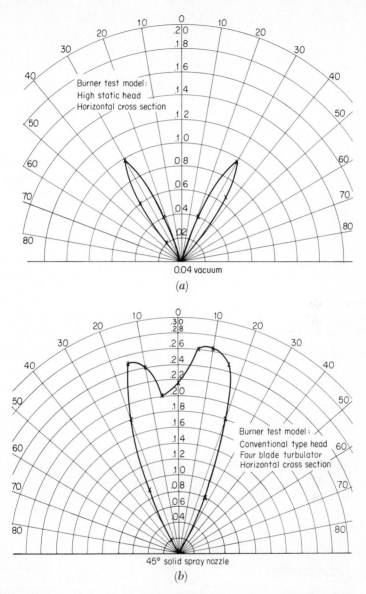

Fig. 2-49 Boston Machine method of graphically showing the air-diffusion characteristics of a burner as the air passes through the combustion chamber. This provides a practical, visual method of matching the nozzle's oil-spray pattern to the burner's air-diffusion pattern. (*a*) Chart of air from a sunflower-type-flame burner head. This pattern has a vacuum in the center, and no air goes down the middle. This air pattern would require a hollow-spray nozzle for best results. (*b*) Chart of air from a conventional type burner, with an ordinary turbulator and end cone. This air pattern would require a solid-spray nozzle for best results, as there is plenty of air going down the center opposite the nozzle.

what this air diffusion is. It covers an angle span of about 40 deg and
operates at a higher air pressure—as high as 0.26 in. of water. The
burner air pattern shown in Fig. 2-49(*a*) reaches a pressure of approximately 0.09. It is obvious that the air-diffusion pattern of the burner
shown in Fig. 2-49(*b*) would require a nozzle with a 45-deg angle of spray
producing a solid cone of atomized oil.

AIR-HANDLING MODERNIZATION

The air-handling modernization kit shown in Figs. 2-50 and 51 has a
special nozzle and was designed as a package approach to the problem
of modernizing older high-pressure gun-type burners already installed
and in operation for a considerable number of years. If their air-handling
parts were modified or replaced, many of these burners could be as efficient as brand-new burners and even almost as efficient as comparable
unitary equipment. The kit comes in two ranges, one of which will up-
grade burners from 0.65 to 1.50 gal per hour and the other burners having
a capacity of from 1.65 to 2.50 gal per hour.

   Air-handling parts of this head (Fig. 2-50) consist of an end cone, a
sleeve, static-pressure disks, and a special patented nozzle somewhat
different from the conventional high-pressure nozzles discussed earlier in
this chapter. The disks and end cones vary in diameter, as determined
by two factors: the nozzle capacity in gallons per hour and the size of the
blast (air) tube which carries the air from the fan and is an integral part
of the whole burner housing. The addition of a complete assembly such
as this provides a quick, easy, and comparatively inexpensive way of

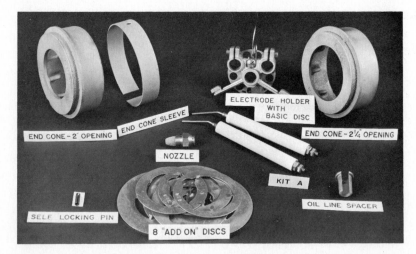

Fig. 2-50   Parts for Gulf Econojet modernization kit.

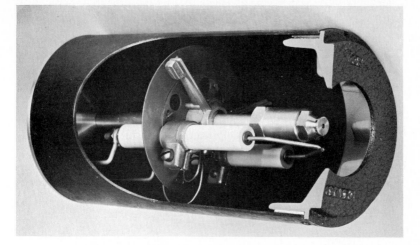

Fig. 2-51 Assembled Gulf Econojet modernization kit.

bringing the performance of older burners up to the efficiency of newer equipment.

Figure 2-52 shows the special nozzle used with this combustion head assembly.   It is a high-pressure nozzle in the conventional sense, as it is designed to operate at 100-psi oil pressure.   However, in addition, to the usual high-pressure nozzle parts, it has incorporated in its design an outer chamber containing air-inlet holes and a second orifice for discharging a

Fig. 2-52 Exterior view of Gulf Econojet nozzle.

mixture of atomized fuel and air.   The inner tangential slots and the small inner orifice are sized to impart a higher velocity to the atomized fuel. This velocity aspirates air through the inlet holes shown at the tip of the nozzle housing just before and at right angles to the nozzle oil-spray outlet.   The air drawn in through these holes (aspirated) is premixed with oil spray in the outer chamber formed between the small oil orifice and the larger orifice in the outlet of the nozzle.   This is an added feature of this high-pressure nozzle.   It admixes oil and air before they have left the nozzle tip by keeping air in close proximity to the oil spray so that it may be caught up by the atomized oil, thereby improving the mix.

The addition of air-control devices such as those mentioned above is extremely valuable.   They mean good operating efficiencies, less servic-

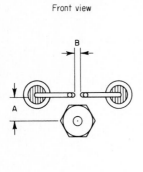
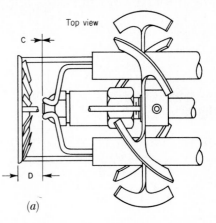
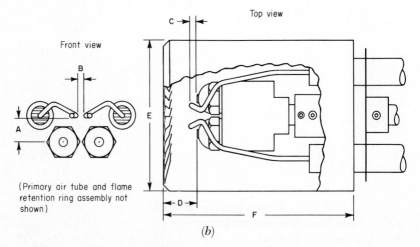

Fig. 2-53   Carlin flame retention head.   Note flame retention ring.   (*a*) Single-nozzle application; (*b*) dual-nozzle application.

(a)

Dimensions (in inches) for Combustion Head Settings of Carlin Flame Retention Head

Model number	Bottom of electrode wires to orifice of nozzle(s)	Spark gap at bends of electrode wires	Relation of electrode wire tips to face of nozzle(s)	Nozzle face to outside rim of flame retention ring	Primary air tube and flame retention ring assembly: Outside diameter	Overall length
150N-2R	½	⅛	Flush	⅝	—	—
150N-3R	½	⅛	Flush	⅝	—	—
400N-2	½	⅛	Flush	⅝	—	—
400N-3	½	⅛	Flush	⅝	—	—
450FR-1	⁷⁄₁₆	⅛	⅛ ahead	½	2¾	4
450FR-2	⁷⁄₁₆	⅛	⅛ ahead	½	2¾	4
700FR	⁷⁄₁₆	⅛	⅛ ahead	⅝	3⅛	4
950FR-1	⁷⁄₁₆	⅛	⅛ ahead	¾	3½	4
950FR-2	⁷⁄₁₆	⅛	⅛ ahead	¾	3½	4
1200FR-1	⁷⁄₁₆	⅛	⅛ ahead	¾	3½	4
1200FR-2	⁷⁄₁₆	⅛	⅛ ahead	¾	3½	4

(b)

Fig. 2-54 (a) Closeup of Carlin flame retention head. (b) Dimensions for combustion head settings.

ing, and an economy of operation that is highly desirable. They should not be looked upon as added work or unnecessary adjustments. They are definitely needed and desirable. In truth, the last frontier of development on the highly standardized high-pressure gun-type burner is its air delivery.

TRANSFORMERS AND IGNITION ASSEMBLIES

High-pressure gun-type burners use electric ignition exclusively. The ignition system is fairly simple and consists of a step-up transformer, high-tension leads, electrodes, and ceramic insulators. The transformer furnishes the high-voltage current; the ignition leads carry the current to the electrodes; and the electrodes are insulated from the surrounding metal surfaces by the ceramic insulators. The spark or electric arc set up by the high-voltage current is pushed into the path of the oil spray by the air moving down the blast tube from the fan, and ignition of the oil spray is then accomplished. The voltage required to produce the spark is about 10,000 volts, although some burners have one 7,000-volt electrode.

The voltage needed to initiate the electric arc requires the use of a step-up ignition transformer. This usually comprises a primary coil and two secondary coils, which are wound over a laminated iron yoke or core and are connected and grounded to the iron core. The metal case provides the gound for this core. The ignition leads are connected by means of terminals to the other side of the secondary coils. These types of transformers are referred to as "mid-point grounded," since the secondary coils are grounded to the case.

An ordinary ignition transformer primary is 110 to 115 volts, while the secondary is 10,000 volts and about 23 ma. This high voltage is not normally dangerous, because of the very low amperage. Actually, such

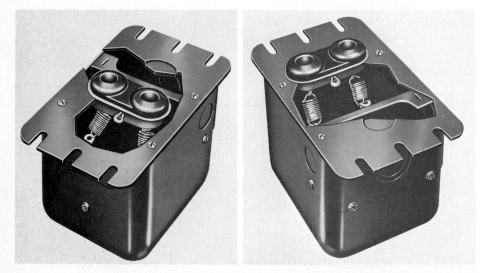

Fig. 2-55 This Webster (Sta-Rite) ignition transformer utilizes one model to provide replacement for about 75 per cent of those in use today. The secondary (high-voltage) terminals may be located at any of three locations on the transformer base. The illustrations above show two of these locations.

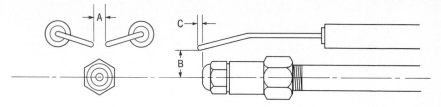

Fig. 2-56 Important spacings in setting electrodes.

high voltage is necessary only to get the spark across the gap, and once it is established, we have for all practical purposes what amounts to a short circuit of the secondary. The ignition transformer is capable of sustaining this short circuit over long periods of time without overheating.

The voltage produced in the secondary depends upon the ratio of turns between the primary coil and the secondary coil. The secondary coil contains the larger number of turns—anywhere from 60,000 turns of fine wire—and because of this it is a step-up transformer. The primary coil consists of several hundred turns of comparatively heavy wire. These coils as they rest in the metal case are covered with a tarlike compound that is heated and poured over them. This provides adequate protection against corrosion, dampness, etc. For this reason also, it is impractical to service transformers in the field, since they must be heated in an oven to soften the sealing material in order to remove it and reach the coils. A defective or weak transformer should be immediately replaced, for properly placed hot ignition in one all-important factor in preventing a puffback. Occasionally, oil-burner transformers will cause radio interference, but this is rare with mid-point grounded transformers as they exist today. If it does occur, a small condenser should be installed. These condensers are usually sold under the name of "radio interference eliminators," "suppressors," or "static eliminators" (see Chap. 25).

Multistrand copper wire with heavy insulation (or metal bars) carries the current to the electrodes, which are metal rods usually of nickel-

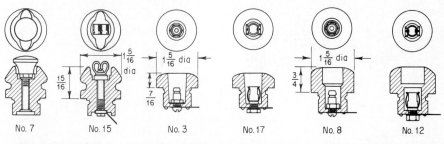

Fig. 2-57 Various types of ignition terminals. (*Heating Div., Sta-Rite Industries*)

Fig. 2-58 Porcelain insulators.

chromium alloy. These electrodes are rounded at the tips to provide a greater surface of dispersal for the spark and to prevent arcing or burning away of the metal. They are held by ceramic insulators, the only material that will properly insulate under such high voltage. Electrode settings are important, and Chap. 25 gives general recommended settings. It is wise to follow the burner manufacturer's directions in this matter.

Gun-type burners may employ either constant or "intermittent" ignition. With constant ignition, the spark is present all the time the burner is on. Intermittent ignition provides a spark when the burner starts, for a period varying from 1 to 2 min. Most burners employ intermittent-type ignition. Whether ignition is of one type or the other depends upon the kind of primary control used.

BOILER-BURNER AND FURNACE-BURNER UNITS

The use of unitary equipment, of which the burner, boiler or furnace, and controls are integral parts, has dominated the residential heating field since the early 1950s. Prior to that time, most installations were

Fig. 2-59 Typical transformer mountings on top and lower side of oil-burner housing.

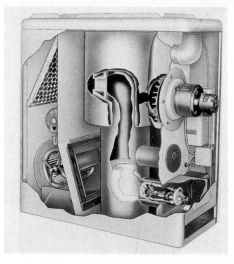

Fig. 2-60   A Space Conditioning unit with high-pressure burner.   Parts are assembled on furnace in specific locations not usual when compared with conventional gun-type burners.

of the conversion type, consisting of an oil burner and a combustion chamber which replaced the grates and ash pit in former coal-burning boilers.

The advent and mass installation of burner-boiler or furnace units brought a great degree of mechanical and engineering sophistication to

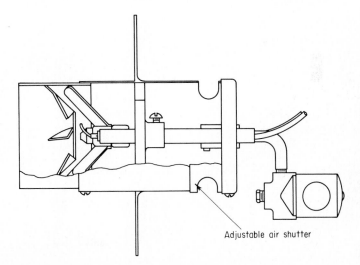

Adjustable air shutter

Fig. 2-61   Space Conditioning combustion head, shown in lower-right part of Fig. 2-60.

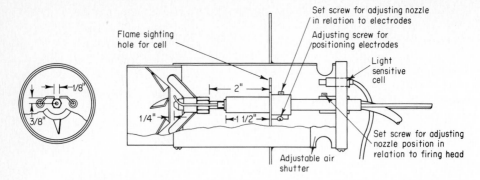

Fig. 2-62 The same head as shown in Fig. 2-61, but this one is equipped with mounting for a light-detection cell for use with a primary control requiring this. Note electrode settings. *(Space Conditioning)*

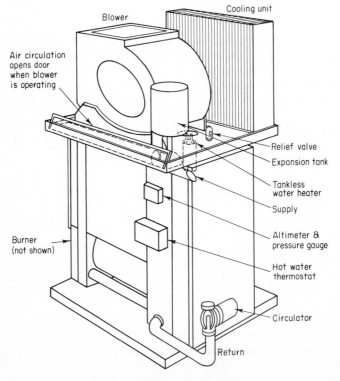

Fig. 2-63 This Unitron combines warm air and hydronic heating with domestic hot water in a single unit. *(Thermo-Dynamics Inc.)*

the oil-heating field. Designed from the start for integral operation of the burner and boiler or furnace, they represented the "truly engineered" approach to residential oil heating. This engineering approach, as opposed to the pragmatic approach necessitated by the application of a burner to an existing coal burner, helped the residential oil-heating industry tremendously. Not only did such units decrease operational costs and increase efficiency, but their package design and compactness did much to increase consumer confidence in, and acceptance of, oil heating.

Service was also substantially reduced and simplified. This led to better overall performance for the cost. This improvement is evidenced by the fact that the average number of service calls for an oil-burner installation in 1950 was about 4.5 per year. This number declined to an average of 2.0 calls per year by 1960 and to 1.4 calls per year by 1968. The oil-burning furnace or boiler unit plus organized service training and better technical schools account for this decline.

Although there are dozens of brands of well-made and -engineered oil-fired units on the market, only a few can be discussed here. Figure 2-60 shows one well-known, advanced-design unit employing the high-pressure burner. The Custom Mark II series, which is built only as an integral part of domestic furnaces and boilers, has an induced draft fan at the flue outlet. The ID fan motor also operates the fuel unit. The blast-tube assembly, including combustion head, nozzle, ignition assembly, air shutter, and flame scanner, is located in the inlet to the combustion zone. Owing to the high negative fire-box pressure, this system is used only in sealed furnaces and boilers.

Its special-design combustion head with an adjustable air shutter and conventional high-pressure nozzle is shown in Fig. 2-61. This is the typical nozzle-and-flame-cone assembly for this unit. All air for combustion flows at a relatively high velocity through air ports of special shape and size. The position of the nozzle in relation to the air cone is critical. Fins attached to the nozzle adapter maintain the nozzle location and also act as heat radiators to maintain a nozzle temperature of only a few degrees above that of the entering air. The nozzle size, make, and type recommended by the manufacturer must be used. The air-flow rate is largely determined by the fan pressure and air-slot size, but may be modified over a range of approximately 20 per cent by the adjustable air shutter.

In checking combustion with the ID unit for true excess air determination, CO_2 samples must be taken ahead of the fan because of dilution by cooling air drawn in around the fan shaft. Combustion efficiency, determined by CO_2 and gas temperature, is the same when measured ahead of or after the fan, because the total heat content of the vented gas remains the same even though both temperature and CO_2 are reduced by

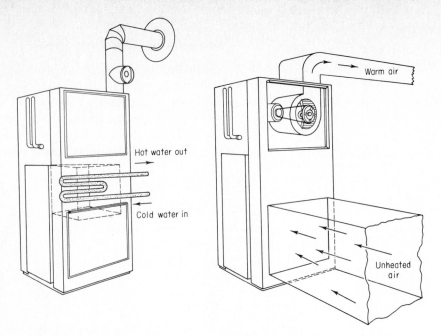

Hot water out

Cold water in

Warm air

Unheated
air

Fig. 2-64 Separate hot water and warm air circulation in Unitron. (*Thermo-Dynamics Inc.*)

Fig. 2-65 This shows how Unitron can be adapted to cooling by installing the evaporator coil at top. The finned-coil heat exchange shown at the bottom is used for hot-water heating applications.

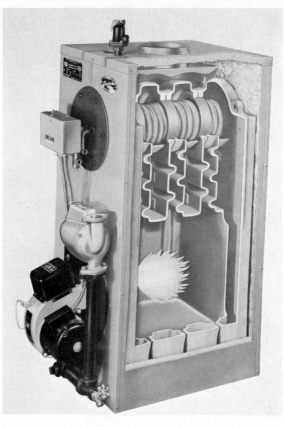

Fig. 2-66 A cast-iron boiler, in this case with high-pressure gun-type burner, comprises a complete unit. The unit, equipped with circulator, primary, and water-temperature controls, and an instantaneous domestic hot-water coil, provides a long-life heating package. (*H. B. Smith Co. Inc.*)

dilution. Near-zero Shell-Bacharach smoke readings should be expected without a warm-up period.

The unit shown in Figs. 2-63 and 2-64 is a completely sophisticated engineering approach to almost every phase of residential comfort climate control. This multiple-application "unitary equipment" is the next step in the evolution of oil-heating equipment from (1) the conversion installation to (2) the burner furnace or boiler heating unit to (3) the burner "climate-control" unit. Unitary equipment has progressed through heating, hot water, and humidification to heating-cooling, humidification-dehumidification, and domestic hot water plus warm air and hydronic (wet heat) applications with all control in a single package.

By a series of heat exchangers and other devices providing a high

Fig. 2-67   A typical oil-fired tank-type hot-water heater.   (*Carlin*)

Table 2-3   Btu Requirements for Heating Swimming Pools

Pool pickup time, hr	Pool size, gal					
	15,000	**20,000**	**25,000**	**30,000**	**35,000**	**40,000**
12	260,000	345,000	433,000	519,000	606,000	693,000
24	130,000	172,000	216,000	260,000	303,000	346,000
36	87,000	116,000	144,000	173,000	202,000	231,000
48	65,000	87,000	109,000	130,000	152,000	173,000

Based on a temperature rise of 25°F for a 30° rise, add 20 per cent. Most people will accept a 48-hr pickup time, since it happens only once a year when the pool is first heated. Water-heater output should be about 20 per cent higher than BTU demand for pool size and time required. (Table courtesy of Oil Heat Institute of Washington State.)

degree of flexibility, this unit provides all these features and can be used for warm-air or hot-water heating, alone or in combination.

Another unitary piece of oil-fired equipment which is growing rapidly in popularity because of low operating costs and high recovery rates is the water heater (Fig. 2-67). These oil-fired water heaters, which come in a variety of sizes, ranging from 30-gal tanks on up to tanks for sizable commercial applications, utilize conventional high-pressure gun-type burners and sometimes low-pressure burners with low firing rates.

Most of these hot-water heaters have special linings, such as glass, ceramic, "stone," and copper. They have applications other than supplying the domestic hot-water market, one of which is the heating of water for swimming pools. The oil-fired hot-water heater is especially suitable for this purpose because of its rapid recovery rate (see Table 2-3).

COMMERCIAL-INDUSTRIAL HEATING UNITS
Using No. 2 oil

Many commercial and industrial installations now utilize high-pressure gun-type burner units. These include garages, gasoline stations, factories, warehouses, etc. Ideal for these, the commercial-industrial oil-fired unit comes in several basic designs: (1) unit heaters, (2) special large air heaters, and (3) blower heaters. Vented to the atmosphere, they have high heat-producing capacities along with the feature of rapid heating.

(a)   (b)

Fig. 2-68 (a) Front and (b) back view of PowRmatic unit heater. This thermostatically controlled blower-type commercial-industrial heater (three models) has an output range of 84,000, 140,000 and 184,800 Btu per hour, utilizing nozzle sizes, respectively, of 0.75, 1.25 and 1.65 gal of No. 2 fuel oil per hour.

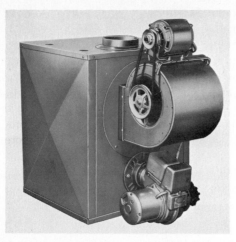

Fig. 2-69 A PowRmatic blower-type heater identical in output and nozzle size with the unit heater shown in Fig. 2-68. Note that this unit employs a sirocco- (squirrel-cage) type fan. This is designed for ducted delivery of the heated air.

Fig. 2-70 A large industrial-type PowRmatic space heater.

Within a few moments of starting, they are producing and delivering large quantities of heated air.

Conventional-pressure gun-type burners used with this equipment are easy to service and are comparatively trouble free. This burner is applied in increasing gph capacity to the blower heater (typical of the conventional warm-air furnace), the unit heater, and the air heater. The latter is for large industrial applications. The oil-fired unit heater shown in Figure 2-68 is typical of this equipment. Manufacturers usually provide a range for this equipment running from 70,000 to 200,000 or more Btu per hour.

A larger-capacity air heater is shown in Fig. 2-70. Outputs range from half a million to a million Btu per hour. They may be floor-mounted, wall-mounted, or suspended from the ceiling, as the application requires.

QUESTIONS

1. What are the characteristic parts of a high-pressure gun-type burner? Explain each.
2. What is meant by a single-stage pump; a two-stage pump? When should each be used?
3. What are the parts of a "fuel unit"?
4. How many different types of pressure regulating valves are used on domestic oil burners? What are they?
5. Give the threefold function of a pressure regulating valve.
6. How does a pressure regulating valve maintain constant pressure at the nozzle?
7. What is the purpose of the nozzle? How does it accomplish its purpose?
8. What effect has viscosity on the capacity of a nozzle? Why?
9. How many cubic feet of air are theoretically required to burn 1 gal of fuel oil?
10. What is the function of a combustion head?
11. What are the parts of the ignition assembly? Explain the function of each part.
12. Explain the primary and secondary circuits of the ignition transformer.
13. What are the three evolutionary types of oil-heating equipment? How do they differ in function and application?
14. What are the performance advantages of oil-fired water heaters?

CHAPTER 3
LOW-PRESSURE
ATOMIZING BURNERS

Low-pressure domestic gun-type atomizing burners are unique in the one respect that oil and air meet prior to leaving the nozzle. With high-pressure gun-type burners oil and air do not make contact until they both have actually left the burner and entered the firebox. The stream of secondary air moving down the blast tube is utilized to create turbulence and provide the necessary oxygen for combustion. Thus, there are actually two streams of air utilized by the low-pressure domestic gun-type burner. That air which atomizes the oil upon leaving the nozzle is referred to as "primary" air, while in this case the air moving down the blast tube and meeting the mixture in the combustion chamber is "secondary" air. The operating pressures of these burners normally range from 1 to 5 psi, as against the 100 psi used by high-pressure burners. Some low-pressure domestic burners use as high as 15 psi atomizing and operating pressure.

The application of the air-pressure atomization principle requires special types of nozzles, and the maintenance of air pressures at anywhere from 1 to 15 psi requires special pressure-making devices. Thus, every brand of low-pressure burner is essentially unique and different from that of other manufacturers. In principle they are somewhat the same, but they are different in mechanical operation and application. In this respect, they differ radically from the high-pressure burner, with its characteristic parts standardization. Because of this unique mechanical application of low-pressure-air atomization, it is necessary to discuss these burners separately.

WILLIAMS OIL-O-MATIC

The Williams Oil-O-Matic (Fig. 3-1) is a well-known low-pressure burner with capacities of from $\frac{1}{2}$ to 25 gph extending through a number of models. As the mechanical application of the low-pressure atomization principle is practically the same in all Williams Oil-O-Matic models, the following diagrams and description will serve for all except the Fifty-Ten and R160A.

The characteristic parts of the Williams Oil-O-Matic are the bellows-type valve control assembly, the thrift meter, the pressurotor and air-intake muffler, the sump stabilizer, and the nozzle. If the tank is buried and the oil requires lift to get to the burner, an ordinary gear pump is attached to perform the suction lift. If the oil flows by gravity

Fig. 3-1 Cutaway view of older-model Williams Oil-O-Matic low-pressure burner.

to the burner, the oil line is connected directly to the valve housing and no suction pump is required.

When the burner is not running, the oil valve in the bellows assembly is in the OFF position, and no oil can reach the metering device. As the motor begins to rotate on the starting cycle, the metering device and the pressurotor begin to turn. The pressurotor draws in air and commences to build pressure, which is exerted through two channels (see Fig. 3-5). One carries the pressure back to the bellows valve assembly and one to the float chamber (sump-stabilizer assembly). When the pressure created by the pressurotor reaches about 1 psi, the bellows opens and lifts the valve, allowing the oil to flow through to the thrift meter.

The thrift meter, a positive displacement pump, has a piston in a cylinder. Together, they form a rotor surrounded by a steel ring and driven from the motor shaft.

In the pump body there are two curved ports—one suction, one discharge. As the rotor passes the suction port, the piston is on the "out" stroke and picks up a fixed quantity of oil, which is released at the discharge port where the piston completes its downstroke.

The rate of oil flow can be increased or decreased by manually varying the position of the ring or casing against which the piston head

Fig. 3-2 Exposed view of vaned pressurotor in the Williams Oil-O-Matic (Fig. 3-1).

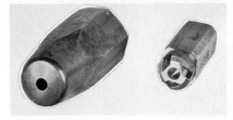

Fig. 3-3   Williams Oil-O-Matic nozzle.

presses.   The greater the eccentricity, the longer must be the stroke of the piston.

The oil now passes to the pressurotor, which consists of six vanes of fiber-type material (Figs. 3-2 and 3-5).   While rotating, the vanes press against the casing because of centrifugal force.   This pressurotor also draws in air through an intake muffler.   The air is used to create the necessary pressure to atomize the oil (by the jet of air) just before leaving the nozzle orifice.   The pressure created by this pressurotor is adjustable, and the adjusting screw opens a bypass that allows a portion of the oil-air mixture to go back to the suction side of the pressurotor, thus lowering the pressure on the sump chamber.   As this bypass is closed, all the oil and air are forced through to the sump, thereby raising the operating pressure.

The oil-air mixture is now discharged into the sump-stabilizer chamber where the oil, being heavier, drops to the bottom and the air remains on top.   As the oil level in the sump rises, the float also rises, lifting the valve stem.   At this point the oil feeds into the oil tube, which has its opening near the bottom of the sump.   The oil is now forced by the air pressure above it to move through the tube to the nozzle.   The air moves through an outer channel created by the wall of the oil tube and the outer casing (Fig. 3-5).   The oil and air meet in two streams just before the nozzle orifice.   This air jet serves to bring about complete

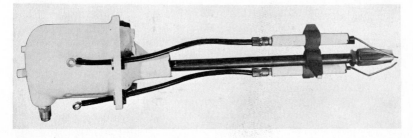

Fig. 3-4   Nozzle-assembly electrodes and sump-stabilizer housing.   (*Williams Oil-O-Matic*)

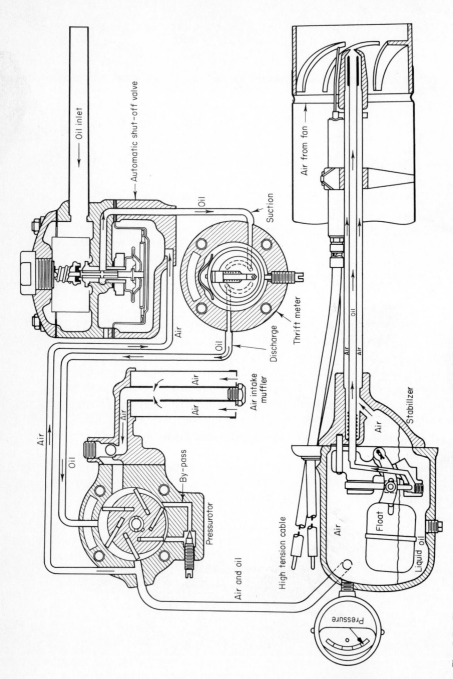

Fig. 3-5 Flow diagram: primary air and fuel oil. (*Williams Oil-O-Matic*)

atomization of the oil as it leaves the nozzle. It is not, however, sufficient to support combustion. The major air supply comes from the conventional impeller-type fan, moving through the burner blast tube. An air cone at the end of the tube furnishes the turbulence necessary to provide the proper oil-air mixture. A rotational-type shutter controls the air input to the fan.

The stabilizer consists of a float-actuated needle valve and provides a means to conduct oil and air separately to the oil-air nozzle. In operation there is always a uniform level of oil in the housing. This causes the float to ride in a fixed position whether the burner is operating or idle. When the firing rate is increased, the level of this oil will rise, seek its own level, and remain constant. As the firing rate is decreased, the oil level will drop. In either case, the action of the stabilizer precludes sudden pressure changes at the oil-air nozzle.

When the pressure drops, the bellows in the main oil-control valve assembly expands, and spring pressure causes the valve stem to descend and close off the main oil supply. At least 1 psi of pressure is required to reopen this bellows, and it is important therefore that the operating pressure is not set below 1 psi, for in such case the burner would be unable to start.

A later model of the Williams Oil-O-Matic known as the Fifty-Ten has been designed to be handled as a sealed unit much in the manner of some modern electric refrigerators. This unit contains the strainer, fuel pump, oil-pressure regulator, metering pump, and pressurotor. The oil valve is not enclosed in the sealed unit.

This model has a built-in gear pump and requires no auxiliary pump for use with an outside tank. To use this burner with a gravity-fed single-line system, one must remove the bypass plug shown in Fig. 3-8. No return line is then necessary. Motor speed is 3,450 rpm.

Fig. 3-6 Air cone. (*Williams Oil-O-Matic*)

Fig. 3-7 Williams-Oil-O-Matic model Fifty-Ten.

Figure 3-9 shows the path followed by the oil and air through this burner. As the flow diagram shows, the oil enters the fuel unit at the strainer housing. From here it passes down through the fuel pump into the oil-pressure regulator, where the oil is divided. Part of the oil bypasses the pressure regulator and flows into the metering pump. The excess oil passes the port of the pressure regulator and is returned to the strainer housing. A ball check in the rotor of the pressure regulator is held in a closed position by centrifugal force until enough pressure is built up by the pump to force the ball off its seat.

As pictured by the flow diagram, the oil channel between the pump and pressure regulator connects with the hydraulic valve. Thus, pressure built up by the pressure regulator in these channels opens the oil valve at maximum pressure and provides a full-sized flame immediately. When the motor speed drops to 2,800 rpm, the regulating pressure drops and the valve closes, eliminating any possibility of afterdrip.

Air for atomization of the oil at the nozzle is drawn in by the pressurotor through openings in the sealed unit housing. It passes through the enclosed muffler into the rotor cylinder. From here, air under pressure passes through the hydraulic valve to the manifold and then to the oil-air connection at the base of the blast tube. The air pressure is adjustable by means of the atomizing pressure adjusting screw (bypass) located in the fuel unit housing. The pressurotor is lubricated through a passage from the hydraulic valve to the rotor cylinder. Clearance between the stem and valve body allows ample oil to flow to the rotor for lubrication.

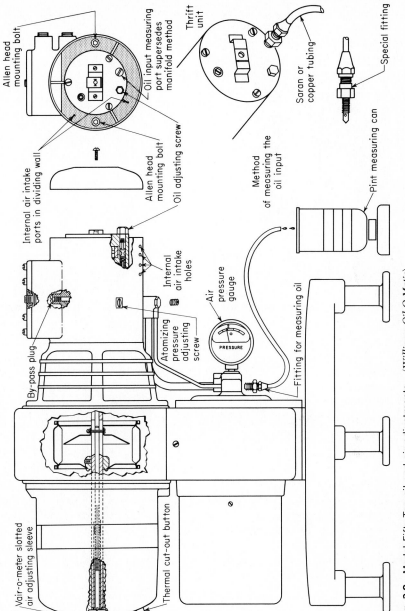

Allen head mounting bolt

Oil input measuring port supersedes manifold method

Thrift unit

Special fitting

Internal air intake ports in dividing wall

Allen head mounting bolt

Oil adjusting screw

Saran or copper tubing

Pint measuring can

Method of measuring the oil input

Internal air intake holes

Atomizing pressure adjusting screw

Air pressure gauge

PRESSURE

Fitting for measuring oil

By-pass plug

Vair-o-meter slotted air adjusting sleeve

Thermal cut-out button

Fig. 3-8 Model Fifty-Ten oil and air adjustments. (*Williams Oil-O-Matic*)

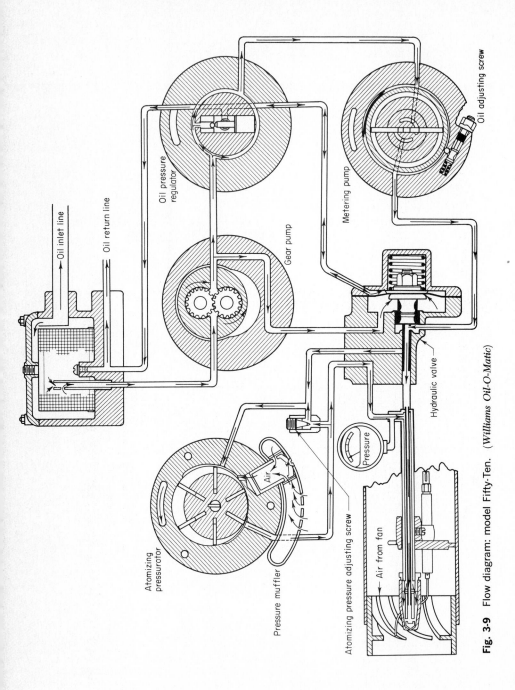

Fig. 3-9 Flow diagram: model Fifty-Ten. (*Williams Oil-O-Matic*)

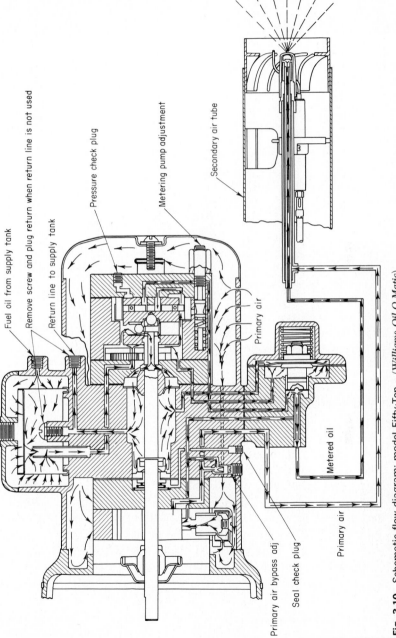

Fuel oil from supply tank

Remove screw and plug return when return line is not used

Return line to supply tank

Pressure check plug

Metering pump adjustment

Secondary air tube

Primary air

Metered oil

Primary air

Primary air bypass adj

Seal check plug

Fig. 3-10 Schematic flow diagram: model Fifty-Ten. *(Williams Oil-O-Matic)*

The following are recommended operating pressures for the Fifty-Ten:

Gph rate	Pressure, psi
½–1¼	1½–1¾
1¼–2	1¾–2
2 –3	2 –2¼

Fig. 3-11   Williams Oil-O-Matic R160 burner.

R160 BURNER OPERATION
Fig. 3-12

After the burner has been started and motor speed has reached approximately 3,150 rpm, an air pressure of 6 to 8 psi is developed in the air pump (*GG*) and transmitted to the aspirator assembly (*I*). This air is forced through the aspirator assembly (*I*) and discharged into the oil-supply container (*N*). Primary air for fuel atomization is supplied to the nozzle (*EE*) from this container (*N*) through the port (*T*). The atomizing pressure is controlled by the pressure regulator (*H*), which will bypass excess air back to the intake side of the air pump (*GG*). Any normal operating pressure between 1 and 1½ psi can be maintained in the oil-supply container (*N*) by proper positioning of the pressure regulator adjustment screw (*E*).

When the supply of primary air from the air pump (*GG*) is forced through the aspirator assembly (*I*), a vacuum is created in the float housing (*L*) through the open port (*J*). The same amount of vacuum

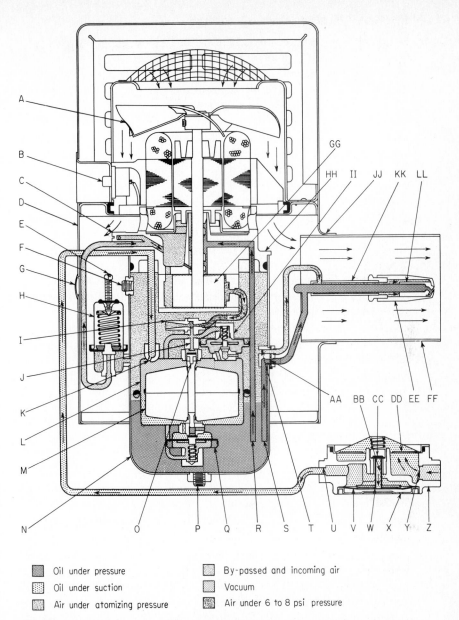

A

B

C

D

E

F

G

H

I

J

K

L

M

N

GG

HH II JJ KK LL

AA BB CC DD EE FF

O P Q R S T U V W X Y Z

■ Oil under pressure

▦ Oil under suction

▦ Air under atomizing pressure

▦ By-passed and incoming air

▦ Vacuum

▦ Air under 6 to 8 psi pressure

Fig. 3-12 Flow diagram: Williams Oil-O-Matic R160 burner. (*A*) Fan assembly. (*B*) Switch thermal manual reset. (*C*) Air-intake muffler. (*D*) Access panel. (*E*) Pressure-regulator adjusting screw. (*F*) Pressure-gauge port. (*G*) Snap fastener. (*H*) Pressure-regulator assembly. (*I*) Aspirator assembly. (*J*) Port aspirator to float housing. (*K*) Port-float housing oil intake. (*L*) Float housing assembly. (*M*) Float assembly. (*N*) Oil-supply container. (*O*) Float-valve-stem assembly. (*P*) Drain plug. (*Q*) Lower valve. (*R*) Tube oil to bearings. (*S*) Tube oil to nozzle. (*T*) Port air to nozzle. (*U*) Oil-valve discharge port. (*V*) Diaphragm oil valve. (*W*) Guide-pin oil valve. (*X*) Vent-hole oil valve. (*Y*) Port oil-valve intake. (*Z*) Oil-valve assembly. (*AA*) Orifice metering. (*BB*) Porting through oil-valve guide pin. (*CC*) Disk-retainer oil valve. (*DD*) Strainer oil valve. (*EE*) Nozzle. (*FF*) Draft-pipe assembly. (*GG*) Air pump. (*HH*) Bearing-body assembly. (*II*) Upper valve. (*JJ*) Burner case. (*KK*) Nozzle and electrode assembly. (*LL*) Oil spiral.

will be drawn on both sides of the diaphragms in the upper valve (*II*) and lower valve (*Q*) and in the oil inlet through the port (*K*). The amount of vacuum drawn in these chambers (*L, II, Q,* and *K*) will be that vacuum necessary to lift oil from the storage tank to the burner. Both the upper valve (*II*) and the lower valve (*Q*) will be held in the closed position by spring forces during the pump cycle. The springs will hold the valves (*II* and *Q*) closed during the pump cycle because equal amounts of vacuum are drawn on both sides of the diaphragms.

The oil valve (*Z*) will open when a vacuum of 3 to 5 in. of mercury is drawn in the chamber above the oil-valve diaphragm (*V*). When the diaphragm (*V*) is pulled to the UP position, the guide pin (*W*) will force the disk retainer (*CC*) up against the spring and allow oil to be pulled from the storage tank into the port (*Y*), through the strainer (*DD*), around the disk retainer (*CC*), through the ports (*BB* and *U*), and on to the float housing (*L*).

As oil is being pulled into the float housing (*L*), the float (*M*) and float-valve-stem assembly (*O*) will rise with the oil level until the port (*J*) is sealed. The float-housing chamber (*L*) is now sealed from the aspirator (*I*). Since the aspirator (*I*) is pulling on a sealed chamber, rather than a column of oil, a deeper vacuum will be pulled on the spring sides of the diaphragms in the upper valve (*II*) and lower valve (*Q*). This vacuum, applied across the area of the diaphragms, is enough to force the upper valve (*II*) open against the force of the spring. The upper valve (*II*) will open momentarily ahead of the lower valve (*Q*) because of a weaker spring in the upper valve (*II*). This is done to break the vacuum in the float housing (*L*) before the lower valve (*Q*) opens to prevent oil from being pulled into the float housing (*L*) from container (*N*).

When the upper valve (*II*) opens, air under pressure in the container (*N*) will flow into the float housing (*L*), breaking the vacuum in the float housing (*L*) and oil inlet line. When the vacuum in the oil inlet line is broken, the oil valve (*Z*) will close. The lower valve (*Q*) will now be forced open, allowing oil to flow through the lower valve (*Q*) and into container (*N*) until both levels are equal.

The air pressure in the oil-supply container (*N*) forces oil from the oil-supply container through the tube (*S*) and metering orifice (*AA*) and onto the nozzle (*EE*). As the oil level in the oil-supply container (*N*) drops, the oil level in the float housing (*L*) will also drop. When the float (*M*) drops, the float-valve-stem assembly (*P*) will be pulled away from the port (*J*), starting the next pumping cycle.

The air pressure in the oil-supply container (*N*) and the orifice (*AA*) in the oil line regulates the amount of oil delivered to the nozzle. Besides forcing oil through the nozzle (*EE*), the air pressure in the oil-supply container (*N*) also forces fuel oil up the tube (*R*) to the bearing body (*HH*) for lubrication of the bearing. Excess lubricating oil enters the air pump (*GG*) with the incoming air, lubricates the air pump (*GG*), and is discharged through the aspirator (*I*) into the supply container (*N*).

Secondary air for combustion is forced into the burner case (*JJ*) by the fan assembly (*A*). The burner case, serving as an air plenum, is under positive pressure. A sliding-disk assembly regulates the amount of air entering the draft pipe (*FF*). This disk can be adjusted for the correct amount of air needed to support combustion.

When the burner is stopped, the air pressure in the oil-supply container (*N*) is immediately dissipated through the pressure regulator (*H*), air pump (*GG*), and air line to the nozzle (*EE*) to provide a clean "shutoff." All oil in the nozzle (*EE*) or oil line to the nozzle, at the time of shutdown, will be siphoned back to the oil-supply container (*N*). This eliminates the carbonization of the oil in the nozzle (*EE*) by reflected heat from the combustion chamber after shutdown.

When the burner is started, there will be a delay in oil delivery to the nozzle (*EE*) of approximately 7 sec. This is due to the time necessary to build up air pressure in container (*N*) and to refill oil tubes leading to the nozzle.

WINKLER LOW-PRESSURE BURNER

The Winkler low-pressure burner is manufactured by the Stewart-Warner Corp., Heating & Air Conditioning Division. This burner does not separate the oil-air mixture during its travel through the burner. Its range runs from $\frac{1}{2}$ to 6 gph.

The characteristic parts of this burner are the metering assembly, which comprises the fuel aerator (air meter) and the fuel meter; the turbanozzle; and the secondary-air-control combustion head at the mouth of the blast tube.

The fuel aerator (air meter), the fuel metering device, and the fan are all on the same shaft and are driven at motor speed by means of a flexible coupling between the fan and the motor. The fuel aerator consists of a spring-loaded single vane (Fig. 3-14) riding an eccentric impeller of meehanite. It is a nonadjustable, positive metering and mixing means for the air that is premixed with the fuel. Flexible-face-type seals are used on each side of the fuel aerator, and the shaft runs in bronze bearings. It is self-lubricated by the fuel oil passing through it.

The fuel meter is made up of three castings. The bottom casting is the piston housing in which the metering pistons operate. The middle casting houses the eccentric shaft and worm-gear reduction (Fig. 3-14). In one end of this housing is a 20-mesh strainer to remove the coarse sediment. The speed of the eccentric shaft is reduced from 1,740 to

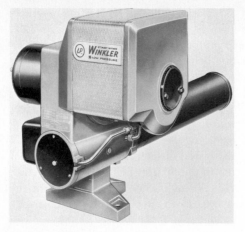

Fig. 3-13 Winkler low-pressure burner. (*Stewart-Warner Corp., Heating & Air Conditioning Div.*)

50 rpm. Twice the eccentricity of this shaft equals the stroke ($\frac{1}{8}$ in.) of the metering pistons. By means of the wobble action of a fork and clevis, the pistons are given an oscillating motion to open and close the intake and discharge ports. Low-speed, positive fuel metering is obtained thereby at no pressure, irrespective of the oil viscosity. The top casting of the fuel meter houses the piston that operates the automatic shutoff valve.

The turba-nozzle consists of three parts: the housing, stem, and cone. The fuel-air mixture flows through a series of passages in the stem and swirls around the cone and through the large orifice in the nozzle housing.

The air-control combustion head divides the air into three streams. The flame shape is controlled by the combination of electrode holder, adjustable flame controller, blast tube, and blast-tube head.

Operation

When the motor starts, the fuel aerator builds up a pressure of approximately $3\frac{1}{2}$ psi in the air-cushioning chamber (Fig. 3-14). This pressure acts on one side of a piston to overcome spring pressures and thus opens the automatic fuel-shutoff valve. Fuel flows by gravity through the strainer chamber into the fuel meter, covering the inlet ports to the pistons that measure the fuel. While one piston is moving up, allowing oil to fill the space under it, the other piston is moving down, forcing the metered fuel to the fuel aerator. A metered amount of air is mixed with a measured amount of fuel in the aerator and forced through the percolating chamber and nozzle tube to the nozzle.

The percolating chamber in conjunction with the air-cushioning

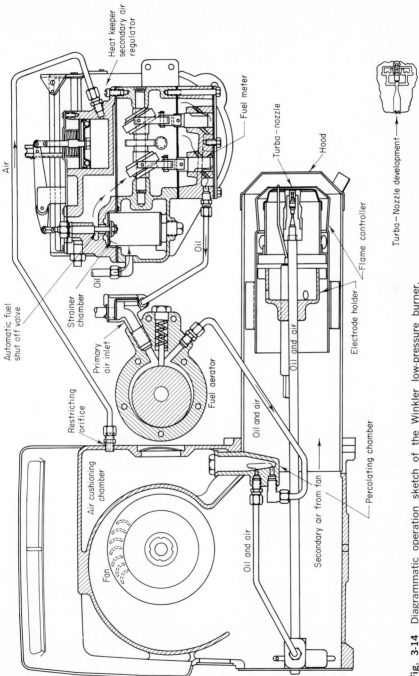

Air

Heat keeper secondary air regulator

Fuel meter

Turba-nozzle

Hood

Flame controller

Electrode holder

Oil and air

Automatic fuel shut off valve

Strainer chamber

Primary air inlet

Oil

Oil

Fuel aerator

Restricting orifice

Air cushioning chamber

Fan

Oil and air

Oil and air

Secondary air from fan

Percolating chamber

Turba-Nozzle development

Fig. 3-14 Diagrammatic operation sketch of the Winkler low-pressure burner. (*Stewart-Warner Corp., Heating & Air Conditioning Div.*)

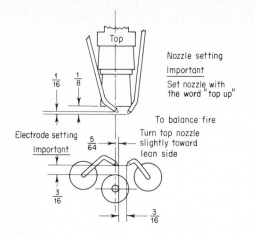

Fig. 3-15 Nozzle and electrode settings for Winkler low-pressure burner.

chamber provides a steady flow of air and a properly proportioned fuel-air mixture. The fuel and air are kept in intimate contact from the time they are mixed in the fuel aerator until they reach the nozzle in the form of foam and oil-saturated vapor.

In the nozzle, this mixture is dashed against a series of passage walls (see nozzle development, Fig. 3-14) by several abrupt changes of flow, dividing the mixture into four separate streams. These streams are hurled inwardly through tangentially drilled holes against and around the nozzle cone, giving the thoroughly atomized fuel-air mixture a swirling action as it passes through the $\frac{5}{32}$-in.-diameter nozzle orifice to be mixed with secondary air from the fan.

The secondary air supplied by the fan is controlled by the heat-keeper secondary air control. Air pressure, which is built up in the air-cushioning chamber by the aerator, is slowly bled through an orifice to the air-piston-chamber assembly of the fuel shutoff valve. As the piston is forced upward by the air pressure, the fuel shutoff valve is opened. The heat-keeper air-control damper is connected to the beam of the fuel shutoff valve with a bead chain, and the upward motion of the shutoff valve releases the tension on the bead chain and permits the heat-keeper air-control damper to be opened by spring tension.

The air-control damper and the fuel shutoff valve are not completely opened until after the flame has been established, and as a result of this a smoother, quieter start is obtained.

The air delivered through the blast tube by the fan is divided into three streams. The inner air stream is given a twisting motion by the vanes on the outside of the electrode holder, and the outer stream is given a similar motion by the vanes on the outside of the adjustable flame controller.   With the flame controller in the back position, a small amount of air passes through the holes in the outer surface to form a center stream of straight air.   As it is moved toward the forward position, the space between the front of the controller and the hood is restricted. This decreases the outer stream of twisting air and increases the center stream of straight air, which results in lengthening and straightening the fire.

When the motor stops, the air continues to flow from the air-cushioning chamber until the pressure is dissipated.   This extra air removes any remnants of fuel in the nozzle lines.

If oil is fed by gravity to the burner, no suction pump will be needed.   The requirement of a suction lift necessitates the addition of a gear pump to the metering unit.   To change the capacity of this burner, the pistons and piston housing on the bottom of the fuel meter are removed and replaced with pistons and housing of desired capacity.

GENERAL ELECTRIC LOW-PRESSURE BURNER

This low-pressure burner was produced in two types: the conversion burner and the boiler-burner unit.   One basic difference between these two lies in the delivery of secondary air.   With the conversion gun-type burner shown in Fig. 3-16, the secondary air and oil travel in the same direction and meet in the firebox.   With the boiler-burner unit, the air stream is divided (Fig. 3-18), part traveling in the same direction as the oil (primary air) and part being directed through a channel in such

Fig. 3-16   GE conversion burner. This model has not been manufactured for years.

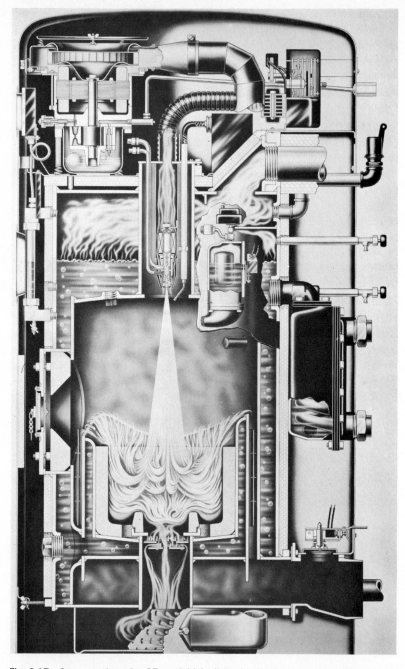

Fig. 3-17 Cross section of a GE model LA oil-fired boiler-burner unit. Although no longer produced, many thousands of these units are still operating, especially in New England.

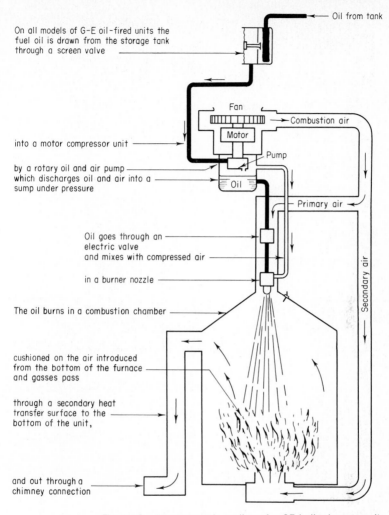

On all models of G–E oil-fired units the
fuel oil is drawn from the storage tank
through a screen valve

Oil from tank

Fan

Motor

Combustion air

into a motor compressor unit

Pump

by a rotary oil and air pump
which discharges oil and air into a
sump under pressure

Oil

Primary air

Oil goes through an
electric valve
and mixes with compressed air

in a burner nozzle

The oil burns in a combustion chamber

Secondary air

cushioned on the air introduced
from the bottom of the furnace
and gasses pass

through a secondary heat
transfer surface to the
bottom of the unit,

and out through a
chimney connection

Fig. 3-18   Diagrammatic outline of a GE boiler-burner unit.

manner as to come up opposed in direction to the oil stream and thereby
meet the flame from the bottom of the unit. Thus, the down-fired oil
spray has air traveling with it and further air meeting the mingling with
it from an opposite direction. In addition, the oil meets with compressed
air in the nozzle (Fig. 3-21). This compressed air within the nozzle
atomizes the oil.

The GE burner and unit both make use of a rotor-type pump with
two vanes that operate tangentially from slots. These vanes rotate
eccentrically from the shaft-driven rotor. As they come up to speed,
they are moved outward by means of centrifugal force, pressing against

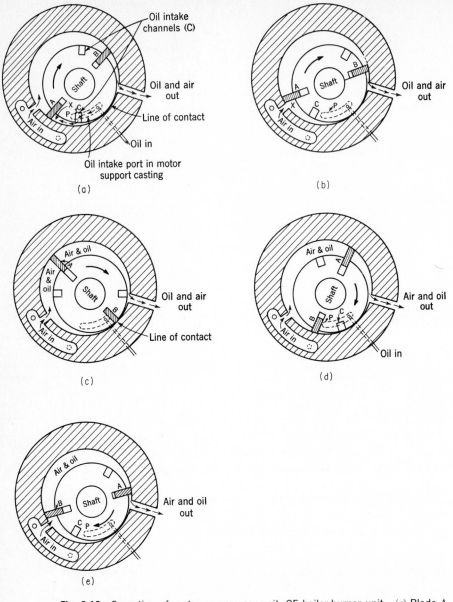

Fig. 3-19 Operation of motor-compressor unit; GE boiler-burner unit. (*a*) Blade *A* is drawing oil through channel *C* in rotor and port *P* in upper casting as space *x* becomes larger. (*b*) Oil channel *C* is now beyond port *P*, so more oil cannot be drawn in. Blade *A* has passed air-inlet port and now draws air as space *x* becomes larger. (*c*) Blade *A* is still drawing air. Blade *B* is passing the "line of contact." Blade *A* is forcing out air and oil previously drawn in by blade *B*. (*d*) Blade *B* is beginning to draw oil through *C* and *P*. Blade *A* is still drawing air. (*e*) Blade *B* has finished drawing oil and has started drawing air. Blade *B* is pushing air and oil just drawn in by *A*. Blade *A* is completing the discharge of air and oil previously drawn in by *B*.

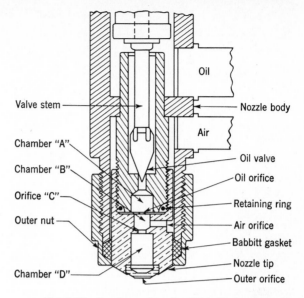

Fig. 3-20   Nozzle used on the GE boiler-burner unit.

the outer casing.   Their rotation creates a vacuum.   Figure 3-19 shows
the stages of operation of the eccentric rotor and the centrifugally
operated vanes.   As they rotate, they draw in oil and air, respectively,
through the ports provided.   As the rotation continues, pressure is
developed and the mingled oil-air mixture is forced out through the
opening provided (Fig. 3-19).   This mixture now passes under pressure
to the sump (Fig. 3-18).   The oil in the sump is used for lubrication
and combustion.   A very tiny opening passes enough fuel oil to furnish
lubrication to the motor bearings.   Because of this fact, it is important
that the unit not run for any length of time unless fuel oil is flowing
through it.   The oil in the sump then passes on to the burner head and
thence to the nozzle.   There is a float valve in the sump (Fig. 3-22)

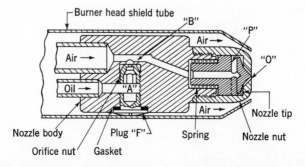

Fig. 3-21   Nozzle used on conversion burners.   *(General Electric Co.)*

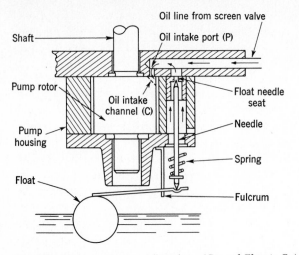

Fig. 3-22 Float-operated needle valve. (*General Electric Co.*)

which controls the oil level therein by allowing air to bypass around to the suction side of the pump when the level is high.

The compressed air furnished by the dual-vaned rotor fills the sump and passes out through the top into a tube that takes it to the burner head and nozzle, where it is used for atomizing the oil.   The pressure of this air determines the oil pressure and is controlled by an air-pressure regulator.   As the air leaves the sump, it passes through a channel to a needle-type spring and bellows-operated valve equipped with an

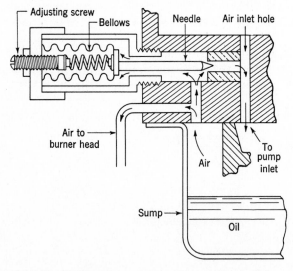

Fig. 3-23 Air-pressure regulator. (*General Electric Co.*)

adjusting screw (Fig. 3-23). This is really an air bypass; and as it is opened, more air is bypassed around to the suction side of the pump. If it is closed, less air can be bypassed, the pressure of the air going to the burner head will be greater, the quantity of oil consumed will also increase. This gives some control over the quantity metered by the oil orifice disk.

The oil-feed line and the compressor air line meet in the nozzle, and the projection of the stream of compressed air against the oil results in its atomization. A disk-type orifice governs the rate of oil flow and must be removed and replaced with a larger or smaller orifice if more or less oil is required. This orifice is made in several sizes up to 3 gph. Figures 3-20 and 3-21 show a cross section of the nozzles used in the boiler-burner unit and the conversion burner.

The necessary air for combustion is supplied by the fan, and the stream is divided as explained above. Operating pressure for the boiler-burner unit is about 15 psi; for the conversion burner, 3 to $6\frac{1}{2}$ psi. This unit does not require an additional gear pump for suction lift in the event that the tank is below the level of the burner. The compressor unit is capable of developing a high vacuum and thus can lift the oil itself, as well as provide the necessary air pressure of atomization.

QUESTIONS

1. What is the purpose of primary air in low-pressure burners?
2. What is the purpose of secondary air?
3. Explain the principle of low-pressure atomization.
4. What is the function of the sump stabilizer on the Williams Oil-O-Matic?
5. Explain simply the operation of the Winkler burner.
6. How is the rate of oil flow governed in the GE burner?
7. How are low-pressure burners affected by changes in viscosity of the oil?
8. Explain how the heat-keeper secondary air control of the Winkler burner works.
9. What is its purpose?

CHAPTER 4

COMMERCIAL OIL BURNERS

Using Nos. 4, 5, and 6 oil

Gun-type commercial oil burners of varying sizes, extending from the commercial to the industrial range, are becoming increasingly popular owing to the compactness of their design and especially to their lower operating cost resulting from the use of No. 4 or heavier oils instead of No. 2.

These commercial gun-type burners using Nos. 4 and 5 oil take two forms, those for (1) low-pressure operation and those for (2) high-pressure operation. This breakdown is comparable to that of the gun-type burners used for domestic purposes, requiring No. 2 heating oil.

The burner shown in Fig. 4-1 utilizes the low-pressure principle for atomization of the oil. It has been on the market for a considerable number of years. It has a capacity, in a number of models, ranging from 5 to 150 gph.

This burner is essentially an assembly, consisting of a blower to furnish all the combustion air required, a variable-delivery piston-type metering fuel-oil pump, and a sliding-vane primary-air pump. The oil and primary air are mixed in the nozzle at low pressures by the process known as *air atomization*. Oil and air are at the same pressure in the

Fig. 4-1 An AM6OF Hev-E-Oil burner, maximum capacity 40 gph. Left front view. (*Industrial Combustion*)

nozzle, which varies according to the size of the burner, the quantity of oil being burned, and the viscosity of the oil. It may be as low as 12 or as high as 50 psi.

The secondary-air blower furnishes air at a considerably higher pressure than is customarily used for oil burners. This air passes through an air diffuser around the nozzle, which tends to intimately mix the secondary air with the atomized oil and maintains a steady, constant fire with no pulsation. The "drawer assembly" consists of the air diffuser, nozzle, atomizing-air tube, oil-delivery tube, starting-oil heater, thermostat, and electrodes. The whole assembly may be easily and quickly removed from the rear of the burner for cleaning and adjusting.

The operation of the burner is as follows. The thermostat or operating control calls for heat, the circulating-oil pump starts, and the starting-oil heater heats the oil lying in the oil-delivery pipe in the drawer assembly. When this oil is at the correct temperature, the thermostat starts the burner blower, the metering oil pump, and the primary-air pump and causes a spark of 10,000 volts to jump between two electrodes in front of the nozzle. When the atomizing-air pressure is high enough, a pressure control opens the oil solenoid valve, allowing the hot oil to be delivered to the nozzle, where it is ignited by the electric spark.

The burner starts on low fire, the secondary-air damper and the metering oil pump set for low fire with the proper amount of air for high CO_2 and a high efficiency. As the air pressure increases, an air motor slowly moves the burner to high-fire position, increasing the stroke of the pistons of the oil pump and opening the secondary air to a set position, giving the highest CO_2 and highest efficiency for the size flame required. Both high and low flames can be adjusted to any size flame between minimum and maximum.

An oil burner that uses No. 6 oil is shown in Fig. 4-24 at the end of this chapter. Its operation is almost identical with the one described above. However, it utilizes a gas pilot to assist in igniting the No. 6 oil.

A simple pressure control or temperature control can be used to release the air from the air motor and therefore modulate the burner between high and low flame. An electric modulating motor can be furnished if it is found necessary to have complete modulation.

When the burner shuts off, the blower motor continues to run, as does the primary-air pump, for a short post-purge period, in order to purge the nozzle of oil, thus preventing "afterdrip" and ensuring a clean, positive start on the next cycle. The secondary-air blower operates through the post-purge period, removing all the gases from the combustion chamber.

Since the operation of this burner is somewhat different from conventional gun-type burners as explained above, it is necessary to have knowledge of the operation of its major components in order to understand it fully.

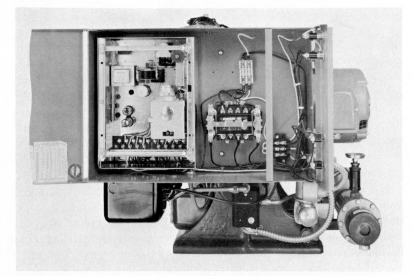

Fig. 4-2   Model AM5CF, back view showing control panel and Fireye control. (*Industrial Combustion*)

Fig. 4-3 Side view of model AM3CH, showing air-modulating motor, fuel-oil pump, oil solenoid valve, and lube-oil tank. (*Industrial Combustion*)

THE DRAWER ASSEMBLY

The drawer assembly shown in Fig. 4-4 consists of a diffuser, nozzle-tip and swirler assembly, electrodes, electrode bracket, drawer-preheater assembly [(8) in Fig. 4-7, cylindrical tube on lower part of illustration], and the drawer thermostat at the rear of the assembly. It can be removed from the burner as a unit to make any necessary adjustments and periodic inspections or cleanups.

DRAWER PREHEATER

The drawer preheater is designed for use except when distillate oil is to be burned. It preheats the oil uniformly throughout the entire length of the oil tube within the drawer assembly before the burner is started, so that the oil can be readily ignited by an electric spark.

When the room thermostat or pressure control calls for heat, this heater automatically begins to warm up and the burner will not start until the drawer thermostat [(28) in Fig. 4-7] is satisfied. This means that the oil in the preheater has been heated sufficiently for positive ignition and that a low fire has been started.

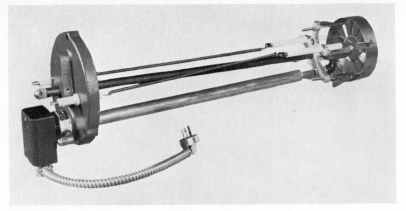

Fig. 4-4 The drawer assembly is readily removable and contains a fuel-oil heater. The burner cannot start until this heater is at proper temperature. (*Industrial Combustion*)

DRAWER THERMOSTAT

The tube on the outside of the drawer-thermostat element has a greater coefficient of expansion than the rod on the inside. When heat is applied to the element, the tube will expand faster than the rod. This action operates the microswitch in the drawer thermostat and starts the burner. Oil in the drawer preheater must be heated to 110°F before the microswitch will start the burner. If light oil is used, the light-heavy oil switch should be turned to LIGHT OIL. This will disconnect the drawer preheater and shunt out the drawer thermostat, allowing the burner to start immediately when the controls call for heat.

The drawer thermostat has a three-position temperature switch: low, medium, and high. The position used depends on the viscosity of the oil. If viscosity is low, nozzle trouble may occur if temperature is set too high.

NOZZLE BODY AND NOZZLE ASSEMBLY

Figures 4-5 and 4-6 show, respectively, the paths of the air and oil through the nozzle and the component parts of the covering assembly. This assembly consists of the nozzle body, the swirler, and the nozzle tip. The swirler is held rigidly against the nozzle tip by the compression spring to produce a well-atomized oil cone. Nozzle tips are available in a number of sizes.

The nozzle body provides the means for connecting the air and oil lines together in back of the nozzle swirler. Here the air and oil mix under pressure within the nozzle body. Oil enters at the bottom of the

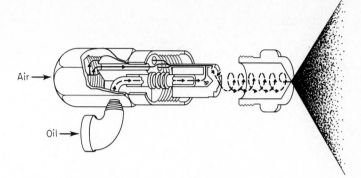

Fig. 4-5 How oil and air mix in the nozzle. (*Industrial Combustion*)

nozzle body, passes through the swirler, comes out of the holes in the swirler grooves, and comes in contact with the primary air fed by the primary-air pump. This primary air enters the rear of the nozzle body and passes through three holes within the body and through the swirler grooves, along with the oil coming out of holes in each groove. The air and oil pass through the groove at the front of the swirler and out the nozzle tip to form an atomized cone of oil. This is sprayed into the secondary-air stream passing through the blast tube.

IGNITION TRANSFORMER

A standard high-voltage ignition transformer is provided with built-in filter. Ignition is by electric spark only and is interrupted except in special applications. Any one of several standard commercial controls for interrupted ignition may be used.

OIL SOLENOID VALVE

The oil solenoid valve is operated by a pressure control in the primary-air line. Each time the burner starts, the solenoid valve remains closed

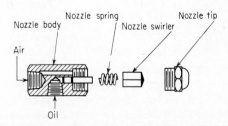

Fig. 4-6 Nozzle assembly. (*Industrial Combustion*)

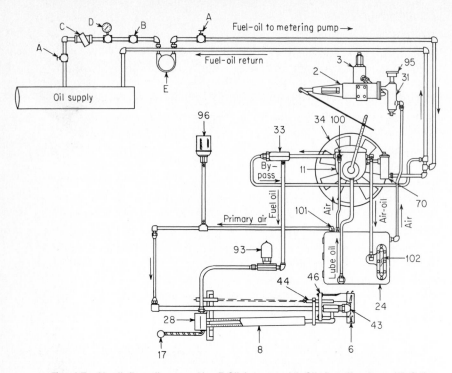

Fig. 4-7 Air-oil flow diagram, Hev-E-Oil burner. (*A*) Oil-shutoff valve. (*B*) Swing valve check. (*C*) Suction-line strainer. (*D*) Vacuum gauge. (*E*) Fuel-oil pump. (2) Modutrol motor. (3) Solenoid air-bleed valve. (6) Diffuser. (8) Heater tube. (11) Air-oil metering pump. (17) Heater and thermostat plug. (24) Air-oil tank. (28) Thermostat. (31) Air strainer. (33) Pressure-relief oil valve. (34) Secondary-air damper. (43) Nozzle assembly. (44) Ignition electrode. (46) Diffuser-support spider. (70) Burner strainer. (93) Solenoid oil-control valve. (95) Air-pressure gauge. (96) Pressuretrol. (100) Primary-air adjustment valve. (101) Lube-oil filler plug. (102) Lube-oil-level sight glass. (*Industrial Combustion*)

and does not open. Thus no oil is discharged until the primary-air pressure reaches 3 to 5 psi. This prevents oil from running out of the nozzle until there is sufficient air pressure to atomize it. A relief valve bypasses oil while the oil solenoid valve is closed.

AIR MODULATOR

The air modulator (Fig. 4-9) is an air-operated cylinder which utilizes the pressure of compressed air from the oil-air tank. The purpose of this air-operated motor is to increase the size of the burner flame from "low-fire" to "high-fire" operation after the burner has started. The low-fire to high-fire starting operation is explained in the following paragraph.

AIR AND OIL FLOW

Figs. 4-7 and 4-8

When the burner motor starts, air pressure is built up in the oil-air tank (24) and is carried through the air line (52) past the modulator-speed adjustment valve (53) into the chamber (Fig. 4-8) where pressure is exerted upon the piston (62), forcing it back against the resistance of the spring (49). As the piston and shaft are moved back, the air shutter (34) is gradually opened by means of the air-shutter adjustment rod (36). At the same time, the metering-pump adjustment rod (57) pulls the metering-pump adjustment lever (29) back, thereby increasing the delivery of the oil-metering pump (11). The high-fire stop (56) on the piston shaft limits the movement of the piston (62) and thus the size of the maximum fire. When the burner shuts down, the oil-and-air metering pump (11) stops and air pressure in the oil-and-air tank (24) is released. This permits the retracting spring (49) in the modulator (2) to force the piston forward to its original starting position, as limited by the low-fire stop (55).

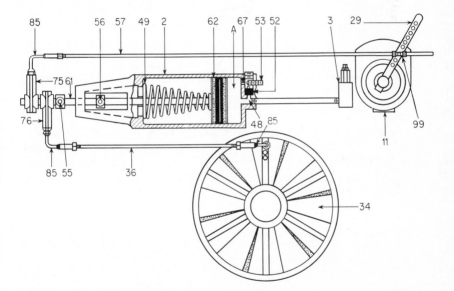

Fig. 4-8 Modulating motor with air solenoid. (2) Modulator. (3) Air-bleed solenoid valve. (11) Oil and air pump. (29) Metering-pump adjustment lever. (34) Air shutter. (36) Air-shutter adjustment rod. (48) Air-check valve (modulator). (49) Piston retracting spring. (52) Modulator air line. (53) Modulator-speed adjustment valve. (55) Low-fire stop. (56) High-fire stop. (57) Oil-metering pump adjustment rod. (61) Modulator piston shaft. (62) Modulator piston assembly. (67) Air-check-valve removal plug. (75) Modulator oil-adjustment arm. (76) Modulator air-adjustment arm. (85) Ball swivel joint (90 deg). (99) Ball swivel joint (straight). (A) Primary-air pressure chamber. (*Industrial Combustion*)

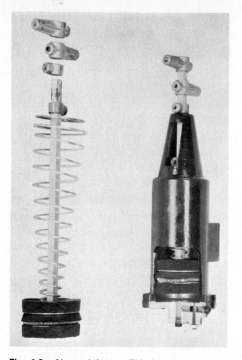

Fig. 4-9 Air modulator. This is an air motor that allows the burner to start at low fire. As the air pressure gradually builds up, the burner goes to high-fire position. (*Industrial Combustion*)

Adjustment is made by means of the modulator-speed adjustment valve (53). The adjustment valve is turned clockwise to force back the piston (62) more slowly; counterclockwise to force it back faster. Full modulation may be obtained with the use of a modulating motor. This involves additional controls.

AIR-BLEED SOLENOID VALVE

Fig. 4-8 (3)

The air-bleed solenoid valve (normally open) is used in conjunction with the air modulator (2). It is connected to the modulator back cap so that when the valve is deenergized, the pressure within the cylinder of the modulator can be released. On flame failure or burner shutdown, the release of pressure within the primary-air pressure chamber (A) allows the piston (62) to return automatically to the low-fire or starting position to be sure of a low-fire restart. If the air-bleed solenoid valve (3) is to be used in a high-low fire operation, then a boiler-mounted temperature or pressure control is wired in series with the air-bleed solenoid valve. The air-bleed solenoid valve is operated within a small range of temperature or pressure variation, allowing the modulator piston to move back and forth between the limits set by high- and low-fire stops.

LIGHT-HEAVY OIL SWITCH

This is a single-pole single-throw switch used in conjunction with the drawer preheater and thermostat. If light oil is to be used, the light-heavy oil switch is put in the LIGHT OIL position; and if heavy oil is to be used, the switch is put in the HEAVY OIL position, and the heavy oil will be preheated for ignition purposes only.

COMMERCIAL HIGH-PRESSURE GUN BURNER

Burners which use a conventional high-pressure oil-burner pump and high-pressure nozzle for Nos. 4 and 5 heating oil have now been developed. Figure 4-11 shows a front view of one of these burners. Its resemblance to its prototype, the No. 2 gun-type burner, is marked. The fundamental difference between this and the original high-pressure gun-type burner using No. 2 heating oil lies in a device called the thermax converter. The thermax converter is a compact built-in electric oil heating unit that heats only the small quantity of oil to be burned. This changes the high-viscosity heavier oil to a light viscosity that can be readily atomized and discharged through the conventional high-pressure nozzle and thereby burn with the characteristics of No. 2 oil. The

Fig. 4-10 Air-oil pumps for Hev-E-Oil burner. (*Industrial Combustion*)

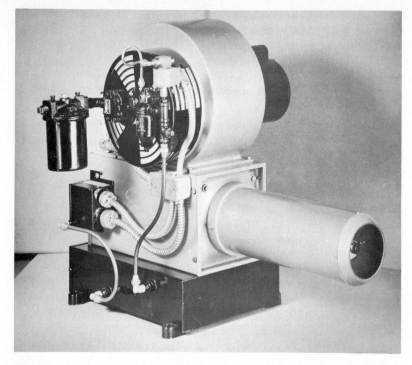

Fig. 4-11 A Sun-Ray No. 4 and No. 5 oil burner. It uses a conventional high-pressure pump and nozzle with a built-in electric oil heating unit that is thermo-statically controlled. The oil heater is in the burner base. (*Sun-Ray Burner Mfg. Co.*)

thermax converter is systematically controlled by a thermostat and is accessible along with the nozzle assembly. Otherwise the major components of this burner are comparable except for size and capacity to those of the high-pressure gun-type burner using No. 2 heating oil. This burner incorporates an electrically operated firing assembly with built-in safety shutdown and a positive mechanical oil cutoff in the nozzle fuel line. Actual point of cutoff is directly behind the atomizing oil nozzle.

NOZZLE ASSEMBLY

As shown in Fig. 4-12, the nozzle assembly consists of (1) a preheating system of two 350-watt elements; (2) a temperature-control unit of an operating and reverse-safety remote switch, and (3) a spring-loaded bellows and pin cutoff for pressurized oil-flow control.

The oil enters the converter (B) through the oil line (A) where it reaches a final temperature of 180°F. Thermoswitch (D) in series with the limit switch closes and allows the flame safety control to pull in if there is a call for heat. The oil under pressure is forced through (E)

into the pressure tube at a pressure of 100 psi, which collapses the bellows (*G*) pulling the rod (*H*) off pin (*I*), allowing the oil to flow to the nozzle.

The oil is drawn from the tank through the filter (*A*) by means of the suction created by the gears in the pump (*B*). The oil under pressure now enters the pressure regulating valve (*C*). This is a spring-bellows-type valve with pin cutoff and bypass. The cutoff will not open until pressure reaches 140 psi. At this pressure, valve (*F*) will open and bypass the excess oil to the tank. The oil under regulated pressure passes on to the nozzle assembly. When the burner shuts down, any back pressure

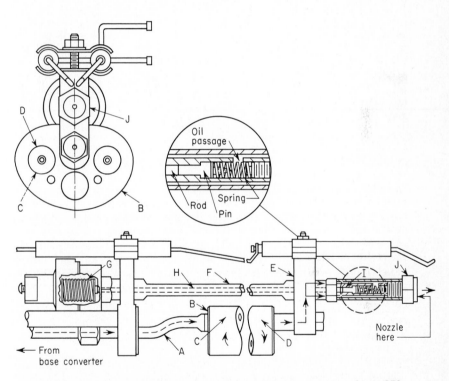

Fig. 4-12 The nozzle assembly consists of (1) a preheating system of two 350-watt elements. (2) A temperature-control unit of an operating (set at 180°F) and reverse-safety thermoswitch (set at 140°F) (*D*). (3) A spring-loaded bellows and pin cutoff for pressurized oil-flow control. Oil enters converter *C* through oil line *B*. Here oil reaches a final temperature of 180°F. Thermoswitch *D* (which is in series with the limit switches) closes and allows the flame safety control to pull in if there is a call for heat. The pressurized oil is forced through *E* into *F*. At a pressure of 100 psi it collapses the bellows *G*, pulling rod *H* off pin *I* and allowing oil to flow at the nozzle. (*A*) Fuel line. (*B*) Nozzle converter. (*C*) Operating thermoswitch. (*D*) Reverse thermoswitch. (*E*) Bracket assembly. (*F*) Pressure tube. (*G*) Bellows. (*H*) Rod. (*I*) Pin. (*J*) Nozzle adapted assembly. (*Sun-Ray Burner Mfg. Co.*)

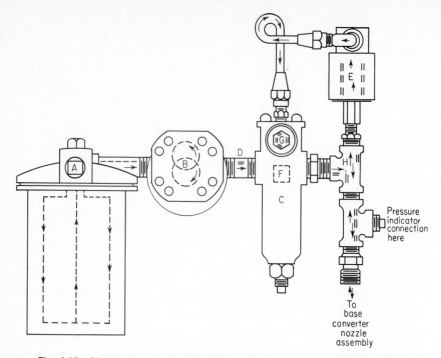

Pressure
indicator
connection
here

To
base
converter
nozzle
assembly

Fig. 4-13 Oil is drawn from tank through strainer A by suction side of gears of pump B. Pressurized oil enters pressure regulator C through line D. Regulator is a spring-bellows type with pin cutoff and bypass. Cutoff will not open until 140 psi. At this pressure, setting valve F opens and bypasses excess oil through G to tank. Regulated pressure passes through series of T's (where a pressure indicator may be installed) to nozzle assembly. On shutdown, any back pressure caused by heating of oil is bypassed to normally opened solenoid valve E through pressure-regulator bypass F and finally back to tank via G. 30-mesh strainer on models J-5 and J-7. 100-mesh strainer on J-3. (A) Strainer. (B) Pump. (C) Pressure regulator. (D) Pressure line. (E) Solenoid valve. (F) Pressure valve. (G) Return line. (H) Regulated pressure. – – Path of oil suction. = = Path of pressurized oil. (*Sun-Ray Burner Mfg. Co.*)

caused by the heating of the oil is bypassed to the normally open solenoid valve (E) through bypass (F) and back to the tank.

Other parts of this burner—transformer, fan, housing, and motor—all follow those of the conventional high-pressure gun-type burner used with distillate oils.

The burner shown in Fig. 4-15 utilizes principles similar to the one just discussed. Referring to Fig. 4-16, it can be seen from section 1 that when the burner stands by, only the heater C is hot. The cutoff at the nozzle is closed to prevent oil drippage, and the magnetic oil valve is open.

In the "start" position (section 2), hot oil at practically no pressure

Fig. 4-14 Rear view of burner shown in Fig. 4-11.

Fig. 4-15 Electrol burner using heavy No. 4 oil.

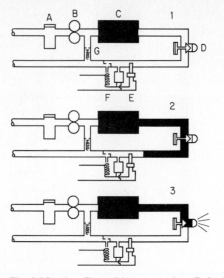

Fig. 4-16 How Electrol burner works. Referring to the schematic diagrams, it can be seen in section 1 that on burner stand-by only the heater is hot; the cutoff at the nozzle is closed to prevent oil dripping, and the magnetic oil valve is open. When the burner is in the "start" position, as in section 2, hot oil at almost no pressure flows up to the rear of the nozzles, thereby heating them. The hot oil then progresses back to the temperature-check control, causing its electric contacts to close. This, in turn, closes the magnetic oil valve, and oil pressure is built up in the system. In the "running" position, as in section 3, the oil pressure opens the cutoff valve at the nozzle and allows the burner to fire. After the oil pressure is built up, the pressure-check control takes over and supervises the oil pressure in the system. Should the temperature or pressure of the oil drop below the proper preset values, the oil burner will stop or trip into safety. Shaded area indicates hot oil. (A) Strainer. (B) Pump. (C) Oil heater. (D) Cutoff valve and nozzle. (E) Temperature check. (F) Oil valve. (G) Pressure regulator. (*Electrol Mfg. Co.*)

flows up to the rear of the nozzles, thereby heating them. The hot oil then flows back to the temperature-check control, causing its electric contacts to close. This in turn closes the magnetic oil valve, and pressure builds up in the system. In the running position (section 3), the oil pressure opens the cutoff valve at the nozzle, allowing the burner to fire. After the oil pressure is built up, the pressure-check control takes over and controls the oil pressure. If the temperature or pressure of the oil drops below the proper preset values, the oil burner will stop or trip into safety.

A newer model series of the commercial high-pressure burner shown in Fig. 4-11 has been developed (Figs. 4-17 and 4-21). The burner also utilizes grades 4 and 5 oil. The new features of this series MJ include a redesigned fuel-delivery system that enables the burner to start and operate at low fire. After a predetermined period of time has elapsed and the fire is proved, it then modulates to high fire by increasing the quantity flow of oil and the volumetric flow of air.

With this model, the MJ series added new methods of regulating oil pressure and air delivery (Figs. 4-18, 4-19, and 4-20) and eliminated the mechanical nozzle cutoff by replacing it with one operated electrically.

This device provides a higher efficiency for varying process or heating demands. The high fire provides for start, pickup, and load, and the low fire maintains the load. Thus peak, operating, or standby loads are met by varying the amount of oil burned, thereby increasing or decreasing the flame size. The low-fire position is adjusted by a bypass pressure regulator, and high fire is adjusted by the pressure regulator incorporated in the fuel unit. Solenoid valves operated from the control panel mounted at the back of the burner regulate the firing.

The burner control panel mounted at the top back of the burner

Fig. 4-17   A newer Model series of the burner shown in Figs. 4-11 and 4-14. Designated as the model MJ series, this newer development incorporates a special combustion head (Golden Cup) and provides a pre-purge period, low-fire start, and high-fire run. Low and high fire can be adjusted by pressure regulators. This burner will not go to high fire unless the high-fire rotary shutter moves from the closed position. (*Sun-Ray Burner Mfg. Corp.*)

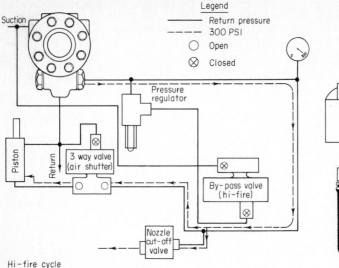

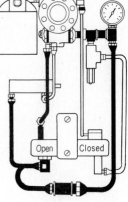

Legend

— Return pressure
- - - 300 PSI
○ Open
⊗ Closed

"HI-FIRE"

Suction

Pressure regulator

Piston

Return

3 way valve (air shutter)

By-pass valve (hi-fire)

Nozzle cut-off valve

Open   Closed

Hi-fire cycle

On energizing hi-fire cycle, the 3 way (air shutter) valve for operating the hi-fire shutter piston, recieves pressure from the nozzle line and actuates piston to extend position. When hi-fire shutter opens, lo-fire proving switch is energized and closes by-pass valve. The delivery pressure to the nozzle is now 300 PSI. The input GPH will increase approximately 50%

Fig. 4-18 Model MJ Sun-Ray Burner hydraulic system when unit is operating at high fire.

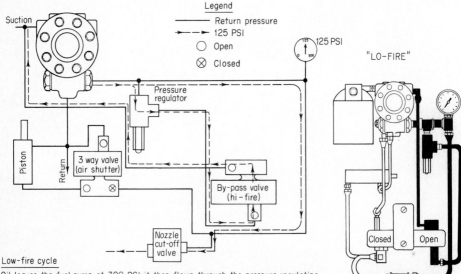

Legend

— Return pressure
→- - → 125 PSI
○ Open
⊗ Closed

125 PSI

"LO-FIRE"

Suction

Pressure regulator

Piston

Return

3 way valve (air shutter)

By-pass valve (hi-fire)

Nozzle cut-off valve

Closed   Open

Low-fire cycle

Oil leaves the fuel pump at 300 PSI it then flows through the pressure regulating valve and is reduced to 125 PSI. The discharged oil from the pressure reguator then passes through the normally open solenoid valve (by-pass), and back to suction line. The pressure to nozzle is now 125 PSI, and burner is on lo-fire

Fig. 4-19 Model MJ Sun-Ray Burner oil-flow diagram showing burner at low-fire position.

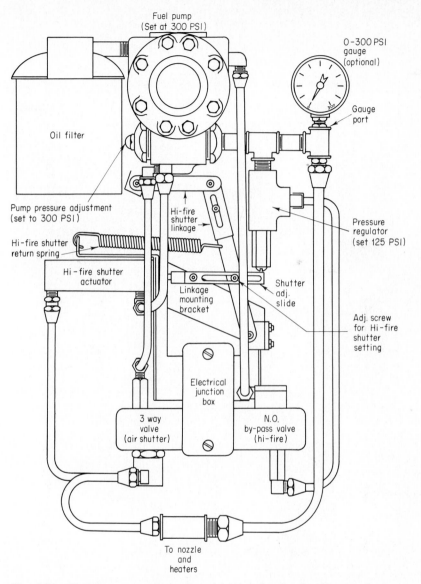

Fuel pump
(Set at 300 PSI)

0-300 PSI
gauge
(optional)

Gauge
port

Oil filter

Pump pressure adjustment
(set to 300 PSI)

Hi-fire
shutter
linkage

Pressure
regulator
(set 125 PSI)

Hi-fire shutter
return spring

Hi-fire shutter
actuator

Linkage
mounting
bracket

Shutter
adj.
slide

Adj. screw
for Hi-fire
shutter
setting

Electrical
junction
box

3 way
valve
(air shutter)

N.O.
by-pass valve
(hi-fire)

To nozzle
and
heaters

Fig. 4-20 Oil piping arrangement of model MJ series Sun-Ray Burner, showing piping, linkages, and points of adjustment for low and high firing rates.

housing controls all functions of the burner and provides sequential operation. These include (1) prepurge air flowing through the unit prior to introduction of oil, (2) low-fire start, and (3) high-fire run. In this third stage, there is a 50 percent increase in fuel pressure.

Other operations-control features provided by the burner-mounted panel (Fig. 4-21) are a proved low-fire start wherein the burner will not

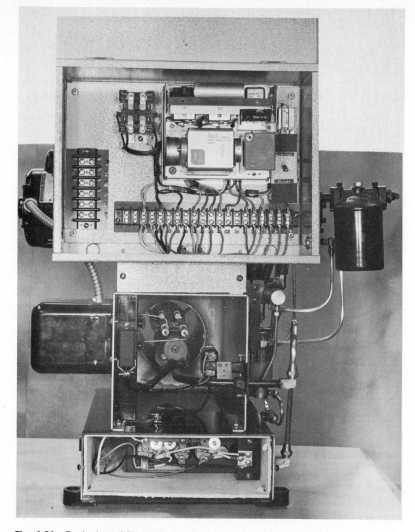

Fig. 4-21 Back view of Fig. 4-17 showing wiring and control panel (upper portion); back view of nozzle and air tube with electrodes (lower center); filter (right); motor and ignition transformer (left).

operate unless the high-fire air shutter is in closed position and conversely will not go to high fire until the high-fire rotary shutter moves from its closed setting. There is also a manual switch in the panel, providing for constant low-fire operation if desired.

The sequence of the operation of this burner is given below.

OPERATING SEQUENCE
Prepurge

Control-energized, the burner starts its prepurge cycle, approximately 30 sec. Air is now flowing through the heating unit.

Oil leaves the fuel pump, which has been regulated for 300 psi. It then flows through the pressure regulating valve and is reduced to 125 psi. The discharged oil from the pressure regulator then passes through the normally open solenoid (bypass) valve and back to the suction line. The pressure to the nozzle line is now 125 psi.

Low fire (trial for ignition)

The electric nozzle cutoff valve opens and oil is delivered at 125 psi to the nozzle. Low fire is now established. There is an approximate 25-sec delay between low and high fire. The gases are now flowing through the unit.

High fire (main burner)

On energizing the high-fire cycle, the three-way (air-shutter) valve for operating the high-fire shutter piston receives pressure from the nozzle line and actuates the piston to the extend position. When the high-fire shutter opens, the low-fire proving switch, located in the air cage, is energized and closes the bypass valve. With the bypass closed,

Fig. 4-22 WhirlPower forced-draft commercial oil burner. Models range from 3 to 9.5 gph. (*Space Conditioning*)

delivery pressure to the nozzle is now 300 psi. The input gph will increase by approximately 50 percent.

Postpurge

This cycle is approximately 15 secs. The high-fire shutter closes and the nozzle cutoff is deenergized to the closed position. Control after this purge cycle terminates the power to the burner. It is ready to start the next cycle with prepurge.

The low-fire-proving microswitch inside the air cage will not allow the burner to go to highfire unless the shutter is moved off its closed position. If the rotary high-fire shutter is not moved from the closed position (a fraction of an inch), the bypass valve will not be actuated. This is a safety feature.

GUN TYPE BURNER—FORCED DRAFT-SEALED COMBUSTION

Figure 4-22 shows a conventional gun-type, one-piece arrangement with a forced-draft blower. These blowers are capable of higher pressures than conventional gun burners. In boilers which can be reliably sealed against leakage, this makes possible operation with the firebox under pressure. Forced-draft sealed combustion eliminates the need for draft regulation.

These WhirlPower burners are not dependent upon firebox size or shape and do not require refractory to aid combustion. In its application to a converted heating system the burner is frequently installed through the fire door of the boiler, and the ash-pit section is partially or completely filled or sealed off. Elimination of the usual large refractory firebox improves response and reduces heat loss. Figure 4-23 shows a typical application in a compact sealed firebox boiler.

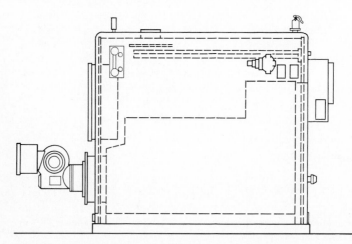

Fig. 4-23 WhirlPower burner applied to a sealed firebox boiler. (*Space Conditioning*)

Fig. 4-24 This Hev-E-Oil burner utilizes No. 6 fuel oil and has a firing range extending from 25 to 125 gph. (*Industrial Combustion*)

These burners are built in a variety of sizes for firing rates from 1 through 30. The performance of this type of burner is dependent upon precise air- and oil-flow rates and patterns; therefore, alterations or deviations from the manufacturers's recommendations should not be made.

QUESTIONS

1. What forms do commercial gun-type burners take, using Nos. 4 and 5 oil?
2. The low-pressure Hev-E-Oil burner discussed in Chap. 4 is essentially an assembly consisting of what parts?
3. How does this burner start?
4. Explain the function of the following parts: (*a*) drawer assembly; (*b*) nozzle assembly; (*c*) oil solenoid valve; (*d*) air modulator; (*e*) air-bleed solenoid.
5. Explain how a high-pressure gun-type burner using Nos. 4 and 5 oil operates.
6. What is the function of the "electric eye" in the primary control?
7. Why are electronic controls used with these burners?
8. What is the purpose of heating the oil?

CHAPTER 5
ROTARY BURNERS

HORIZONTAL ROTARY BURNER

The principle of mechanical centrifugal atomization is demonstrated and applied by the horizontal rotary burner. This type of burner, which has a range running from below 5 gph to 200 gph, has the broadest application of any type of burner and successfully utilizes all grades of fuel oil from No. 2 to No. 6. The use of the heavier type of fuel oils is achieved by preheating them before they reach the cup, thereby assuring that the viscosity will be within a range that the cup can handle. This burner has been and is found in all types of installations, whether domestic, semicommercial, commercial, or heavy industrial. They are usually used with No. 5 and No. 6 oil.

This burner receives its name from the fact that it enters the boiler on a horizontal plane, in the same manner as the gun-type burner, and prepares the oil for combustion by centrifugal force, spinning it off a cup rotating from 3,450 to 4,900 rpm.

The heart of this burner and its characteristic part is the atomizing cup (Figs. 5-1 and 5-2), which by its spinning action finely divides the oil. These cups are made in many sizes in order to accommodate them to various burner capacities. The cups are turned from castings and

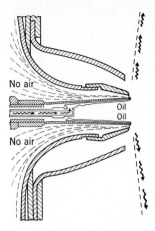

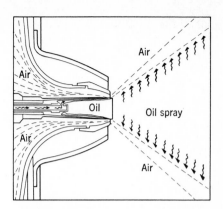

Fig. 5-1 Direction of oil spray leaving spinning cup before being deflected by the air. (*Petro*)

Fig. 5-2 Deflection of oil spray by air from fan. (*Petro*)

are long and tapering in order to permit the centrifugal motion to create a thin film of oil for dispersion from the edge of the thin cup. Oil reaches this cup at a rate of flow controlled by an oil-metering valve that can be manually or automatically adjusted. As the oil flows through the oil tube into the rotating cup, the centrifugal action causes the oil to spread out into an unbroken film over the entire inside area of the cup. It then follows the widening taper through the cup to the outside edge. At this point, it is thrown off in a very fine film or spray.

The spray, if it were allowed to follow the pull of the forces on it, would leave the cup at right angles to the edge, as shown in Fig. 5-1. This is prevented, however, by the action of the air being delivered by the fan. The fan rotates at the same speed as the cup and moves air from the fan housing into an air nozzle (Fig. 5-2) which projects out over the atomizing cup to a point just short of its outer edge. The air is thus delivered to the actual point of atomization.

The vanes within the air cone are absolutely concentric to the cup and deliver the air with velocity and a swirling motion that is *opposite* to the rotation of the cup and oil spray. This deflects the oil spray from its normal tangential travel, thoroughly mixing it with air and providing the necessary turbulence for clean, efficient combustion.

An adjustable shutter controls the air. By the use of interchangeable cups and air nozzles, it is possible to alter the shape of the flame from a short, bushy structure to a long, narrow type, which gives a flexibility that enables this type of burner to be adapted to variously designed boilers or furnaces.

The oil supply to the cup may be provided through a hollow shaft or rigid tube (Fig. 5-3) within a steel shaft. The pump is gear-driven by a worm gear. The main shaft drives the cup and fan, receiving its power from the electric motor within the burner housing. Oil is supplied in nearly all cases by a pump.

Another operating characteristic of these burners is that of modulated firing. This enables the capacity and flame size of the burner to be controlled automatically and is accomplished by means of a modulating motor, which is controlled by steam pressure. A change in steam

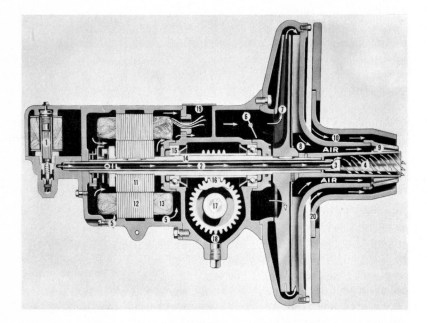

Fig. 5-3 Cutaway view of a Petro model W commercial horizontal rotary. (1) Oil-metering valve which connects with (2) rigid fuel-oil tube; thence to (3) Oil-distributor head. (4) Extra-long conical rotary automizing cup. (5) Induced-air passages, ensuring cool motor. (6) Adjustable shutter controlling primary air. (7) Air fan, statically and dynamically balanced. (8) Large primary air pass, streamlined. (9) Interchangeable, adjustable, angular-vaned air nozzle. (10) Induced air to cool burner front plate and sleeve. (11) Electric motor rotor, air-cooled. (12) Electric motorstator, air-cooled. (13) Stator windings, extra-heavy insulation. (14) Cantilever steel shaft assuring perfect cup alignment. (15) Heavy-duty annular ball bearings. (16) Steel worm on main shaft; drives pump through. (17) Bronze worm gear keyed on pump shaft. (18) Splash-feed lubricating-oil reservoir. (19) Motor-wiring junction box. (20) Long sleeve to permit adequate refractory wall and clearance of water legs and dead plates.

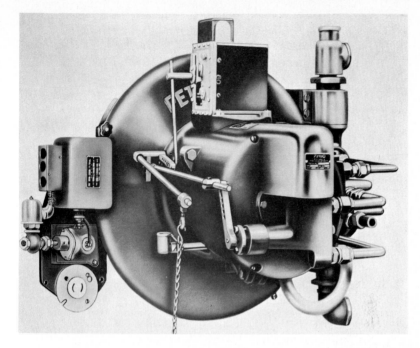

Fig. 5-4   Petro WD-AH rotary burner equipped with modulating motor.

pressure actuates this motor and drives a shaft which, by means of a connecting rod and additional linkage, passes its motion on to the burner through an arm.   The arm on the burner adjusts a shutter to regulate air intake and operates the valve or metering pump controlling the flow of oil to the cup.   This lowers or raises the oil consumption capacity, as the case may be, and the flame changes in size.   The oil-air mixture is kept in the exact ratio necessary for good combustion.   Such modulation provides a means of always matching the burner capacity to the load and thus enabling steam pressures to be kept constant.

The ignition used on these burners may be manual or automatic. The term "manual ignition" implies what it is.   The burner is ignited by hand, usually by means of a torch consisting of a long rod with combustible material at the end.   This flaming torch is inserted into the firebox in such a manner as to be placed in the path of the oil spray. The oil-feed valve is then turned on and ignition accomplished.   In this

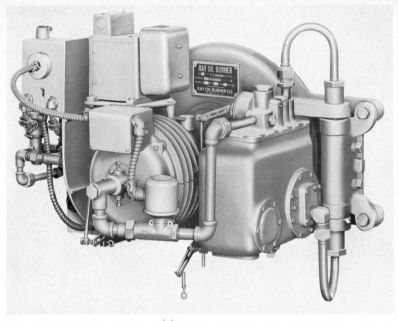

(a)

(b)

Fig. 5-5 (a) A direct-drive horizontal rotary burner, motor, shaft, and rotary cup all in direct drive. (b) Horizontal rotary with belt drive. (*Ray Burner Co.*)

case, care must be exercised to have the torch in the firebox before the oil is delivered, in order to prevent a starting puff. However, manual ignition is rarely used today.

Gas-electric ignition, with electronic sequence combustion control, is now standard. The initial pilot ignition is furnished to the gas by an electric spark. In this case, as the burner goes on, the electric spark furnished by a step-up transformer comes on first. Then the solenoid is energized and the gas comes on at full flow. The spark ignites the gas if the control senses a satisfactory pilot. The oil valve then opens and the oil is ignited; after a short period both the gas and the electric ignition go off and the control monitors the burner flame.

VERTICAL ROTARY BURNERS

Vertical rotary burners consist of two types: the wall-flame burner and the sunflower-flame burner. The motor speed of the wall-flame type is 1,450 to 1,550 rpm, and that of the sunflower-flame type, 3,450 rpm or higher. The wall-flame vertical rotary is a combination centrifugal-action and vaporizing burner. The sunflower-flame type is a straight high-speed centrifugal atomizer, as is the horizontal rotary. The high-speed vertical centrifugal atomizer as represented by the sunflower-flame type of burner is not manufactured in any quantity today, and the larger producers of this burner have discontinued its production altogether. This burner was a costly, though finely made, device, and the advent of less costly and simpler burners has resulted in its discontinuance. For that reason, this book will not concern itself with any further description of it other than that found in Chap. 1. This, however, is not the case with the wall-flame-type vertical rotaries.

The vertical rotary gets its name from the fact that it stands vertically within the boiler itself and produces a blue-yellow flame that burns as a ring around the inner wall of the boiler or furnace. Figure 5-6 shows a typical wall-flame vertical rotary, and Fig. 5-7 shows the location and shape of the fire, from whence comes the term "wall wiping." This burner utilizes centrifugal force to disperse the oil over the circular hearth onto a ring, where it vaporizes. These vapors rise and burn about the ring, producing a blue flame with yellow-white tongues. The fact that a large portion of this flame is blue demonstrates that combustion is thorough and complete and of a certain chemical type.

Oil is fed by gravity to this burner, but in order to assure a constant rate of flow from the tank regardless of the head pressure created by the oil therein, a constant-leveling valve is placed in the line at a prescribed height above the burner. The discharge side of the constant-

Fig. 5-6   Model F Torridheet vertical rotary burner; capacity: ½ to 2½ gph.

level valve has a float located in a chamber which is vented to the atmosphere. The float operates a valve which controls the rate of oil flow into the float chamber and thus maintains constant oil level in the vented float chamber at all times. In addition to this constant-leveling valve, there must be an adjustable metering-type needle valve to control the amount of oil entering the burner.

With constant oil level on the metering valve and a fixed needle-valve setting, the rate of flow to the burner is constant regardless of how much or how little oil is in the tank.

The positive cutoff of the oil upon stopping is achieved by a solenoid valve. This valve closes the oil line as soon as current to the motor is cut off and thereby stops the gravity-flow oil to the burner.

In recent years, many of the factory-assembled units fired at 1 gph or less use a constant-level metering valve similar to the control valve used on the pot-type vaporizing burner. This valve combines the constant-level valve and metering valve in a single control and, by proper positioning relative to the burner motor, will eliminate the necessity of a solenoid shutoff valve.

In the event of a sunken tank being used with this burner, an auxiliary wall-mounted lift pump must be used, since the burners have no pumping mechanism whatsoever whereby the oil can be lifted. They depend entirely upon a regulated gravity flow of oil.

Most rotary burner designs introduce the oil through the bottom or base of the motor into an oil well inside the motor stator assembly.

A cone-shaped cup attached to the motor rotor and shaft assembly dips into the oil well.   When the rotor-cup distributor-tube assembly rotates, the oil passes by centrifugal action up the sides of the cup into the distribution tubes; air from the fan is propelled with it, and the oil moves from the distribution head outward toward the furnace walls, where it impinges on the metal rim.   In other designs the oil flows up through an oil-feed channel inside the motor shaft, and thence up into the oil-distributor tubes.   At one or two points on the rim, the oil comes in contact with a hot spot generated by the electric spark, at which location it ignites.

The heat from the flame at these points quickly spreads throughout the metal rim, and soon the flame is burning in a complete ring around the wall of the furnace.

The oil is now thoroughly vaporized and mingles with the air from

Fig. 5-7   Cutaway view of model OFC-140/170, Silent Automatic oil-fired forced warm-air furnace, showing burner being fired.

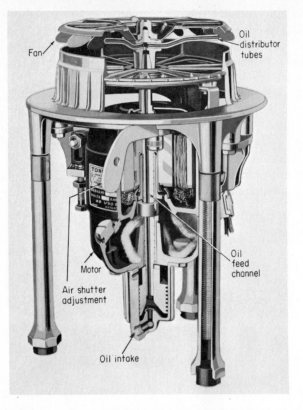

Fig. 5-8   Cutaway view of a model C Torridheet vertical rotary with "ropellor."

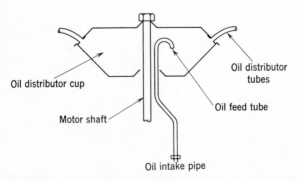

Fig. 5-9   An oil-feed line and distributor cup.

Fig. 5-10 View of circular hearth and oil-distributor head showing impingement and vaporizing of the oil on the metal rim. (*Silent Automatic*)

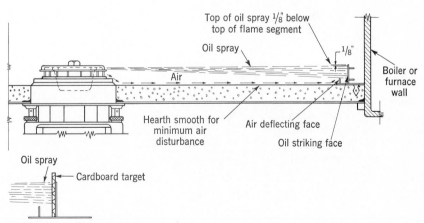

Top of oil spray $1/8"$ below
top of flame segment

Oil spray

$1/8"$

Boiler or
furnace
wall

Air

Hearth smooth for
minimum air
disturbance

Air deflecting face

Oil striking face

Oil spray

Cardboard target

Method of Checking Oil Strike

Fig. 5-11 Dimensions show location and checking of oil strike on one type (Fluid Heat) of vertical rotary burner (no longer manufactured).

the fan. As it vaporizes, the gaseous fuel rises and burns about $\frac{1}{4}$ in. above and in back of the metal grilles around the furnace or boiler walls. Once the grilles and ring are thoroughly heated, combustion becomes thorough and complete and the blue section of the flame at the bottom is about 2 in. in height with about 6 in. of yellow flame above that.

Earlier models of these burners used gas ignition with a constant-burning gas pilot, but now they primarily utilize electric ignition, usually with two electrodes at opposite sides of the ring, either 7,000 or 7,500 volts each. Later model burners employ one electrode of 7,000- or 8,500-volt capacity.

It can be seen from the above that this type of burner is truly a vaporizing type, the centrifugal force in this case being used to throw and direct the oil into the rim, where it is vaporized. The capacity of these burners runs from about 0.3 up to approximately 7 gph.

The installation of vertical rotary burners does not require the use

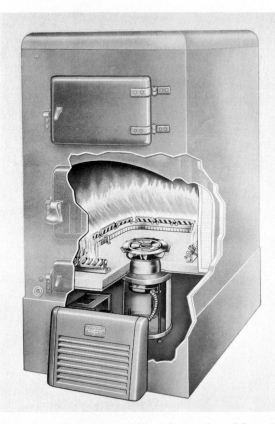

Fig. 5-12 Cutaway view of Silent Automatic wall-flame burner in a rectangular boiler.

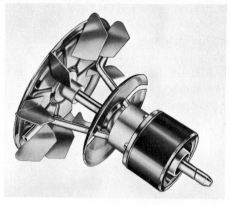

Fig. 5-13   The Mono-Rotor is the only moving part in the Silent Automatic rotary burner.

of the conventional firebox or combustion chamber found with guntype and horizontal rotary burners.   Instead, the vertical rotary is installed on a hearth.   Set into the center of the furnace, the head and oil-distributor assembly protrude above the hearth.

The hearth is a very critical part of the installation of this type of burner.   Its efficient and trouble-free operation depends upon correct construction and installation of the hearth.   The burner manufacturer's

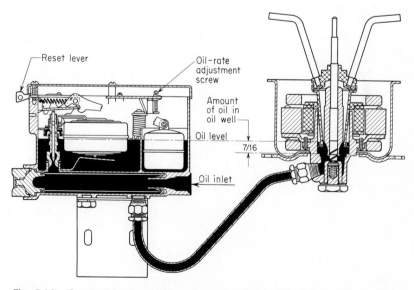

Fig. 5-14   Constant-level metering valve as applied to Silent Automatic product-model J burner.   (*Silent Automatic*)

specifications should be followed exactly in constructing it. The hearth is constructed of a refractory material poured over a supporting metal platform or hearth pan and formed to shape in much the same manner as concrete would be.

The shape of the boiler or furnace determines whether the hearth segments are curved or straight, or whether the flexible metal rim will be curved or rectangular. The burner must be perfectly level. The importance of this is obvious, for if the burner were not level, the oil would not strike at the proper spot on the rim.

Later models of these burners, such as are shown in Figs. 5-11 and 5-16, are very compact units driven by a shaded-pole motor of $\frac{1}{100}$- to $\frac{1}{30}$-hp capacity. The rotor of this motor contains the oil-distribution tubes and oil-feed tube, and to it is attached the fan. It is the only moving part of these burners. It is lubricated by the fuel oil passing through it. The removal of the head of this burner for servicing purposes is very simple, since the entire rotor lifts off the bearing on which it rests (Fig. 5-13).

Wall-flame vertical rotary burners are adaptable to boilers or furnaces of any shape and to all types of heating surfaces. The flame produced by this burner, being blue at the base, does not radiate heat to any great

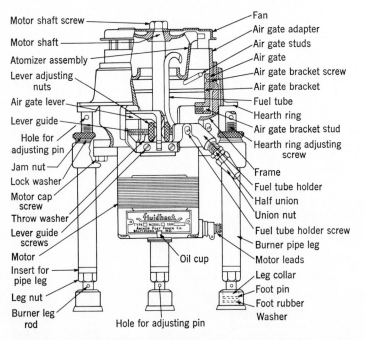

Fig. 5-15 Model SM Fluid Heat vertical rotary burner, showing component parts (no longer manufactured).

Fan and oil distributor

Ignition transformer

Burner motor

Solenoid metering valve

Junction box

Fig. 5-16 Silent Automatic OCA-18B vertical rotary burner.

extent. This enables the head of the burner to remain within the furnace and still not overheat. The air drawn in by the fan also passes the head and thus assists in keeping it cool.

QUESTIONS

1. In what types of installation is the horizontal rotary burner found?
2. Explain how the oil spray is produced and shaped by the horizontal rotary burner.
3. What is meant by centrifugal force?
4. What types of ignition are used with horizontal rotaries?
5. Is manual ignition used very much today?
6. Why?
7. What is the difference between direct drive and belt drive?
8. Why are each utilized?
9. What are the two types of vertical rotary burners? Explain how they differ.
10. How is the rate of oil flow to a wall-flame vertical rotary kept constant?
11. What is the motor speed of a wall-flame rotary? Of a sunflower-flame rotary?
12. How is the oil prepared for combustion by a wall-flame rotary? By a sunflower-flame rotary?
13. What is the purpose of the hearth ring?
14. Name the principal parts of a wall-flame rotary.

CHAPTER 6
VAPORIZING POT-TYPE BURNERS

Vaporizing pot-type burners can be divided into two groups: the *natural-draft* type and the *forced-draft* type. The natural-draft burner is most widely used in dwellings where there is no application of central heating. These cabinet-type burners depend upon manual ignition and must be ignited by hand whenever their use is required. The size of the flame and the amount of oil consumed are controlled by a hand adjustment that regulates the flow of oil through a needle-valve-controlled orifice.

In many instances these natural-draft vaporizing burners are regulated by a simple, float-operated constant-leveling valve equipped with a rotating flow-adjustment device which is turned manually. There are usually four adjustments: OFF, LOW, MEDIUM, and HIGH.

These burners may also be wick-fed or have nothing but a metal vaporizing pot consisting of two or more perforated sleeves. In the latter case, the oil flows right into the pot and no wick exists. The oil is ignited; air is drawn in by *natural draft* through the perforations in the sleeve and mingles with the oil vapor. As the pot gets hotter, combustion becomes more thorough and stable, and eventually an all-blue flame occurs. This burner is completely dependent upon natural draft for its combustion air.

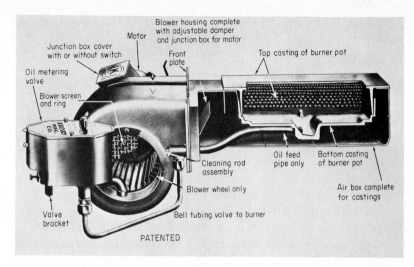

Fig. 6-1 Cutaway view of a Kresky vaporizing burner equipped with manually operated metering valve. Note rectangular shape of pot.

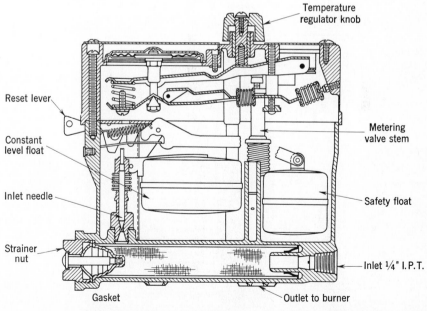

Fig. 6-2 Automatic Products model 240 W-YP oil-control valve.

Vaporizing burners, whether they use forced or natural draft, depend upon a volatile type of oil for good combustion and smoke-free performance. Usually they are designed for No. 1 or No. 2 distillate fuel oil, which easily vaporizes under heat. However, there are pot-type vaporizing burners that can use and have used heavier grades of fuel oil. These are successful because of preheating devices, either gas- or electrically operated, that heat the oil to a nearly gaseous state before it reaches the pot (Fig. 6-4). As a result of this preheating, the consumption of heavier grades of oil is attained by these burners with good combustion efficiencies. On the whole, however, vaporizing burners can be regarded as being sensitive to the grade of oil and are designed primarily for most efficient operation with light distillate fuel oils.

The application of the vaporizing burner to central heating is usually achieved by the use of forced draft. With forced draft, the oil-consumption capacity rate can be increased and the range of these forced-draft vaporizing burners runs from $\frac{2}{3}$ up to as high as 2 or $2\frac{1}{2}$ gph.

The method of operation of these burners is comparatively simple. Since they depend upon heat to prepare the fuel for combustion, it is essential that the pot or retort, as it may be called, be kept warm throughout the periods when the burner is not being called on to produce

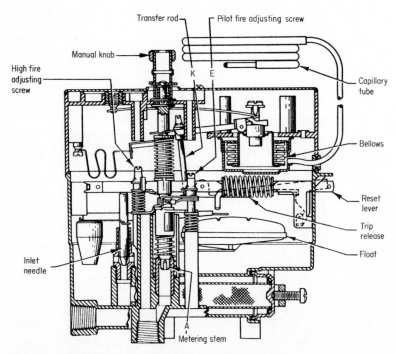

Fig. 6-3   Detroit Lubricator model CRC-239-WA float valve.

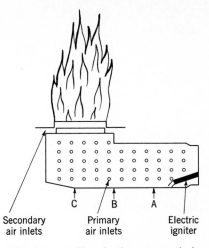

| C | B | A |
| Secondary
air inlets | Primary
air inlets | Electric
igniter |

Fig. 6-4   H. C. Little natural-draft vaporizing burner. Vaporization progressively increases in rate from *A* to *B* to *C*. Ignition was accomplished electrically.

heat. In old models of these burners, the retort or a section of it was kept warm by a small constant-burning gas pilot which provided the necessary ignition for each firing cycle. This gas ignition system is no longer used on modern vaporizing pot burners. Instead, it has been replaced by the high-low fire method. Figure 6-1 shows a burner using the high-low fire method of ignition to provide initial vaporization. During the OFF period when no demand is being made for heat, the oil fire is sustained at a very low pilot rate within the retort. Air may be furnished for the pilot flame by the fan.

Some burners operate the fan at constant speed whether the burner is in full or pilot operation, but the burner shown in Fig. 6-1 has a two-speed fan. When the burner is on pilot-fire operation, the fan operates at a much lower speed than when the burner is at high fire. This low-fire or oil pilot flame with an oil-consumption rate as low as $\frac{1}{30}$ gph serves two purposes: (1) to provide ignition and (2) to keep the retort or a section of it warm in order to facilitate gasifying the oil when a demand is made for heat.

The retorts of these burners may be of various shapes, rectangular or round, and are of such construction as to have the air pass between the walls of the pot and enter the oil vapor through perforations in the inner shell or wall. Some have the retort set horizontally instead of vertically, and in this case the burner fires in much the same direction as do the gun types.

As the call comes for heat, a bimetallic strip is heated by the action of the thermostat and expands, thereby opening the oil valve. Oil now flows into the retort and is ignited by the pilot fire, and the oil proceeds

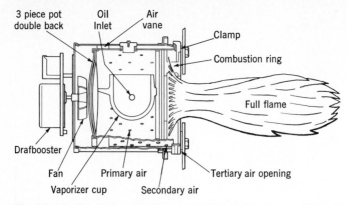

Fig. 6-5   Sectional view of a Breese model D horizontal vaporizing oil burner.

to burn.   As the retort becomes hotter, the rate of vaporization increases so that the oil is vaporizing faster than it can be consumed within the pot.   Consequently, the flame rises until it reaches the flame spreader head.   Here vaporization and combustion conditions are stabilized and the fire burns off the spreader in the form of a large sunflower, covering the hearth and the furnace diameter.

When these burners are operating on high fire, the flame is extremely hot and efficient, and for the most part its surface is a brilliant yellow-white color.   As the thermostat is satisfied and the oil valve closes, the flame gradually diminishes in size until it reaches the pilot-fire point, at which it remains.   When these burners are first fired, the initial ignition is usually accomplished manually.

The oil supply to these burners is of the gravity-flow type, and if a buried tank below the level of the burner is used, an auxiliary wall lift pump must be employed to provide gravity flow of oil to the burner. The rate of flow is maintained by a metering-type oil-flow control valve (Fig. 6-2).   This type of valve usually consists of two floats, one of which controls the oil supply rate and the other of which acts as a safety in the event that the valve becomes flooded.   Upon being actuated by an abnormally high oil level within the valve, this safety float trips a lever that is spring-operated.   This action automatically shuts off the flow of oil, which cannot be resumed until the valve is reset manually.   The safety action afforded by the trip mechanism prevents the retort from being flooded with oil.   All oil that enters the valve passes through a fine mesh strainer that eliminates the dirt so that it may not reach the metering orifices and cause trouble.

The pilot or low-fire flow rate in these valves can be increased or decreased either by using a screw-type adjustment or by replacing the metering stem of the pilot-flow valve with one of a larger or smaller

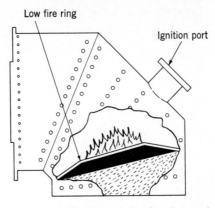

Fig. 6-6 Evans horizontal firing vaporizing burner, showing pot, low-fire ring, and ignition port.

pilot-flow rate. Metering valves are usually stamped with the minimum-flow rate in cubic centimeters per minute.

The installation of forced-draft vaporizing pot burners requires the construction of a proper type of hearth, as is the case with wall-flame vertical rotaries. The proper installation of this hearth with the proper material is essential to trouble-free operation of the burner. The hearth and burner must be level and at the correct height. Materials used to construct the hearth should be such that they will withstand high temperatures without shrinkage. For this reason, powdered asbestos should never be used, since its workability is overridden by its great tendency to shrink. The castable-type refractories recommended for this work by the burner manufacturer should be used. Hearths should be airtight to prevent the infiltration of air into the combustion process, thereby lowering its efficiency? With these burners, no refractory other than the hearth is needed, and it is not necessary to fill the ash pit with any material, insulating or otherwise.

Since even forced-draft vaporizers are sensitive to chimney draft conditions, a draft control should always be installed with these burners. This will take care of fluctuating draft conditions at the breeching, rather than pass them on to the fire. The use of a draft control with these burners is essential if stable combustion conditions and fires of proper height are to exist.

QUESTIONS

1. Into what classifications can vaporizing burners be divided? Which is used primarily for residential central heating?

2. What characteristic must fuel oil have to be properly suited to use with vaporizing burners?
3. How is ignition accomplished with vaporizing burners?
4. Give two purposes for low-fire position.
5. Explain the action of the safety float mechanism on a float-operated oil valve.
6. Explain the operation of a thermostatically controlled float valve.
7. What conditions must be observed when installing these burners?
8. Why is powdered asbestos considered a poor material of which to construct a hearth?
9. How does draft affect a vaporizing burner?
10. Why should a draft control be installed with vaporizing burners?
11. Contrast the on-off operation of the high-pressure gun-type burner with that of the vaporizing burner.

PART TWO

HEAT LOSS CALCULATIONS, BURNER AND UNIT SIZING, INSTALLATION, CONTROLS AND CONTROL SYSTEMS

CHAPTER 7
DETERMINING THE GPH RATE
OF THE OIL BURNER

The methods of determining the number of gallons of liquid fuel to be consumed per hour and thereby finding the size and capacity of the oil burner to be installed are many and varied. The Btu survey method is the most thorough, accurate, and complete. For this reason it will be discussed first, and Chap. 8 will discuss a half-dozen shorter methods of determining the gph rates.

All oil burners are rated according to the gallons of fuel they consume per hour, regardless of the type of burner and the grade of fuel concerned. This standardization provides an easy and accurate method of finding the heat-giving output of any oil burner. Fuels have standard heat-giving values rated in Btu per gallon burned per hour, and all we have to know to have a complete knowledge of the heat-giving value of a fuel is the type or grade of that fuel. The following are the accepted figures for the approximate Btu values of the standard commercial grades of fuel oil:

Commercial grade no.	Gravity range, deg API	Btu per gallon
1	48–36	137,000
2	36–32	140,000
5	24–18	148,000
6	18–12	152,400

Commercial grades of No. 3 and No. 4 oil are not mentioned because now they are not handled to any extent, and if they are demanded, a blending of the other oils is usually made to obtain an oil equal to the No. 3 or No. 4 grade in gravity and Btu content.   For heating-survey purposes they can be disregarded and No. 2 fuel-oil heat content made the basis for figuring.   Since we are concerned primarily with domestic oil burners, we will deal with the No. 2 grade oil with approximately 140,000 Btu per gal, and the 140,000 figure will be of great interest to us.

Roughly defined, the Btu is the amount of heat necessary to raise 1 lb of water 1°F, and since a gallon of No. 2 oil contains 140,000 Btu, it follows that it *could* raise 140,000 lb of water 1°.   There are 8.3 lb of water to the gallon, so if we divide 140,000 lb by 8.3, we get 16,866 gal.   This means that 1 gal of No. 2 fuel oil has enough heat in it to raise 16,866 gal of water 1° or about 168 gal of water 100°.

The average domestic heating boiler contains about 20 gal of water or less; thus there is enough heat in 1 gal of No. 2 fuel oil, if properly burned and *completely* utilized, to drive the water up 100° in about eight average domestic boilers.   Actually, though, when the oil is burned, a good portion of this total heat is lost because of failure of the burner and boiler or furnace to do the job with 100 per cent efficiency, and the necessary allowances for this must be made.   They will be provided for in the system herein explained.

THREE IMPORTANT CONDITIONS TO BE CONSIDERED

Three conditions affect the amount of heat that we must furnish to a house.   Each of these is important because they govern the rate at which heat is lost by the building.   We must balance the heat lost with the heat furnished in order to obtain comfort, and the effectiveness of every heating system in achieving physical comfort depends upon how accurately the input-output balance is figured and maintained.   Hit-or-miss systems are not of too much value to the heating man because they are not good engineering and every heating man is, in reality, a "comfort engineer."

The three conditions upon which the rate of heat loss is dependent are (1) *the outside temperature,* (2) *the material of which the building is constructed,* and (3) *the volume of air contained in the room, as well as the number of times per hour this volume of air changes.*

The temperature determines the speed with which the house will lose heat.   The lower the outside temperature or the greater the differential between inside and outside temperature, the faster the heat will pour through the building.

The construction materials determine how much heat will be lost.

They are concerned with quantity of heat (the actual Btu). In an uninsulated house, more Btu will be lost to the outside than in any insulated house of similar construction.

A specific number of Btu will be lost through 1 sq ft of any substance in 1 hr for a 1°F temperature change, and we know this number for all types of construction materials. Therefore, we can compute the number of Btu lost through a number of square feet of material simply by multiplying the known constant Btu loss per square foot by the number of square feet of that material.

For example, 1 sq ft of brick wall 8 in. thick with ½ in. of plaster on the wall will allow 0.46 Btu per sq ft to pass through for a 1° temperature change. One hundred square feet of brick wall would allow 46 Btu per hr to pass through for a 1° temperature change (100 times 0.46 = 46).

If we wish to raise the temperature 70° instead of 1°, we merely multiply 46 × 70, finding that 3,220 Btu per hr will be lost through 100 sq ft of brick wall 8 in. thick with ½ in. of plaster on one side. We multiply Btu lost per square foot by the number of square feet by the temperature differential expected between inside and outside temperatures expressed in degrees Fahrenheit. This equals total Btu lost *per hour* through that material.

We compute this only for outside walls and surfaces and for roofs or cold floors, that is, surfaces which require heat on one side and which are exposed to the winter temperature on the other.

The third condition that governs the heat loss is the volume of air contained in the house we wish to heat and the number of times per hour this volume of air changes. The losses due to this air can be easily found with some degree of accuracy by the "volume method." The volume method consists of finding the cubic contents of the room by multiplying the length by the width by the height and then applying the following rules:

Windows on one side: multiply cubic contents by 1.
Windows on two sides: multiply cubic contents by 1.5.
Windows on three sides: multiply cubic contents by 2.
Windows on four sides: multiply cubic contents by 2.
Halls and stairways: multiply cubic contents by 2.5.

The resulting figure will be the required number of Btu that must be furnished per hour to provide heat for the necessary air changes in that space. If tight weather stripping is used, the number may be reduced by 50 per cent. There are more accurate methods of determining the Btu loss due to air changes, but for all practical purposes the foregoing method will serve.

CONSTRUCTION LOSSES MUST BE DETERMINED

From the foregoing we can see now that we have three things to consider in any Btu survey in order to arrive at the number of gallons per hour of fuel we must burn, namely, the *temperature*, the *construction materials of the exposed walls*, and the *volume of air that changes constantly*. Once we have determined the total Btu lost from any house due to these three factors, the finding of the necessary fuel consumption per hour becomes an easy matter.

Table 7-1 contains some of the most common factors used in determining exposed-wall losses. It is far from complete. If the reader wishes complete tables for all types of construction, they may be found in *Handbook of Fundamentals* published by ASHRAE.

Table 7-1   Exposed-wall Losses (for 70° Temperature Difference Between Inside and Outside)

Material	Heat loss, Btu per sq ft
Single glass windows	78
Double glass windows	32
Doors 1 in. thick	50
Doors 2 in. thick	30
8-in. plain brick wall	35
8-in. plain brick wall plastered on one side	32
Brick-veneer 8-in. hollow tile, plaster on lath and furred	17
12-in. solid brick, plaster on lath and furred	18
Wooden frame with brick-veneer 1-in. wood sheathing, plaster on lath on studs	19
Stucco 8-in. hollow tile, plaster on lath and furred	19
Frame building siding, 1-in. wood sheathing, plaster on lath on studs	21
Ceiling lath and plaster, no floor above with attic on top	25
Ceiling lath and plaster, floor above with attic on top	16
Ceiling as part of roof, no attic, lath and plaster, sheathing, shingles	22
Roof, pitched, wooden shingles on strips	21
Roof, pitched, slate or tile shingles	23
Roof, flat, composition roofing on 1-in. wood, beams and air spaces with plastered ceiling	24
Floors, wood over unheated cellar, double on joists	10
Concrete, basement, on earth	1.5

From the information we have thus far, we can take an example and work it out.

Example 1   Given a building of brick veneer on 8-in. hollow tile, plaster on lath and furred; 20 ft wide by 30 ft deep and 20 ft high; exposed on three sides with 13 double-hung wood sash windows each with 12 sq ft of area and two doors front and back of 20-sq-ft area each; flat composition roof on 1-in. wood with plastered ceiling; concrete basement floor. Find the gph rate of consumption of No. 2 fuel oil necessary to heat this dwelling. Temperature differential 70° (0° outside average, 70° inside average).

1. Find cubic contents.

   Width 20 ft × length 30 ft × height 20 ft = 12,000 cu ft

2. Find Btu loss per hour due to air volume changes. Windows on three sides.

   12,000 cu ft × 2 = 24,000 Btu

3. Find gross exposed wall area.

   First exposed wall area: 20 × 20 =   400 sq ft
   Second exposed wall area: 30 × 20 =   600 sq ft
   Third exposed wall area: 20 × 20 =   400 sq ft
   Gross wall area   = 1,400 sq ft

4. Find net exposed wall area.

   13 windows each 12 sq ft =   156 sq ft
   2 doors each 20 sq ft   =   40 sq ft
   Total glass and door area =   196 sq ft
   Gross wall area (3)   = 1,400 sq ft
   Less glass and door area   =   196 sq ft
   Net wall area   = 1,204 sq ft

5. Find net exposed wall area (4) Btu loss. Multiply 1,204 sq ft by construction factor 17.

   For brick-veneer building: 1204 × 17 = 20,468 Btu

6. Find glass and door area Btu loss.

   Glass windows: 156 × 78 = 12,168 Btu
   Door 1 in. thick: 40 × 50 =   2,000 Btu
   Loss   = 14,168 Btu

7. Find roof Btu loss per hour.

   Length 30 × width 20   = 600 sq ft
   Sq ft × factor: 600 × 24 = 14,400 Btu

8. Find concrete basement floor Btu loss per hour.

   Length 30 × width 20   = 600 sq ft
   Sq ft × factor: 600 × 1.5 = 900 Btu

9. Find total Btu loss for house.

Volume air changes (2)	=	24,000 Btu
Net exposed wall area (5)	=	20,468 Btu
Glass and door area (6)	=	14,168 Btu
Roof area (7)	=	14,400 Btu
Basement floor area (8)	=	900 Btu
Total Btu loss	=	73,936 Btu

We now have determined the total Btu loss per hour for the house for each of the three conditions: temperature, construction materials, and air volume changes. Now we will go on to determine the gph firing rate in a series of systematic steps that will apply the foregoing example.

Example 2
1. Total Btu loss for air changes (2)   = 24,000 Btu
2. Total Btu loss for construction factors (5, 6, 7, 8) = 49,936 Btu
3. Add Steps 1 and 2 together: Total   = 73,936 Btu
4. Allowance for piping and pickup. Multiply total in Step 3 by 1.40 for steam, 1.30 for warm air, 1.60 for gravity hot water, 1.40 for forced hot water.

$1.40 \times 73,936 = 103,510$ Btu

5. To obtain gph firing rate, divide the figure found in Step 4 by 91,000.

$103,510 \div 91,000 = 1.13$ gph

Choose the next closest nozzle size: 1.25 gph.
Divide by 105,000 if boiler (or furnace) is 75 per cent efficient.
Divide by 98,000 if boiler is 70 per cent efficient.
Divide by 91,000 if boiler is 65 per cent efficient.
Divide by 84,000 if boiler is 60 per cent efficient.
Divide by 77,000 if boiler is 55 per cent efficient.
Divide by 70,000 if boiler is 50 per cent efficient.
6. Multiply the gph rate (Step 5) by 90 to obtain combustion-chamber size (area of combustion chamber floor).

$90 \times 1.25 = 113$ sq in.

113 is number of square inches of floor space area of combustion chamber to be allowed for that amount of oil.
A chamber 10 by 11 in. or 10 by 12 in. would give floor space area close enough to this requirement.

Any system that can give with fair accuracy the total number of Btu per hour required to heat a dwelling can be substituted for the Btu survey method. Once the total Btu loss is determined, begin with Step 3 of the "six-step method" and continue on through to obtain the gph rate and combustion-chamber size.

The following formula, which is a derivation of the old Mills rule, can be used as a substitute for the Btu survey on frame and brick-veneer homes. It eliminates much of the figuring in Steps 1 and 2 that is necessary if the Btu survey is used. The formula is as follows:

1.30 × (cubic content + 10 times net exposed wall area
$$+ \text{ 100 times glass and door area}) = \text{Btu lost per hour}$$

In this formula the net exposed wall area figure should include roofs and cold basement floors. This gives the total Btu loss for construction and volume air changes based on a 70° temperature difference between indoors and outdoors. If the temperature difference is to be 80°, multiply the answer by 1.14; if the difference is to be 60°, multiply by 0.85.

If this rule is to be used, it should be handled with some discretion. It does not apply to all construction, and a comparison with the figures of a complete Btu survey should be made if there is any doubt in the estimator's mind. In the case of a northern exposure of any considerable area, increase the figure by 10 per cent.

QUESTIONS

1. What is the Btu content of 1 gal of No. 2 fuel oil? Of No. 1 fuel oil?
2. Define a Btu.
3. How many Btu are required to raise 75 gal of water 50°F?
4. What are the three conditions that determine the rate of heat loss from a house?
5. What is the standard method of rating oil burners?
6. Explain how the heat loss through a specific type of construction material is calculated.
7. Explain how the volume method is used to determine the heat loss due to air changes.
8. Why is boiler or furnace efficiency an important consideration in determining the amount of oil to be consumed per hour?
9. How many square inches of combustion floor space are allowed per gallon of oil with the "six-step system"?
10. Give a short formula for determining the Btu loss per hour from a dwelling.
11. How should such a short formula be regarded?
12. What allowance should be made for extreme northern exposure?

CHAPTER 8

SHORT METHODS OF
CALCULATING GPH RATES
FOR CONVERSION INSTALLATIONS

In the conversion of any coal-burning heating system to oil, the most important initial step is to determine the actual necessary amount of oil to be consumed per hour by the oil-burning equipment. By this is meant finding out the number of gallons of oil per hour that *will have to be burned* to furnish the actual amount of heat necessary to fulfill the demands of the heating plant. A number of factors influence this, and all of them must be properly applied if there is to be an economic and service-free operation of the heating plant.

The best possible advertisement for automatic oil heating is the satisfied customer, and the customer is satisfied when his oil bills are within reason and the equipment's performance is relatively free of service, especially that type of service which is caused by *high oil consumption.*

It has become more and more necessary to establish in all new installations, and in many old ones, the correct firing rate per hour. Whether a burner is a gun type, a rotary type, or a vaporizing pot type, the same rule applies because the use of a fuel in a furnace or boiler in relation to the load is rigidly governed by certain mathematical laws, and the application of these remains the same, regardless of the type of burner used.

FACTORS AFFECTING FIRING RATE

This chapter will give five different short ways of determining the firing rates for oil burners. They should be used with discretion. Some of them will be qualified by various limitations set on them by conditions inherent in boiler or furnace design, the type of system, and the efficiency of the burner used.

In other words, the gph rates are affected directly by the *actual heating load placed on the plant by the installed radiators or ducts;* this is normally referred to as "standing radiation."

In addition to this, there is a second factor, that of the *mains and risers or the leaders, which require an important part of the total heat produced by the oil flame.*

Third, we have the *domestic faucet hot-water load* which, in certain cases, must be computed because of the demands it makes upon the total boiler output. Heat must be provided to take care of this hot-water load, especially if the demand for it is made at the same time the heat demand occurs.

The fourth condition that consumes part of our heat output is the *pickup demands of the boiler or furnace.* The mass of metal that comprises the boiler or furnace absorbs a specific amount of heat before any is passed into the system, and it also radiates a portion of the heat to the surrounding surfaces in the basement; this may be considered for practical purposes as a loss and is generally referred to as the "pickup factor."

The fifth condition which will have a bearing upon the actual amount of oil we burn is the *boiler efficiency itself,* which depends to a great extent upon the heat transfer qualities of the boiler or furnace. We may put a definite amount of heat into the boiler or furnace and find that because of its design a certain percentage of the heat that we put in will not be absorbed by the boiler, but will pass on up the chimney.

The *intensity* of this loss can be measured or gauged fairly accurately by taking a *stack temperature* reading. This loss, occasioned in the actual transfer of the heat because of the boiler flue-passage design, etc., is really the inability of the boiler to absorb totally and pass on all the heat fed to it. This is a percentage factor, and we refer to it by the common term, "boiler efficiency" or "furnace efficiency."

The boiler may be 50 percent efficient, which means that it will absorb only half the heat passed into it; thus for every gallon of oil we fire, we get only half the heat from it that we possibly could.

Efficiencies of coal-burning boilers when converted to oil are usually quite low (50 to 55 per cent), while the efficiencies on oil-burning boilers may run from 70 to 85 per cent or higher on larger units. These are average figures. The consideration of this factor of boiler efficiency is often neglected in converting from coal to oil, and yet this is the one time when it is most important.

The sixth and final factor to be considered is the *ability of the burner to mix the oil and air properly* and thereby consume all the fuel with an intense hot flame. This is usually measured by a carbon dioxide analysis of the stack gases, a topic that will be discussed in Chap. 21. If an oil burner performs so poorly that a great portion of the oil it is using is deposited out in the form of soot or smoke, a considerable portion of the fuel is going to waste.

For instance, a heating plant that consumes $1\frac{2}{3}$ gph with a 5 per cent CO_2 reading will require only $1\frac{1}{3}$ gph if the CO_2 can be raised to 13 per cent.

The importance of high CO_2 rates on fuel-oil consumption has not been fully appreciated, since CO_2 has been normally referred to as a guide in determining the correct amount of excess air. It is considerably more than that, for it has a direct mathematical relationship to fuel wasted and is a good guide in evaluating the mechanical performance of the oil burner in properly mixing oil and air, just as much as the "miles per gallon of gas" rate in an automobile can be an index of carburetor performance and engine efficiency.

In analyzing the actual methods of calculation for determining the gph rate for oil to be consumed, we will see how some of these factors just discussed will come into play and exert their influence so they may be provided for in the total heat output in Btu per hour given off by the quantity of oil burned.

METHODS OF CALCULATION

The installed radiation method, which is well adapted for conversion installation, consists merely of determining the total number of feet of radiation represented by the radiators in each room. Add these together, allowing a 40 per cent increase for piping and pickup.

The next step is to multiply the gross load in square feet of radiation by 240 Btu, which will convert the load into Btu. This figure should now be divided by 65,000 in the case of *round sectional boilers* with a maximum of *four sections,* or by 75,000 in case of *sectional boilers with fairly restricted flue passages,* or *round boilers with six sections or more.*

A certain amount of judgment is to be used in these cases. If a boiler has a restricted or narrow flue passage, its efficiency may be increased—or the boiler may be baffled to force the flue gases against the heat-absorbing surfaces of the boiler and thereby increase its efficiency.

If we divide by 65,000, we are *roughly* estimating the boiler to be 50 per cent efficient; if we divide by 80,000, we are considering the boiler to be about 65 per cent efficient. The resultant answer will be the gph rate at which the plant should be fired. For example:

Total standing radiation loads of all rooms:	400 sq ft
Add 40 per cent increase for piping and pickup (multiply the total standing square feet of radiation by 1.40 to obtain this increase):	560 sq ft
Gross radiation load:	560 sq ft
Multiply by 240 to convert to Btu:	134,400 Btu

In the case of *round boilers converted to oil* this figure would be divided by 65,000 and the resultant answer would be approximately 2 gph. In the case of a more efficient boiler we would divide by the higher figure, which is 75,000, and the resultant answer would be 1.80 gph. Since a 1.80 nozzle is not a standard size, we could use the nearest size, a 2-gal nozzle.

If the actual boiler efficiency in per cent is known (as, for instance, we know a boiler to be 60 per cent efficient), then we can take 60 per cent of 140,000 Btu (the amount of Btu in 1 gal of No. 2 fuel oil) and divide it into the gross Btu load to get the accurate rate.

In the *constant radiation allowance method* we allow a specific number of square feet of radiation per gallon of oil fired. This constant has been developed through experience and should be carefully used. On the average conversion job with this system we divide the total standing square feet of steam radiation load by 300, and the resulting answer is the gph rate. This figure should apply fairly well in boilers with a fair operating efficiency and stack temperatures not above 700°F.

In the event that a *coal-fired* round boiler of four sections or less is involved, it would be wise to divide by 250. This would give higher gallonage per hour and take up for the extra general inefficiency occasioned by the lack of proper restricted flue passages in some round boilers. Another answer to this is to baffle the boiler to increase its efficiency (see Chap. 29). The basis for this computation is that we expect to get 300 sq ft of radiation from each gallon of oil fired in the average boiler, while we expect to get only 250 sq ft of radiation for each gallon of oil fired in a coal-fired round boiler of four sections or less.

It is wise to avoid the installation of an oil burner in a coal-fired round sectional boiler that has only three sections. An installation of this sort should be made only if the customer can be convinced of the wisdom of installing another section. *There should be at least four sections in every coal-fired round boiler that is being fired by oil.*

The total volume of flue gases and their velocity are so much greater than is the case in coal firing that there must be a necessary increase in flue-passage restriction and total heating surface, if the boiler is to absorb properly the intense amount of heat put into it, which is characteristic of intermittent oil firing, without a large percentage of that heat passing up the stack.

The method of *determining the firing rate from boiler output rating* is based upon obtaining the actual total boiler output rating given in square feet of radiation. This can be obtained usually from a plate or marking on the boiler itself or from the boiler manufacturer or any of the boiler reference guides.

Multiply the total boiler output rating in square feet by 240 (600 sq ft of radiation × 240 = 144,000 Btu boiler output), and this will give the total boiler output in Btu.

Next take the boiler efficiency in per cent and divide it into 100 (100 ÷ 70 = 1.43). Take the resultant figure (1.43) and multiply the total boiler output by it (144,000 Btu × 1.43 = 205,920 Btu). Divide this figure (205,920) by the Btu in 1 gal of No. 2 fuel oil (140,000). The resultant figure will be the gph firing rate (205,920 ÷ 140,000 = 1.47 gph). Since there are no nozzles of this particular size, the next closest size (1.50 gph) should be chosen.

Calculating the firing rate from the boiler heating surface is one of the most accurate methods of determining the actual firing rate to be applied to a boiler. By "boiler heating surface" we mean the actual part of the boiler that has hot flue gases on one side and water on the other.

Engineers are able to determine the heat-transfer capacity of a boiler, and by knowing the actual specific heat-transfer rate per square foot of the boiler heating surface we can determine the constant rate of heat transfer.

In automatic oil-fired boilers we regard 4,000 Btu per hr per sq ft of boiler heating surface as a practical heating transfer rate, but this figure provides us with a constant that is only fairly accurate.

The only thing necessary in this case is to find the total number of square feet of boiler heating surface. Sometimes this is not easy to obtain.

On older types of boilers that have been in the field for a number of years, it may prove to be difficult to determine the firing rate from the boiler heating surface. The number of square feet of boiler heating surface is multiplied by 4,000. For instance, 40 sq ft of boiler heating surface × 4,000 = 160,000 Btu. Assuming the boiler to be 60 per cent efficient, the firing rate should be 266,667 Btu per hr. Divide this by 140,000 and we will find that the firing rate will be 1.91 gph.

One of the best-known but least accurate methods of determining gph rate is by the *grate area method*. This method must be used with some caution and is really effective only in the case of small boilers or furnaces. Since there is no definite proportion between boiler heating surface and boiler grate area, it follows that boiler capacities cannot be accurately determined from grate size. Some boilers have a small amount of heating surface per square foot of grate area, while others have as high as 20 sq ft of boiler heating surface per square foot of grate area.

As boilers get larger in size, the relationship between grate area and boiler heating surface begins to vary widely, and for this reason it is best to use the grate area method only with small boilers.

Determine the square feet of grate area by multiplying the length in feet by the width in feet of the grate; then multiply the total number of square feet of grate area by 70,000 (3.50 sq ft of grate area × 70,000 = 245,000 Btu). Divide the number of Btu thus obtained by 140,000, and this will give the maximum rate at which that boiler can be fired (245,000 ÷ 140,000 = 1.75 gph).

In using this method it is wise to check with a stack thermometer. If stack temperatures run over 700°, the nozzle size should be reduced, for the boiler does not have enough heating surface to absorb the heat properly; or it should be so baffled as to increase its heat-absorption rate.

SUMMARY OF GPH FLOW RATE FORMULAS

Much of the foregoing material in this chapter can further be simplified if it is expressed as arithmetic formulas. Since the basic point to be established is the nozzle size, the answer furnished by these calculations is expressed in gallons per hour (gph) firing rate. These answers can be arrived at if certain data are known. The most important of these known data are: (1) the unit rating in Btu per hour *input*, (2) the unit rating in Btu per hour *output*, (3) the total square feet of steam radiation (including piping), or (4) the total square feet of hot-water radiation (including piping).

If any one of these is known, then the following formulas apply:

1. Btu *input* known:

$$\text{gph} = \frac{\text{Btu input}}{140,000}$$

2. Btu *output* known:

$$\text{gph} = \frac{\text{Btu output}}{\% \text{ efficiency} \times 140,000}$$

3. Total square feet steam radiation (including piping) known:

$$\text{gph} = \frac{\text{total sq ft steam radiation} \times 240}{\% \text{ efficiency} \times 140,000}$$

4. Total square feet hot-water radiation (including piping) known (based on 180°F water temperature):

$$\text{gph} = \frac{\text{total sq ft hot-water radiation} \times 165}{\% \text{ efficiency} \times 140,000}$$

The application of any of these methods in determining gph rates can be successfully achieved if some care is taken and a knowledge of the various factors involved is present. A good point to remember is that in order to change the total number of Btu for any room or house into square feet of steam radiation, one should divide by 240, since 240 represents the number of Btu emitted in 1 hr by 1 sq ft of cast-iron radiation exposed to the air on one side at 70°F and filled with steam at 215° on the other.

With a vapor-heating system, 200 is the constant by which we divide or multiply in order to obtain radiation or Btu.

With a closed forced-circulation hot-water system, 200 is the constant.

With a closed gravity-circulation hot-water heating system, 180 is the constant.

With an open gravity-circulation hot-water system, 150 Btu per hr is the constant.

Therefore, we can estimate *roughly* that in a steam system 1 gal of oil per hr will normally give us 300 sq ft of radiation, while in a vapor system 1 gal of oil per hr will furnish us with 360 sq ft of radiation.

In a hot-water closed system with forced circulation, 1 gal of oil per hr will furnish approximately 360 sq ft.

In a hot-water closed system with gravity circulation, 1 gal of oil per hr equals about 410 sq ft.

In a hot-water gravity-circulation open system, 1 gal of oil per hr should furnish 470 sq ft of radiation.

QUESTIONS

1. What are some of the factors that must be considered in calculating the gph rate for conversion installations?
2. How should these short methods be used?

3. What is the average efficiency of a coal-burning boiler converted to oil?
4. Explain the "installed radiation method" of calculating the gph rate.
5. Explain the "constant radiation allowance" method.
6. Explain the "grate area method."
7. What are the limitations of the grate area method?
8. Why is it advisable to check with a stack thermometer when using the grate area method?
9. Give short formulas for determining GPH rate when (a) BTU input is known, (b) BTU output is known, (c) square feet of steam radiation required and boiler efficiency are known, (d) square feet of hot-water radiation required and boiler efficiency are known.
10. Give the constants for changing square feet of radiation into Btu, or vice versa, for (a) vapor-heating systems, (b) forced-circulation hot-water systems, (c) gravity-circulation hot-water systems.

CHAPTER 9

COMBUSTION CHAMBERS: PART I

In order for oil to burn properly, a number of conditions must be complied with. A review of these conditions will lead us to the subject of this and the next chapter.

As we have seen from a previous chapter, the purpose of the oil burner is to *prepare fuel for burning.* This is accomplished in two steps. First, the oil is broken up or, as it is popularly termed, "atomized." Second, it is mixed with air to supply the necessary oxygen to support combustion.

By the time the oil has been atomized and mixed with air from the blast tube of the burner it is a distance from the burner itself. At this point the burner has already done its job and a new set of conditions steps in to govern the burning process that is going on. From this we can see that two of the rules concerning the burning of oil have already been complied with. These first two rules, namely, (1) that *the oil must be broken up or finely divided into very small particles* and (2) *mixed with air* in order to burn, are met by the burner itself. Other conditions that must be met are to be reckoned with without the burner.

The other two conditions that now enter the picture and must be complied with if we are to have hot, efficient, and clean combustion are dependent on the combustion chamber and the way it is designed.

The two further rules are: (1) *the oil must be burned in suspension* and (2) *the neighborhood or environment in which this combustion takes place must furnish enough heat to the burning oil to speed up vaporization considerably and also maintain a surrounding temperature high enough to prevent any oil from escaping unburned.*

It is obvious that the agency which can properly fulfill these conditions must be the combustion chamber or firebox.

The first rule, that of burning the oil in suspension, has its purpose achieved if the firebox is *proper in design and shape and accurate in size.*

Burning oil "in suspension" simply means that the burning oil must not touch any cold surfaces. The particles of oil as they burn depend on high temperatures to complete combustion. All throughout the flame these tiny particles of oil are breaking down into gases and carbon and burning through to completion. They need the high temperatures furnished by the fire itself to enable them to complete their job. The tips and sides of the flame are filled with these droplets being vaporized and, being on the outer reaches of the flame, they are not as hot as the droplets within the flame itself. They are, therefore, more sensitive to any decline in temperature.

If these flame tips brush against cold surfaces or surfaces that are considerably cooler than the flame itself, the oil particles cease to vaporize and begin to settle out as unburned carbon or soot. Smoke can also be an evidence of such cooling.

The combustion chamber is the area in which this burning takes place; therefore, it follows that it must be of such size and material as to prevent directly this chilling of the oil droplets in the outer portions of the flame. This does not mean that the flame cannot ever touch the chamber walls, but it does mean that if the flame does touch, it must be in such a hot state that the oil particles in it are already completely vaporized and in the final stages of combustion. Or, the chamber walls must be hot enough so as not to interfere with the combustion process that is taking place. Either of these two circumstances can eliminate the deposit of soot that may result from such flame *impingement.* The above conditions can be easily complied with if the combustion chamber is of the right material and of proper size, design, and construction.

The actual dimension, design, and construction of chambers will be discussed more completely in Chap. 10. This chapter concerns itself with the principles that necessitate the use of fireboxes and the materials with which they should be built in order to achieve their purpose properly. However, there are burners that can operate without fireboxes.

HOW TO BURN OIL PROPERLY

In order to burn oil properly in suspension, we must limit the combustion process to a specific environment which will provide it with the necessary space to prevent impingement of the partially burned oil on the surrounding walls, and which will also provide an area of intense heat that is reflected and radiated and reradiated back upon the fire itself. Thereby, we furnish an intensely hot locality in which the oil particles can vaporize freely and completely without any physical interference.

This means that the combustion chamber must use the heat of the fire itself *quickly* and efficiently to provide the necessary conditions for burning oil thoroughly and efficiently.

If the combustion chamber must use the heat of the fire to help the combustion process complete itself, then we can readily see that it is important for the firebox to get intensely hot as soon as possible.

If we were to burn the oil in a boiler without any refractory brick or other type of insulation, the large quantities of soot and smoke that arise would quickly demonstrate it to be impractical. The cold metal surfaces of the boiler, behind which rest large quantities of water, would cool the tip and sides of our flames so quickly that the combustion would be dirty and inefficient. Not only that, but the hot fire brushing against the cold metal sides of the boiler or furnace could seriously harm them.

Unequal strains and stresses due to uneven heating of the metal could seriously shorten the life of the boiler. Unequal distribution, by radiation and convection, of the heat would lead to uneven circulation of the water and a wasteful application of the heat.

It is quite evident that the metal surfaces of the average boiler cannot provide the proper environment for the fire. We must have some intermediate material that will give the flame the environment it requires and protect the boiler or furnace. This protective material is the refractory of which our combustion chamber is built.

A refractory brick or material, in order to do its job properly with a domestic burner, must be able to get up to intense heat quickly on the surfaces coming into close contact with the oil flame. The refractory

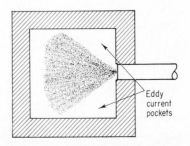

Fig. 9-1 Square chamber for short, wide flame.

material must also be able to withstand high temperatures with little or no effect on itself.

Of these, the first is most important: getting up to intense heat as quickly as possible on the side where the flame is located. This will give us maximum combustion efficiency in a minimum amount of time.

Refractory material

The type of refractory material that is best suited to the intermittent firing of domestic oil burners is the modern *lightweight insulating firebrick*. This brick, which is highly porous, is light in texture, and its weight is but a fraction of that of the standard heavyweight refractory brick and is excellent for small fires.

Heavy brick is not suited to the short intermittent firing periods that are characteristic of domestic oil-burner heating installations. This heavy firebrick takes a long time to become heated to the high surface temperature (on the inner side of the chamber) that is necessary to facilitate the complete combustion of the oil. What actually happens is that this heavy type of brick passes the heat of the flame right on through its entire area because it is a good conductor. This means that instead of concentrating the heat on the surface of the brick adjacent to the flame such heavy brick passes the heat *immediately* through its own body to surrounding surfaces.

Because of this, no initial concentration of heat takes place on the inner chamber wall close to the fire where and when we need it most—*at the start, when everything is comparatively cold.*

As a result, brick of this heavy variety achieves the proper surface heat for good combustion a considerable time after the burner has been operating. The result is soot, smoke, and odor on starting, all of which combine to give us poor initial combustion efficiency expressed in low CO_2 readings.

In the continuous firing that we find in industrial jobs with a minimum of starting periods and a maximum of constant operating periods, this heavy brick with its high heat transfer ability and lack of insulating qualities offers no real disadvantage and is necessary because of its long-term resistance to breaking down under constant firing.

With the on-and-off periods of domestic burners, however, and with the emphasis on running as short a time as possible to heat evenly, heavy firebrick is inefficient and offers serious disadvantages on each cold starting cycle.

The type of refractory material that is admirably adapted to the numerous on-off cycles of domestic oil-burner operation, as mentioned previously, is *lightweight insulating firebrick*. This insulating firebrick resists the flow of heat through the brick itself for a longer period of

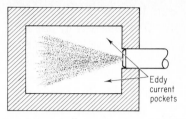

Fig. 9-2   Rectangular chamber for long, narrow flame.

time than is the case with the heavier type of brick.   This is due to its porous, light, insulating type of construction and material.

When the burner is started and combustion begins, the heat from the flame passes to the adjacent surfaces of the light brick.   Instead of dissipating this initial surface heat right on through the brick, its insulating qualities hold and concentrate the heat right on the surface of the chamber that is closest to the fire.   Thus the firebrick surface which faces the fire reaches a glowing red heat in a mere fraction of the time it would take the ordinary heavy firebrick to reach the same surface temperature.   The rest of the brick is still comparatively cool.

Because this initial heat is not immediately passed through the brick but held at the surface, the light brick surface actually becomes much *hotter* as well as heats more rapidly.   The result of this is more quickly balanced combustion.   The rate of flame propagation stabilizes quickly, and flames are hotter and more intense.   Thus the initial firing cycles are more efficient and less smoky, and produce higher CO_2 readings; less heat is wasted up the stack, and substantial fuel savings can be made.

These hotter flames mean a much shorter period of waiting for heat, since boilers and furnaces with the greater heat applied more quickly will naturally furnish heat to the house at a more rapid rate.

A good point to remember in regard to the use of these insulating firebricks is that there is less chance of flame impingement causing soot deposits, since the brick surface heats so rapidly.   As a result, chambers can actually be built smaller with insulating brick, thus saving material and time.

Whenever light brick is used, the special type of high-temperature bonding mortars provided for them should be employed.   Insulating firebrick does not make a good bond with ordinary types of fire clays.

Stainless-steel chambers are now frequently used because of their ability to heat quickly and help combustion equilibrium.   Newer combustion chambers, discussed in the next chapter, using insulating material developed for jet engines, are now becoming more popular and undoubtedly will be utilized to a great extent in the future.

BASIC COMBUSTION-CHAMBER DESIGN

In the fulfillment of the second purpose of the combustion chamber, that is, to furnish an area that will properly provide heat for the combustion process, the problem of basic chamber design is encountered.

In the field there are chambers of many sizes, but basically of only three major designs (see Figs. 9-1 to 9-3). These are the *square,* the *rectangular,* and the *circular* chambers.

Observation might lead one to believe that the design of the boiler or furnace or grate area would be the main factor in determining the shape of the chamber. Undoubtedly this is so in a vast number of installations, but it definitely is not the correct procedure.

The real factor that governs the shape of the chamber to be used is the *flame shape produced by the burner to be used.* This is the most important consideration.

Next is the location and design of the heat-receiving surfaces of the boiler, that is, the crown sheet or sections right over the flame. These two conditions—burner flame shape and crown-sheet height and placement—are the most important considerations in proper firebox design.

An installer should never at any time build a combustion chamber without knowing the flame characteristics of the burner he is to install. The burner should be observed under actual operation and the air-handling parts adjusted to see if such adjustments *alter the shape of the flame.*

If the flame shape is not adjustable or changeable, then it follows that only one of the basic design types—the square, rectangular, or circular chamber—will be correct. If the flame is *short and wide,* the *square* chamber is the best. If the flame is *long and narrow,* the *rectangle* is best. If it is of the *round, ball* type or shows a tendency to be *irregular,* the *circular* chamber is best.

These are general rules that can be easily and safely followed, but they do not mean that conditions may not arise that alter these general design applications.

Rounded or curved surfaces of a combustion chamber *generally* lend themselves to better and more thorough mixing of the oil and air. This

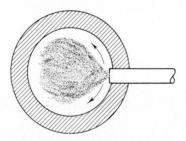

Fig. 9-3 Round chamber for ball-shape or short, wide flames.

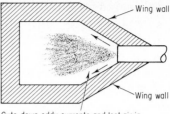

Fig. 9-4   Combustion chamber with wing walls.

is due to the fact that the flow of air over the rounded surfaces is less erratic, smoother, and more inclined to follow the contours of the chamber and thereby be directed into the fire, provided that the chamber is of the proper size.

In chambers with regular square corners there are eddy currents formed in these angles that cause quantities of air to miss the fire completely and pass on up the stack without ever entering the combustion process. This is especially so at the front of the chamber where the burner blast tube enters. The fire is narrower at this point, and the air in the corners often never reaches it (Figs. 9-1 and 9-2).

The use of "wing walls" at this point forces the air to contact the oil by "squeezing" it into the spray at the beginning of the flame. This makes for better combustion and more even distribution of heat throughout the surface of the chamber wall. The use of wing walls on the pear-shaped chamber is of especial value in larger fireboxes.

The heat built up in the chamber is radiated back into the firebox from all directions. This means that the heat from the fire, after being passed on to the chamber, is radiated and reflected back on the flame, and so used to help the burning process and increase the speed with which the oil is gasified.

The design of the chamber can effectively help or hinder this condition. A chamber should, because of this, always be large enough to encompass at least 90 per cent of the flame, so that no major portion of the combustion is going on outside the environment that is most helpful to it.

QUESTIONS

1. What are the four conditions that must be complied with when one is burning oil?
2. What is the purpose of the combustion chamber?
3. What happens when an oil flame touches a cold surface?

4. What are the two types of firebrick? Explain the difference between the two.
5. Which type of firebrick is better for small oil fires? Why?
6. What type of firing is best with standard firebrick?
7. What are the three basic combustion-chamber designs? To what shape of flame is each best fitted?
8. What are the advantages of wing walls?

CHAPTER 10

COMBUSTION CHAMBERS: PART II

Once the gph rate has been calculated, the next step is to build the combustion chamber of proper size and design. The size depends upon the actual amount of oil burned per hour, and the design depends upon the shape of the flame produced by the burner to be installed. Both these factors should be known if any success is to be achieved in building the chamber.

Ignoring either of these two factors will result in decreased operating efficiencies as mirrored by low CO_2 readings, or soot deposits, smoky fires or even pulsations.

Many well-designed burners have characteristically shaped fires with a standard angle of spray regardless of gallonage. This is due to the rapid development of specially designed air-handling parts that result in stable flame shapes.

Older burners and even some of the newer ones are not yet equipped with these air-turbulating devices and as a result are still quite dependent upon changes in the angle of spray to help fit the flame to the chamber.

An installer should quickly determine *whether or not the selected burner has a definite flame shape,* for this will be of great importance when it comes to firebox building or selecting a precast firebox.

If the burner uses a single spray-angle pattern, say a 45-deg angle, as recommended by its manufacturer, then the installer can usually be sure that it has a fixed flame shape and can always use a chamber of the same design, varying only in size. This is a great help, for the installer then will have a fixed type of chamber to work with at all times and thus be assured of attaining higher operating efficiencies more easily.

If the burner has no definite flame shape and the shape depends on the angle of spray, then the installer will be faced with a variable problem on each installation.

In cases where no standard angle of spray is required by the burner because of its lack of special air-handling parts (which in turn results in no specific air pattern), the shape and design of the boiler may become the deciding factor in determining the shape of the chamber. Once the chamber is built to shape in this case, the proper angle of spray is selected so that the fire shape may conform as much as possible to the form of the chamber. In a rectangular chamber, which is narrow in width, a 45-deg angle of spray, or possibly a 60-deg angle, will be preferable. In a square or round chamber, a 70-, 80-, or even a 90-deg will be the best.

It must be remembered at this point that the air delivery of a burner will alter considerably the spray-angle pattern, and some experimenting with angles of spray may have to be done. The flame should fill the chamber but not impinge on the sides or back wall. Any deposits of carbon, signified by a blackening of the wall on starting cycles, show that there is impingement and the flame is too large, too wide, or too long provided the firebox is of proper size. In this case, a narrower angle of spray or a smaller nozzle should be selected. A CO_2 analyzer should be used to check the results of the changes in the spray-angle pattern.

The proper spray angle will result sometimes in a startling increase in the CO_2 reading (as much as 2 or 3 per cent), especially on the starting cycle when this increased efficiency is needed the most.

Once the basic design, whether square, rectangular, or round, has been selected, the next problem becomes one of proper sizing. This refers to the dimensions of the chamber, especially length and width.

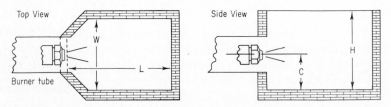

Fig. 10-1   Basic chamber dimensions referred to in Table 10-1 (page 157).

The height may often be standardized because of the boiler or furnace design characteristics.

The most important factor in chamber dimension is the actual area in square inches of the floor of the chamber. We can get the area of the floor of the chamber by simply multiplying the length in inches by the width in inches. Thus, if we needed a chamber of 100 sq in. of floor space, we could use a length and a width of 10 in. each. The square area in inches of floor space in the chamber is the all-important factor in small-burner installations, for it furnishes a definite and constant guide to which we may refer.

With high-pressure gun-type burners allow approximately 90 sq in. of floor space per gallon of oil to be burned. With low-pressure gun-type burners allow approximately 100 sq in. of floor space per gallon of oil to be burned. Follow the manufacturer's instructions.

Of course there may be cases in which, because of boiler or furnace design, these exact dimensional requirements cannot be met, but every effort should be made to adhere to them as closely as possible.

In square or round chambers, an addition of up to 10 sq in. to the above figures will do little harm, but such an addition with a rectangular, narrow chamber will definitely decrease operating efficiencies.

Remember that, in field installations, one of the greatest single factors in causing increased fuel consumption and the consequent waste of oil is *improperly sized chambers*. Even a chamber of wrong shape or poor design can do a fairly good job if it is of the proper size.

After an installer has had considerable experience with chambers, these figures can be reduced to 85 sq in. for high-pressure gun-type burners and to 90 sq in. for low-pressure burners. But such close dimensions can only be undertaken when there is a tailored design chamber and where the firing period is not too constant.

The smaller the space provided per gallon of oil, the shorter should be the ON periods of the burner. Constant, long ON periods with the chamber size down to 85 sq in. of floor space can very well result in the destruction of the firebox due to "peeling" away of the brick surface and its consequent deterioration. The surface cell structure of soft insulating bricks is destroyed in such cases.

Not much economy is involved when a very small chamber saves oil but then the chamber itself has to be replaced every 2 years. This becomes doubly important in view of the fact that when using light-weight insulating firebrick, it will break down more quickly if overfired than will the heavy type of brick.

It should be kept in mind that reductions in floor area below the 90 sq in. per gal of oil figure for increased operating efficiencies can be undertaken only if the gph rate is low (below 1.50); the ON periods are not above 25 to 30 min; and the shape of the chamber is carefully tailored to the shape of the flame.

The side walls should always be high enough to cover the mud ring on the bottom of the water leg of the boiler. High side walls mean higher CO_2 readings. The side-wall height should roughly be $2\frac{1}{4}$ times the distance of the nozzle from the chamber floor. In the warm-air furnace, the side walls should be higher than in the steam or hot-water boiler. This is especially so with the gravity-fed warm-air furnace, where a chamber that is too low can cause overheating at the base of the furnace.

Such overheating of the base could well cause reverse circulation through the return ducts. Side walls in such cases should be $2\frac{1}{2}$ to 3 times the nozzle height from the floor.

The height of the nozzle from the inner floor of the combustion chamber is really dependent on the gallons of oil burned per hour. The more oil burned, the larger will be the flame and the higher the gun must be placed. If the angle of spray is not specified and any angle may be chosen, this too must then be considered.

The flame created by an 80-deg angle of spray will be more sensitive to height from the floor than is the case with a 45-deg angle of spray. This is due to the fact that the flame will be wider. Table 10-1 gives dimensions that will govern most installations and can be used with some freedom.

If there is any doubt about the height the nozzle should be from the floor and the angle of spray that is to be used is not known at the time of the installation, a good guide is to be certain that the nozzle is two-thirds the width of the chamber above the floor for gph rates up to 1.65.

For gph rates above 1.65, the nozzle should be about half the width of the chamber above the inner combustion-chamber floor. This applies

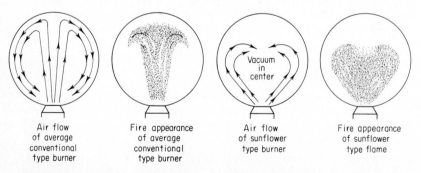

Fig. 10-2 Air-pattern characteristics are important to combustion chamber design. Note how air characteristics determine type of fire. Also observe how round shape of chamber helps to use the air to best advantage.

Table 10-1 RECOMMENDED COMBUSTION-CHAMBER DIMENSIONS

| Nozzle size or rating, gph | Spray angle, deg. | Square or rectangular combustion chamber | | | | Round chamber |
		Length (L), in.	Width (W), in.	Height (H), in.	Nozzle height (C), in.	Diameter, in.
0.50–0.65	80	8	8	11	4	9
0.75–0.85	60	10	8	12	4	*
	80	9	9	13	5	10
	45	14	7	12	4	*
1.00–1.10	60	11	9	13	5	*
	80	10	10	14	6	11
	45	15	8	11	5	*
1.25–1.35	60	12	10	14	6	*
	80	11	11	15	7	12
	45	16	10	12	6	*
1.50–1.65	60	13	11	14	7	*
	80	12	12	15	7	13
	45	18	11	14	6	*
1.75–2.00	60	15	12	15	7	*
	80	14	13	16	8	15
	45	18	12	14	7	*
2.25–2.50	60	17	13	15	8	*
	80	15	14	16	8	16
	45	20	13	15	7	*
3.00	60	19	14	17	8	*
	80	18	16	18	9	17

*Recommended oblong chamber for narrow sprays.

Notes:

These dimensions are for average conversion burners. Burners with special firing heads may require special chambers.

Higher backwall, flame baffle, or corbelled backwall increase efficiency on many jobs.

Combustion chamber floor should be insulated on conversion jobs.

For larger nozzle sizes, use the same approximate proportions and 90 sq. in. of floor area per 1 gph.

SOURCE: Delavan Mfg. Co.

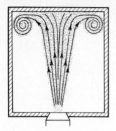

Fig. 10-3   Air action and pattern of average conventional burner in a square chamber.   Eddy currents in 90-deg corners are unavoidable.   This air is never used in combustion.   It simply passes through heater, wasting heat, and must be replaced with added air from fan of burner.

mainly to rectangular chambers.   *In every case, the burner must be high enough to prevent flame impingement upon the floor.*

If a mound of carbon builds up on the floor of the chamber, it can be evidence of flame impingement provided that it is not caused by oil leaking from the nozzle after the burner has been cut off.   If this carbon is soft and sootlike, there is just a slight impingement, and raising the burner an inch or so will usually correct it.   If the carbon is hard and crustlike, however, there is serious impingement and a large amount of liquid oil is striking the floor.   In such a case, the *burner should be raised several inches immediately.*   If it is not possible to do this right away, a nozzle with a considerably narrower angle of spray can be used as a temporary measure.   Such a nozzle will ordinarily produce a longer, narrower flame.   Do not make such a substitution, though, if the chamber is too short and the flame then strikes the back wall.   Such a procedure just substitutes one evil for another.

At this point, the question arises about how far to place the gun of the burner into the chamber.   The edge of the gun should be flush with the inner wall of the chamber or should extend back about ½ in. from the edge.

Do not have the edge of the blast tube or gun protruding beyond the inner wall into the combustion space.   This is to invite trouble that

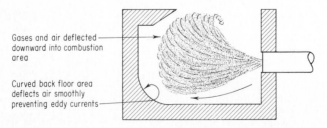

Gases and air deflected
downward into combustion
area

Curved back floor area
deflects air smoothly
preventing eddy currents

Fig. 10-4   Chamber with curved rear floor surface (side view).

can result in the front of the blast tube melting down and burning off, carbonized nozzles, carbonized electrodes, and resultant puffbacks. Check the burner manufacturer's specifications on this and follow them closely. Years of experience and adjustment have gone into his directions, and they should be followed in this respect. Some burners, because of special design of the air-handling parts, can bear close proximity to the fire without harm, but this is the exception rather than the rule.

In boilers of round design, there is only one opening in front of the boiler through which to place the burner, and this also is true of many steel boilers. A large number of cast-iron, rectangular, sectional boilers may be fired from either end. This presents a problem both from the choice of the firing position and from the chamber design viewpoints.

The burner with a narrow flame should not be fired from the end opposite the first flue-pass opening. It should be fired on the same side as the first flue-pass opening. This forces the gases to wipe over the entire crown sheet and then reverse their direction to reach the flue pass, which enables us to extract more heat due to this double wiping action.

The use of corbels or shelves on the back or front walls of the chamber aids materially in increasing the heat absorption rate of the boiler as well as assuring more complete combustion. These corbels should be on every chamber back wall even though they may do nothing

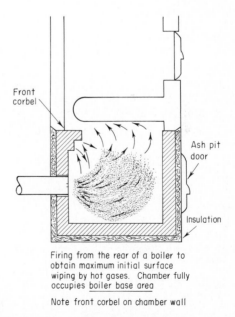

Front corbel

Ash pit door

Insulation

Firing from the rear of a boiler to obtain maximum initial surface wiping by hot gases. Chamber fully occupies boiler base area

Note front corbel on chamber wall

Fig. 10-5 Location of burner mounting is determined by position of first flue-pass opening.

to deflect the gases as they flow, because they radiate heat back into the firebox, helping thereby to create a hot locale for combustion. They also catch any unburned oil vapors and force them back over the fire, where they are properly consumed (see Figs. 10-6 to 10-8).

A corbel has the advantage of deflecting the hot gases when such is required because of boiler design, but they always help make combustion more complete by affording increased surface for direct radiation of additional heat back into the fire, thereby increasing flame temperature.

The deposit of oily soot found in so many boilers, a condition that seriously decreases the boiler's heat-absorbing efficiency, can be eliminated by using the proper type of corbel. Corbels have distinct limitations as regards size, however, and must never be so large or cover so much area as to interfere with the direct radiation of heat from the flame to the surrounding boiler surfaces.

CONSTRUCTING THE CHAMBER

In building the combustion chamber, the first item is *laying the floor.* The brick used for the floor should be of the same type as that used for the walls, that is, insulating firebrick for low gph rates.

Do not use hard firebrick for the floor and insulating brick for the

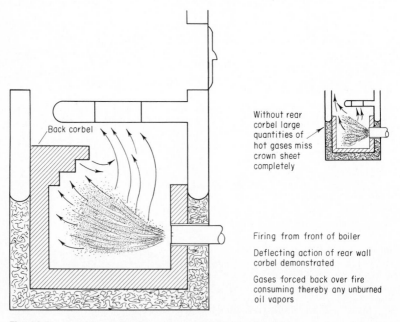

Back corbel

Without rear corbel large quantities of hot gases miss crown sheet completely

Firing from front of boiler

Deflecting action of rear wall corbel demonstrated

Gases forced back over fire consuming thereby any unburned oil vapors

Fig. 10-6   Use of corbel helps assure complete combustion.

Chamber with front and rear
corbel and sloped corners

Excellent for small fires

Fig. 10-7 Corbels and sloped corners help increase flame temperatures of small fires.

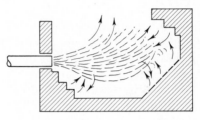

Chamber with rear corbel and front floor corbel

Heat radiated from floor corbel increases combustion efficiency

Floor corbels prevent air from escaping combustion process

Fig. 10-8   Additional corbel location at front floor of chamber.

walls.   The different rates of expansion may result in cracking and damage to the walls; in addition, heat will be lost to the basement floor if standard firebrick is used.   Place the firebrick flat side down on the ashpit floor and be sure at this point that there will be enough distance between the blast tube and floor to furnish the required clearance for the flame.   If there is not, use a hacksaw, cut the insulation firebrick in half and use this split.

Table 10-2   Miscellaneous Data

1 cu ft of wall requires 17 bricks
1 sq ft wall 2½ in. thick requires 3.6 bricks
1 sq ft wall 4½ in. thick requires 6.4 bricks
1 standard 9-in. firebrick weighs 8.0 lb
1 insulating 9-in. firebrick weighs 1.48 lb
Length (in.) × width (in.) = area of floor, sq in.
Radius^2 × 3.1416 = area of a circle
Diameter^2 × 0.7854 = area of a circle
90 sq in. floor space per gal of oil for high-pressure gun-type burners
100 sq in. floor space per gal of oil for low-pressure gun-type burners

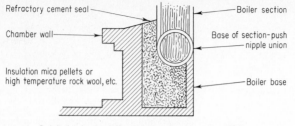

Refractory cement seal

Chamber wall

Insulation mica pellets or
high temperature rock wool, etc.

Boiler section

Base of section-push
nipple union

Boiler base

Detail showing insulation between chamber wall and boiler

Fig. 10-9 Insulating behind chamber wall protects boiler base.

Do not, however, resort to the use of splits for the floor unless it is necessary. In fact, it is preferable, if feasible, to pit the boiler a few inches and keep to the whole brick, thus being sure of its full insulating quality being used to prevent transfer of heat to the floor. After the floor brick has been laid with flat side down, the cracks in the floor should be sealed with the proper high-temperature mortar.

It is not necessary to seal the floor bricks with mortar over their full joining surface; in fact, in most chambers mortar is not used between the bricks laid as the floor. It is a good idea, though, to seal the spaces or cracks at the top where the floor bricks join, in order to prevent any excess air from leaking in at these points and thereby lowering the CO_2.

The mortar used should be of the special type made for insulating firebrick. This mortar should be diluted to a consistency where it will flow slowly if poured. The insulating firebrick should be dipped in the mortar on the abutting surfaces only. That is, on surfaces where it will meet and join the other brick. A strong bond is then established by this thin wall of mortar. Avoid, at all costs, any *thick* application of mortar as a bond between the bricks.

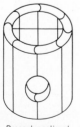

Precast sectional
round chamber

Fig. 10-10

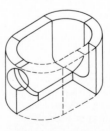

Precast chamber oval
streamline type

Fig. 10-11

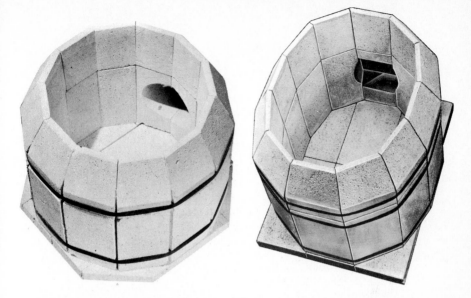

Fig. 10-12 Precast insulating firebrick chambers. These chambers are keystone fitted and are quickly assembled on the job, eliminating the labor and time required for handmade chambers. (*Boston Machine Works*)

If heavy firebricks are used, any ordinary high-temperature refractory cement will do, and a layer of insulation between the cellar floor and the firebrick floor is a must. However, standard heavy firebrick will make an excellent floor for a firebox built within a *wet-base* boiler.

After the brick has been laid, covering the entire interior floor of the furnace or boiler base, the walls are now ready to be built. The bricks used in the side and back walls should be staggered.

The joints where the back and side walls meet should be interlocked and if there is enough room between the corner joints and the boiler base, the extra brick can be left jutting into the space. If there is not enough room, cut the brick with a keyhole saw or hacksaw blade.

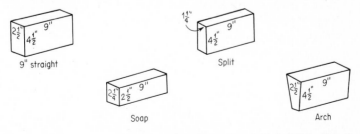

Fig. 10-13 Standard firebrick shapes.

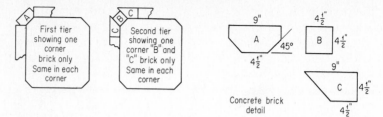

Fig. 10-14   Larger chambers need special attention to design details. Above 5.0 gph, when properly designed insulating brick chambers are not available, it is necessary to construct the chamber from insulating brick. Because of width limitation in most boilers such chambers should be rectangular but should be kept as near square as possible. All 90-deg corners should be eliminated, and the sketches show a most practical and satisfactory way of doing this. 45-deg corners help direct air trapped at back of chamber to the front of the firebox where it can be used in the combustion process. (*Boston Machine Works*)

Insulating firebrick can be easily cut into any shape desired, and do not hesitate to take advantage of this fact and make perfectly fitted joints.

Bring the side and back walls up to the specified height and then pour insulation between the boiler base, boiler walls, and the brick wall. Use mica pellets, high-temperature rockwool, or powdered asbestos and be sure to tamp it lightly so that it will not settle later and leave gaps between the chamber wall and furnace or boiler base.

Do not use dirt, waste, rubble, sand, broken concrete, etc., as insulation between the chamber and the boiler base.

Materials used for back- and side fill must be capable of withstanding high temperatures. The back wall is then ready to have a corbel tied into it of whatever size or height is required.

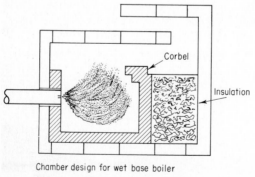

Chamber design for wet base boiler

Note short chamber occupying only part of boiler base area

Fig. 10-15

The next step is the front wall, which is interlocked with the two side walls and built up, leaving an opening for the blast tube. When the burner is set in, be sure that it is level and follow the instructions previously given on how far in the gun should be inserted. Fill in around the burner gun with loose pieces of brick, the whole to be held in place with bonding mortar.

At this point the top edge of the chamber should be sealed over with mortar between the brick and the boiler or furnace, as shown in Fig. 10-6. All leaks and cracks around the boiler or furnace base and between the boiler sections should be tightly sealed to prevent excess air from seeping in.

Once the chamber is completed, the burner can then be fired. Run the burner for 10 min and shut it off for 10; then increase the running time to 15 min and the OFF period to 5. Repeat the 15-min ON and 5-min OFF period several times, and the chamber then will be ready for ordinary operation.

At this point, it is wise to "candle" the installation to make sure

Fig. 10-16 A Cerafelt chamber showing outer serrated stainless-steel covering. (*Johns Manville*)

that there are no air leaks. Run a lighted candle around all the places where air leaks might occur: the top and bottom of the ashpit, between sections, around firing and cleanout doors, or where the boiler sections meet the base. Any leaks will draw the flame to the point where the air is getting in and they are thus easily located. When doing this, have the draft regulator completely closed so that the highest possible draft is obtained. Every unit should be so tested just before the beginning of the winter season. A draft gauge may be used for this purpose.

Many installers prefer precast boxes because of the ease and facility with which they are installed. If a precast chamber is used, be sure to select the proper size for the gph rate. Then put a layer of insulation (powdered asbestos, high-temperature rockwool, etc.) on the floor and place the precast chamber upon it. Use a good refractory cement between the joints and insulate in the same manner as with hand-built chambers.

Precast chambers have fewer joints, and their design often lends itself to creating the proper turbulence so necessary to efficient combustion.

BLANKET-TYPE INSULATING CHAMBERS

The development of special wrap-around blanket-type insulating materials for jet engines has resulted in these materials being applied for use as combustion-chamber material for oil-burner fireboxes. The use of this material, as shown in Figs. 10-17 and 10-18, allows for smaller floor area for combustion chambers than is the case when firebrick is used. Using such material allows the chamber to be reduced in size to 70 sq in. per gal.

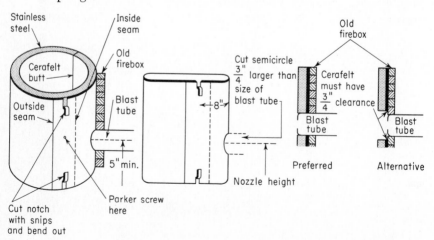

Fig. 10-17   Some pointers for installing Cerafelt chambers. Loose backfill such as mica pellets should not be more than 3 in. high.

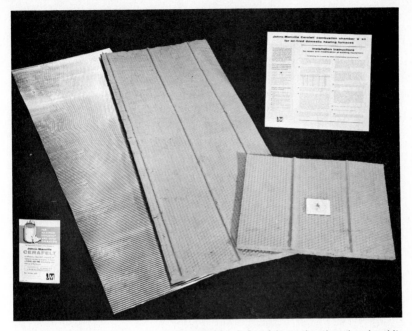

Fig. 10-18   A Cerafelt combustion-chamber kit.

Absorbing little heat, the material will glow in as short a period as 10 sec after firing is started.   It is comparatively simple to install, since it wraps around the interior of an old chamber like a blanket.   It can be applied with equal simplicity to new installations.   It has a sustaining working temperature of 2500°F, a temperature very seldom reached by smaller oil burners.

Surrounded by a stainless-steel outer covering, as shown in Fig. 10-17, it is easily installed and will give good performance if installation instructions are followed closely.

Table 10-3   Length of Cerafelt Firebox Material Needed for Various Firing Rates

Nozzle size, gph	Inside firebox diameter, in.	Length of Cerafelt, in.
0.50–0.75	9	30
0.85–1.00	10	33
1.10–1.25	11	36
1.35–1.50	12	39
1.65–1.75	13	42

QUESTIONS

1. What is the importance of having a definitely shaped fire?
2. What does increasing the angle of spray do to an oil-burner flame?
3. What is the most important factor in chamber dimension?
4. What amount of floor-space area should be allowed for a gallon of oil with a high-pressure gun-type burner? A low-pressure gun-type burner?
5. How does the length of the burner firing period affect the size of the chamber?
6. Why are air-pattern characteristics important to combustion chamber design?
7. Explain the air-flow pattern of a sunflower-flame-type burner.
8. What special design details should be considered for chambers over 5.0 gph?
9. How should bonding mortar be applied to insulating firebrick?
10. What is a usual indication that the burner is placed too close to the floor?
11. How far into the boiler or furnace should the burner gun be placed?
12. What is the purpose of a corbel?
13. Where can corbels be placed?
14. Explain the procedure for constructing a combustion chamber.
15. How should a chamber be "fired in"?
16. Why should a new installation be "candled"?

CHAPTER 11

TANKS, PIPING, AND CENTRAL SYSTEMS

ONE- AND TWO-PIPE SYSTEMS

Before discussing the surface and underground tank and the best means of piping either, it would be well to understand what is meant by the popular terms "one-" and "two-pipe" systems when used in reference to the storage and pumping of domestic fuel oil.

These terms refer to the system used in bypassing the excess oil delivered by the pump. Every oil burner will have a pump capable of delivering a considerably larger amount of oil than is needed. This extra oil is either returned to the oil-storage tank or circulated back to the suction side of the pump. If it is returned to the oil-storage tank, we have what is called an *external bypass* or a *two-pipe* system. If it is returned only to the suction side within the pump, as is the case in modern fuel units, it is an *internal bypass*.

In all installations, the *external* bypass should be used with a tank below the level of the burner, whether buried or not, and when so used will utilize a two-pipe system. One pipe or line carries the oil from the tank to the burner and is called the *suction line*. The other line returns the excess oil to the tank. This is called the *return line*.

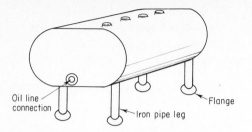

Fig. 11-1   A 275-gal oil-storage tank, horizontal mounting.

The two-pipe system should always be used when the pump has a definite suction function to perform, that is, when we are dependent on the pump not only to furnish the oil under pressure to the nozzle but also to pull the oil from some distance, as in the case of a buried tank.

When the tank is above the surface of the burner and the pump does not have to exert any appreciable suction because the oil is delivered to it by gravity, we do *not* make use of the two-pipe system. Instead, by making use of certain channels designed within the casting of the pump, we bypass the excess oil through the pump itself back to the strainer on the suction side. This eliminates the necessity for a return line to the tank, and thus we have a one-pipe system comprised of the suction line only, from tank to pump. The *internal bypass* arrangement of the pump is used in this case (see Chap. 3).

In the event that there is a sunken tank and an auxiliary *wall lift pump* is used, the system, in such case, would be a one-line system with an internal bypass used on the burner pump, as the oil is fed by gravity from the reservoir of the lift pump to the burner pump.

However, a return line to the tank from the *lift pump* may be used as a safety precaution in the event that its float mechanism failed to shut it off when the reservoir was full. This would not be a true return-line type of two-pipe system, but merely the addition of a line to take care of an accidental overflow due to the failure of the float mechanism in the wall pump. A true two-pipe system is one in which the excess oil constantly being delivered by the *burner pump* is returned to the fuel-oil storage tank.

DISTINCTION BETWEEN ONE- AND TWO-STAGE PUMPS

At this point it may be well to make a review of one- and two-stage pumps and their place in one- and two-pipe systems. Domestic oil-burner fuel pumps can be either single stage or double stage. These terms refer to the separation of the suction and pressure functions within the pump. If the same set of gears is used for suction and for pressure delivery of the oil (in other words, if the pump has only one set of pumping gears), it is a *single-stage* pump. If the pump has two sets of gears, one for pulling the oil from the tank and the other for delivering it under pressure to the nozzle, it is a *two-stage* pump (two sets of pumping gears) (see Chap. 3).

The single-stage pump should always be used with a one-pipe gravity-fed system. This will enable the pump gears to be used entirely for the pressure delivery of oil and also to be relieved of any suction work, since the oil will be delivered to them by gravity.

The employment of a two-stage pump on a gravity system with the tank above burner level results in no use being made of the suction set of gears, since they have no suction function to perform.

With a two-pipe system a two-stage pump should always be used. The suction set of gears will draw the oil from the tank and deliver it to a tiny reservoir in the pump. Here the second set of gears (second stage) will pick it up and deliver it to the nozzle. The pressure and suction functions are performed by separate sets of gears. This results in greater pulling power, greater capacity, quieter operation, and longer life for the pump. A single-stage pump can do the job on a sunken tank with a two-pipe system but not with the quietness of operation or efficiency of a two-stage pump.

The use of a single-stage pump where there is any great lift involved may be a major cause of service. The better procedure is to use a two-stage pump with a two-pipe system on all tanks below the level of the burner.

The pump on a one-pipe system will have to be vented in the event that the oil tank runs dry, since the pump will become air-bound. If oil is delivered, the pump will not be able to operate until the air trapped in it is released to the atmosphere. That is not the case with a two-pipe system when the tank runs dry. In such case, the pump will vent itself and return the air bubbles by way of the return line to the tank and thus operate normally.

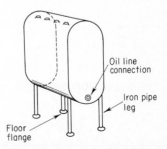

Fig. 11-2 A 275-gal oil-storage tank, vertical mounting.

Even with a two-pipe system, it is wise to prime the pump with oil or vent it to the atmosphere through the plug or port on the pressure side, providing there is a long pull. This prevents the gears from rotating for any length of time without fuel oil flowing between them, upon which they depend for lubrication.

TANK INSTALLATION

Outside tanks

In many cases where the homeowner so desires or where there is sufficient space, a sunken tank, usually of 550 or 1,080 gal capacity, is installed. These tanks are placed underground and require a two-pipe system with a two-stage pump.

In most sizable communities there are local ordinances governing the installation of such storage equipment. If there are no local regulations, the recommendations set up in the Standards of the National Board of Fire Underwriters should be followed.

These standards recommend that all oil-storage tanks be buried outside of buildings when feasible. The top of the tank should be at least 1 ft below grade and the backfill of earth covered with a concrete slab 4 in. thick.

A tank that is to be used for underground service should be covered liberally with asphalt or any good rust-resistant paint. Such tanks should never be set on a bed of cinders or ashes, since the moisture in the earth as well as water seepage cause chemical reactions with such material that is either corrosive or caustic in nature and will result in rapid destruction of the steel walls of the tank.

Once the excavation is completed to the proper depth and the bottom is free of stones, the tank should be lowered into it gently. This can be accomplished with ropes. A tank should never be dropped into an excavation, for damage to the seams is likely to result.

The tank should set in the excavation in such a manner that it will pitch about 3 in., the low end being opposite to the side from which

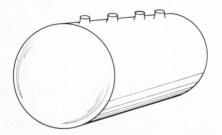

Fig. 11-3 Typical tank for location underground.

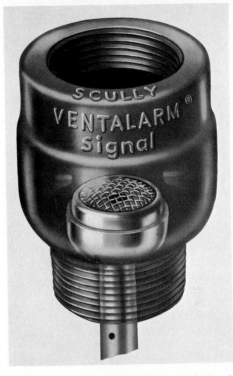

Fig. 11-4   Ventalarm® whistling tank signal.

the suction line will be taken.   This provides for the accumulation of water within the tank, resulting from condensation, *to take place at the end of the tank opposite from the suction line.*   The return line can run to the bottom of the tank at this lower end and thus be used as an emergency suction line to remove such water when it collects in any appreciable quantity.

If wet conditions prevail, precautions must be observed to prevent the tank from floating out of the ground.   This can best be done by pouring a base of concrete in the bottom of the excavation and setting eyebolts therein.   The tank can be strapped down by passing wire rope through the eye bolts and around the tank, assuring that it will be held in place.

If such a procedure is not feasible or practical, the concrete slab may be poured over the tank, thus pressuring it firmly in position from the top.

Inside tanks

As in the case with outside tanks, local ordinances govern the position and manner of installation of inside fuel tanks.   The 275-gal tank is the

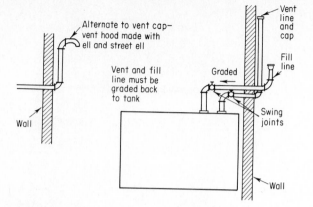

Fig. 11-5   Detail showing vent and fill lines.

standard indoor surface tank, and some communities allow the installation of two such tanks side by side on the surface of the cellar. Such surface tanks must not be closer than 5 ft to the burner, boiler, or furnace and do not have to be enclosed.

Tank capacity located on the cellar surface (550 gal) must be enclosed in a concrete or brick vault in many communities. If concrete, the enclosure should be at least 6 in. thick and if brick, 8 in.

The bottom of the vault should have weep holes 1 in. in diameter about 1 ft apart so that the oil will be noticed in the event of a leaky tank and not trapped in any quantity within the vault.

However, many communities now allow 550-gal maximum inside storage, without the tank or tanks being enclosed.

An inside tank should always be located in such a manner as to avoid

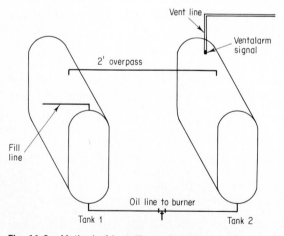

Fig. 11-6   Method of installing twin 275-gal tanks.

the blocking of doors, passageways, staircases, and windows either by the tank or by the necessary piping to it. Once the location is established, the bottom of the tank should be about 1 in. above the top of the burner pump to ensure proper gravity flow of the oil.

The height of the tank is determined by the lengths of pipe that form the legs. These pipe lengths thread into flanges at the bottom of the tank. If the surface tank is below the level of the pump for any appreciable portion of its height, a two-pipe system should be used.

PIPING

The common term used to denote the oil line from tank to burner is "suction line." For the average domestic burner installation, this line should be of ⅜-in. copper tubing or larger, depending on the amount of oil and the distance lifted (Table 11-1), and it should run from the tank to the burner under concrete.

If there is a concrete floor, a V-shaped trough should be cut into it. The suction line should be run in this trough and then cemented over. Never run a suction line exposed, as the soft copper tubing is easily crushed or kinked.

A gate valve should be placed in the line at the tank, and a globe valve installed just where the line meets the burner pump.

Avoid running oil lines above the burner level as air in the line has a tendency to collect at the highest point. This will cause air locks,

Table 11-1 Inches of Vacuum Required to Lift Oil for Combined Horizontal Run and Vertical Lift (Based on Performance of Sundstrand Single-stage Pump, Model S-1)

Lift, ft	Diameter of tubing, in.													
	⅜	½	⅜	½	⅜	½	⅜	½	⅜	½	⅜	½	⅜	½
	Vacuum, in.													
10	9	8	9½	8½	10	9	10½	9½	11	10	12½	11½	14	13
9	8	7	8½	7½	9	8	9½	8½	10	9	11½	10½	13	12
8	7	6	7½	6½	8	7	8½	7½	9	8	10½	9½	12	11
7	6¼	5¼	6¾	5¾	7¼	6¼	7¾	6¾	8¼	7¼	9¾	8¾	11¼	10¼
6	5½	4½	6	5	6½	5½	7	6	7½	6½	9	8	10½	9½
5	5	4	5½	4½	6	5	6½	5½	7	6	8½	7½	10	9
4	4½	3½	5	4	5½	4½	6	5	6½	5½	8	7	9½	8½
3	4	3	4½	3½	5	4	5½	4½	6	5	7½	6½	9	8
2	3½	2½	4	3	4½	3½	5	4	5½	4½	7	6	8½	7½
1	3	2	3½	2½	4	3	4½	3½	5	4	6½	5½	8	7
Length of run, ft	10		20		30		40		50		75		100	

the elimination of which, in overhead tubing, is extremely difficult. Suction lines from surface tanks are connected to nipples or tappings provided for that purpose at the base of the tank. These outside bottom tappings are not used with sunken tanks. In the unusual event that they do exist on a tank that is to be buried, they should be plugged with a screw fitting that has been coated with an oilproof pipe-joint compound.

With buried tanks the suction line should be inserted through the top of the tank on the higher side of the canted tank. This suction line should extend into the tank within 3 or 4 in. of the bottom, but no closer. This leaves ample space for sediment to collect and still have the suction opening clear.

Be certain that this section of the suction line inside the tank is in one piece, because it is inadvisable to have joint fittings within the tank. Such joints may admit air to the suction line when the oil level is low, and, for this reason, they should be avoided. If it is possible, a single length of tubing should run from the bottom of the tank to the burner without any fittings. The fewer joints or couplings, the less frictional resistance to the flow of oil and the less strain on the pump.

The return line must also enter all buried tanks at the top and should extend down into the tank within 3 in. of the bottom. This can provide an emergency suction line in the event of trouble or a break in the suction line proper. Avoid installing any type of valve on the return line. If there seems to be danger of the oil tank settling because of a soft fill, use swing joints where the suction line and return line enter the tank.

In order to prevent the pump from dropping its prime when the tank is below the level of the burner, a check valve should be installed

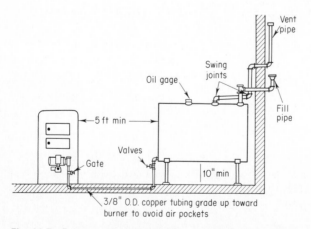

Fig. 11-7 Basement tank installation, single-pipe system.

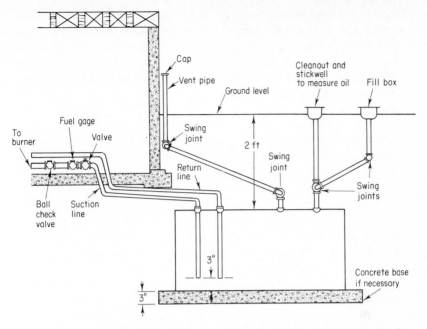

Fig. 11-8 Underground tank installation below burner level.

in the suction line as close to the burner as possible. Avoid using a foot valve at the end of the suction line inside the tank. These may become clogged with dirt and cause trouble. There is nothing that an inaccessible foot valve can accomplish that cannot be done just as well by a check valve in an *accessible* portion of the suction line.

Some communities require the suction line to come through the top of the tank wherever the tank is higher than the burner. In such cases an antisiphon valve is required at the highest point in the line to prevent the siphoning of the oil from the tank if the line is broken. These antisiphon valves demand a fairly high vacuum to be opened and thus throw an excessive work load on the pump. Since the Board of Fire Underwriters regulations no longer require such a valve, avoid using one, unless so required by local law.

FILL AND VENT LINES

All oil-storage tanks must have a vent line to permit the escape of air and vapors as the tank is filled as well as to permit the escape of fuel oil in case of overflow, without setting up excessive back pressures. This vent line should be at least $1\frac{1}{4}$ in. in diameter and should be protected by a cap to prevent water from entering the tank thereby.

When the vent pipe joins the tank, it *must not extend into the tank* whereby it may become blocked off by the rising oil. If a whistling tank signal, such as a Ventalarm®, is installed, there will be no problem about its extending into the tank. This will be taken care of by the installation of the Ventalarm® signal. Be certain that it grades back toward the tank and terminates outside the structure, *not less than 2 ft* in any direction from any type of building opening and well above the ground, the latter to prevent its obstruction by refuse or snow. *The vent must not under any circumstances be tied in with the fill line.*

The fill line should be at least 2 in. in diameter and its terminal point or fill-box cover must not be closer than "2 ft from any opening in the building at the same or lower level." * Check local regulations on this, since some communities are strict regarding the location of fill- and vent-line openings.

Fill-line openings must be closed with a metal cover. The special fittings used to comprise this cover are referred to in the composite as the "fill box." Of course, the fill line must be graded back to the tank and should provide a well with buried tanks to allow "sticking" the tank in order to check on the quantity of oil therein. It is wise to provide swing joints with buried tanks on both the fill and vent lines.

Consult the illustrations accompanying this chapter for the standard methods of piping lines to the tank.

A gauge or gauge line to show the amount of oil should be installed in one of the tank openings provided. All other openings should be closed tightly with threaded fittings, using an oilproof pipe-joint compound.

In all tank and piping work, the local regulations of the community

* Standards of the National Board of Fire Underwriters.

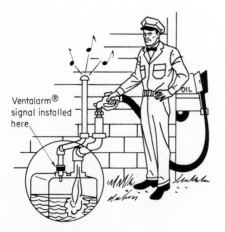

Ventalarm®
signal installed
here

Fig. 11-9

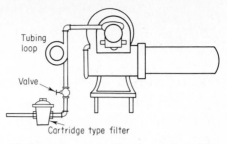

Fig. 11-10   Tubing loop at burner aids in cutting down vibration and provides easier servicing.

involved should be consulted and adhered to closely.   In the event that no local regulations exist, the Standards of the National Board of Fire Underwriters, some of which are mentioned in this article, should be the rigid guide for all installations.

The following is a list of things that should and should not be done in piping and installing tanks:

1. Avoid burying a tank too deeply.   Twelve inches of vacuum should be the maximum required to get the oil to the burner (see Table 11-1).

2. Be sure that oil lines running to the burner do not render inaccessible those burner parts which may have to be reached later for servicing, and that such lines do not exert a pull or strain on the burner.   This can cause misalignment between pump and motor shafts.

3. Be certain that the fuel pump is set up for a one- or two-pipe system and used that way.   Check the pump manufacturer's instructions about the position of the bypass plug or strainer cap for gravity- or suction-fed systems requiring either one- or two-pipe runs.

4. Be careful in selecting the spot for a buried tank.   Consult the owner so that you do not run into water, soft mud, or even rock.

5. Be sure that the fill- and vent-line openings are not in a position to provide easy access for water resulting from rain, snow, or ice or from upper surfaces, such as porch roofs.   The fill line should be well above the level of the ground if it is in any sort of a hollow.

6. Never use a single-line system on a buried tank.   It is only inviting trouble.   Always use a two-stage pump and a return line when the tank is below the level of the burner.

7. Always install a replaceable cartridge-type filter on the suction line, placed in an accessible location.

8. Be sure that the tank location conforms to all local rules and regulations, and always have at least a $1\frac{1}{4}$-in. vent line and a 2-in. fill line.

9. Do not have any high spots in the oil suction line where air can be trapped.   Grade the oil-feed line up to the burner where the air can reach the pump and be vented.

CENTRAL FUEL-OIL SYSTEMS

The newest development in the tank and piping picture is the central fuel-oil system, which provides for delivery of fuel oil to individual homes via underground piping from a central storage source.   These systems are especially adaptable to industrial parks, shopping centers, mobile home parks, and residential building developments.   Undoubtedly newer applications will be uncovered for the practical, low-cost method of delivering fuel oil to the individual burner or location where it is required.

Fig. 11-11   This standpipe marks the location of a 10,000-gal underground fuel oil tank at a mobile home park near Cleveland, Ohio.   This installation of the American Oil Company delivers oil via standpipe and gravity flow through underground lines to 129 mobile home units spread over a considerable area.

Fig. 11-12   Two views of the fuel oil meter used for central fuel distribution.   This unit is the "heart" of the fuel measurement for each unit served.   (*Service Recorder Co.*)

This system permits direct piping of fuel oil to individual home or commercial units from large-capacity central oil-storage tanks or reservoirs.   This eliminates the individual storage tank (usually a 275-gal tank) at each "point-of-use" location (Fig. 11-11).

The vital, practical element that makes a system like this workable is an accurate metering system for each home or "point of use" location. Such meters provide accurate measurement of the fuel oil consumed by each home.   The device precisely measures and records the fuel-oil consumption at each point.   Thus periodic readings of the meter supply the oil distributor with the amount consumed, and the customer is billed accordingly.   These fuel meters are about 12 in. long, $3\frac{1}{2}$ in. wide, and 7 in. deep and may be post-mounted outdoors or wall-mounted inside the home.   The meter has a pilot flow rate as low as $\frac{1}{20}$ gph and up

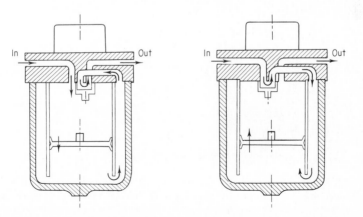

Fig. 11-13   Flow diagram of meter shown in Fig. 11-12.

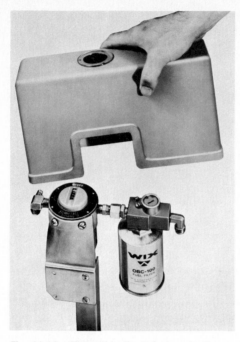

Fig. 11-14 This "thin line" fuel meter is more compact than previous models. It is shown with a filter on the oil line preceding it. These meters guarantee accuracy only if the fuel is filtered free of impurities. (*Service Recorder Co.*)

Fig. 11-15 A new optional safety device for central oil supply systems in this "fail safe" valve, that shuts off the flow of fuel if there is a line break between the device and the burner. It also keeps pressure at the burner from exceeding the recommended 3 psi. (*Service Recorder Company*)

to 5 gph. At 5 gph, it has a pressure drop across the meter of 1 lb per sq in. Its operating temperature range extends from 20° to 140°F. The flow diagram is shown in Fig. 11-13.

QUESTIONS

1. What is meant by a one-pipe system?   A two-pipe system?
2. What is an external bypass?   An internal bypass?
3. Define "suction line"; "return line."
4. When is a wall lift pump used?
5. Explain the difference between a one-stage pump and a two-stage pump.
6. When should a two-stage pump be used?
7. What happens when the oil tank of a single-pipe system runs dry?
8. What regulations should be followed when installing oil-storage tanks if no local regulations exist?
9. How should a tank to be used underground be treated?
10. Why should an underground tank be tilted?
11. What are the advantages of running the return line within a few inches of the bottom of the tank?
12. When should a check valve be used?
13. What is the purpose of the vent line?   What should be its minimum size?
14. Give five precautions that should be observed when installing oil-storage tanks.
15. Explain the newest development in fuel-oil distribution.
16. What are the advantages of central system distribution?
17. What is the vital element or "heart" of such a system?
18. Explain what it does.
19. What is the flow-rate range of the fuel meter?
20. What is its operating temperature range?
21. What condition is an absolute requirement for the proper operation of such a meter?

CHAPTER 12
AUTOMATIC
OIL-BURNER CONTROLS

THERMOSTATS

The most commonly known of all oil-burner controls is the thermostat. This is due to the fact that it is the one control that is known and handled by anyone who has anything to do with an automatic heating plant. The purpose of the thermostat is to provide a means of regulating the temperature and of operating the oil burner in response to temperature changes. Because of this, the thermostat must be very sensitive to temperature variations, must respond quickly to such variations, and must be able to conduct electric current.

One part of the thermostat which does all these necessary things is the bimetal. A bimetallic element consists of two metal strips welded together. Each of these strips expands or contracts when heated or cooled at different rates of speed. This difference in the rate of expansion and contraction develops a stress that causes the strip to bend or move. In so doing, it makes or breaks a contact, which in turn opens or closes a circuit.

The bimetallic element is not, however, the only method of providing movement by temperature changes. Often a bellows filled with a highly volatile liquid is used (Fig. 12-1). This liquid vaporizes at comparatively low temperatures and creates a pressure that makes the bellows expand and close a circuit. The opposite action results on cooling.

The number of degrees difference in surrounding temperature required to make a thermostat open or close its contacts is referred to as its "differential." Thus if a thermostat has been set at 70° and the temperature drops to 69° before it closes its contact, that thermostat has in effect a 1° differential. Usually, the smaller the differential, the more rapid will be the thermostat action. In practice, however, the differential is adjusted to the characteristics of the type of heating system, whether it be steam, hot water, or warm air. It is best to observe the control manufacturer's directions on this.

Control manufacturers achieve this differential and the sharp opening and closing of the contacts in various ways. It is necessary for smooth starting and stopping of the burner to be certain that the thermostat contacts close quickly and securely and open in the same manner. If the contacts were to float back and forth in response to very minute temperature changes, the result would be a rapid, inefficient, and even dangerous on-off action of the oil burner.

Figures 12-2 and 12-3 show a thermostat that uses a magnet to achieve firm and secure closing of the contacts. As the temperature drops, the bimetallic element (in Fig. 12-3, a spiral element; in Fig. 12-6, a U-shaped element) moves the contacts to close them. As they come within the field of force of the magnet, they are abruptly pulled into contact and close the low-voltage circuit (snap action). With the Mercoid thermostat, the magnet pulls a small prong into a pool of mercury through which the contact is completed.

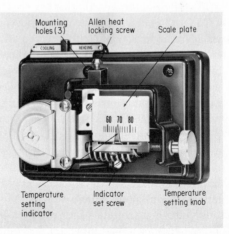

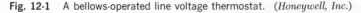

Fig. 12-1 A bellows-operated line voltage thermostat. (*Honeywell, Inc.*)

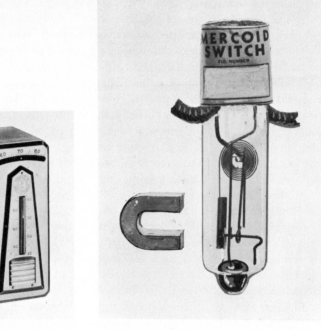

Fig. 12-2   Mercoid low-voltage thermostat.

Fig. 12-3   Mercoid mercury-tube-type low-voltage switch used with thermostat in Fig. 12-2.

Many thermostats make use of artificial heat to accelerate the shutdown once the room begins to warm. They thereby prevent the accumulation of excess heat within the system. Without an artificial heater the thermostat must be very sensitive to do its job properly.

If, for instance, the thermostat on a steam heating system was set at 70° and it did not shut off the burner until the room reached 70°, considerable heat could still be given off by the radiators after the unit had shut down. This causes overheating and is characterized as "overshooting." Heat acceleration, which is the application of artificial heat to the thermostat *before* it is satisfied by room temperature, helps prevent this condition. When the artificial heat (from a small resistor heater built into the thermostat) is applied to the bimetallic element, it breaks its contacts more quickly, shutting down the burner to prevent excessive room temperature. In this way "overshooting" is minimized.

Low-voltage thermostats close a circuit on the low-voltage side of the primary control, which in turn energizes a coil that creates a magnetic field; this closes a line-voltage circuit by pulling in a relay clapper. Line-voltage thermostats interrupt the hot line circuit to the primary control and turn the burner on and off in that manner. Figure 12-1 shows a line-voltage thermostat.

Fig. 12-4 Penn "Rimset" low-voltage thermostat. This type T888 thermostat unit contains the bimetallic element, silver contacts, thermometer, temperature-setting dial, and cover.

The Honeywell series 10 thermostat (Fig. 12-6), although out of production, is still operating by the millions in the field. It does not use a magnet to avoid arcing and to provide sharp opening and closing of contacts. It employs the well-known U-shaped bimetallic element and establishes the opening and closing of the contacts along with the necessary differential for regular operation by having two blades, one stiff and one flexible. These two blades are part of the red-wire circuit. The flexible blade contacts the white wire (see Fig. 12-7), and the blue

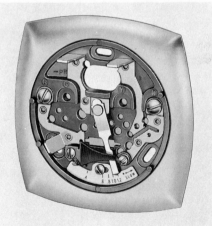

Fig. 12-5 888, Penn thermostat sub-base. These sub-bases are available for heating only, cooling only, and combination heating-cooling systems. The thermostat sensing unit, as shown in the preceding illustration, plugs on to this sub-base.

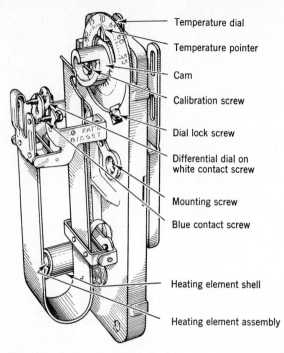

Temperature dial

Temperature pointer

Cam

Calibration screw

Dial lock screw

Differential dial on
white contact screw

Mounting screw

Blue contact screw

Heating element shell

Heating element assembly

Fig. 12-6   Honeywell three-wire series 10 low-voltage thermostat.

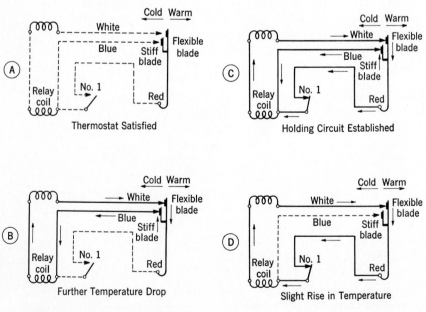

Fig. 12-7   Honeywell series 10 circuit.

contact is met by the stiff blade. Heat acceleration is included with this thermostat. The heater element is connected permanently to the red circuit. This thermostat closes a low-voltage circuit which energizes a relay, which in turn passes on line voltage to the burner.

The series 10 circuit of the Honeywell thermostat operates in the following fashion. When the thermostat is satisfied, as shown in Fig. 12-7, the relay (No. 1) will be deenergized. As the room cools, the flexible white contact will close first, but nothing will occur since there is no completed circuit for the current. On a further drop in temperature, the rigid blue blade will make contact and the starting circuit is made. The relay coil is not energized and the No. 1 relay is making contact, establishing thereby a holding circuit. The burner will now be operating. Upon a rise in temperature, the rigid blade breaks from the blue contact. The starting circuit has now been broken. The low-voltage circuit, however, continues via the red and white circuit. A further rise in temperature will break the white contact and the No. 1 relay will be deenergized, stopping the operation of the oil burner. The circuit will now be open, as shown in Fig. 12-7. If heat acceleration is incorporated with this thermostat, the resistor used to furnish the artificial heat to the bimetallic element will be connected permanently into the red circuit. During such time as blue and white are both making contact, very little current will flow through the heater. Upon a slight rise in temperature, however, the blue contact will break. All the current then flows through the red and white circuit, energizing the small heater element. The artificial heat given off by this resistor accelerates the shutdown by heating the bimetallic element, hastening thereby the breaking of the white contact which will shut off the burner.

In order to provide still further automatic thermostat operation, a clock-operated switching mechanism is incorporated with the thermostat. These clock thermostats provide for an automatic temperature cutback at night and automatic return to the day setting in the morning. The time when these temperature changes will occur is adjusted for by making certain settings, and from there on the action is completely automatic.

To simplify wiring and reduce costs, Honeywell is replacing their series 10 thermostats (three-wire, low-voltage) with series 80 (two-wire, low-voltage) thermostats. For this reason the Honeywell Round T87F thermostat is being used, in most installations, in place of the one illustrated in Fig. 12-6. The T87F employs a mercury switch and an adjustable heat-anticipator resistor (Fig. 12-8).

The clock thermostat shown in Figs. 12-9 and 12-10 accomplishes this night setback by means of a mechanical lever system operated by a synchronous-motor electric clock.

The temperature-sensing element is a spiral bimetal which tells the

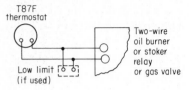

Fig. 12-8   The T87F provides 24-volt temperature control for residential heating or cooling or heating-cooling systems. For control of heating systems the T87F mounts on a wallplate, and for cooling or heating-cooling it must be used with the Q527 sub-base. The SPDT switch makes one set of contacts on a temperature fall to operate the heating system. The other set of contacts makes on a temperature rise, and operates the cooling system when the T87F is used to provide cooling control. This single-pole double-throw thermostat is adaptable to most two-wire, 24-volt heating control systems and to most three-wire, 24-volt heating systems controlled by an SPDT thermostat. (*Honeywell, Inc.*)

mercury switch to open or close the circuit to the heating system. The time dial, accessible by opening the thermostat, as shown in Fig. 12-10, revolves once every 24 hr and is equipped with two indicators marked DAY and NITE. These indicators can be independently set and locked at whatever time the changeover from day temperatures to night temperatures, and vice versa, is desired.

The T852 electric-clock thermostat (Fig. 12-12) provides completely

Fig. 12-9   General Controls clock thermostat, Tempotherm. Note day-night adjusting dials.

Fig. 12-10   Interior view of Tempotherm shown in Fig. 12-9.

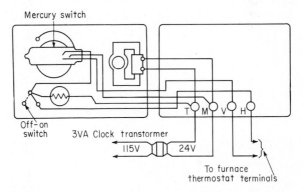

Fig. 12-11   Interior wiring schematic of General Controls clock thermostat.

Fig. 12-12   Honeywell T852 clock thermostat. May be used in series 80, series 10, or self-powered millivolt systems and employs a cam-operated day-night assembly.

automatic day-night temperature control. It may be used in two-wire (series 80) and most three-wire (series 10) *low-voltage* control circuits. Also, it is suitable for use in Powerpile (*millivoltage* pilot generator) burner control systems. The T852 is not for applications requiring a thermostat that makes contact on both a rise and a fall in temperature. On three-wire systems (other than Honeywell series 10), consult the control manufacturer to determine the possible two-wire thermostat applications for their three-wire controls.

The T852 consists of a bimetal-operated, snap-acting, open-contact thermostat, a universal carbon heater for heat anticipation, and an electric clock which controls the night-setback and day-return mechanism. A transformer is included in the package to provide the proper power supply for the electric clock. Of additional importance is the fact that the universal carbon heater element is energized by the clock transformer (only when thermostat switch is made) and is not affected by the current requirements of the heating controls.

Three other thermostats are shown in Figs. 12-13 to 12-15. These are White-Rodgers temperature controls. Figures 12-13 and 12-14 are low-voltage thermostats. The former is equipped with an adjustable heater that enables it to match all White-Rodgers primary controls as well as most of those of other manufacturers. The latter has a fixed-output heater which comes in varying capacities. The proper heat anticipator must be used to match the current sent through the thermostat by the primary control.

The type shown in Fig. 12-15 is a line-voltage temperature control used to operate unit heaters, boilers, furnaces, pumps, or other applications requiring a heavy-duty room thermostat.

Fig. 12-13 Low-voltage, Astro-Stat, Type 1E30, White-Rodgers thermostat.

Fig. 12-14   A horizontal type White-Rodgers thermostat for use with zone control.

Fig. 12-15   Heavy-duty, line-voltage White-Rodgers thermostat.

LIMIT CONTROLS

Hot-water temperature controls

The application of hot-water temperature limit controls to domestic oil-fired heating systems usually takes three forms.   They are used either to give low-limit protection for domestic faucet hot water or to give high-limit protection for hot-water heating systems.   They can also be used in hot-water heating systems to give low-limit protection for operation of the circulator.   In this case, the circulator cannot operate if the water falls below a certain temperature.   "Low-limit" protection means that the water is not allowed to drop below a certain temperature.   If it does, the hot-water temperature control will bring the burner

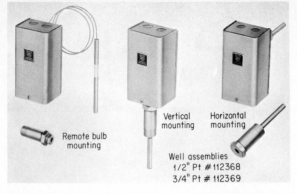

Fig. 12-16 General Controls immersion-type hot-water temperature controls.

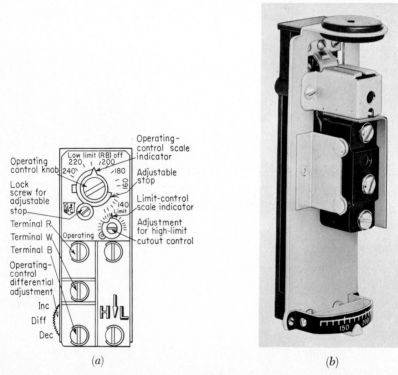

(a)   *(b)*

Fig. 12-17 (*a*) L53 General Controls combination hot-water temperature control. (*b*) General Controls strap-on type of hot-water limit control.

on to restore the water to the temperature for which the control is set. "High-limit" protection means that the water temperature is not permitted to go above a certain point. If it does, the hot-water control interrupts the circuit and shuts down the burner.

Hot-water temperature controls may be direct- or reverse-acting as is the case with all limit controls. If they are direct-acting, they will make contact on a drop and break contact on a rise in temperature. If reverse-acting, they will make contact on a rise and break contact on a drop in temperature. Some units are a combination of both functions and act as a high-limit, low-limit, and circulator control in one case. These are as shown in Fig. 12-17(a).

These hot-water temperature controls usually make use of three different types of actuating mechanisms: the conventional bimetallic strip or helix, the fail-safe, fully liquid-filled element, and the bellows. The switching mechanism itself may be either the metal-to-metal open-contact type or the mercury-tube type. For domestic usage these water-temperature controls have a range from about 90° to 220°F.

Immersion-type hot-water limit controls may be either vertically or horizontally mounted into wells provided for that purpose. In addition, these controls may be surface-mounted, or if faster response to varying water temperatures is required, these may be mounted using a spud-and-

Fig. 12-18   The L4006 Aquastat controller uses a liquid-expansion temperature-sensing element to rapidly detect and respond to temperature changes. Switching action is performed by an enclosed snap switch. The Aquastat is mounted with the element inserted horizontally into a boiler, tank, or other vessel. Models are available to break or make contact on temperature rise or with SPDT action. The visible control-point scale is easily set by an external screw-driver adjustment.

pressure nut arrangement so that the element is in direct contact with the water. Immersion aquastats usually give more accurate control than the surface-mounted types. This is due to the fact that they are in closer contact with the medium that is to be controlled.

BOILER MASTER CONTROLS

Combination circulator relay, transformer, high-limit control, combination low-limit and circulator control in single casing (series 4200–4300)

The series 4200 and 4300 Penn Boilermasters combine a circulator relay, a transformer, a high-limit control, and/or a combination low-limit and circulator control in a compact wiring center. They are designed for use on hot-water boilers which contain instantaneous or tankless domestic hot-water coils, although the units incorporating the high-limit temperature control are adaptable to any hot-water boiler.

This control can be located as a compact wiring center at the point where the high-limit control and the low-limit–circulator control perform in the best manner on the boiler, or one of the units which incorporates the high-limit control and uses a remotely located low-limit and circulator control can be chosen. Likewise the compact wiring center could be located at the point where the low-limit and circulator control operate most satisfactorily and a remote high-limit control can be used. An important feature of the sensitive temperature element on all controls is a safety feature which opens the high-limit contacts if there is an element failure.

Operation

Low-voltage burner circuit with power supplied from the Boilermas-

Fig. 12-19   Penn combination series 4200–4300 Boilermaster control.

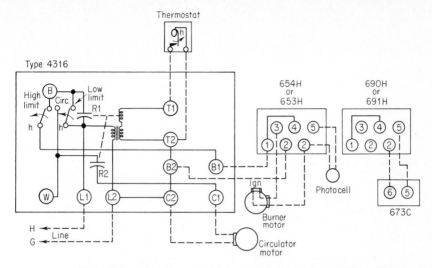

Fig. 12-20   Internal and typical external wiring of type 4316.   (*Penn*)

ter: The diagram for the type 4316 shows the internal circuit of the boilermaster incorporating both the high-limit control and the combination circulator and low-limit control.   When the thermostat is not calling for heat, the low-limit control operates the burner by closing this circuit between T1 and T2 as required to maintain an adequate temperature in the boiler for domestic hot water.   When the room thermostat calls for heat, the burner starts and the circulator relay makes the contact between L1 and C1 to start the circulating pump, providing the water in the boiler is warmer than the low-limiting setting.   The circulator motor may turn on and off even though the room thermostat is calling for heat because the low-limit control is maintaining a sufficient quantity of hot water in the boiler to assure adequate hot water for domestic use.   If the water in the boiler reaches the high-limit setting, the burner will turn off.   If this occurs while the thermostat is calling for heat, the circulator will continue to run.

Pressure controls

Limit controls that respond to changes in steam pressure are called pressure controls.   Usually they open or close the circuit by opening contacts or by employing a mercury-tube switch.   The normal pressure range on these switches that are used for domestic heating units is from 1 to 15 psi.   In the case of vapor-vacuum heating systems, the range may be anywhere from 22 in. of vacuum to 16 oz of pressure, depending on whether the system operates with a vacuum pump or with pressure so low as to be measured in ounces.   The mechanism used to actuate the switch may be either a diaphragm, bellows, or liquid-filled element.

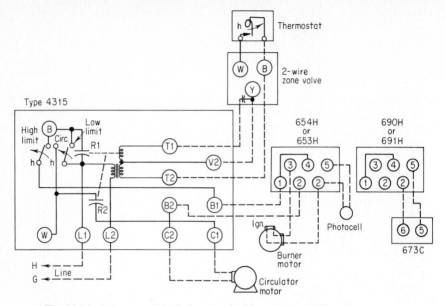

Fig. 12-21 Internal and typical external wiring of type 4315. (*Penn*)

Settings on the General and Honeywell pressure controls are furnished by a double scale. One side is an adjustable cut-in setting, and the other is a differential setting. The sum of the two gives the cut-out point at which the high-limit protection is achieved. At this point the control interrupts the line-voltage circuit and shuts off the burner. When the pressure drops to the cut-in point, the circuit is restored.

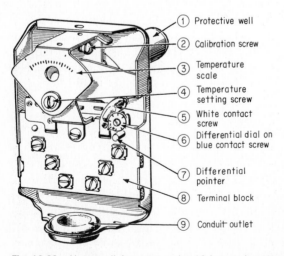

1. Protective well
2. Calibration screw
3. Temperature scale
4. Temperature setting screw
5. White contact screw
6. Differential dial on blue contact screw
7. Differential pointer
8. Terminal block
9. Conduit outlet

Fig. 12-22 Honeywell Aquastat series 10 immersion type (three-wire, low-voltage).

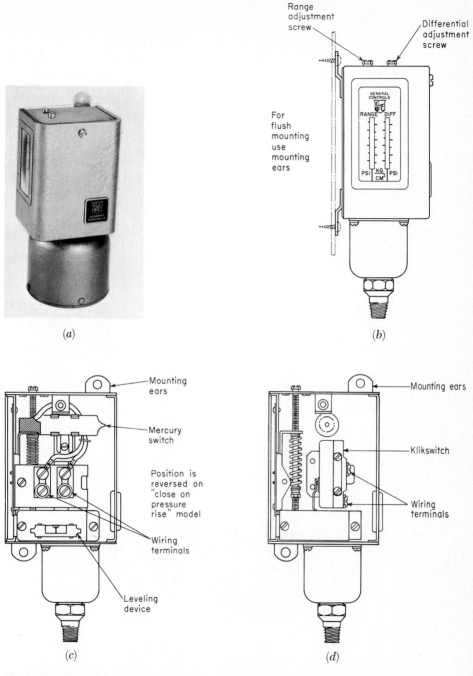

Fig. 12-23 General Controls pressure-limit controls. (*c*) and (*d*) show interiors of mercury-tube and enclosed-shap-switch types, respectively.

Fig. 12-24 Honeywell L4007 immersion-type Aquastat.

Fig. 12-25 Mercoid mercury-switch type pressure control.

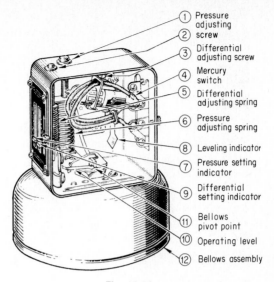

1. Pressure adjusting screw
2.
3. Differential adjusting screw
4. Mercury switch
5. Differential adjusting spring
6. Pressure adjusting spring
8. Leveling indicator
7. Pressure setting indicator
9. Differential setting indicator
11. Bellows pivot point
10. Operating level
12. Bellows assembly

Fig. 12-26   Honeywell Vaporstat.

The Mercoid pressure switch has a high and low setting.   When the pressure reaches the high setting, the bourdon tube tilts the mercury switch, interrupting the line circuit.   Upon a drop in pressure to the low setting, the circuit is restored.   The differential in this case is the difference between the high and low settings.

Pressure controls may be direct- or reverse-acting.

Warm-air controls

The warm-air control, which is usually operated by a helix-type bimetallic element, has two applications.   These are *bonnet air-temperature control and fan-operation control.*

In the first case, the control has as its purpose high-limit protection (that is, it prevents the heated air in the plenum of the furnace from going above a certain temperature, thus preventing overheating) and also low-limit protection in restoring the circuit when the plenum air temperature drops below a certain point.   In this way, it acts much as does the pressure control.   It may employ either metal-to-metal contacts or a mercury-tube switch to do this.

When the fan is being controlled, limit protection is so provided that the fan cannot operate when the bonnet temperature is below a certain minimum setting.   This is to prevent cool air from being circulated through the ducts and into the rooms during cold weather.   Many fan controls have a manual knob that provides for fan operation during the summer for ventilation purposes.

The warm-air limit control shown in Fig. 12-27 combines the fan and limit controls into one mechanism with two separate enclosed-contact switches for fan and burner limit operation. Both these switches are operated by the same helix-type bimetallic element. Two settings are provided, one for the fan and one for the limit, both of which are adjustable over ranges extending from 60° to 210°F and 70° to 230°F, respectively.

The combination fan and limit warm-air control shown in Fig. 12-28 operates on the principle of expansion and contraction of a liquid against a diaphragm. The temperature-sensitive element is completely filled with a special liquid from which all air, gas, or any other compressible matter has been entirely removed. Whenever changes in temperature occur at the bulb of the element, this liquid expands or contracts with uniformity, causing an instantaneous movement of the diaphragm. The diaphragm movement actuates the switch, which may be set to operate at any desired temperature within the range of the control.

PRIMARY CONTROLS

Primary controls, relays, or stack switches, as they are popularly called, have two functions. One is to provide a safety feature whereby the burner is shut down in the event of lack of combustion; and the other is an integrating and operating function whereby the action of

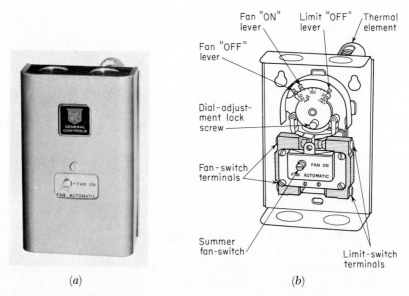

(a)   (b)

Fig. 12-27   (a) Exterior view of General Controls combination fan and limit control. (b) Interior view of same control.

Fig. 12-28   White-Rodgers combination fan and limit control with remote mounting elements.

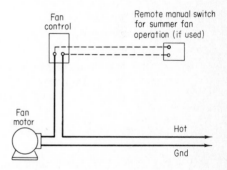

Fig. 12-29   Fan control. This separate control operates the fan only on changes in bonnet air temperature. (*White-Rodgers*)

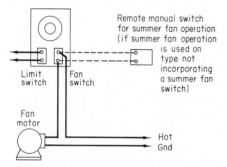

Fig. 12-30   Location of combination fan and limit control in line wiring.

Fig. 12-31   Location of fan control in line wiring.

all the controls may be integrated, so that the normal operating sequence is observed.   Thus a primary control must turn the burner on and off in response to the low-voltage operating controls, it must furnish ignition at each start, and it must provide for a shutdown of the burner in the event that combustion does not take place.

When a low-voltage thermostat closes its circuit, it makes low-voltage current, from a step-down transformer in the primary control, available to a coil.   The coil thus energized pulls in a switch by magnetic force.   The switch transfers line-voltage current to the burner, and it begins to operate.   However, it may be that the burner will not ignite, and as a result no flame will appear.   It is then the job of the primary control to shut off the burner.

This is accomplished by having a temporary circuit through a safety switch. The safety-switch heater heats up while current flows through it. If it heats up for over 90 sec on the average, a bimetallic strip will warp from the heat and break the circuit, shutting off the unit. This switch will then have to be reset by hand before the unit will operate.

If the burner ignites normally and the flame appears, the hot gases going up the stack will heat the bimetallic element of the primary control, and this will actuate a mechanism that will shunt out the heater in the safety switch, ending the possibility of its warping out and shutting down the burner. Thus the safety-switch *temporary* circuit is shunted out, and a *permanent* circuit established through another set of contacts. Control manufacturers accomplish these features in various ways.

Primary Control Terminology

The following terms are frequently used when describing a particular type of oil-burner primary control:

Low Voltage   Denotes that the primary control is for use in a low-voltage thermostat circuit.

Line Voltage   Denotes that the primary control is for use with a line-voltage thermostat or operating control.

Constant Ignition   Denotes that the ignition electrodes spark during the entire running part of the burner cycle. (Underwriters Labs., Inc., refer to this type of ignition as *intermittent* ignition.)

Intermittent Ignition   Denotes that the ignition electrodes spark only for a timed period at the beginning of the running part of the cycle. (Underwriters Labs., Inc., refer to this type of ignition as *interrupted* ignition.)

Non-recycling   Denotes that, in event of flame failure, the primary control will allow the burner to run for a short period of time in an attempt for reignition. If the flame is not reestablished, the primary control will then lock out on safety, shutting down the burner.

Recycling   Denotes that, in event of flame failure, the primary control will stop the burner for a short period of time (called the scavenger period) before it allows the burner to recycle in an attempt for reignition. (In case of momentary power interruption, scavenger period is also required before primary control will let burner recycle.) If flame is not reestablished, the primary control will then lock out on safety, shutting down the burner.

Safety Timing   At the beginning of each cycle the safety heater is energized. If ignition fails to establish the burner flame, the safety heater will lock out the safety contacts, stopping the burner. The length of this period is called the safety timing.

Scavenger Timing   On recycling type primary controls, the length of time from flame-out (or momentary power interruption) until the primary control allows the burner to recycle.

Ignition Timing On intermittent ignition primary controls, the length of time from start of the burner cycle until the ignition electrodes quit sparking.

SCR Silicon Controlled Rectifier (solid-state device).

MERCOID PYRATHERM

The Mercoid JMI and JM Pyratherms, which are intermittent and constant ignition, respectively, are stack-mounted combustion controls that do not employ a shunt to break the temporary safety-switch circuit. Instead, the safety-switch heater is removed from the bimetal loop mechanically. The operation of this control is as follows (refer to Fig. 12-32):

When the relay is in the normal starting or cold position, the ignition switch J is in the ON position and the heater coil C is in the bimetal loop E. As the thermostat calls for heat, the coils A and B are energized and a *repulsion* force is set up. Coil A rises as a result of this force, and the ignition and motor circuits are energized through mercury-tube switches J and D. Low-voltage current flows from secondary relay coil A through the thermostat and also through heater C. As normal combustion occurs, the hot stack gases will actuate the bimetal helix S in the smoke pipe and cause the safety heater coil C to move away from the bimetal loop E, simultaneously opening the ignition circuit by tilting mercury-tube switch J. The burner is now in normal operation. When the room thermostat is satisfied, or in the event of momentary power interruption, the burner will stop immediately and will be unable to

Fig. 12-32 Mercoid JMI Pyratherm.

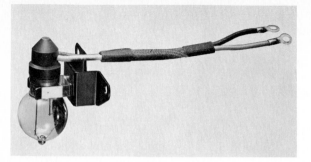

Fig. 12-33 Mercoid Visaflame bulb.

start again until the control has returned to the "cold" normal starting position.

If ignition fails upon starting, the heater coil C will remain in bimetal loop E owing to inaction of helix coil S. This heater coil will heat up the bimetal loop E and stop the burner after the predetermined time for which it was set has elapsed. As bimetal E expands, it moves away and ceases to support mercury-tube switch F. This switch falls to the OFF position and interrupts the flow of current to the burner. It must then be reset manually by turning knob H.

Flame failure causes the heater coil C to return to the bimetal loop E. This heats up the loop and causes it to release the safety switch F, stopping the burner, the ignition switch being held in the OFF position. Since current always flows through C, it is already hot when entering loop E, and an accelerated shutdown occurs.

VISAFLAME CONTROL

The use of the Visaflame bulb (Fig. 12-33), which is actuated by radiant energy from the fire, replaces the usual helix-coil element used to operate primary controls. Rays from the fire pass to the mirror-surfaced reflec-

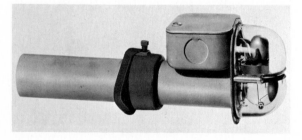

Fig. 12-34 Mercoid Visaflame mounting assembly.

tor, which reflects and concentrates them on a small bimetal coil. This coil absorbs the light waves and converts them to heat. The coil then expands and moves an electrode into a small pool of mercury to close the contact.

This bulb can be used in conjunction with type K-2-I or K-2 safety relay panel for intermittent or constant ignition, respectively. The type K-2-I panel operates as follows: When the thermostat calls for heat and closes its contacts, the primary coil is energized. Magnetic repulsion forces the secondary coil to rise, tilting the motor switch to the ON position. Current is thus supplied to the motor and also to the burner ignition transformer through the ignition mercury tube and ignition heater, all of which are in series. The current flow through the ignition heater causes it to heat and expand a bimetal coil which moves the ignition mercury-tube switch to the OFF position. Since the ignition switch, ignition heater, and motor are in series, no current can flow through the ignition heater when the motor switch is in the OFF position. In the event of power failure, the ignition switch will resume the ON position and a full ignition period will be provided for.

Fig. 12-35   Mercoid K-2-I-relay panel for use with visaflame bulb.

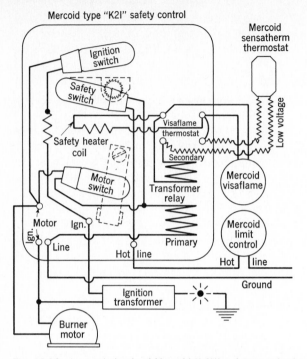

Fig. 12-36 Internal circuit of Mercoid K-2KI safety-panel relay.

In the event of normal operation, light from the flame will cause the Visaflame bulb to close its contacts and shunt the current away from the safety heater coil, which is *stationary* in the bimetal loop. This safety heater coil does not move out of the loop, as was the case with the JMI Pyratherm previously described.

If the flame fails to appear, the Visaflame bulb will not close its contacts. As a result current will continue to flow through the safety heater coil, expanding the bimetal loop to the point where it will trip the latch and cause the safety-switch mercury tube to tilt to the OFF position, shutting off the flow of current to the burner. The safety switch will then have to be reset manually. On a start, about 70 sec will be required for the safety shutdown. After the burner has been in operation, however, a safety shutdown will require the 70 sec for the heater coil plus the time required for the Visaflame bulb to break its contacts.

GENERAL CONTROLS PRIMARY CONTROL

The General Controls series 5520-D21 primary control, shown in Fig. 12-37, is an intermittent-ignition relay with factory-set ignition time. Ignition is therefore independent of stack temperature changes. There is also a constant-ignition model.

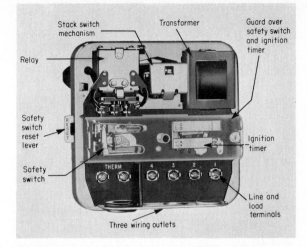

Fig. 12-37 General Controls 5520-D21 stack mounted primary control.

After being properly installed and wired, the control operates the burner in the following manner: When the thermostat calls for heat, the relay closes, starting the burner motor and ignition. After a predetermined time, ignition is cut off by means of the ignition timer. The safety-switch operating heater is also energized when the thermostat calls for heat, and if this heater is not shunted out by the closing of the stack switch, a safety shutdown will result (see Fig. 12-38). On recycling controls a drop in stack temperature indicating a flame failure will cause

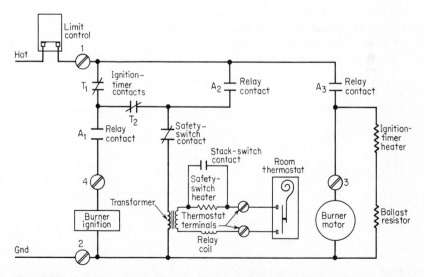

Fig. 12-38 Schematic wiring diagram of General Controls 5520-D21 primary control.

a burner shutdown. After an enforced purge period, another attempt to establish flame will be made by the primary control. If flame is not established on recycle, a safety lockout will occur.

In its starting position, the stack-switch arm rests against the cold (upper) stop. When the flame is established, the rise in stack temperature causes the stack thermal element to expand and the stack-switch arm moves downward, closing the stack switch and shunting out the safety-switch heater. It then proceeds to the hot (lower) stop. Additional expansion of the stack thermal element is absorbed by the slip-friction unit. The burner will continue to operate until the thermostat contacts open. The relay then opens and stops the burner. The drop in stack temperature causes the stack thermal element to contract, open the stack switch, and return the stack arm to its initial starting position. Continued contraction of the stack thermal element is absorbed by the slip-friction unit.

If for any reason combustion is not established, the stack element mechanism will remain in the cold position, the safety-switch heater will remain energized, and a safety shutdown will result after approximately $1\frac{1}{2}$ min.

In the event of flame failure during burner operation, the drop in stack temperature causes opening of the stack switch. This results in the energizing of the safety-switch heater, and a safety shutdown will occur approximately $1\frac{1}{2}$ min after the stack switch opens.

After the safety switch has opened, it must be manually reset before operation can be resumed.

OPERATION OF THE GENERAL CONTROLS
R96 SERIES COMBUSTION SAFETY SWITCH
IN CONJUNCTION WITH
THE CT-99 FLAME DETECTOR

In this control the flame detector replaces the stack element. When the thermostat contacts close, the relay coil will become energized, the initial flow of current being through the safety-switch heater, flame-detector switch, relay coil, thermostat, and safety switch. As soon as the relay coil is energized, contacts $A1$, $A2$, $A3$, and $A4$ (Fig. 12-40) will close, starting the burner motor and ignition. The ignition timer heater, energized through $A3$, operates a bimetallic snap-acting switch, whose contacts $T1$ and $T2$ open simultaneously after an adjusted time delay of approximately 60 sec. Opening of this switch cuts off the burner ignition. Contact $A2$, paralleling $T1$-$T2$, provides the holding circuit for the transformer primaries.

Also, following the initiation of flame, the flame-detector switch will open in 5 to 15 sec, depending on the rate of firing. After the flame-

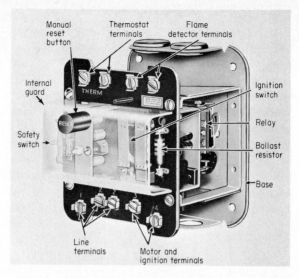

Fig. 12-39 General Controls R96 safety combustion relay (burner-mounted).

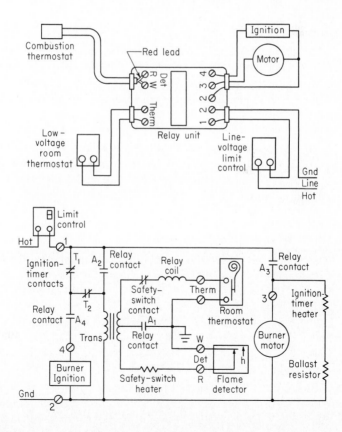

Fig. 12-40 Schematic wiring diagram of General Controls R-96 burner-mounted primary control.

detector switch opens, the safety-switch heater becomes deenergized, preventing lockout of the control. $A1$ is a holding contact for the relay coil.

When the room temperature opens the thermostat contacts, the relay coil will become deenergized, opening contacts $A1$, $A2$, $A3$, and $A4$ and causing burner shutdown. Upon cessation of flame, the flame detector (combustion thermostat) will cool and close the flame-control switch in a period of 15 to 30 sec, depending on the rate of cooling of the immediate surroundings of the flame-detector (combustion thermostat) unit. Also, with the opening of $A3$, the ignition timer heater will cool, and after an approximate 1-min purge period, the switch $T1$-$T2$ will close, putting the circuit in condition for the next normal start cycle.

Ignition failure

If, after the beginning of a normal start cycle, there should be no flame because of ignition failure, the flame-control switch will remain closed, heating the safety-switch heater and causing the safety switch to open after approximately 60 sec.

Flame failure

If, during a normal running cycle, the flame should be extinguished, the flame detector (heat actuated) will cool, causing the flame-control switch to close, energizing the safety-switch heater, and causing lockout of the control. Series 96B recycles on flame failure.

Power failure

If there should be a momentary power failure during a normal burner cycle, the control will automatically recycle after a period of approximately 1 min, which is the time required to cool the ignition timer heater and close switch $T1$-$T2$.

HONEYWELL PROTECTORELAYS

The Honeywell RA116A and RA117A relays are bimetal-operated relays for use with domestic oil burners. The RA116A is constant ignition and the RA117A is intermittent. With the intermittent-ignition relay, the ignition timing is adjustable.

The operation of the RA117A intermittent-ignition relay is as follows (refer to Fig. 12-44): Any time the burner is idle, the cold contacts 6 and 7 are closed and the hot contact 8 is open. Safety-switch contact 5 is closed, and the relays are in the OUT position.

Upon a call for heat by the thermostat, the low-voltage circuit is closed. This energizes the relay coils and the right-hand relay pulls in. Contact 15 closes, starting the ignition. Contacts 9, 10, and 11 are also

Fig. 12-41   Flame detector mounted on nozzle, General Controls CT-99 Perfxray.

closed to complete the circuit to the left-hand relay.   The burner motor is started through contact 16.   As the stack temperature rises, hot contact 8 is made, shunting out the heater element in the safety switch.   A further rise in stack temperature breaks cold contacts 7 and 6, in that order.   This interrupts the circuit to the right-hand relay and it drops out, shutting off ignition.   The burner is now operating normally.

As the room temperature rises, thermostat contact *B* will open first. The holding circuit through *R* and *W* (red and white) will hold in the

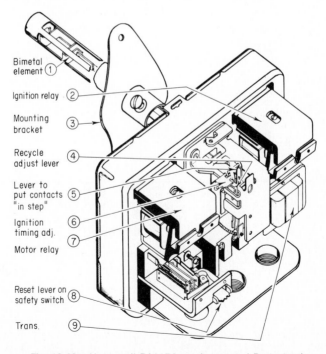

Bimetal element ①

Ignition relay ②

Mounting bracket ③

Recycle adjust lever ④

Lever to put contacts ⑤ "in step"

Ignition timing adj. ⑥
⑦

Motor relay

Reset lever on ⑧ safety switch

Trans. ⑨

Fig. 12-42   Honeywell RA117A stack-mounted Protectorelay.

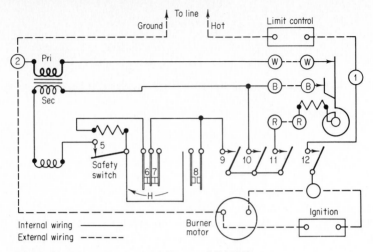

Fig. 12-43 Schematic circuit of Honeywell RA116A.

left-hand relay.   When the thermostat is satisfied, the white contact *W* will open, breaking the circuit to the left-hand relay.   This will stop the burner.

If combustion fails to take place, the hot contact 8 will not be made. This means that current will continue to flow through the safety-switch heater.   In about 90 sec, safety-switch contact 5 will open, shutting down the burner.   The safety switch will then have to be manually reset.

In case of flame failure while the burner is running, the hot contact

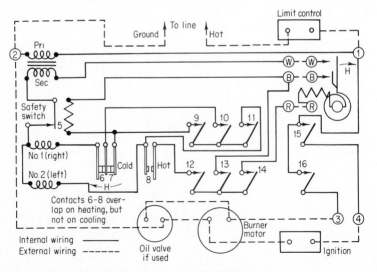

Fig. 12-44 Schematic circuit of Honeywell RA117A.

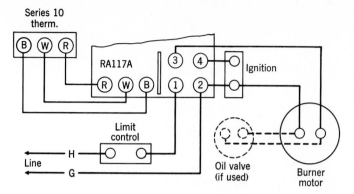

Fig. 12-45   Connection diagram for a Honeywell RA117A Protectorelay.

8 will break.   This breaks the circuit to the left-hand relay and the burner stops.   Further cooling will remake the cold contacts and the burner will start again.   If a flame appears, the burner will run normally. However, if the oil fails to ignite, then the relay will "go into safety" after about 90 sec.   In the event of power failure, the relay will recycle normally and restart the burner.

HONEYWELL RA817A PROTECTORELAY

The two-wire stack mounted Protectorelay shown in Figs. 12-47 and 12-48 has replaced the RA116A and RA117A controls.   Two-wire controls simplify operation and service and are less costly to install. Although millions of series 10 three-wire low-voltage controls are in use, new installations will be two-wire low-voltage (series 80).

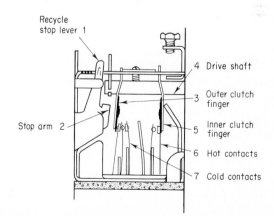

Fig. 12-46   Hot and cold contacts on a Honeywell RA116A Protectorelay.

Fig. 12-47   Honeywell RA817 two-wire low-voltage series 80 Protectorelay.

The RA817A is a stack-mounted intermittent-ignition Protectorelay designed to cycle and safeguard the operation of domestic oil burners. The U-shaped bimetal that operates the simple Pyrostat mechanism is designed to operate quickly and reliably in low stack temperatures. The terminal board is flat so that the terminals are easy to locate and terminal connections are simple.   A small low-voltage transformer which is part of the RA817A supplies electric power for a thermostat or other type of controller.   The safety switch is ambient-temperature-compensated so that changing temperatures do not affect its timing.

If flame is not properly established when an attempt to start the burner is made, the safety switch will "lock out" and the burner cannot be operated until the safety switch is manually reset.   If the flame goes out during the burner running cycle, the Protectorelay will recycle (attempt to restart) after a scavenger period.   If flame is reestablished, normal operation continues.   If not, the Protectorelay locks out.   If the power supply is interrupted, the relay returns to the starting position and operates through a complete starting cycle when power is restored.

The complete sequence of operation is as follows:

Normal operation

1. When the system is satisfied, the Pyrostat cold contacts 1 and 2 and the safety switch 4 are closed; hot contact 3 is open; and both relays are open.

2. On a drop in room temperature, the thermostat contacts close. The ignition relay circuit is then completed from the transformer secondary through the safety-switch heater, Pyrostat cold contacts

(1 and 2), ignition relay (Ig), safety switch, thermostat, and back to the transformer.

3. The ignition relay closes, energizing the ignition through relay contact Ig3 and terminal 4, and energizes the motor relay coil through contacts Ig1 and Ig2.

4. The motor relay closes, energizing the burner motor through motor relay contact MR2, and closes contact MR1.

5. Normally, flame is established at once. Subsequent expansion of the Protectorelay bimetal element closes hot contact 3 and opens cold contacts 2 and 1. The ignition relay opens as soon as contact 1 opens.

6. The burner will normally continue in operation until the thermostat is satisfied and opens the low-voltage control circuit. The motor relay then opens, deenergizing the burner motor, shutting down the burner.

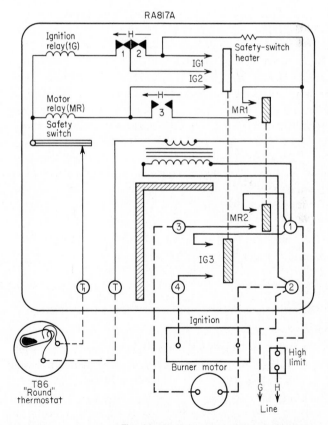

Fig. 12-48   Schematic circuit of RA817A.

7. Following burner shutdown, the bimetal cools and contracts. This contraction opens the hot contact and closes the cold contacts so that the burner can be recycled on the next closing of the thermostat contacts.

8. If temperatures in the system reach the setting of the high-limit control before the thermostat is satisfied, the limit control will open the line-voltage supply circuit to the system, causing it to shut down. When the temperature of the system and flue has fallen below the limit setting and the Pyrostat has cooled, the thermostat can again pull in the relay and start the burner if heat is still needed.

Ignition failure

If flame is not established at the start, hot contact 3 remains open and cold contacts 1 and 2 remain closed. The current flow in the control circuit will continue through the safety-switch heater until, in approximately 90 sec, the safety switch, contact 4, opens. Opening the safety switch shuts down the system, and the safety switch must be reset manually before the system can be recycled.

Flame failure

If the flame goes out while the thermostat is calling for heat, hot contact 3 opens on the first drop in stack temperature. The motor relay drops out, and the burner stops. A scavenger period follows in the time taken for the stack to cool. By the end of the scavenger period, cold contacts 2 and 1 have closed, in that order. The ignition relay is again energized, and the Protectorelay will attempt to restart. If the flame is reestablished, the burner continues to run, but if the flame is not reestablished, safety shutdown occurs through the operation of the safety switch.

Power failure

An interruption of power causes the relay to return to starting position following a scavenger period.

NEW MODELS RA116A, RA117A, RA816A, AND RA817A

No low-voltage oil-heating control series has had as numerous installations as the series 10 circuit just discussed. In the course of progress, it was superseded by a more simply designed series 10 circuit, as well as a more simple series 80 circuit, which substituted a two-wire low-voltage operating circuit for the three-wire low-voltage circuit of series 10.

Nevertheless, because approximately half of all the oil-burner control systems for the 11 million residential oil-heating systems in the United

Fig. 12-49   Honeywell RA816A Protectorelay provides ignition during all the ON cycle.

States are still operating on the series 10 circuit, all the foregoing discussion of this circuit continues to be appropriate in spite of the fact that this particular series 10 circuit is no longer manufactured.

The series 10 circuit itself has undergone revision and simplification as Fig. 12-51 shows. This newer series 10 three-wire, low-voltage circuit operates in a sequence similar to that of the new series 80, RA817A that superseded it. For this reason, the sequence of operation of the *revised* RA116 and RA117 will be covered simultaneously with the RA817. This sequence is as follows:

Operation

The schematic diagrams in Figs. 12-50 and 12-51 show all systems in the idle condition: burner off, no call for heat, Pyrostat "cold" contacts closed, "hot" contacts open, safety switches closed, and all relays de-energized.

Normal Sequence   On a call for heat by the thermostat (or line voltage controller for RA116A, RA117A), a circuit is completed through relays to start ignition and burner motor. Flame is normally established at once, and a rising stack temperature expands the Pyrostat bimetal element, closing the "hot" and opening the "cold" contacts. This shunts the safety-switch heater and, in the RA117 and RA817A only, deenergizes the ignition circuit. The ignition timer in the RA817C heats and opens the timer contacts, cutting off ignition.

When heat demand is satisfied, the system returns to idle condition.

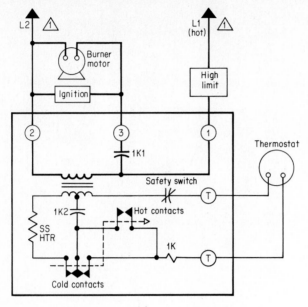

(a)

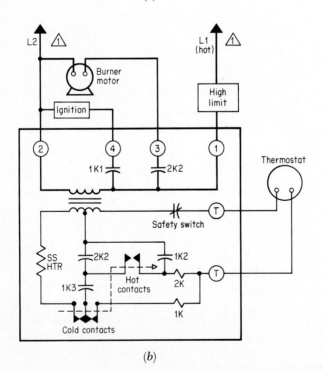

(b)

Fig. 12-50   Schematic circuits of newer model Honeywell RA816A and RA817A Protectorelays.   (a) RA816A; (b) RA817A.

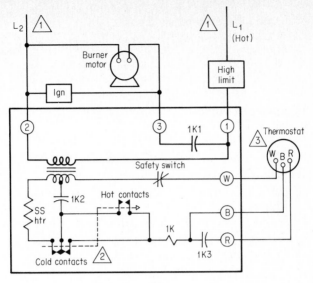

(a)

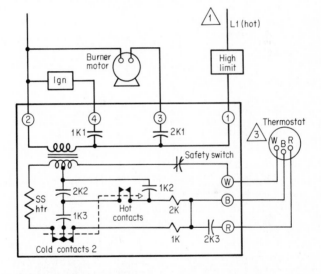

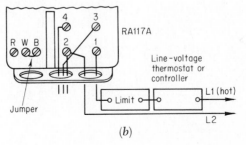

(b)

Fig. 12-51 Schematic circuits of newer model RA116A and RA117A Protectorelays. (a) RA116A; (b) RA117A.

Ignition Failure If flame is not established within approximately 80 sec, the Pyrostat "hot" contacts remain open, causing the safety switch to heat and open its contacts. This shuts off the burner, which cannot be started again until the safety switch has been reset manually.

Flame Failure during Running Cycle The resulting drop in stack temperature causes the Pyrostat "hot" contacts to open, and the system shuts down for approximately 1 min (scavenger period) until the Pyrostat "cold" contacts are remade. If controller is still calling for heat, the Protectorelay then attempts to restart the system. If flame cannot be established in 80 sec, the safety switch locks out.

Power Failure Power interruptions shut off the burner and ignition. When stack cools enough to open "hot" contacts and close "cold" contacts, the system will start when power is restored if thermostat is calling for heat.

THE HONEYWELL R890E ELECTRONIC PROTECTORELAY
(Fig. 12-52)

The RA890E Protectorelay provides electronic-flame safeguard protection for industrial and commercial gas, oil, or combination gas-oil burners. The *normal sequence* of operation is shown in Table 12-1.

PROTECTORELAYS (R8184) UTILIZING CAD CELL DETECTORS

Series 80 (R8184) Protectorelays are available for use with cadmium-sulfide (cad) cell flame detectors. The term "cad cell" is now commonly used throughout the control industry as the popular term to identify the cadmium cell, which senses the oil flame. The R8184 controller

Fig. 12-52 Honeywell RA890E electronic Protectorelay.

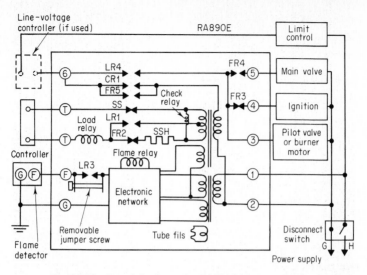

Fig. 12-53   Internal schematic: RA890E Honeywell Protectorelay.

shown in Fig. 12-55, is designed for such use with appropriate 24-volt heating thermostats.   The C544A cad cell is usually installed on the burner by the burner manufacturer.

Operation

When the low-voltage thermostat calls for heat, the relay pulls in, energizing the burner motor, oil valve, and ignition.   The safety switch starts to heat.   If the cad cell sees flame within 70 sec, another relay pulls in, deenergizing the safety-switch heater, preventing the control from locking out by going into safety.   It continues to operate until

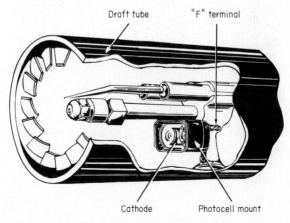

Fig. 12-54   Typical installation of photocell.

Table 12-1   Sequence of Operation: RA890E Honeywell Protectorelay

Low-voltage controller		Line-voltage controller
Power off	Entire system is deenergized	Power off

Power on	Vacuum tube heats
	Component check:
	    Flame relay pulls in
	    Check relay pulls in
	    Flame relay drops out
		Power on

Controller start	Load relay pulls in
	Safety-switch heater is energized
	Gas:
	    Pilot valve opens
	    Ignition starts
	    Burner motor starts (if used)
	Oil:
	    Burner motor starts
	    Ignition starts
	    Oil valve opens
		Controller start

Flame is proved	Flame relay pulls in Ignition stops (if connected to terminal 4) Safety-switch heater is deenergized Gas: Main fuel valve opens	Flame is proved

Controller stop	Load relay drops out
	Ignition stops
	Gas:
	    Both valves close
	Oil:
	    Oil valve closes
	    Burner motor stops
	    Flame-signal circuit is broken
	    Flame relay drops out
		Controller stop

Power off	Entire system is deenergized	Power off

the heat demand is satisfied.   The relay then drops out, shutting off burner motor, oil valve, and ignition.

If the burner fails to ignite, the cad cell sees no flame and the relay feeding current to the safety-switch heater continues to be energized. After 70 sec, the safety switch opens, deenergizing the relay and shutting off the burner motor, oil valve, and ignition.

In the event of flame failure during the burner operating cycle, the cad cell will sense and see "no flame." The relay shunting out the safety-switch heater circuit drops out. The safety switch then opens

Fig. 12-55 Series 80, Honeywell, R8184 cad-cell Protectorelay.

in 70 sec, and a shutdown occurs. The control is then manually reset and operation is reestablished if flame appears in 70 sec.

A power failure will cause the control to shut down safely. It will automatically return to normal operation when power is restored. A check-out of the control in order to verify safety features is as follows:

Check-out

1. Flame failure: Simulate by shutting off oil-supply hand valve while burner is on. After 70 sec the safety switch locks out, the ignition stops, the motor stops, and the oil valve closes. This condition requires resetting the safety switch.

2. Ignition failure: Test by closing oil supply while burner is off. Run through starting procedure, omitting step 3. The safety switch locks out as in flame failure.

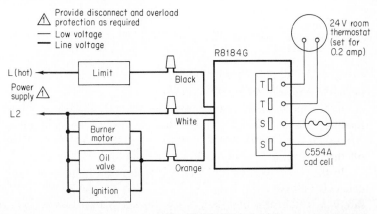

Fig. 12-56 Typical hookup for the R8184G.

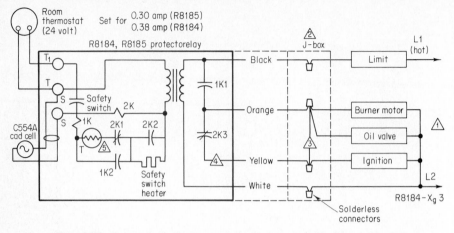

Fig. 12-57 Internal schematic and typical hookup for R8184 and R8185 Protectorelay controllers.

△1 Power supply. Provide disconnect means and overload protection as required.

△2 Supplied with "A" and "C" models. Purchase locally for "B", "D", and "E" models (or use frame provided on burner).

△3 Connection for R8184 only.

△4 Connection for R8185 only.

△5 Thermistor is in R8184E and R8185 circuits only. R8184A and B have wire connections in place of thermistor.

3. Power failure: Turn off power supply while burner is on. When burner goes out, restore power and burner will restart.

4. If operation is not as described, check wiring and installation first. If trouble still persists, follow the complete procedure for checking out the relay and cad cell printed on the inside of the control cover.

COMBINATION PROTECTORELAY, OPERATING, AND LIMIT CONTROLS

See also Figs. 12-19, 12-20, and 12-21.

Forced-circulation hot-water heating systems with domestic hot-water supply

The combination Protectorelay and hydronic heating control (R8182A) shown in Fig. 12-58, is a combined Protectorelay and immersion-type aquastat which includes as part of the latter operating and limit controls. This single-unit device provides a high-limit-protection, minimum water-temperature control for a domestic (faucet) hot-water supply, and a circulation (pump) switching control.

Some models of this control provide for circulation switching through a relay in the control circuit. Another model (R8182C) provides both

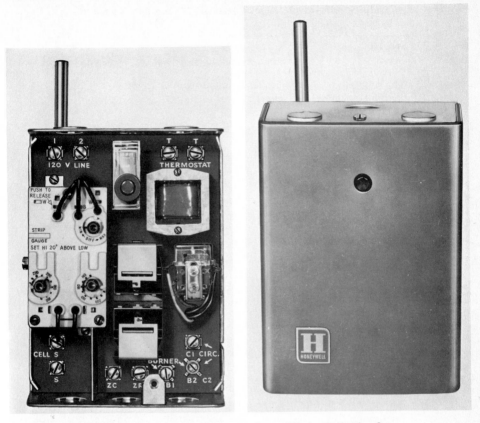

Fig. 12-58 Honeywell R8182 combination Protectorelay and Hydronic Heating Control. This single control includes combustion safety protection, high limit hot water temperature control, domestic (faucet) hot water low limit control and circulator operation on-off control.

high-limit protection and circulator switching from the aquastat. All models use a 24-volt thermostat and a C544A cad-cell flame detector to control the line voltage to the constant-ignition oil burner. Specifications for the various models (R8182A, -B, and -C) are shown in Table 12-2.

Operation

R8182A   A call for heat by the thermostat pulls in relays 1K and 2K to turn on the burner. A safety switch starts to heat. If the burner ignites within 70 sec, the cad cell sees flame, and relay 3K pulls in to deenergize the safety-switch heater. The burner operates until the call for heat is satisfied. The circulator operates when relay 1K pulls in *only* if Aquastat R-W contact is made. When the R8182A is used to control

Table 12-2   Specifications for Various Models of Honeywell Combination Protectorelay and Hydronic Heating Control

Model	Provides burner control	Provides Aquastat switching	Water temperature control ranges
R8182A*	Line voltage, constant ignition oil burner, using C554A cad cell and 24-volt room thermostat.	High limit (spst) to turn off burner if boiler overheats.	120 to 240° F, adj. with fixed differential of 10°
		Low limit, circulator (spdt) to maintain a minimum water temp. for domestic hot water service and to prevent circulator operation if water temp. is low.	100 to 220°F, adj. with adjustable differential 5–20°
R8182B	Same as above.	High limit (spst) to turn off burner if boiler overheats.	180 to 240°F, adj. with fixed differential of 15° (nominal).
R8182C	Same as above.	High limit (spst) to turn off burner if boiler overheats.	120 to 240°F, adj. with fixed differential of 20° (nominal).
		Circulator (spst) to prevent circulator operation if water temp. is below comfort level.	100 to 220°F, adj. with fixed differential of 15° (nominal).

*Auxiliary ZC and ZR terminals may be used to provide zone control through an R845A switching relay.

zone circulators, the R845A relay and thermostat for each succeeding zone will control the zone circulator *only* if the Aquastat R-W contact is made.

When Aquastat R-B contact is made by a drop in water temperature, it acts as a call for heat, pulling in relay 2K to burn on the burner. The circulator cannot operate [Fig. 12-59(a)].

R8182B   The burner and circulator operate whenever the thermostat calls for heat. Relays 1K and 2K pull in. Relay 3K pulls in when the cad cell sees flame, deenergizing the safety-switch heater [Fig. 12-59(b)].

R81829C   The thermostat call for heat pulls in relay 2K to turn on the burner. The relay 3K pulls in when the cad cell sees flame, deenergizing the safety-switch heater. The circulator is independent of the thermostat circuit, being controlled only by the Aquastat switch [Fig. 12-59(c)].

The Penn primary (stack) control

The Penn Stackswitch, Fig. 12-62(a) and (b), is also designed for use on continuous or intermittent-ignition domestic oil burners. They can also be used with small commercial or industrial burners.

The main functions of these controls are:

1. To prevent operation of the burner and ignition if there is no flame established when starting.

2. To start and stop the burner at the demand of the thermostat or other controlling device.

3. To cut off ignition spark on intermittent oil burners after the flame has been established.

4. Automatic recycling (on types 682, 683A, and 685A) in case of flame failure or power interruption during "burner on" cycle. A scavenger period of approximately 1 min is provided to allow fumes to leave the combustion chamber and assure a safe start.

5. Automatic recycling (on all types) in case of power outage or opening and reclosing of thermostat circuit while burner is running. A temperature fall of 100°F is necessary to move the contacts to the start position.

These controls with bimetal helix flame detectors may be mounted on the stack, heat exchanger, or suitable location where temperatures will not exceed 1000°F.

Two-unit models are available for applications in which it is desirable to mount the relay unit separately from the flame detector.

The 680-685A stack controls provide low-voltage protection in addition to automatic recycling should low-voltage conditions occur. The relay will drop out to stop the burner. The control will recycle after low voltage and permit the burner to restart if voltage has returned to normal. Since a scavenger period is required, puffs caused by momentary low-voltage conditions are prevented.

Upon flame failure, with the control in running position, the relay of the intermittent ignition burner control will drop out. Approximately 1 min later; if the thermostat or limit switch still calls for heat, the burner will try to start again. If no combustion occurs, the stack switch will lock out on safety in approximately 90 sec, requiring manual reset.

The bimetallic element (helix) will withstand temperatures up to 1000°F. A safety warp switch compensates to provide uniform control, regardless of surrounding air temperatures.

A teflon (tetrafluoroethylene) facing works against a stainless steel clutch disk, providing consistently smooth clutch action. This assures constant contact pressure as the stack temperature rises beyond the temperature change required to signal the presence of burner flame.

The stack tube can be inserted from $3\frac{1}{4}$ in. minimum to $6\frac{1}{2}$ in. maximum, thus permitting installation in tight places, should such conditions be encountered. This also assures proper positioning of the helix in the stack pipe.

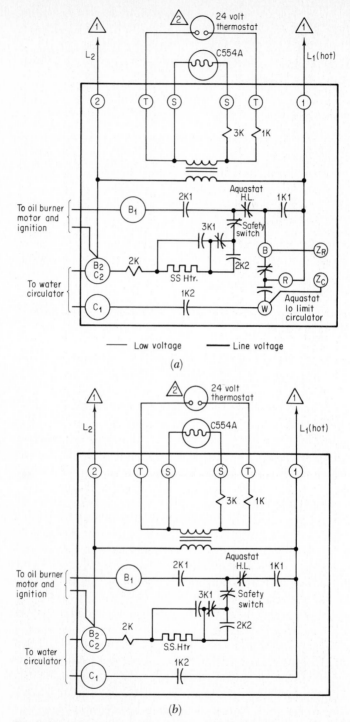

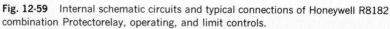

Fig. 12-59 Internal schematic circuits and typical connections of Honeywell R8182 combination Protectorelay, operating, and limit controls.

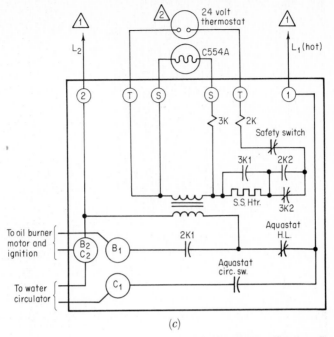

(c)

Fig. 12-59 (Continued)

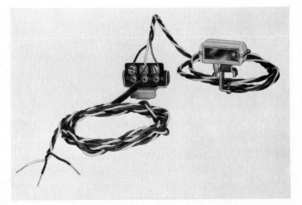

Fig. 12-60 The C549 is a radiant-heat-actuated flame detector designed for use with the R866A and R867A Protectorelay primary controls. The C549A clamps onto the oil line in the blast tube immediately behind the nozzle adapter. Its SPDT bimetallic switch is hermetically sealed in a ceramic body. The radiant heat from the flame passes through a special glass window in the face of the body to actuate the switch. A small magnet on the switch ensures that the starting circuit is maintained even though the switch is subjected to off-cycle vibration and high ambient temperatures. An auxiliary terminal strip to secure the lead wires from the C549A is available for mounting on the burner housing.

Fig. 12-61   The R866 Protectorelay is a constant-ignition domestic oil-burner control for use with a remote-mounting flame detector.   Safety lockout on ignition failure.   Automatic recycle on flame or power failure.

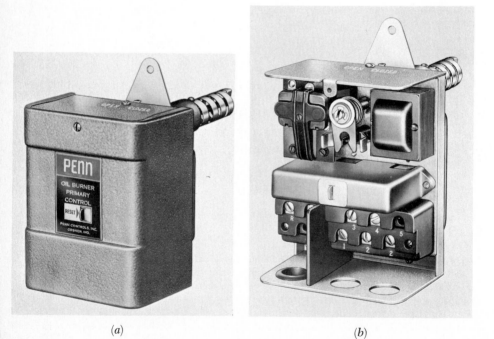

(a)

(b)

Fig. 12-62   (<i>a</i>) Exterior and (<i>b</i>) interior views of Penn Type 680 stack switch.

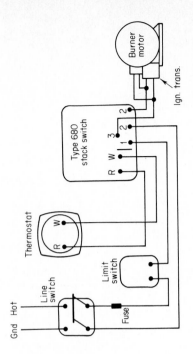

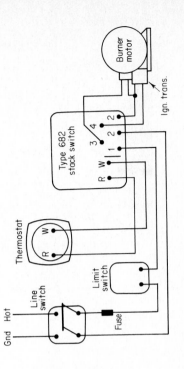

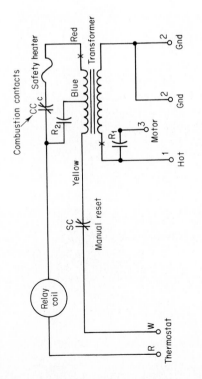

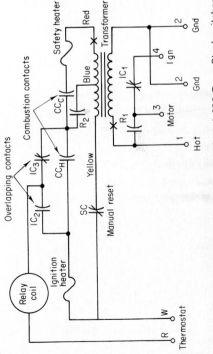

Fig. 12-63 Wiring diagrams for Types 680 and 682 Penn Stackswitches.

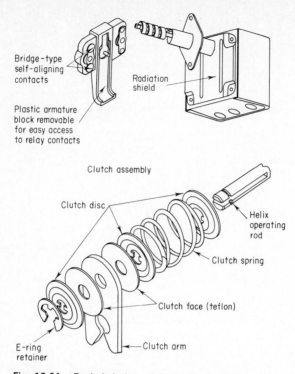

Bridge-type
self-aligning
contacts

Radiation
shield

Plastic armature
block removable
for easy access
to relay contacts

Clutch assembly

Clutch disc

Helix
operating
rod

Clutch spring

Clutch face (teflon)

E-ring
retainer

Clutch arm

Fig. 12-64 Exploded view of Penn Stackswitch clutch mechanism. Note Teflon clutch disk face.

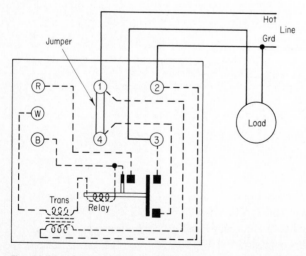

Jumper

Hot
Line
Grd

R
W
B

1
2
4
3

Load

Trans
Relay

Fig. 12-65 General Controls 5010 transformer relay with line and load circuits wired in common.

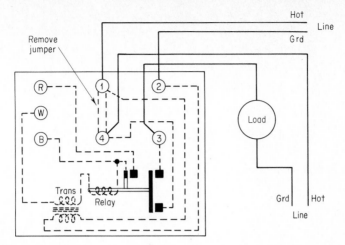

Fig. 12-66   Same relay as in Fig. 12-65 with line and load circuits separated.

SWITCHING RELAYS

In oil-fired heating systems, there will often be auxiliary devices such as fans, circulators or pumps, and dampers that are motor-operated. This necessitates the use of an intermediate switching relay if a low-voltage thermostat is used to operate these auxiliary devices.   Closing of the thermostat circuit energizes the relay, pulling in the clapper to pass line current to the motor.   Figures 12-65 and 12-66 show an internal circuit of this type of relay with and without separated line and load circuits.

'WHITE-RODGERS OIL-BURNER PRIMARY CONTROLS

Types 610 and 611 White-Rodgers oil-burner primary controls shown in Figs. 12-68 and 12-69 are of the intermittent- and constant-ignition types, respectively.

The type 610 primary oil-burner control has been designed for use on heating plants having gun- or rotary-type oil burners where it is desired to have ignition only at the start of every cycle.

Principle of operation

Operation of Normal Cycle   When the thermostat calls for heat, the burner motor starts and ignition is simultaneously turned on.   When the oil ignites, the heat of the flame raises the temperature in the stack which operates the combustion switch.   In about 1 min, the ignition is turned off.

When the thermostat is satisfied, its contacts open, breaking the

Fig. 12-67   Exterior view of White-Rodgers primary control.

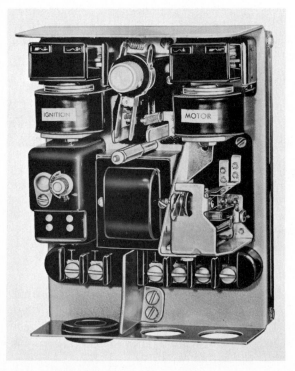

Fig. 12-68   White-Rodgers primary control.

low-voltage circuit. This immediately stops the burner motor. It is then impossible to restart the burner until after a scavenger period of about 1 min.

Operation during Power Failure If the electric power fails while the thermostat is calling for heat, the burner will shut off. Even if the power is immediately resumed, the burner will not operate until after an approximate 1-min scavenger period. Then the burner and ignition come on as in a normal demand for heat.

Operation during Ignition Failure If the oil fails to ignite when the thermostat calls for heat, both the ignition and the burner motor will shut off in about $1\frac{1}{2}$ min. The red manual reset lever on the control must then be pushed upward to recycle the mechanism. (A waiting period of 3 min is recommended before pushing the reset lever.)

Operation during Flame Failure If the flame fails during the time that the thermostat is calling for heat, the burner motor will stop in a short period of time. About 1 min later the burner motor and ignition will start again. If flame is not established this time, the burner motor and ignition will shut off in about $1\frac{1}{2}$ min. The red manual reset lever on the control must then be pushed upward to make further attempts at ignition. (A waiting period of 3 min is recommended before pushing the reset lever.)

The mechanisms that govern the safety time, ignition time, and scavenger time are not affected by variations in temperature in the room where the heating plant is located.

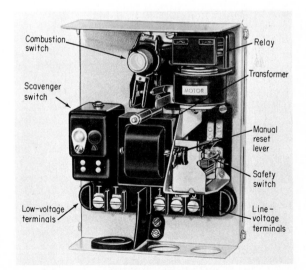

Fig. 12-69 White-Rodgers constant-ignition primary control.

Circuit analysis

Type 610, White-Rodgers Primary Control
See schematic circuit (Fig. 12-70)

Normal Cycle   When the room thermostat calls for heat, it closes its contacts, completing the circuit from the transformer X through the safety switch, through the thermostat, through the ignition scavenger switch, to the ignition relay coil, and back to the other side of the transformer Y. This pulls in the ignition relay, which closes both sets of ignition relay contacts. The ignition transformer is excited. Then a circuit is established from the transformer X through the safety switch, through the thermostat, through the ignition scavenger switch, through the top ignition relay contacts, through the safety heater, through the cold contacts of the combustion switch, through the motor relay coil, and back to the other side of the transformer Y. This pulls in the motor relay, which causes the oil-burner motor to run. (The above sequence transpires in a fraction of a second, so that actually the transformer and burner motor start simultaneously.)

After ignition is established, the bimetal of the combustion switch heats up and goes from cold to hot (the switch action is such that hot is made before cold is broken). This causes the circuit to be broken to the safety heater and made to the scavenger heater. In about 45 sec (adjustable) the scavenger heater opens the ignition scavenger switch, and then the ignition relay drops out, thereby shutting off the ignition transformer.

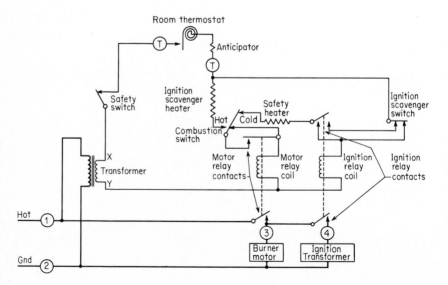

Fig. 12-70   Internal-wiring schematic: White-Rodgers type 610 primary control.

When the room thermostat is satisfied, it opens its circuit and the motor relay drops out, thereby stopping the burner motor. It is now impossible to restart the burner until the scavenger heater cools off enough to permit the ignition scavenger switch to close.

Flame Failure   If the flame fails after it has been established, the combustion-switch bimetal cools off rapidly, which causes the combustion switch to go from hot to cold. Since the circuit through the cold contact is broken at the ignition relay contacts and at the ignition scavenger switch, the motor relay drops out and the motor stops. When the scavenger heater cools off, the ignition scavenger switch closes and the system starts off the same as explained under normal cycle.

Ignition Failure   If the flame is not established when the thermostat calls for heat, the combustion switch stays on the cold contact. The current is maintained through the safety heater, which opens the safety switch in about $1\frac{1}{2}$ min. It is then necessary to raise the red reset lever before the system will start again.

Power Failure   If there is a momentary interruption of electric service while the thermostat is calling for heat, the motor relay drops out, but it cannot again pull in until the ignition scavenger heater cools off, and then the cycle restarts.

WHITE-RODGERS KWIK-SENSOR TYPE 668 OIL BURNER CONTROL

White-Rodgers primary controls type 668 known as "Kwik-Sensor" are used for the same purpose as all basic primary controls. However, they are supplied as part of the burner, furnace, or boiler unit. These devices are located and mounted on the unit by the burner, furnace, or boiler manufacturer. The type 668 controls are used with the 956 Flame Detector. Later models employ SCR "solid-state" flame-detection circuits. "Solid state" refers to the employment of the silicon-controlled rectifier. These devices will be discussed later. All 668 oil-burner primaries utilize a 25-volt cad cell circuit.

THE TYPE 956 FLAME DETECTOR

This detector fits into a socket assembly that positions the cad cell to a direct view of the oil fire. The combination of the cad cell and socket assembly is known as the "956 Flame Detector" (see Figs. 12-71 and 12-72).

The cad cell is actually a resistor that varies its electrical resistance according to the amount (and kind) of light it sees. It acts like a switch; when it sees the light of an oil flame, it has very low resistance and conducts electricity (switch closed). When exposed to darkness, the cad cell has very high resistance and breaks the circuit (switch open).

Fig. 12-71   White-Rodgers "Kwik-Sensor" oil-burner control.   The above model covers types 668, 6L68 and 669.   At the circled left is the type 956 Flame Detector used with all Kwik-Sensor controls.   The Flame Detector shows the cad cell mounted in the socket assembly.

This flame detector will respond immediately to an oil flame, but is not to be used with any other fuel.

Operation: Type 668 Kwik-Sensor

The operation of a Kwik-Sensor can best be understood by considering how its operation differs from that of the more familiar stack-mounted type of primary control.   The basic difference is the method used for detecting the presence or absence of a burner flame.   Whereas stack-mounted controls rely upon the heat from the flue gases for their operation, Kwik-Sensor controls rely solely upon the light from the oil flame.

Instead of using a bimetal type of flame detector to operate a combustion switch, Kwik-Sensors use the type 956 Flame Detector to operate a low-voltage relay (called the flame relay) or an SCR "solid-state" switching device.   The description of the SCR switching circuit is explained at the end of this chapter.

Normal Cycle   When the thermostat calls for heat, the motor relay coil pulls in, closing its two sets of contacts.   As the motor relay contacts No. 2 close, the burner motor and ignition start.

When the flame is established, the 956 Flame Detector instantly

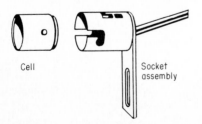

Cell   Socket
                        assembly

Fig. 12-72   The 956 Flame Detector unit showing cad cell separated from socket assembly.   (*White-Rodgers*)

decreases its resistance and allows current to flow through the flame-relay coil. The flame-relay coil pulls in, snapping the normally closed flame-relay contacts from the "cold" to "hot" side. This drops the safety heater out of the circuit. Burner operation continues, owing to the hold-in circuit through motor-relay contacts No. 1.

When the thermostat is satisfied, the motor-relay coil drops out, stopping the burner. "Seeing" darkness, the 956 Flame Detector instantly increases its resistance, stopping the flow of current through the flame-relay coil. The flame-relay coil drops out, snapping the flame-relay contacts back to the "cold" side. The primary control is now ready for the next burner cycle.

Ignition Failure   If the flame is not established on start-up, the resistance of the 956 Flame Detector remains very high and prevents the flow of current through the flame-relay coil. The flame-relay contacts remain on the "cold" side to keep the safety heater in the circuit, and the primary control locks out on safety.

Flame Failure   If the flame goes out after a successful start-up, the 956 Flame Detector instantly increases its resistance to stop the flow of current through the flame-relay coil. The flame-relay coil drops out, snapping the flame-relay contacts back to the "cold" side and putting the safety heater back in the circuit. If flame is not reestablished, the primary control then locks out on safety.

Momentary Power Interruption   Flame can be reestablished as soon as power is resumed.

False-light Condition   If the 956 Flame Detector senses enough light from a source other than the burner flame, it would register the

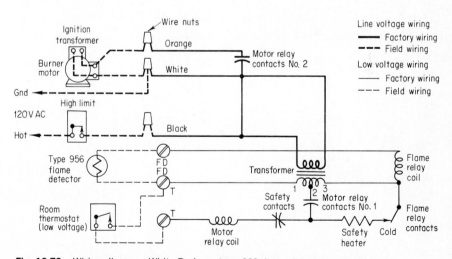

Fig. 12-73 Wiring diagram, White-Rodgers type 668, low-voltage, constant-ignition, nonrecycling primary control with type 956 Flame Detector.

existence of a burner flame even though the burner might be off, but it cannot be fooled into starting the burner under such conditions. On low-voltage models such as the type 668, the flame-relay contacts would be open (on the "hot" side) on a call for heat from the thermostat, and the burner motor would not start since the motor-relay coil could not pull in. On line-voltage models such as type 6L68, the flame-relay coil would pull in before the motor-relay coil when the thermostat called for heat, and the burner could not start.

Damaged Flame Detector   The 956 Flame Detector will fail safe in the event of either type of damage to the Flame Detector. If damaged so its circuit is shorted, the Flame Detector will not allow the burner to start. If damaged so its circuit is open, the Flame Detector will cause the primary control to lock out on safety.

TYPE 663-1 AND 663-3 KWIK-SENSORS

Low-voltage, intermittent-ignition, recycling type (wiring diagram, Fig. 12-74)

Operating features

Normal Start   On a call for heat from the thermostat, the ignition-relay coil pulls in through the scavenger contacts, closing the ignition relay contacts 1, 2, and 3. The motor-relay coil then pulls in, closing motor contacts 1, 2, and 3. The burner motor and ignition start.

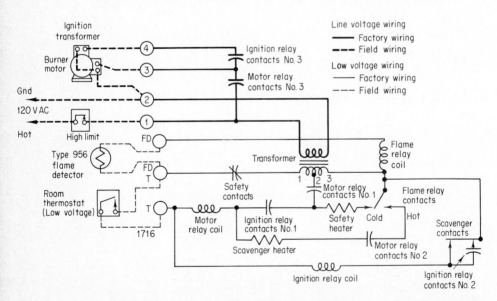

Fig. 12-74   Wiring diagram, White-Rodgers, Kwik-Sensor, low-voltage, intermittent-ignition, nonrecycling type 663-21 (no longer available) and 663-22 oil-burner primary controls.

Normal Operation   As the 956 Flame Detector sees light from the oil flame, it instantly decreases its resistance, allowing current to flow through the flame-relay coil.   The flame-relay coil pulls in, snapping the flame-relay contacts from the "cold" to "hot" side.   This completes a circuit through the scavenger heater and drops the safety heater out of the circuit.   A short time later, both sets of scavenger contacts open, dropping out the ignition-relay coil and stopping the spark.   The burner operation continues due to the hold-in circuit through the motor-relay contacts no. 2 and the scavenger heater.

Ignition Failure   If the flame is not established on start-up, the resistance of the Flame Detector remains very high, preventing the flow of current through the flame-relay coil.   The flame-relay contacts remain on the "cold" side, and the control locks out on safety.

Flame Failure   If the flame goes out after a successful start-up, the 956 Flame Detector instantly increases its resistance, stopping the flow of current through the flame-relay coil.   The flame-relay contacts snap from the "hot" to "cold" side, dropping out the motor-relay coil and stopping the burner motor.   When scavenger contacts reclose, the burner will try for reignition.   If flame is not reestablished, the control will then lock out on safety.

Momentary Power Interruption   The flame can be reestablished as soon as the scavenger heater has had sufficient cooling time.

SOLID STATE OIL-BURNER PRIMARY CONTROLS
Figs. 12-76, 12-77, and 12-78

A new development in oil-burner primary control circuits is the "solid state" switching device.   This switching device performs the same function as a switching relay but achieves this in a manner far different from that familiar device.   The SCR, as it will be referred to, has no moving parts and responds with great speed to the commands of the cad cell.

An SCR can "conduct" a flow of current (like the closing of normally open relay contacts), or it can "block" a flow of current (like the opening of normally open relay contacts).

Operation

When an SCR conducts, it permits current to flow from anode to cathode.   When an SCR blocks, it stops the flow of current from anode to cathode.

To make an SCR conduct, two conditions must be met, as follows:

1. A voltage difference must exist between anode and cathode.   (This can be accomplished in Fig. 12-77 by closing the hand switch.)

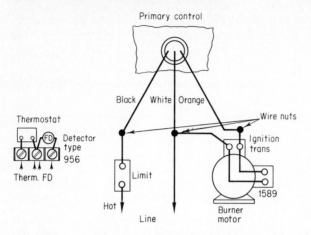

Fig. 12-75   If no special wiring instructions are supplied, then electrical connections should be made as shown on the above diagram for type 668, constant-ignition, nonrecycling oil burner primary control.   (*White-Rodgers*)

2. A sufficient voltage (about 1 volt) must be applied to the gate (FD-FD terminals).

Thus, with the hand switch closed, the SCR will conduct (from anode to cathode) when an excess of 1 volt is applied to its gate (FD-FD terminals).   The SCR will block when this gate voltage drops sufficiently below 1 volt (about ¼ volt).

Figure 12-78 shows the complete 25-volt circuit for a type SCR Kwik-Sensor.   It should be pointed out that capacitors C1 and C2 do not affect control operation in any way.   Their sole purpose is to protect the SCR against momentary surges in voltage.

First, assume that the two leads of the type 956 Flame Detector are disconnected.   Then, whenever the thermostat contacts close, 25 volts will be applied across the series resistance of R1, R2, and R3. Thus, the voltage drop across resistances R1, R2, and R3 must also be 25 volts.

Now, if R3 has a resistance in excess of 1/25th of the sum-total resistance of R1, R2, and R3, the voltage across R3 would be greater

Fig. 12-76   Wiring symbol for a silicon controlled rectifier (SCR).

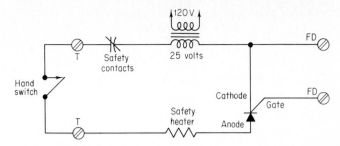

Fig. 12-77 This diagram shows how a voltage difference which must exist between anode and cathode (the SCR) can be achieved by closing the hand switch. (See text for full sequential explanation.)

than 1 volt. This voltage is also the gate voltage, so the SCR would make contact, starting the burner and sending current through the safety heater. Burner shutdown would occur, however, since the safety heater would lock the control out on safety.

Next, consider the case in which the type 956 is connected to the FD-FD terminals and is "seeing" darkness. Since the type 956 has a resistance of about 10 million ohms when it "sees" darkness, the voltage across R3 would remain above 1 volt because no appreciable current flows through the type 956 when it "sees" darkness. Thus, the gate voltage is greater than 1 volt with the type 956 "seeing" darkness.

When the type 956 "sees" the light of an oil flame, its resistance drops to about 500 ohms. The current now flows through the type 956, which lowers the voltage across R3 (also the gate voltage) to about $\frac{1}{4}$ volt. The SCR now blocks, stopping the flow of current through the safety heater.

The foregoing explained the purpose of the R3 resistance. The purposes of the R1 and R2 resistances are as follows:

1. R2 is an adjustable resistor which is factory adjusted (and sealed) to compensate for normal production tolerances of transformer and

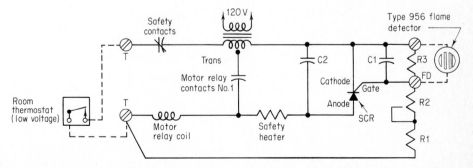

Fig. 12-78 The complete 25-volt circuit for the SCR Kwik-Sensor.

other component parts. R2 is adjusted to put the proper voltage across R3 with the type 956 disconnected.

2. R1 serves to protect the SCR while factory adjustment of R2 is being made. Without R1, it would be possible to apply 25 volts to the gate of the SCR while making factory adjustments of R2. A 25-volt source should never be applied to the gate of the SCR since it would instantly render the SCR inoperative.

NOTE Do not touch thermostat wires to FD flame detector terminals.

QUESTIONS

1. What is a bimetallic element?
2. What devices besides the bimetallic element are used to actuate controls?
3. Explain what is meant by differential.
4. Give two different methods of achieving thermostat differential.
5. Explain the function of a clock thermostat.
6. What is meant by the term "low-limit" control? "High-limit" control?
7. What is a "direct-acting" control? A "reverse-acting" control?
8. What is the purpose of a pressure control? Give two methods by which they are set.
9. Explain the function of a combination fan and limit control.
10. What are the purposes of a primary control?
11. Explain the operation of the Mercoid JMI Pyratherm; the General Controls 5520-D21 primary control; the Penn 680 stack switch; the Honeywell RA117A Protectorelay.
12. What devices are used to actuate primary controls?
13. What are some uses for switching relays?
14. Explain the operation of a White-Rodgers stack-mounted primary control (intermittent ignition).
15. What is the normal sequence of operation that occurs with a stack-mounted primary control when flame failure occurs?
16. What is meant by the term "recycles on flame failure"?
17. How does a series 10 circuit differ from a series 80 circuit?
18. How does the electronic primary control differ from the stack-mounted electromechanical primary?
19. What is a cad-cell flame detector?
20. Who usually installs the cad-cell detector?
21. Explain the check-out procedure for the R8184 cad-cell primary control.

22. Prepare a diagram showing the typical hookup for the R8184G.
23. How does a combination Protectorelay, operating, and limit control operate?
24. What is meant by the term "Kwik-Sensor"?
25. Name the parts of the White-Rodgers 956 Flame Detector.
26. What is meant by a "false-light" condition?
27. Give five operating features of the White-Rodgers Kwik-Sensor 663-1 and 663-3 primary control.
28. Prepare a diagram showing the basic electrical connections for White-Rodgers type 668, constant-ignition, nonrecycling, oil-burner primary control.
29. Draw the wiring symbol for an SCR.   What does SCR mean?
30. What is meant by the term "solid state"?

CHAPTER 13
INSTALLING
THE THERMOSTAT

The purpose of the thermostat is to furnish a means of regulating temperature within the living quarters. It does this by starting and stopping the heat-giving equipment in response to small temperature changes. For these temperature changes it depends primarily upon air circulation, and thus, in installing a thermostat, it is essential that its position in relation to air currents be seriously considered.

In selecting the location for the thermostat, extreme care should be exercised. Evenness of heat levels throughout a structure depends to a great extent upon proper thermostat location and differential setting. In general, it should be placed where it can maintain the proper warm temperature of the home or space to be controlled. It should *never* be in the path of cold or hot air currents (drafts), nor close to radiation, warm air registers, lamps, chimneys, or in the direct path of the sun's rays. Neither should it be mounted on outside cold walls, close to windows, or adjacent to surfaces covering hot or cold water or steam pipes. As free air circulation over the thermostat is so important, no cabinets or pieces of large furniture should be placed to interfere with the free passage of air over the control.

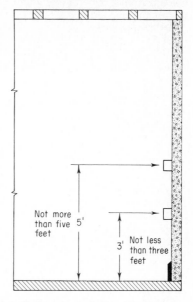

Fig. 13-1   Height limitations for installing thermostats.

The best location is usually on the inside wall of a dining room or living room. This wall should not, if possible, have its other side as the kitchen, for a wall of this type becomes considerably warmer during cooking periods and thus will affect any thermostat mounted on its opposite side.

From 4 to $4\frac{1}{2}$ ft from the floor is usually accepted as the proper height for a thermostat. If it is placed any higher, discomfort may result for the occupants of the room when seated. Warm air rises and as a result the temperature of a room is always higher as it approaches the ceiling. This means that the higher a thermostat is on the wall, the longer it will be in a satisfied state and the cooler will be the lower portions of the room, becoming progressively cooler closer to the floor. Such a condition can result in discomfort for seated persons and especially small children if some thought is not given to placing the thermostat at the proper height. The control should never be more than 5 ft nor less than 3 ft above the floor.

Thermostats generally used with domestic oil-burner installations are of three types: three-wire low voltage, two-wire low voltage, and two-wire line voltage. Regardless of the number of wires or their voltages, the basic method of running the cable is the same. Once the location has been selected, the following procedure should be followed.

Remove the quarter-round molding from the baseboard right below the selected thermostat location and at this point drill a small guide

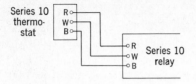

Series 10 thermostat, low voltage

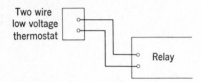

Two-wire low-voltage thermostat

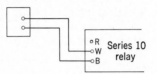

Two-wire thermostat with series 10 relay

Fig. 13-2   Wiring diagrams for two-wire or three-wire thermostats.

hole at an angle through the floor and basement ceiling, as shown in Fig. 13-3. Now at the basement ceiling drill up with a larger drill at the point where the small drill hole appeared.

At the location selected for the thermostat, drill a ½-in. hole in the wall for the thermostat cable, directly in line with the small hole drilled at an angle through the floor. This ½-in. hole in the wall will be covered by the thermostat when it is mounted.

Through this hole at the thermostat location drop a weighted cord until it touches the floor. Insert a piece of hooked wire up through the hole in the basement floor and "fish" through this cord.

Fasten the end of the thermostat cable securely to the cord and draw it up between the walls through the hole at the thermostat location. A good type of thermostat cable (usually No. 18 wire) conforming to local and Underwriters' standards should be used.

Leave about 6 in. of thermostat cable showing *and then plug up the hole in the wall.* This will provide adequate protection against drafts coming up from the basement through the wall space and reaching the thermostat. The plugging of any hole in the wall through which the cable passes is of great value in assuring true and accurate thermostat operation.

Drafts pass through the spaces between the walls; therefore, if the basement does not have a finished ceiling covering the joists there may be considerable air currents, and any opening such as that for a thermostat cable will result in these drafts moving into the room.

With the hole behind the thermostat bracket not plugged, it is obvious that these drafts will circulate about the thermostat or carry heat away from it by reducing the temperature of the mounting bracket. This, of course, will affect its operation and result in overheating. There should never be an unsealed opening in the wall adjacent to or behind the thermostat mounting bracket.

At this point fasten the thermostat bracket and attach the wires. Figure 13-4 shows the mounting bracket for a Honeywell T11A thermostat with wires attached, as well as for General and Mercoid controls.

If a line-voltage thermostat is used, the following procedure should be followed: Select the location for the thermostat and install a conduit box. Run conduit or BX from this box to the unit that is being controlled, leaving a length of wire about 6 to 8 in. for connection to the control terminal posts.

Attach the thermostat mounting plate to the conduit outlet box after drawing the wires through it. Screw the plate tightly into position.

Fasten the wires to the terminals on the mounting plate and mount the thermostat base on the plate, screwing it on securely (Fig. 13-6).

In wiring the series 10 circuit, care must be taken to see that the red, white, and blue thermostat terminals are hooked into the proper, similarly colored, marked, or lettered terminals on the relay (Fig. 13-2).

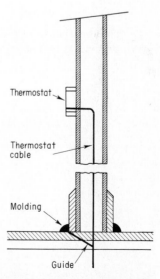

Fig. 13-3   Method of locating thermostat cable.

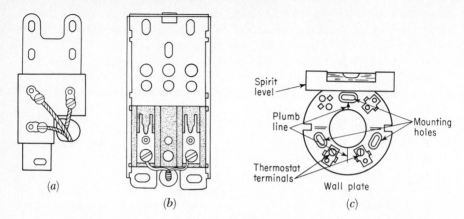

(a)   (b)   (c)

Fig. 13-4 (*a*) Mounting bracket for Honeywell T11A three-wire low-voltage thermostat. (*b*) Mounting bracket for Mercoid two-wire low-voltage thermostat (Sensatherm). (*c*) Mounting bracket for General Controls two-wire low-voltage thermostat. A mercury-tube switch control requires that the mounting bracket be installed perfectly level (note spirit level in the illustration) to give proper temperature control. If not level, the control point will be altered and the dwelling will overheat or underheat.

With a two-wire low-voltage circuit, it does not make any difference in which order the two are attached to a two-terminal relay panel.

The T87F Honeywell thermostat, a series 80 two-wire low-voltage control, now replaces the series 10 T11A, of which there are millions installed. Instructions for the T87F mounting and low-voltage connections are as follows:

Mount the backplate on the wall with the screws furnished (it is recommended that a pilot hole be drilled to prevent stripping threads), using the mounting holes shown by arrows. The "up" line of the

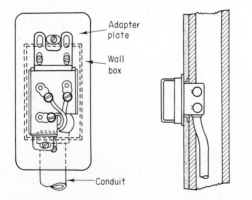

Fig. 13-5 Installing low-voltage wire with conduit. Conduit joins junction box. (*Honeywell, Inc.*)

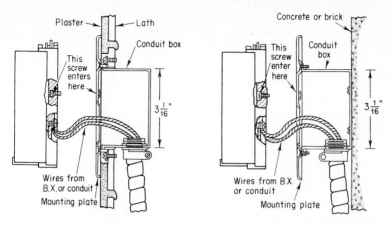

Fig. 13-6   Installing a General Controls line-voltage thermostat.

backplate must be vertical for the thermostat to be accurately calibrated.   To find the vertical, hold the back plate on the wall and level
across the top ears or the horizontal center line with a spirit level; or
hold a plumb line in front of the "up" line.

To connect the low-voltage wiring, slip the exposed end of the

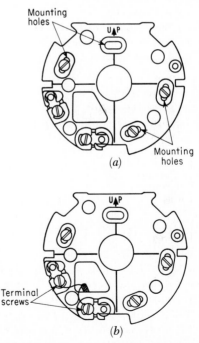

Fig. 13-7   (*a*) The T87F Honeywell thermostat back plate, showing mounting
holes.   (*b*) Terminal screws on the T87F.

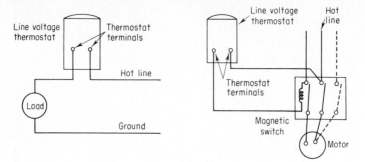

Fig. 13-8 Wiring diagrams for line-voltage thermostat.

thermostat cable through the four-sided hole in the back plate and connect the wires to the back plate terminals as indicated by arrows. Push the excess cable back through the wall hole and plug any free space to prevent drafts from the basement from affecting the thermostat.

If a two-wire thermostat is used with a series 10 stack-mounted relay, only the blue and white terminals on the relay are used and either of the thermostat terminals can be connected to the blue or white.

A three-wire series 10 thermostat should not be used with a two-wire low-voltage relay circuit.

When a line-voltage (110-volt) thermostat is used, the control acts as a switch that breaks the hot line. Thus the hot line should run to one terminal of the control and the other control terminal should be wired to the load as shown in Fig. 13-8. If the line-voltage thermostat is used with a magnetic switch, the wiring hookup, also shown in Fig. 13-8, can be utilized. It may also be used to interrupt the hot line to the primary control.

These few simple procedures and rules govern the installation of thermostats, and they should be observed strictly. Once a thermostat is installed, it should be checked for the proper calibration and differential setting. Follow the individual control manufacturer's specifications and directions on these two important considerations.

CALIBRATION AND DIFFERENTIAL

Calibration has to do with the thermostat's accuracy in responding to temperature levels. If a thermostat is set for 72° and the room is 69° and it has not made contact, it is obviously not calibrated properly. An accurately calibrated thermostat responds quickly and accurately to temperature fluctuations and maintains normal heat levels.

Thermometers on thermostat covers should be checked carefully when the control is installed to make sure that they are fairly accurate and will agree with the on-off action of the thermostat. At times the thermostat may be in calibration and operating normally, but regarded with suspicion because its on-off temperature setting does not coincide with the thermometer on the cover.

As this thermometer is usually the consumer's only guide or reference point, any of its inaccuracies may be blamed on the thermostat's operation when, in reality, the control may be responding accurately to temperature changes.

The *differential* setting of thermostats is extremely important because it will determine the evenness of the heat level and give protection against under- and overshooting. Differential settings change according to the type of heating system installed and actually determine the amount of time the burner will run and whether or not the room temperature will be the deciding factor in determining the length of this running period.

Actually there are two types of differential, the *mechanical* and the *artificial-heat* type. With a purely mechanical differential, the burner operation commences with the closing of the thermostat contacts and continues *until a rise in room temperature* causes the contacts to open and stop the burner. Therefore, with this type of differential there *must* be a change in room temperature to operate the thermostat, and it is this room air temperature change *alone* that causes the thermostat to operate.

With the application of artificial heat to the thermostat by a built-in heater element, we have a substitute for room-temperature changes as

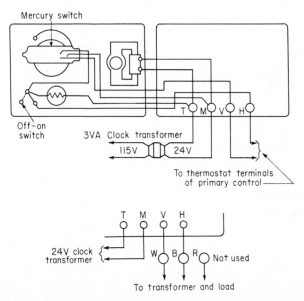

Fig. 13-9 General Controls T-270 Tempotherm connection diagrams.

the operating factor. Thus, there is an artificial-heat differential instead of, or as well as, a mechanical differential established by room-temperature changes.

The artificial heat is a substitute for room air-temperature rise. It can be seen from this that if enough artificial heat is applied to the thermostat to be equal to the thermostat differential, the thermostat will break its contact *without any change in the actual room temperature.* It will then operate the burner only for a specified period of time, according to the amount of artificial heat applied. The more artificial heat applied, the shorter period the burner will run, as the thermostat will be quickly satisfied.

A thermostat such as this can be adjusted for any specific system and thus operate the heating plant to provide measured amounts of heat to balance input against heat loss and maintain constant temperature levels (see Chap. 12).

INSTALLING AN ELECTRIC-CLOCK THERMOSTAT

The installation of an electric-clock thermostat follows the same procedure with regard to mounting as the thermostat does. The cable is "snaked" through the wall in exactly the same fashion.

With the clock thermostat, however, we need two extra wires to supply the current to the clock motor. This motor is normally run on low-voltage current. Because of this we need an added transformer of the step-down type.

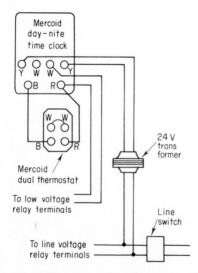

Fig. 13-10 Connection diagram for a Mercoid thermostat and clock.

This transformer steps down the 110-volt current to approximately 20 volts, which operates the clock motor. This means that with a series 10 clock thermostat we will need a five-wire thermostat cable, three wires for the thermostat circuit and two wires for the low-voltage current to the clock motor.

With a two-wire clock thermostat, we would need a four-wire cable. The transformer is wired in directly on the line-voltage side from the junction box and from the low-voltage side to the clock thermostat.

Clocks sometimes referred to as "tork" clocks may be placed in the cellar or basement where they are out of reach. These clocks do not have the conventional time-telling face. They have, instead, a 24-hr dial.

In many cases, the use of a twin thermostat with a "tork" clock gives a flexibility for certain purposes that makes it a desirable method for regulating temperature changeover from night to day and vice versa. Clocks of this type are often utilized for a wide variety of applications where automatically timed switching of electric circuits is desired.

THE TWIN-TYPE THERMOSTAT

With the twin-type thermostat, we have, in reality, two separate thermostats with separate setting adjustments in each case. One is set for night operation at a lowered temperature and the other for normal day operation. Each of these is wired to the relay through the electric time switch.

Thus, during the day the circuit to the relay from the higher-temperature thermostat is completed through the clock, and, at the adjusted time at night, it shunts the circuit over to the night thermostat with the lowered settings. Tests by competent authorities demonstrate that substantial savings of up to 15 per cent of the total annual oil bill can be obtained by maintaining lowered night settings.

The normal day setting of a thermostat should be about 70°F. Settings above this waste oil in considerable amounts. For instance, with a yearly consumption of fuel oil of about 3,000 gal, *a setting of 75°, which is but 5° over the normal setting, will waste 400 gal of oil per year, while a setting of 80° will waste 850 gal of oil per year.* This demonstrates the economy of moderate settings.

Likewise, lowered night settings will afford a saving. With the temperatures lowered from 70° to 60° for 8 hr each night during the winter season, a total saving of 10 per cent of the annual oil bill can be accomplished.

We can see from this that the job is not completed for the installer when the thermostat is installed and the system is operating normally. Oil consumers should be educated to lowered night settings and average

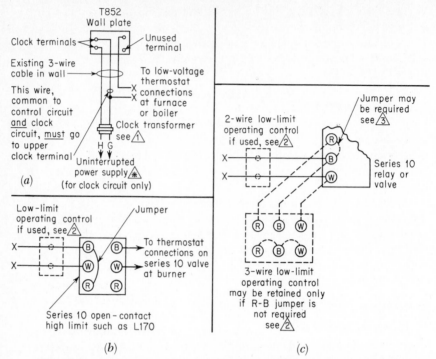

Fig. 13-11 Replacement jobs where three-wire cable is already installed in wall. Connections for thermostat and clock circuit are shown in (*a*); primary controls are shown in (*a*) to (*c*). (*a*) Replacement of older-model two-wire thermostat (in system that has used a series 10 thermostat at some time in the past). (*b*) Replacement of three-wire thermostat in gas-fired system where thermostat is connected to a series 10 open-contact high limit such as L170. (*c*) Replacement of three-wire thermostat in system where thermostat is connected directly to a series 10 valve or relay.

NOTES

⚠1 Use the AT75 or AT82 transformer for the clock; no other transformer may be used. No other device may be powered by the clock transformer.

⚠2 When the R-to-B jumper is required on a series 10, control (if used) must be of the two-wire type.

⚠3 Jumper R to B on series 10 relays that "break the blue" R116, R161, R178, R187A1 to A4, and R190B1 to B8.

*Disconnecting means and overload protection is required. (*Honeywell, Inc.*)

top day settings of 72°. Every opportunity to convince the consumer of the real practical economy to be achieved from the electric-clock thermostat should be utilized.

The figures shown in Tables 13-1 and 13-2 were ascertained by work done by engineers of the Shell Oil Co. and offer evidence in favor of thermostat settings not being over 70° during the day (Table 13-1) and being lowered below 70° during the night (Table 13-2).

Table 13-1 Yearly Oil Waste Due to High Thermostat Settings
(*Shell Oil Co.*)

Average yearly fuel consumption, gal	Oil wasted yearly due to thermostat settings above 70°, gal	
	75°	80°
1,500	214	428
2,000	286	572
2,500	357	714
3,000	428	856
3,500	500	1,000
4,000	571	1,142
5,000	714	1,428
10,000	1,428	2,856
15,000	2,143	4,286

However, while the 70°F noted above will provide optimum conditions for minimum cost of operation in the form of lower fuel bills, studies of the comfort range show some differences in homeowners' tastes in this matter.

ASHRAE publishes a comfort range of from 72° to 78°, and many thermostats manufactured today are so marked. The average home today runs from 72° to 74°, as the preference for comfort overrides economy motives. The technical accuracy of the statements concerning the 70°F daily home temperature is still unaffected, however.

In cases where thermostat settings can be lowered as much as 10° to 20°, care should be taken that the water in the boiler will not become too cold as a result of the long "off" periods caused by such temperature setbacks. The hot-water temperature control can provide an adequate safeguard against this.

In such instances this hot-water temperature control will bring the

Table 13-2 Fuel-oil Savings through Lowered Night-temperature Settings*
(*Shell Oil Co.*)

Lowered night-temperature setting, °F	Per cent savings in fuel oil when thermostat setting is lowered at night for a period of:			
	4 hr	8 hr	12 hr	16 hr
70	0	0	0	0
65	2½	5	7½	9½
60	5	9½	14½	19½
55	7½	14½	21½	28½
50	9½	19½	28½	38½

*Based on inside day temperature of 70° and average outside temperature of 35° for heating season.

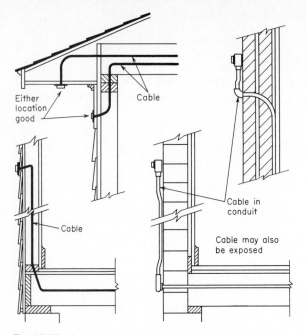

Fig. 13-12   Installation locations for Honeywell outdoor thermostat.

burner on at night for short runs to maintain the temperature of the boiler water at the normal setting of about 160°.   This means that when the thermostat calls for heat in the morning, the boiler water temperature will have to be raised only 52° to reach the steaming point of 212°F.   Had there been no hot-water temperature control on the boiler and the thermostat had a considerable setback, say 15° to 20°, the boiler water might cool down to the ambient cellar temperature before there was a call for heat.

Assuming the cellar temperature to be 60° the burner would now have to run to lift the water temperature 152°F in order to reach the steaming point of 212°F.   As a result, it would take a considerably longer period of time to get heat throughout the house.

With steam and hot-water systems, a low-limit hot-water temperature-operating control furnishes adequate protection against long delays in getting heat when advantage is taken of sharp night thermostat setbacks to obtain increased operating economies.

QUESTIONS

1. Give six locations that should *never* be chosen for a thermostat.

2. What is the proper height for a thermostat?
3. Give the step-by-step procedure for running the thermostat cable.
4. Can a series 10 thermostat be used with a relay that has a two-wire low-voltage circuit?   Why?
5. After a thermostat has been installed, for what should it be checked?
6. Of what importance is the thermometer on the thermostat cover?
7. Explain the two types of differential.
8. What is the advantage of the clock thermostat?
9. What advantage does a low-limit hot-water temperature control have with a steam or hot-water system when a night setback is utilized?

CHAPTER 14

INSTALLING
THE LIMIT CONTROL

The term "limit control," in contrast to the term "operating control," refers to any control that has as its function the maintaining of a definite limit beyond which, or below which, the oil-burning or heat-furnishing apparatus is not allowed to operate.

The prime purpose of an *operating control* is to *initiate operation* of equipment in response to a certain change, whether it be temperature, pressure, or otherwise.

A *limit control* acts as a governor in relation to either an upper or lower level; and we have, therefore, either high-limit or low-limit controls. When the purpose of a limit control is to prevent temperature or pressure from going over a certain point, it is a high-limit control; conversely, when its purpose is to prevent the temperature or pressure from falling below a certain setting, it is a low-limit control.

In certain instances, which will be covered further on, a control may have both a limiting function and an operating function. In such case, the control may serve as a cutoff against a high or low limit and may also initiate the operation of the burner by actuating the relay.

The average applications of limit controls are to limit *temperature* and *pressure* and, in some cases, *humidity*. The heat-giving mediums which are regulated or controlled by the action of a limit control may be steam, vapor, air, or water. The type of limit control to be used will depend upon which of these mediums is used for heating purposes.

Limit controls may be direct-acting or reverse-acting. A direct-acting limit control will *open* its switch and break contact on a *rise* in pressure or temperature. A reverse-acting limit control will make a contact and *close* its switch on a *rise* in pressure or temperature. The two functions described in this paragraph may be combined in a single control.

In the event that we have a steam system, the limit control employed will be a pressure control and its purpose will be to prevent the operating steam pressure from going too high. If we have a vapor system, a vapor control will be the limit control, and it will differ basically from a steam limit control in the fact that the vapor control may be graduated in ounces and may usually run to a maximum setting of from 1 to 4 psi.

From this we get the term *vapor*, for steam, at these low pressures, is regarded as such by the industry. The limit control used on the regular domestic steam heating system, generally known as a *pressure control*, usually has a cut-in range of from 1 to 10 psi with a differential of from 1 to 5 psi. Most modern controls of this type will also carry the metric scale in kilograms per square centimeter.

SETTING A DIRECT-ACTING LIMIT CONTROL

In setting a direct-acting pressure-limit control, two scales must normally be adjusted. One will be the cut-in pressure setting, and the other will be the differential setting. The sum of these two settings determines the cutout pressure or the top level to which the pressure may rise, at which point the switching mechanism will open the circuit. Thus, the low-pressure point at which the control will restore the circuit will be the cut-in point.

The unit will then operate through the differential range until its limit is reached. From this we can see that if the cut-in point is set at 1 psi and the differential at 4, the pressure control will cut back in when the pressure drops to 1 psi and run through the 4 psi of the differential setting. The 1-psi cut-in point plus the 4-psi differential gives the top limit of 5 psi. When 5-psi gauge pressure is reached, the switch will open and the unit will cease operating.

In view of this type of setting, the necessity for a fairly broad differential becomes obvious. The longer the differential, the longer will be the "off" period, and a short differential means shorter intervals between pressure operations.

If the differential is set too low, there may be constant on-off action if it takes any length of time to satisfy the thermostat. For example, if a pressure control were set for a cut-in at 1 psi and a differential of 1 psi, its top limit would be the sum of these two, or 2 psi. At 2-psi pressure, the unit would go off and remain off until it had dropped the 1 psi differential to the cut-in point of 1 psi, which would then close the circuit and bring the burner on.

On an extremely cold day when the system is just about balancing the heat loss, this would lead to constant on and off action through the limit control before the thermostat would be satisfied. This could be remedied by raising the differential setting. On domestic steam systems, the differential setting should be *at least* 3 psi.

Some pressure controls do not use this cut-in plus differential combination to determine the cutout pressure but simply have two adjustments. One is the top limit and the other is the cut-in point at which the switch restores the circuit when the pressure drops. In this case, the operating differential is the difference between the cutout and cut-in points.

If we had a control of this type and set it for a cutout pressure of 5 psi and a cut-in pressure of 1 psi, the differential would be 4 psi, the difference between the two settings.

MOUNTING THE PRESSURE CONTROL

Pressure controls have to be mounted carefully when they are of the mercury-tube type, in order to be certain that they are level. These controls are always mounted in an upright or vertical position. The loop-siphon, or "pigtail," steam trap should always be used with a pressure control.

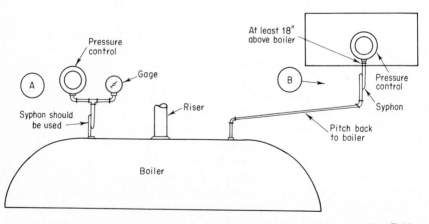

Fig. 14-1 Two methods of mounting pressure control. (*A*) Boiler mounting T'd in with gauge. (*B*) Remote mounting.

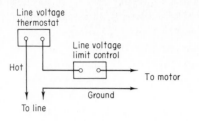

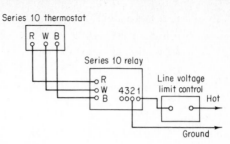

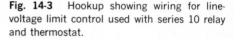

Fig. 14-2 Wiring diagram showing limit control used with line-voltage thermostat.

Fig. 14-3 Hookup showing wiring for line-voltage limit control used with series 10 relay and thermostat.

Trapping the moisture in the loop will allow only air to exert its pressure against the bellows or bourdon tube, whatever the case may be. The use of this loop, by preventing the access of water to the element, materially lengthens its life.

Because the siphon expands upon heating, it must always be placed in such a manner as to have the loop at a right angle to the mercury tube rather than parallel with it. Such a precaution will then prevent the expansion of the siphon loop from disturbing the level setting of the control and distorting its response to the actual adjusted settings.

The siphon to which the pressure control is attached should be tapped into the boiler well above the water line and as far away from it as possible. This will serve as a protection against a surging water level disturbing the control and causing intermittent on-off action.

In making up this connection, pipe dope or any joint-sealing compound must be *carefully* used on the male thread, and care should be taken to see that none of it gets into the siphon, from which it might pass to the pressure control and clog the opening.

If any vibration is expected at the boiler, mount the pressure control away from it at some distant point. In such a case, the control can be securely mounted on a wall and should be at least 1 to $1\frac{1}{2}$ ft above the top of the boiler with the siphon attached. The line from the control, in this case, must pitch back to the boiler to assure the draining of all condensate away from the control and back to the boiler.

Two-wire line-voltage limit controls should always be wired in as shown in Figs. 14-2 and 14-3. If more than one limit control is used, they should be wired in series, as shown in Fig. 14-6.

As these illustrations demonstrate, line-voltage limit controls, regardless of the type used, always break the hot line leading to the relay or apparatus being controlled. This means that they are the first controls to break the line as it leaves the fuse box to run to the burner. In this way, no current at all can get to the burner if the limit control has opened its circuit.

An operating control such as a thermostat may have its contacts closed and be calling for heat, but if the limit-control circuit is opened, the relay will not be energized at the thermostat's demand and will therefore be unable to start the burner. The use of a line-voltage limit control thus furnishes adequate protection in such a manner as to override the operating control's circuit when the limit setting is reached.

If a low-voltage limit control is used, it can be wired as shown in Fig. 14-4. In such a circuit, the limit control breaks the white line (series 10), and the relay cannot be energized. The pressure control (low-voltage type) can be used as an operating control if wired as shown in Fig. 14-5. In this case, the limit-control function and operating function are combined in the one control and the unit will operate on pressure through the adjusted differential.

The addition of a low-water-level-limit control to all steam systems is excellent protection against a cracked boiler. This control is wired in exactly as is the pressure control, breaking the hot line before it reaches the primary control.

As low-water-level-limit controls are float-operated (the falling float tipping a mercury-tube switch that opens the circuit), they are usually equipped with a drain cock whereby they can be blown off and the sediment drained away. Such controls should be drained at least once a month to prevent the sediment from building up in the float chamber. A deposit of any amount will prevent the float from settling if the water line should fall, and as a result the protection that could be offered by the control is lost.

Some low-water-level limit controls come equipped for quick installation in the gauge-glass openings of the average boiler. These types of mountings are shown in Figs. 14-8 and 14-9.

Low-water-level limit controls are sensitive to changing water levels, and precautions should be taken upon installing this type of control to see that the boiler is not priming or surging. If it is, this unsteady water line will constantly trip the float and cause intermittent on-off action. The addition of an equalizer or the use of a good boiler cleaning compound will usually remedy this condition. This type of control will

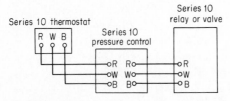

Fig. 14-4 Hookup for low-voltage series 10 Pressuretrol.

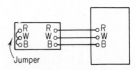

Fig. 14-5 Wiring diagram showing series 10 limit control used as an operating control.

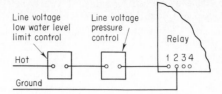

Fig. 14-6   Hookup showing two limit controls: water-level and pressure.

automatically restore the circuit when the water level of the boiler is raised.

Some low-water cutoffs are equipped with an extra circuit which closes an auxiliary line when the water level drops, and the main line circuit is opened.   This auxiliary circuit can be hooked into a bell, buzzer, or light which will give an audible or visible warning when the unit has ceased operating because of the cutoff action of the control. Immediately after the installation of this control the water level of the boiler should be lowered and raised several times to test its action, and this procedure should be repeated at the start of each heating season.

LIMIT CONTROLS ON HOT-WATER SYSTEMS

On hot-water heating systems, the function of the limit control is normally to guard against the hot water reaching too high a temperature.

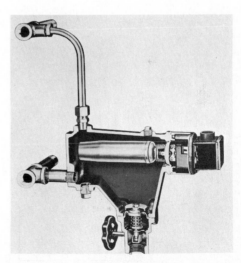

Fig. 14-7   McDonnell & Miller No. 67 low-water fuel cutoff for boilers of any size operating up to 20 psi.   This control provides an independent extra switch for low-water alarm or electric water feeder.   Equipped with quick hookup gauge-glass connections.

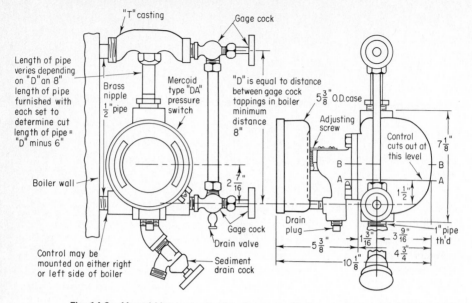

Fig. 14-8   Mercoid low-water-level and pressure-limit control mounted on boiler with independent water column.

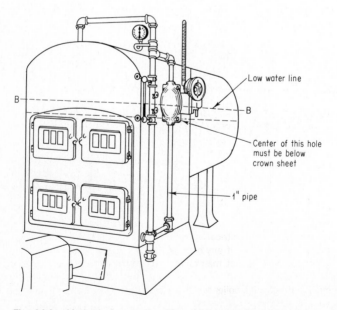

Fig. 14-9   Method of mounting Mercoid combination low-water-level and pressure limit control.

Fig. 14-10   McDonnell & Miller low-water fuel cutoff No. 63, for use on boilers operating at pressures up to 50 psi.   This control is installed with 1-in. equalizer fittings.

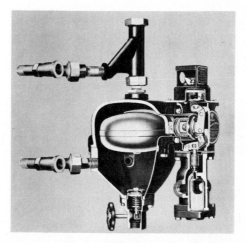

Fig. 14-11   A combination boiler water feeder and low-water cutoff.   This limit control combines mechanical and electrical operation.   It is installed well below the normal operating boiler water level.   If any condition arises in which the water put into the boiler by the feeder does not maintain a safe minimum water level, the cutoff switch stops the burner.

If during normal operation, the boiler water line should drop below its normal operating range, the first function of this combination control is to add a small amount of water, thereby keeping the unit in operation.   If this does not occur, the low-water cutoff will then stop all operation.   (*McDonnell & Miller, Inc.*)

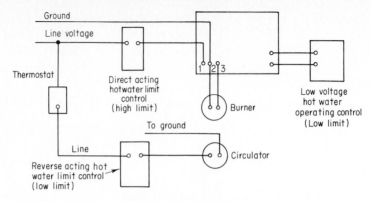

Fig. 14-12 Wiring diagram for hot-water heating system with domestic hot water, showing direct- and reverse-acting hot-water limit controls and low-voltage hot-water operating control.

In such case, it is a high-limit control and is wired into the circuit as shown in Figs. 14-2 and 14-3, respectively, depending upon whether a line-voltage or low-voltage thermostat is used.

With a hot-water heating system, the *direct-acting* hot-water limit control opens or closes the circuit to the burner as the water temperature rises or falls. If a *reverse-acting* limit control is used, it will make or break the circuit to the circulator, making the circuit on a rise in temperature and breaking it on a drop. It is, therefore, a low-limit control.

This is just the reverse of the action of the direct-acting control on the boiler. The use of a reverse-acting hot-water limit control will prevent the circulator from operating if the water falls below the temperature setting of the control.

Hot-water limit controls may have either of two methods of mounting. These can be the *strap-on* type or the *immersion* type, as shown in Fig. 14-13. An immersion-type hot-water temperature high-limit control should always be installed in such a manner that it will not be in the path of water from a hot or cold inlet, but should be placed, if it is direct-acting, in the top of the boiler where the well is in the path of the convection currents set up by the circulation of the water in the boiler. It may also be mounted in the riser, provided that there is free circulation and the riser cannot be closed off.

If the hot-water temperature control is used as an operating control for the purpose of regulating the temperature of domestic faucet hot water, it should be placed in the boiler as close to the generating coil as possible. If an outside generator is used, it should be inserted in that or instead be placed in the hot-water tank itself. The method of connecting a hot-water temperature-limit control when it is functioning as an operating control is shown in Figs. 14-5 and 14-12.

On a gravity hot-water system, the normal setting on the high-limit control is about 180°F. However, this may be varied to any setting that will furnish the desired amount of heat. If radiation is inadequate, a temperature of the setting may have to be raised to 200°F or even higher.

On a forced-feed hot-water system equipped with a tankless coil for domestic hot-water supply, the high-limit control will normally be set at 190°F and even raised as high as 220°F if the severity of the weather demands it.

The operating hot-water temperature control which is used to maintain a constant boiler water temperature should be set at 160°F, or whatever temperature is desirable in view of domestic hot-water requirements. If a reverse-acting hot-water low-limit control is used to control the operation of the circulator, it should normally be set about 140°F.

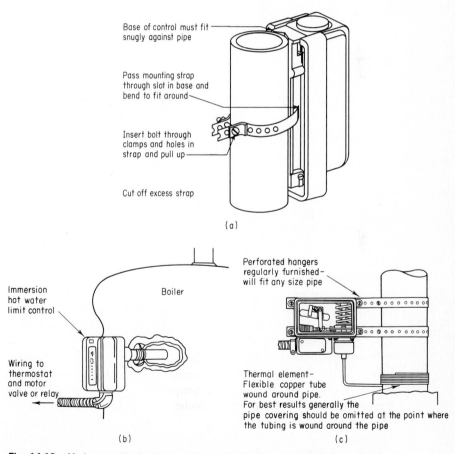

Fig. 14-13   Various methods of mounting temperature-limit controls. (*a*) and (*c*) Strap-on type. (*b*) Immersion type.

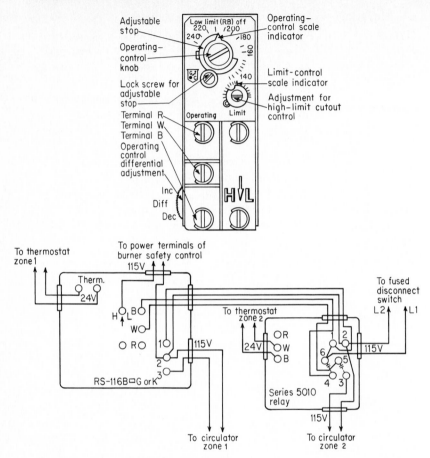

Fig. 14-14 Wiring diagram using RS-116B, -G, or -K in a tankless coil domestic water, gas- or oil-fired, forced hot-water two-zone system. (*General Controls ITT*)

The reverse-acting control must always be set 20° below the operating hot-water control.

With a tankless coil, the use of a reverse-acting low-limit control on the circulator is a must. The action of this control in shutting off the circulator as the boiler temperature drops prevents the hot water from being entirely depleted from the boiler. It thus maintains at all times a reservoir of hot water within the boiler for heating the tankless coil that is furnishing the domestic supply. It is becoming increasingly popular in the industry to combine the function of a forced hot-water system of controls into a single control unit. This eliminates unnecessary costs involved in wiring, tappings, etc. Typical wiring of this type of combination hot-water immersion control as used in a forced hot-water system with tankless coil is shown in Fig. 14-14.

COMBINATION HOT-WATER TEMPERATURE CONTROLLER AND RELAY

The series L8048, L8049, and L8052 Honeywell Aquastat relays are immersion-type controls used with a 24-volt (low-voltage) thermostat on steam and forced circulation hot-water (hydronic) heating systems. They combine (except L8048C) a high-limit water-temperature control with an intermediate switching relay for controlling the burner and water circulator. Some models have a low-limit switch for maintaining minimum boiler-water temperature during thermostat-off periods. They are mounted directly on the boiler. Their liquid-filled sensing bulb is installed in an immersion well at a suitably located boiler tapping.

COMBINATION PRIMARY-CONTROL, HIGH- AND LOW-LIMIT WATER TEMPERATURE AND CIRCULATOR CONTROL

See Chap. 12, Figs. 12-19, 12-20 and 12-21

WARM-AIR LIMIT CONTROLS

The installation of warm-air limit controls follows the same connection diagrams as for steam or hot-water limit controls. The hot line leading to the relay is intercepted by the control as shown in Figs. 14-2, 14-3, and 14-6.

The purpose of this control is to act as a safety device. It prevents the furnace bonnet air temperature from becoming excessive by stopping the burner and restoring the circuit when the bonnet air temperature has dropped to within a safe limit.

With a forced-warm-air system whereby the air is furnished to the rooms by a fan, we have an additional limit control in the form of a fan control. This breaks the circuit to the fan.

The fan control is a reverse-acting limit control which opens its circuit on a temperature drop. Thus it will operate the fan or blower only when warm air is available at the furnace bonnet. The action of this control is the same as the reverse-acting hot-water limit control that operates the circulator pump in hot-water heating systems.

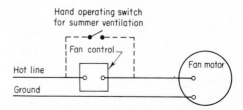

Fig. 14-15   Wiring diagram for fan control (reverse-acting limit control).

If we combine the limit function and the fan-control function into one control, it is then a *combination fan and limit control*. For the connection diagram of this combination control, see Fig. 14-16.

In locating the warm-air limit control or the fan control at the bonnet of the furnace, the thermal element of the control must be placed so that there will be air circulation around it at all times. Care must be taken so that no direct heating surface, metal or otherwise, is closer than an average of 8 in. to the control element.

The reason for this is to prevent heat from radiating from the surrounding metal surfaces to the thermal element of the control and causing it to become satisfied, thereby interrupting the circuit before the proper temperature level in the bonnet is reached. This will result in unsatisfactory operation of the system, causing the burner to shut off before the bonnet temperature-limit level is reached.

If the fan-control element is affected because of radiant heat from the surrounding surfaces, the fan may come on prematurely and deliver cooler air to the rooms. The figure "8 in." given above is but a guide, and the control manufacturer's instructions should be consulted.

Some manufacturers require only a 3-in. distance of the control's element from the bonnet surface, while others require a 12-in. distance. Use a shield or baffle if necessary to protect the element from radiant heat. This, however, should not be done with a limit control if there is danger of reverse circulation with a gravity system.

Avoid the location of any type of warm-air control in a riser. Too many conditions can alter the circulation of air through the riser. For example, on certain occasions a riser could act as a cold-air return, and such air moving around the control element will disturb or prevent its normal operation. Such a condition could cause the burner to run continuously as well as stop the operation of a fan completely in a forced-warm-air system.

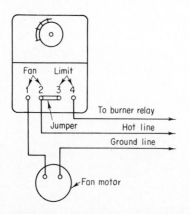
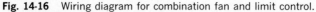

Fig. 14-16 Wiring diagram for combination fan and limit control.

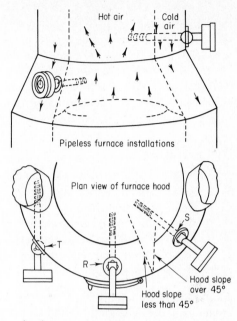

Hot air · · Cold air

Pipeless furnace installations

Plan view of furnace hood

S

T

R

Hood slope over 45°

Hood slope less than 45°

Fig. 14-17 Limit-control mounting, showing use of swivel-type mounting bracket. (*Mercoid Corp.*)

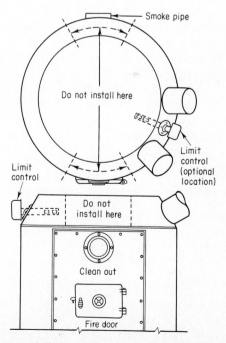

Smoke pipe

Do not install here

Limit control

Limit control (optional location)

Limit control

Do not install here

Clean out

Fire door

Fig. 14-18 Location of warm-air limit control. (*General Controls ITT*)

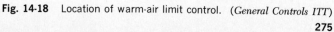

Again with a forced system, the gravity circulation that occurs before the fan is brought on may be slow or extremely sluggish, as is usually the case. The location of the control in an instance such as the foregoing may lead to excessively high and even dangerous bonnet temperatures.

Another case that argues against the installation of such controls in warm-air risers is demonstrated by the almost complete loss of circulation that occurs in the riser when its outlet registers are closed for some reason. In this case, the control will operate erratically.

It can be seen that the three primary rules in installing warm-air limit controls are:

1. Protect the control from radiant heat.
2. Be certain there is a free circulation of air over the thermal element of the control.
3. If separate fan and limit controls are installed, the thermal elements of these controls must be as close together as possible to assure the coordinated response and proper operating sequence of the burner and fan.

In the event that the control body itself is mounted against the bonnet, a layer of asbestos should be placed between the back wall of the control and the bonnet surface, if such surface will exceed 165°F in temperature. This will help prevent the surrounding (ambient) temperature from affecting the operation of the control.

In setting warm-air controls, the primary purpose is to furnish adequate heat to the house with as low a setting as is possible. These settings, of course, will vary first with the type of system, whether gravity or forced circulation, and secondly with the adequacy with which the size of the system makes up the heat losses from the house.

The recommendations in Tables 14-1 and 14-2 are not to be regarded as an absolute indication of what the setting will be, but as a guide to the approximate settings under the conditions indicated. The control manufacturer gives the settings for the average control; consult his directions if there is any doubt.

Table 14-1 Approximate Recommended Warm-air Limit-control Settings for Gravity Warm-air Systems

Control type	System characteristic	Cut-out point (high limit), °F	Cut-in point, °F	Differential maintained, °F
Limit-control setting	Normal-sized average system	250–300	200–250	50
	Furnace oversized; good circulation	200–250	170–220	30
	Furnace too small; poor circulation	350	280	70

Table 14-2 Approximate Recommended Warm-air Limit-control Settings for Forced-warm-air Systems

Control type	System characteristic	Cut-out point, °F	Cut-in point, °F	Differential maintained, °F
Limit-control setting	Average system	200	160	25 (fixed)
	Excessive fan capacity	180	150	30
	Low fan capacity	250	200	50
Fan-control setting	Average system	100	140	40
	Long ducts	140	170	30
	Short ducts	90	130	40

From the foregoing, we can see that the general installation and setting procedure for limit controls varies with the control and type of system. Generally make all connections securely, scraping and cleaning the wires before binding them to the terminal screws.

Do not use rigid conduit in such a manner that it is directly attached to the limit-control casing. In the event of expansion and contraction due to heating and cooling, this may cause the control to be unleveled and affect its accuracy. Use pieces of BX or Greenfield to make the connection from the conduit to the control.

QUESTIONS

1. What is a limit control? An operating control?
2. What determines the type of limit control that will be used?
3. Explain the difference between a direct-acting and a reverse-acting control.
4. What is a disadvantage of a close differential setting on a limit control?
5. How should a pressure control always be mounted?
6. Show with a diagram how two limit controls can be wired into the same system.
7. Why is it sometimes necessary to drain a water-level limit control?
8. Explain the function of a direct-acting limit control on a hot-water heating system; of a reverse-acting limit control.
9. Where should a hot-water temperature operating control be located?
10. How should a reverse-acting hot-water temperature control always be set?
11. What precautions must be observed when installing a warm-air limit control?
12. What is meant by the term "low-limit" control? "High-limit" control?

13. Explain the function of a low-water cutoff.
14. Explain the function of a combination feeder and low-water cutoff.
15. Give three advantages of the combination hot-water temperature and intermediate-relay control.
16. Where is the combination control noted in Question 15 installed?
17. Explain the operation of the Boilermaster control discussed in Chap. 12 and shown in Figs. 12-19, 12-20, and 12-21.

CHAPTER 15

INSTALLING
THE PRIMARY CONTROL

The term *primary control* is used to refer to those combustion safety controls that are usually grouped under the general term of "relay" or "stack relay." These controls also are known by various names, such as "Protectorelay," "Pyratherm," "combustion control," and "stack switch."

In all cases, they are controls which have as their main purpose to prevent operation of the oil burner when conditions exist that make such operation unsafe or hazardous. For example, any delay in the initial ignition cycle will enable a considerable amount of oil vapor to collect in the combustion chamber and the flue passages of the boiler or furnace.

The sudden ignition, after the delay, of these collected oil vapors will result in a *puffback* or explosion of varying degrees of intensity, depending upon how long the ignition may have been delayed. One of the main purposes of the combustion control is to prevent any such occurrence.

The foregoing is but one of a number of conditions in which the primary control may be called upon to perform its function. Another condition might be the failure of the oil supply. In this case there would be ignition, but no fuel, and the control would be called upon to shut down the burner because of its failure to establish a flame. Note that the stack relay directly controls the operation of the burner from the safety as well as the normal operating viewpoint. If the burner is operating normally, the relay does not interfere, but if for any reason there is no fire on a starting cycle or an unwarranted interruption during the normal operating cycle, this stack relay will come into play and shut down the unit.

When a stack relay has *permanently* shut down the unit because of its failure to establish normal combustion, the relay has "gone into safety" and the burner will be unable to operate until the control is reset manually. Upon manual resetting of the control the burner will start again, but if the same difficulty still exists, the relay will go into safety again and continue to do so until the condition has been corrected.

All stack relays, regardless of by whom they are manufactured, will go into safety and shut down the unit if combustion is not taking place within a short period of time after starting, regardless of the cause. If combustion is interrupted during the normal operating cycle (after the burner has been running for a period of time) and the flame suddenly disappears, some relays will go into safety and shut down the unit. Others will recycle and bring the burner on again automatically for another try, in the event that the trouble may clear itself. When a relay performs the latter function, it is said to "recycle on flame failure."

An example of this would be the temporary clogging of a nozzle, which would extinguish the fire. With some relays the extinguishing of the fire by the clogged nozzle would bring the safety shutoff mechanism into play and the control would go into safety. It would have to be reset manually before the burner could start.

This type of action is characteristic of primary controls of the nonrecycling type, but not of a recycling-type primary control. In the latter instance the control would shut down the burner for a short interval and then start it again. If the nozzle were then suddenly blown clean, the unit would operate normally; but if it remained clogged and no fire appeared, the control would then go into safety and shut off the burner. This is what is meant by the term "recycling on flame failure."

SAFETY FUNCTION OF THE PRIMARY CONTROL

The safety function of the primary control is tied up with normal combustion. If a normal fire appears, the burner is allowed to run. If no fire appears or the fire is so defective as not to liberate enough heat, the burner will be shut down and the control has gone into safety. The heat of the flame is the important factor. It is this heat that operates the control.

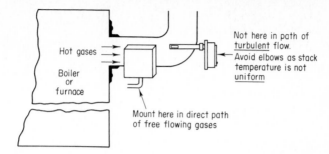

Fig. 15-1 Correct and incorrect methods of mounting primary control.

If the fire appears, its heat causes the control to shunt to a permanent circuit by actuating a heat-driven mechanism, and the burner is allowed to remain on. If no flame occurs, then no heat actuates the heat-driven mechanism of the control and it remains in a temporary circuit which is slowly going to break (by means of a warp-type electrically heated switch) and shut off the burner.

Thus the stack control establishes a temporary circuit by means of which the switch that is feeding line voltage to the burner is operated. This temporary circuit opens after about 90 sec, thereby indirectly interrupting the line circuit to the burner. If a flame appears, this temporary circuit is shunted out and a permanent circuit established to hold in the relay clapper feeding the burner.

These temporary and permanent circuits in the primary control that operate the line switch to the burner are ordinarily opened and closed and maintained by the low-voltage thermostat or hot-water temperature control. We can see that the stack relay also is an integrating control. This means that it integrates the temperature demands of other controls with the safety and operating functions.

Simply stated, the stack relay operates the burner upon the demand of the thermostat. It will allow the burner to continue operation upon the demand of operating controls if the flame conditions are normal.

If no flame or insufficient flame appears, it will shut down the burner and has thus gone into safety. The burner cannot then be started until the control has been reset manually. It will continue to go into safety after each reset until the troublesome condition has been corrected. The control should *not* be reset continually without correcting the cause of trouble.

INSTALLATION OF THE PRIMARY CONTROL

This now leads us to the installation of the control. Since it responds to the heat of the flame and depends upon that heat to actuate its bimetallic operating element, it follows that its location in regard to the heat liberated by the fire is important.

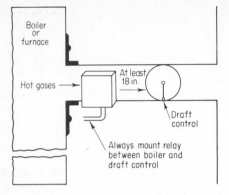

Fig. 15-2   Correct position of stack-mounted relay in relation to draft control.

At this point it would be well to differentiate between the methods used by primary controls to sense the fact that the burner is producing a flame.   There are several ways in which this is done: (1) By a heat-sensitive bimetallic element such as the helix coil, (2) by a heat-sensitive burner-mounted device such as General Control's Combustion Detector, the Mercoid Vis-A-Flame Bulb, or (3) by a *light*-actuated photocell such as Honeywell's Photocell (Fig. 12-54) or the cad cell Flame Detector used with Honeywell or White-Rodgers primary controls.

Those heat- and light-sensitive devices referred to in (2) and (3) are mounted on the burner, usually in the flash tube, by the burner manufacturer.

This chapter concerns itself mainly with primary controls using a heat-sensitive bimetallic element that requires mounting on the stack or boiler at an appropriate opening and well that permits free flow of the combustion gases over the element or helix coil.   Cad-cell controls are covered in Chap. 34.

The bimetal stack element of the primary control must always be in the path of the hot gases rising from the flame.   These gases must flow and circulate freely about the element.   The line of flow of these gases over the bimetal should be direct and not excessively turbulent. This means that the element should be placed in a straight run of pipe and not in any elbows, tees, or offsets.   It should be as close to the boiler or furnace as possible so that the gases coming in contact with it will be reasonably hot.

Usually the minimum temperature to which the primary control element should be subjected is 300°F and the maximum about 900°F. Most relays come with some adjustable device to provide for variations in stack temperature conditions (Fig. 15-4).

In installing a new burner, it is wise to test the stack temperatures to which the primary control may be subjected.   This can be done before wiring the control in permanently.

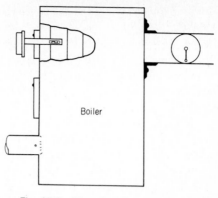

Fig. 15-3   Mounting through boiler door.

Simply run a temporary hot and ground line directly to the burner and start it operating. Test the temperature at the proposed location of the control by inserting a stack thermometer through a small hole drilled in the stack at that point. Leave the stack thermometer in the path of the hot gases until it stops gaining in temperature. This may take 10 or 20 min, and from a cold start even longer. Plug the hole with a sheet-metal screw after the test.

If the stack thermometer reaches 850°F, the location chosen for the control is not the proper one, and a spot more distant from the furnace or boiler should be selected. That temperature should be the hottest to which the control's element will be subjected, for if the stack temperature goes to 850°F on the initial firing of a new installation, it will run *considerably higher* after the unit has run for some time and the flue passages have become coated with soot. This soot will cut down on the amount of heat absorbed by the boiler or furnace and thereby raise the temperature of the gases going up the stack. This means that after a short period of operation the stack temperature will rise well above 850°F and reach too close to the element's temperature limit for com-

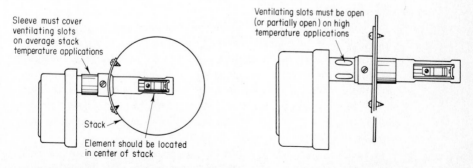

Fig. 15-4   Method of adapting Honeywell Protectorelay to varying stack temperatures by means of a movable sleeve.

fort.   Conversely, if the stack thermometer shows a reading below 300°F, the control should be moved closer to the boiler or closer to the source of heat, that is, the flame itself.

It is not necessary to test every installation this way, but on conversion jobs with round coal-fired boilers it is a wise practice, for such units usually run with high stack temperatures that seriously shorten the life of the control's bimetallic element.

If stack temperatures are excessively high, the body of the control itself may have to be insulated.   This can be done by providing the back plate of the control with a cover of asbestos or other insulating material.

One control manufacturer provides the primary control with a highly polished back plate which reflects the heat away from the body of the control and back upon the stack itself.   Another provides a metal baffle plate that allows air to circulate between the back of the control and the plate.

Relays should be installed with the bimetal element in a horizontal position with mercury-tube-operated relays, as they depend upon being level for normal operation.

All relays that are stack mounted must be on the boiler or furnace side of the draft control with at least 18 in. between the relay and the draft stabilizer (Fig. 15-2).   This is to make certain that cold air entering through the draft-regulator opening will not be able to reach the bimetal element of the relay and affect its performance.

In the event that an oil-burning boiler or furnace that is well designed is being used, it may not be wise to install the control in the smoke pipe as the stack temperature may build up too slowly or not be high enough to operate the control normally.   Use the opening in the fire door or flue passage door usually provided in such cases and be sure when the control is properly inserted so the helix coil or element does not touch any part of the boiler, as this may cause the driving mechanism to bind or operate too slowly, thus throwing the control into safety.

It may even be necessary to tap an opening in the boiler or furnace door if the stack temperature is not high enough and there is no such opening provided.

In mounting the control, make the necessary size hole in the smoke pipe large enough to permit free insertion of the control.   *Always use the flange provided by the manufacturer* when mounting the control on the stack.   The use of this flange is eliminated when a boiler door mounting is utilized.   Seal up with furnace cement any cracks, openings, or gaps around the mounting bracket and thereby prevent cool air from the basement from reaching the control's element and causing it to operate erratically.

When a stack relay is wired in, care should be taken to attach the wire to the terminals as directed by the manufacturer.   Normally No. 1

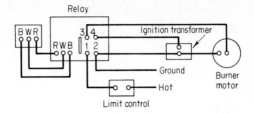

Fig. 15-5   Wiring diagram for a series 10 Honeywell Protectorelay, intermittent ignition.

is the hot line, No. 2 the ground terminal, and No. 3 the motor and transformer terminal if it is constant ignition.   With intermittent ignition, No. 3 is the hot motor terminal and No. 4 the hot ignition terminal (Figs. 15-5 and 15-6).

The transformer and motor always have their ground legs going back to the No. 2 terminal.   Hot lines should be black-colored wire and the ground wires should have white insulation.   The wiring should be done through a junction box, as shown in Fig. 15-8.

Whenever rigid conduit is used, the rigid connection should not be made at the relay, but instead from 8 to 12 in. of Greenfield or BX should be used between the rigid tubing and the control.   This provides freedom of movement for removal of the control and for adjustment of it in the event that future service conditions demand it, as well as for cleaning the element.   No. 14 wire should be used for the line-voltage connections and No. 18 for low-voltage.

Many communities have regulations covering the low-voltage wiring, and BX more than likely is demanded to provide armored protection for this type of wire.   Needless to say, all wiring should conform to local community and Fire Underwriters' regulations.

Where the wires are joined, the splices should be electrically secure without solder.   The splices can then be soldered and covered with

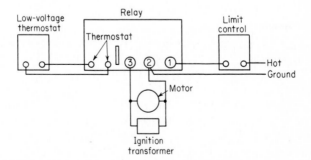

Fig. 15-6   Connection diagram for General Controls two-wire low-voltage primary control.

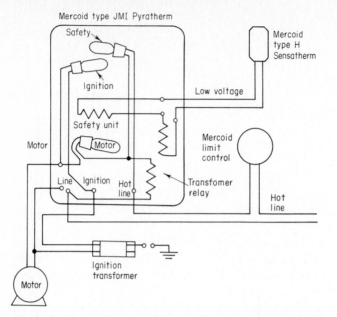

Fig. 15-7 Wiring diagram and internal circuit of a Mercoid JMI Pyratherm.

rubber tape and then friction tape and should be made only in junction boxes.

If the wires are to be connected to screw terminals on the relay connection panel, they should be thoroughly scraped and wrapped around the screw *with the loop made in the same direction of rotation as that of the screw when it is tightened.*

Only the foregoing rules are necessary for installing a primary control properly. However, as this control is the most important in all oil-burner installations, every care should be taken to adhere to these simple

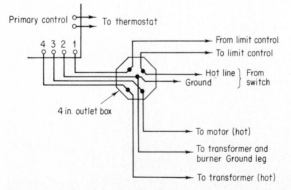

Fig. 15-8 Wiring burner connections to primary control through junction box.

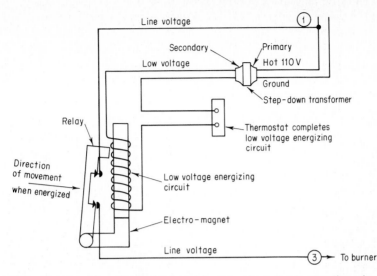

Fig. 15-9   Diagram of how thermostat completes low-voltage circuit, actuating relay and thereby shunting line voltage to burner.

directions.   A carefully installed, easily accessible relay is insurance against unnecessary service demands during winter operation.

Once a season, the relay should be removed from the stack or boiler door mounting and the bimetallic element cleaned thoroughly of the layer of heat-insulating soot that will have collected on it.   This will prevent sluggish response to stack temperature changes and considerably increase the life of the element.

QUESTIONS

1. Explain how the safety mechanism of the primary control performs its functions.
2. What is meant by the term "gone into safety"?
3. What essential condition must always be observed when installing a primary control?
4. What are the usual stack temperature limits for this control?
5. What will happen to the primary control if the stack temperature is too low?
6. What wires go to terminals 1, 2, 3, and 4, respectively?
7. Should a rigid connection be made to the primary control?   Why?
8. Why should the stack element be cleaned at least once a year?
9. What three means or devices does the primary control use to detect whether combustion is taking place?

10. Explain what is meant by a light-sensitive device, a heat-sensitive device.
11. Which of the two mentioned in question 10 acts more quickly?
12. What flame-sensing devices are mounted on the burner by the manufacturer?   Why?
13. What is a cad cell?

CHAPTER 16
CONTROL SYSTEMS: STEAM

Having considered the function, location, and installation of the thermostat, limit control, and primary control, the next step will be to arrange and group these controls to regulate the operation of different types of heating systems.

Control systems as such depend, for the individual controls selected and for the method of grouping, upon the type of heat-giving medium. Thus whether or not a system is supplied by steam, hot water, or warm air will directly determine the controls to be used and the way they will be grouped, installed, and wired.

Because of this, we can divide all domestic oil-burner control systems into three types, namely, those used for *steam, hot water,* and *warm air.* The latter two, hot water and warm air, may further be broken down into *gravity* and *forced-circulation systems.*

In spite of this breakdown of control groupings into systems depending upon the kind of heat being furnished, it will be found that certain controls are always present to provide the basis for normal automatic operation plus safety protection. These controls as we have already seen are the *thermostat,* the *limit control,* and the *primary control.*

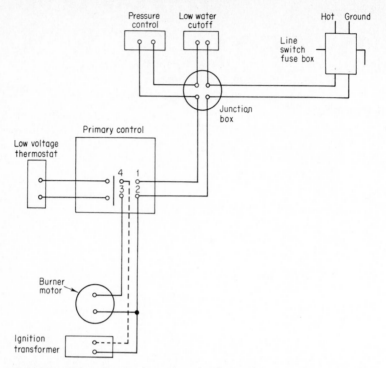

Fig. 16-1   Wiring diagram for a steam heating system.

Different types of thermostats, limit controls, and even primary controls may be required to fit the needs of a system as well as the burner, but the basic function will remain the same. In all cases the thermostat responds to temperature demands and through the *primary control* usually operates the system in response to those demands. The *limit control* stands guard to shut off the flow of current in the event that the temperature or pressure limit for which it is set is reached.

Figure 16-1 shows the control wiring diagram for a *simple steam system*. The hot line running from the main house switch runs through a separate fuse and switch to the junction box and then through the limit (pressure) control to the No. 1 terminal on the primary control. The ground line runs to the No. 2 terminal on the primary control. If the burner is to operate on constant ignition, both the motor and ignition transformer will be connected to the No. 3 terminal and of course to No. 2, the ground terminal. If intermittent ignition is to be used, the ignition transformer will be connected to the No. 4 terminal, through which it will receive its current, and grounded back to the No. 2 terminal.

The thermostat will be connected to the low-voltage terminals on the relay.

DEMAND FOR HEAT

In the event of a demand for heat in a steam system, the thermostat will actuate the clapper in the relay by means of low voltage. As the clapper is pulled in, it transfers current from the No. 1 terminal to the No. 3 terminal on the primary control. The burner motor and ignition will now come on and the unit is operating.

Either one of two controls will now determine the sequence of *normal* operation of the system. These are the *thermostat* and *pressure control*. If the thermostat is satisfied by a rise in room temperature, it will break its contact and deenergize the relay, interrupting the flow of current from the No. 1 terminal to the No. 3 and thereby stopping the burner.

In the event that a considerable period of time is required to bring up enough heat to satisfy the thermostat, the pressure (limit) control setting may be reached and this control will then shut off the flow of current to the No. 1 terminal on the primary control. This will result in deenergizing the primary of the step-down transformer, and the thermostat will no longer be able to hold the clapper in, even though

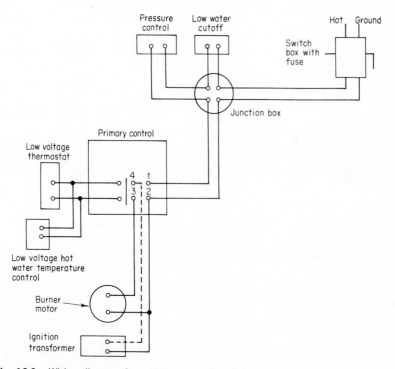

Fig. 16-2 Wiring diagram for a steam system with hot-water temperature control for domestic hot-water supply.

it is making contact. Thus the primary control is deprived of all current and the burner, consequently, is stopped.

When the pressure drops, the circuit will be restored; and if the thermostat is still calling for heat (make contact), the unit will resume operation.

In the event of abnormal operation, that is, no fire or insufficient fire appearing, the safety function of the primary control takes over and the unit is shut down. It has gone "into safety."

It will be noted from Fig. 16-1 that this *control system* provides only for heat and not for domestic hot-water supply. The control system in Fig. 16-2 shows the addition of a hot-water temperature control to provide for this added feature. The control is mounted on the boiler below the water line, to provide a means of furnishing automatic domestic hot-water temperature control. It is also a low-voltage operating control, as is the thermostat, and is wired to the primary control parallel with the thermostat.

Any time the temperature of the boiler water falls below the setting on this control, it will actuate the *primary control* and bring the burner on to raise the boiler water temperature to its setting. If this way, it keeps a supply of hot water in the boiler to satisfy the demands of the hot-water generator.

It should be noted that if the thermostat calls for heat on a steam system, it will be necessary for the water to go to 212°F to provide that steam, and the setting of the hot-water temperature control will be ignored. As a result, the domestic hot-water supply is hotter and more ample in the winter.

A mixing valve is usually provided in this case whereby cold water is bypassed into the hot-water line to bring its temperature down to reasonable limits. The use of a *hot-water temperature control* also will prevent the boiler water from cooling too much during the night if the thermostat is set back for any considerable number of degrees, by bringing the burner on for short runs to maintain the required boiler water temperature setting.

UNIT HEATER HOOKUPS

In the event that *unit heaters* are to be used with a steam system instead of radiators, it will be necessary to add an additional control to the system in the form of a *reverse-acting pressure control*. This control will break the line voltage to the unit heater fan and will not allow it to come on until sufficient steam pressure has been built up.

From Fig. 16-3 it should be noted that the thermostat controls the operation of the burner and the direct-acting high-limit control has its usual function. When unit heaters are used, this direct-acting limit control should be set for at least 7 or 8 psi.

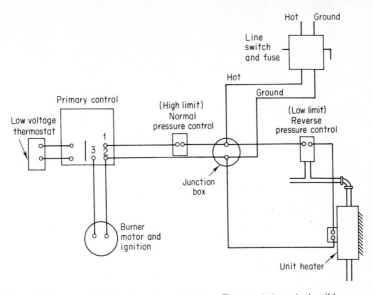

Fig. 16-3   Unit heater hookup with steam sýstem.   Thermostat controls oil-burner operation only.

With the hookup provided for in Fig. 16-3, the burner will go off when the thermostat is satisfied, but the unit heater will continue to operate until the pressure has fallen to the setting on the reverse pressure limit control.

In large halls, stores, etc., this override occasioned by the continued action of the unit heater (after the thermostat is satisfied) until the pressure has been dissipated is hardly noticeable and of little consequence.

If closer control is required on unit heater installations with electrical control systems, the wiring hookup in Fig. 16-4 can be used.   In this case when the thermostat calls for heat, it will energize the switching relay.   Through terminal No. 4, the current passes to the primary control which operates the burner.

Note the jumper across the low-voltage terminals of the primary control.   Through terminal No. 3 of the switching relay, current passes to the unit heater, first being interrupted by the reverse pressure control.   Here, when the thermostat calls for heat, current flows to the burner and unit heater.   The burner will begin to operate but not the unit heater, as the reverse control will keep it off until the low-limit pressure setting has been reached.   When enough pressure is present to actuate the reverse control, the unit heater will come on and remain on until either the thermostat is satisfied or the pressure drops below the 1-psi setting on the reverse pressure control.

Notice that with this hookup when the thermostat is satisfied both the burner and unit heater cease operation; thus the override present

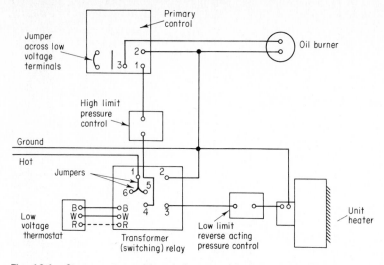

Fig. 16-4 Steam system with unit heater. An "integrated system," since both burner and unit are simultaneously controlled by low-voltage thermostat. (*General Controls ITT*)

in the system in Fig. 16-3 has been eliminated by the use of the relay (switching relay). This is called an "integrated system," because the temperature-controlling device (thermostat) operates both the heat-producing and the heat-delivering mechanisms, that is, the oil burner and unit heater, simultaneously.

A third system for operating unit heaters is shown in Fig. 16-5. This system is somewhat more expensive to operate, as there is no thermostatic control of the burner. The burner operates constantly between the limits set for it on the pressure-limit control, maintaining a "head" of steam pressure that is always available for the unit heater.

The thermostat controls the unit heater directly by energizing the switching relay, which in turn furnishes line voltage to the unit heater through the reverse pressure control. When the thermostat calls for heat, the unit heater comes on immediately, provided that there is enough pressure to close the contact of the reverse pressure control, and will remain on until the thermostat is satisfied or the pressure drops below the 1-psi setting on the reverse control.

With a system such as this, the operating pressure control on the boiler should always be set higher (about 2 psi) than the setting of the reverse control that limits the operation of the unit heater.

One disadvantage of this system is that the pressure control acting as an operating control must also serve as the high-limit control for the boiler. This cannot be regarded as good practice. If for any reason the mercury tube in the control was locked in the on position, or there was a short circuit in the low-voltage wiring to this control, the unit would operate continually. It would, in such case, deprive the boiler of all electrical limit protection.

If steam was produced more rapidly than it was condensed by the unit heater or heaters, the pressure would build up until it was sufficient to open the safety valve on the boiler and blow off. This can be guarded against by installing the *optional line-voltage high-limit pressure control* shown in Fig. 16-5.

Many times instead of using a low-limit (reverse) pressure control to prevent the operation of the unit heater fan until steam at sufficient pressure exists, a hot-water temperature control is used for this purpose.

The control is usually of the surface strap-on type. It is strapped on the return line somewhere between the unit and the steam trap, as shown in Fig. 16-6. This is a better location than strapping it on the face of the unit heater coils proper.

The water-temperature control is usually set at about 215°F, as such a setting will then indicate that some steam pressure exists through the unit heater. This system, as shown in Fig. 16-6, is also equipped with a manual switch, which enables the unit heater to be operated automatically by the thermostat, to be turned off completely, or to operate continuously independent of the thermostat. The latter provides availability of the unit heater fan for air circulation purposes during the summer.

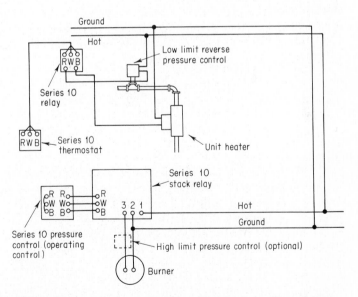

Fig. 16-5 Wiring diagram showing series 10 control hookup with unit heater. Thermostat controls operation of unit heater only, and burner is operated by series 10 Pressuretrol.

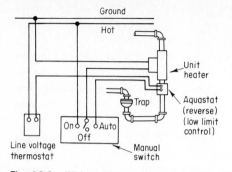
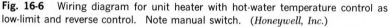

Fig. 16-6 Wiring diagram for unit heater with hot-water temperature control as low-limit and reverse control. Note manual switch. (*Honeywell, Inc.*)

Unique situations sometimes arise in which it may be necessary to furnish additional heat from a system already supplying heat by direct radiation. It may be desirable to furnish this additional supply of heat by means of a unit heater.

The unit heater in such a case is a supplementary source of heat. In a hookup such as this, two thermostats are required, one to operate the burner for the main source of heat, that is, the radiation, and the other to operate the unit heater, as shown in Fig. 16-7.

With a wiring hookup such as this, the position of the unit heater in the system is purely secondary. It cannot begin to operate unless the thermostat controlling the burner in response to the direct radiation demands in operating the unit, for although the line-voltage thermostat operating the unit heater is calling for heat, the unit heater will be unable to perform unless there is sufficient steam pressure on the system to

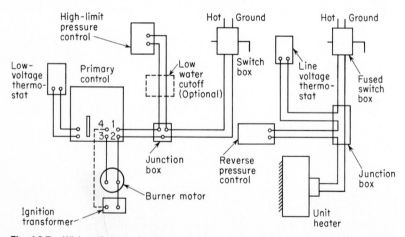

Fig. 16-7 Wiring diagram for steam system using unit heater to supplement direct radiation. (*General Controls ITT*)

actuate the reverse-action pressure control that interrupts the flow of current to the unit heater fan motor.

This steam pressure will exist in the system only if the low-voltage thermostat that responds to the primary radiation output is in the ON position, thus energizing the primary control and bringing the burner on.

Plainly stated, the *line-voltage thermostat can only succeed in operating the unit heater if there is pressure on the boiler to operate the reverse pressure control.*

This pressure can only be furnished by the low-voltage thermostat's operation of the burner. It can be seen from this that the position of the unit heater in such a case is little more than that of an auxiliary or supplementary source of heat.

QUESTIONS

1. What determines the kind of individual controls that will be used and the way in which they are connected?
2. Explain the sequence of operation for a simple steam system equipped for domestic hot-water supply.
3. Draw the wiring diagram for the system in question 2.
4. What is a unit heater?
5. Explain the function of a reverse-acting limit control in a unit heater control hookup.
6. Draw a wiring diagram for a steam system with an auxiliary unit heater.
7. What is meant by an integrated system?
8. Explain the sequence of operation of the system shown in Fig. 16-7.
9. Explain the sequence of operation of the system shown in Fig. 16-4.

CHAPTER 17

CONTROL SYSTEMS: HOT WATER

In applying automatic control systems for oil-fired hot water heating as compared with steam systems, the individual controls to be used will increase in number and vary in type.

With the *steam system* the limit controls used were the low-water cutoff and pressure control. Neither of these appears in the hot-water heating system.

The main limit controls used in hot-water systems are the direct-acting and reverse-acting hot-water temperature-limit controls. These controls respond to changes in the temperature of the water and thus operate on a temperature-limit basis rather than a pressure-limit basis, as is the case with a steam heating system.

Perhaps the best way to ascertain the type of control system that should be installed with a hot-water heating system is to analyze the characteristics of the different types of hot-water systems.

Hot-water heating systems may be broken down into two groups, classified according to the method used to deliver the hot water to the radiators (see Fig. 17-1). These are (1) *the gravity-circulation system* and (2) *the forced-circulation system*.

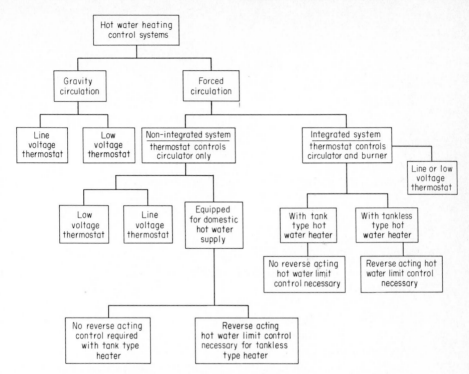

Fig. 17-1 Two groups of hot-water heating control systems.

The basic control system for use with gravity hot water is shown in Fig. 17-2(a). The system is the same as that used with a steam system except that the hot-water limit control takes the place of the pressure control. The thermostat and stack switch are standard in all these systems.

The sequence of operation of this system is simple. The thermostat calls for heat and energizes the relay, bringing the burner on. The burner will run either until the thermostat is satisfied, in which case the burner will cease operating, or until the setting on the high-limit hot-water control is reached.

If it is the latter case, the line-voltage current supply to the stack-switch relay will be interrupted and the burner will go off even if the thermostat is not satisfied.

The radiators in this case, however, will continue to give off heat, as the water circulating through them is hot and, more than likely if the outside temperature is not too low, will satisfy the thermostat before the high-limit hot-water control returns to the on position.

The average setting for the high-limit control on a gravity hot-water system can be said to be about 180 to 190°F. However, this is far from

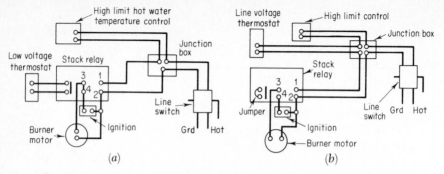

Fig. 17-2 Control wiring diagram for gravity hot-water system with (*a*) low-voltage thermostat and (*b*) line-voltage thermostat.

an absolute figure, for the characteristics of the system will determine just what this setting would be.

With a system that has exceptionally large piping and good circulation in a tight house, it may be that a setting as low as 160° will be ample, especially if the radiation is on the large side. If, however, circulation is poor and radiation is inadequate, it may be necessary to raise the high-limit hot-water temperature control well over the 200° setting in order to achieve the required amount of heat.

It is fairly easy on any hot-water system to achieve a balance between the heat output and heat losses by giving some attention to the high-limit or operating-limit control setting. Raising this setting on cold days and lowering it on milder days will result in a balance between output and losses that can be maintained with extremely close temperature control.

Notice from the foregoing that with a gravity hot-water plant the operation of the control system is comparatively simple.

With the addition of the pump or circulator to achieve forced circulation of the hot water through the system, a number of complications appear that make the control application more complex. Basically, control systems for forced-circulation hot water can be regarded from two aspects, that of the place of the thermostat in the system and the emphasis to be placed on the domestic faucet hot-water supply.

Looking at if from the thermostat viewpoint, hot-water heating control systems may be divided into two distinct types. These are the *nonintegrated* and *integrated control systems*. The terms "nonintegrated" and "integrated" refer to the function of the thermostat.

If we have a control system in which the thermostat, whether it is line or low voltage, controls the operation of the circulator only and has no direct connection with the oil burner, we refer to it as a *nonintegrated system*. In the event that the thermostat, through an intermediate control, can operate both the circulator and the oil burner simultaneously, upon starting.

Integrated systems, whether they use high- or low-voltage thermo-static control of both the circulator and the burner, have pretty well superseded the nonintegrated system. However, in view of the fact that there are many, many thousands of nonintegrated systems in the field it would be well to discuss their sequence of operation.

Referring to Fig. 17-3, we can see that the line-voltage thermostat interrupts the current supply to the circulator, and it is actually nothing more than a line-voltage switch responding to temperature changes.

The operation of the burner is achieved by the operating low-limit hot-water control alone, the thermostat having no direct connection with the burner whatsoever (Fig. 17-3).

On a call for heat by the thermostat, line-voltage current is sent to the circulator and it begins to operate. The hot water is now pumped out of the boiler, the cooler water returning from the radiators. As the cool water returns to the boiler, it will be below the low-limit hot-water control setting. As a result, this control will close its contacts and bring the burner on.

The burner is now operating to bring the temperature of the water up to the low-limit hot-water control setting. The burner does not come on until after the circulator has pumped a considerable amount of cool water back to the boiler.

With this type of system the oil burner is actually chasing the circulator. It is obvious that once the circulator goes on it is going to pump cool water back to the boiler. It is not necessary to wait until this water returns. It would be wiser to bring the burner on simultaneously in anticipation of the water temperature drop that is going to occur.

This is the cause of a basic lag in the nonintegrated system—the continual chasing of the initial losses occasioned by the starting of the circulator before the burner comes into operation.

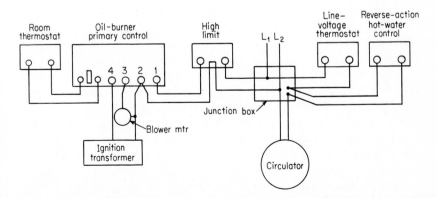

Fig. 17-3 Nonintegrated hot-water control system. Line-voltage thermostat controls operation of circulator only.

In the event that there is a *tankless coil* attached to the boiler, the situation may cause considerable inconvenience if a faucet demand for hot water occurs simultaneously with a demand for heat. In such a case, the circulator will be pumping the hot water out of the boiler and returning the cool water from the radiators just when the faucet water begins circulating through the coil. The result is very little faucet hot water.

In order to prevent this condition from taking place, a reverse-acting limit control is connected into the line leading to the circulator. This control acts in reverse to the direct-acting hot-water limit control. *The direct-acting hot-water limit control will break its contact on a rise in water temperature. The reverse-acting hot-water limit control will make its contact on a rise in temperature.*

With the installation of this reverse-acting hot-water limit control on the line leading to the circulator, we now have an added feature to protect against the condition previously mentioned. This reverse-acting control is set for a certain temperature and any time the boiler water temperature drops below that point, it will open its contacts and prevent the circulator from operating and will also maintain its contacts in an open position until the boiler water rises to the temperature setting for which it is adjusted.

With the addition of this control we would now have the following sequence of operation upon a call for heat by the thermostat in a nonintegrated control system.

The thermostat would start the circulator. The circulator would pump the hot water from the boiler, returning the cooler water from the radiators above. If at any time the water returning to the boiler drops below the setting on this reverse control, the circulator will be shut off and will remain off until the burner has the opportunity to bring the water temperature back up to the setting on the reverse control.

When the water has attained this higher temperature, the reverse control will close its contact and the circulator will assume operation.

This means that if a faucet hot-water demand were made simultaneously with the heat demand, and the amount of hot water drawn from the coil succeeded in lowering the boiler water temperature to any degree, the circulator would not be permitted to operate. The precedence in demand would be given to the domestic faucet hot-water supply rather than to the heat-giving portion of the system.

From this we can see that without the *reverse-acting hot-water temperature limit control,* a nonintegrated system will give precedence to the pumping of the water through the system for heating purposes regardless of its temperatures, but, with the addition of the reverse control, this precedence is changed from heat to domestic faucet hot water, and no water will be pumped for heating purposes until the boiler water temperature is high enough to satisfy the tankless coil demands.

It is important at this point to mention that the operating control, that is, the low-limit hot-water control, which directly operates the burner through the stack-switch relay should always be at least 10° *higher in setting than the reverse-acting hot-water limit control* that controls the operation of the circulator. If the operating low-limit hot-water control is not set higher than the reverse-acting control, the circulator will never operate and, as a consequence, there will be no heat delivered.

It is well to note here that the installation of a reverse-acting hot-water limit control to interrupt the action of the circulator should be considered essential on all hot-water heating systems equipped with *instantaneous tankless coils.*

Figure 17-4 demonstrates an additional control hookup that can be used with nonintegrated systems. The difference between the systems shown in Figs. 17-3 and 17-4 is that the latter utilizes a low-voltage thermostat to control the operation of the circulator.

Essentially, the sequence of operation of this system is exactly the same as that of the foregoing except for the operation of the simple switching relay used to supply the line-voltage current to the circulator upon a heat demand by the thermostat.

The sequence of operation of the nonintegrated systems in Figs. 17-3 and 17-4 is as follows:

Upon a call for heat from the thermostat, the circulator will begin to operate. In so doing, it will return cooler water to the boiler. When the water returned to the boiler drops below the setting of the low-limit operating hot-water control, the burner will begin to operate. The burner will continue to operate until the water is raised to the setting on the operating control. The operating control alone starts or stops the

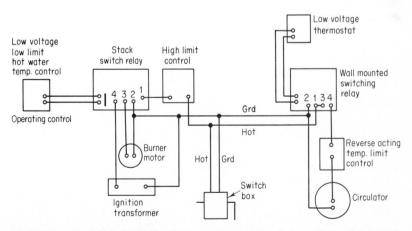

Fig. 17-4 Nonintegrated hot-water control system. A low-voltage thermostat controls operation of circulator only.

burner in response to the changes in temperature of the boiler water.

If, at any time during the operation, the water in the boiler drops below the setting on the reverse hot-water limit control, the circulator will be shut off until the burner returns the water to that temperature.

During times when there is no demand for heat, the thermostat remains in the OFF position and the circulator does not operate.

The flow-control valve effectively seals the line against gravity circulation of hot water to the radiators.

The setting of the hot-water low-limit operating control is lowered for the summer, and it maintains the boiler water temperature constant for domestic faucet hot-water demands.

INTEGRATED HOT-WATER CONTROL SYSTEMS

By the use of additional controls and some wiring changes, the integration of the thermostat to include the control of the burner as well as the circulator can be accomplished. This is an ideal control system for hot-water heating. Figures 17-5 and 17-6 show these types of systems for line- and low-voltage thermostats, respectively.

With the system used in Fig. 17-5 the action is as follows:

The line-voltage thermostat closes the circuit to the burner by furnishing current to the primary control. The low-voltage side of this control has its circuit closed because of the jumper placed across low-voltage terminals. This jumper takes the place of the operating low-limit control shown in Fig. 17-4.

At the same time, the thermostat closes the circuit to the circulator

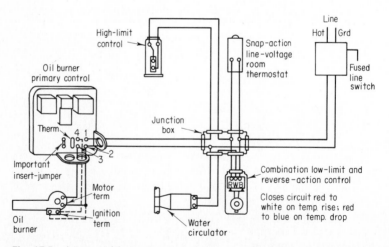

Fig. 17-5 Integrated hot-water control system. Line-voltage thermostat controls operation of burner and circulator. (*General Controls ITT*)

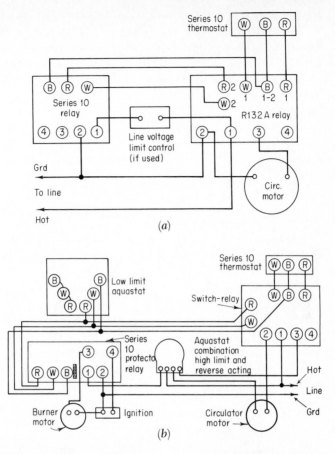

Fig. 17-6 Integrated hot-water control system. Low-voltage thermostat controls operation of burner and circulator: (*a*) without domestic hot water, (*b*) with tankless-type hot water heater. (*Honeywell, Inc.*)

through the *red* and *white* terminals of the combination low-limit and reverse-action control. The red and white terminals are the reverse side; and the *red* and *blue,* the low-limit side.

The burner and circulator are now operating and will continue to do so until the setting of the high-limit control is reached, at which point the burner will be shut off; or until the boiler water drops below the reverse setting on the combination control, at which point the circulator will shut off; or until the thermostat is satisfied, at which point both the circulator and burner will be shut off.

During the summer, the low-limit side of the combination control will close the circuit to the burner and operate it for domestic hot water.

Because of the reverse-action side of the combination control, this system is well adapted for use with a *tankless-type hot-water heater.*

Figure 17-6 shows the use of a low-voltage thermostat and additional switching relay required for integrated operation. In Fig. 17-6(*a*) there is no provision for summer domestic hot water as the thermostat is the only operating control. With this hookup, the burner and the circulator are brought on simultaneously when the thermostat energizes the *switching relay.*

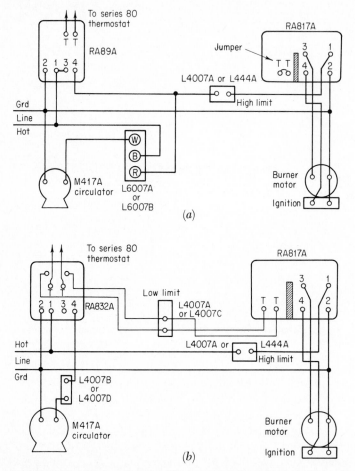

Fig. 17-7 Two Honeywell series 80 summer-winter hot-water systems that provide integrated operation of burner and circulator. (*a*) Typical connections for an oil-fired summer-winter hot-water system with L6007A or L6007B used to prevent circulator operation and start burner on drop in water temperature. NOTE: The combined burner motor, ignition, and circulator motor load rating must not exceed 10.2-amp 115-volt rating of the RA89 relay contacts. (*b*) Typical connection diagram for an oil-fired summer-winter hot-water system with L4007A or L4007C as burner low limit and L4007B or L4007D as circulator low limit.

The *switching relay* closes the low-voltage circuit to the *stack relay,* thereby starting the burner, and at the same time it closes the line-voltage circuit to the circulator.

Either one of two sequences of operation can occur. If the boiler water reaches the high-limit setting, the burner will be shut off, but the circulator will continue to operate until the thermostat is satisfied, or both the burner and circulator will cease operation if the thermostat has been satisfied and the high-limit temperature has not been reached.

With the addition of domestic summer hot water, the control system in Fig. 17-6(*a*) will not do the job [see Fig. 17-6(*b*)].

Figure 17-6(*b*) shows the wiring hookup for low-voltage thermostat operation on an integrated system. This system can be used with a tankless heater because of the reverse-acting side of the combination control.

THE SWITCHING RELAY

When the thermostat calls for heat, the *switching relay* starts the burner by energizing the primary control and also sends line-voltage current to the circulator [see Fig. 17-6(*b*)].

If the boiler water drops below the reverse setting of the combination control, the circulator will be shut off, maintaining a hot-water reserve for any demands created by the tankless coil. As long as the water is

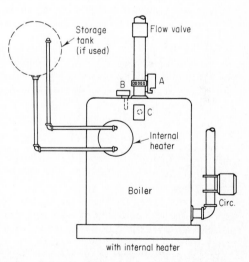

Fig. 17-8   Correct location of various hot-water temperature limit controls with internal water heater. (*A*) High-limit control (strap-on type). (*B*) High-limit control (immersion type). (*C*) High-limit control (immersion type, optional location). (*B* or *C*) Immersion-type operating control. (*B* or *C*) low-limit control. (*A*, *B*, or *C*) Reverse-acting control. (*General Controls ITT*)

above the reverse setting, however, the circulator will operate until the thermostat is satisfied.

If the high-limit setting on the combination control is reached, only the burner will be shut off. If the thermostat is satisfied, the switching relay will be deenergized and both the circulator and burner will cease operating. The low-limit hot-water temperature control (low voltage) will energize the primary control to run the burner for summer hot water.

In the event that a tank-type hot-water heater is used, the combination control could be replaced by a simple high-limit control.

The location of the various types of *hot-water limit controls*, whether they are operating low-limit, high-limit, direct-, or reverse-acting, deserves some mention.

High-limit controls must always be mounted at a point where they will be in contact with the highest temperature in the boiler. This will be at the top of the boiler *and as far away from the tankless or tank-type internal hot-water heater as possible.*

If it is a *strap-on control*, it should be attached to the main riser no further than 3 or 4 in. from the top of the boiler.

When an *immersion-type control* is used for the high-limit control, beware of the use of bushings. Such fittings prevent the element of the control from extending into the boiler water so that it may be in the path of the convection currents.

When a *low-limit control* is used for controlling the domestic hot-water supply (operating control) it should be mounted as close as possible to the hot-water generator if it is the tankless type. If a tank is used, it may be installed in the tank but wired through the high-limit control.

The reverse-acting hot-water limit control that interrupts the action of the circulator should be located so that it is affected by the temperature of the water entering the main riser. It may be strapped on or inserted into the riser. This is the proper location, as its function is to control the circulation of water *from* the boiler.

A combination *reverse-acting* and *high-limit control* may be inserted in the riser also. If the control is a *combination reverse acting and low limit*, it should be installed in the boiler not too far away from the internal heater.

COMBINATION CONTROLS

Controls in combination in a single housing that incorporate the features of primary controls, high- and low-limit controls, and switching relays are now replacing the multiple-control systems used on integrated and nonintegrated hot-water heating systems. Providing easier installation, less and more compact wiring, they are more economical when it comes to first or installation cost.

Table 17-1 Average Settings for Various Hot-water Temperature Controls

Gravity circulation, °F	Forced circulation, °F				
High-limit control	High-limit control	Reverse-acting control*	Operating control	Low-limit zone control	Low-limit control in hot-water tank
180–200	190–220	140–160	165–185	150	130

*Must always be at least 20° lower than operating control setting.

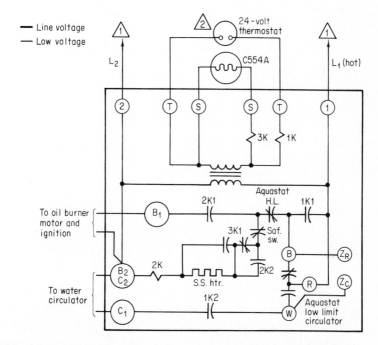

Fig. 17-9 Internal schematic and typical connections for Honeywell R8182A combination primary and hot-water (hydronic) heating control. Operation is as follows: A call for heat by the thermostat pulls in relays 1K and 2K to turn on the burner. Safety switch starts to heat. If burner ignites within 70 sec, cad cell sees flame and relay 3K pulls in to de-energize safety switch heater. Burner operates until call for heat is satisfied. Circulator operates when relay 1K pulls in *only* if Aquastat R-W is made. When the R8182A is used to control zone circulators, the R845A relay and thermostat for each succeeding zone will control the zone circulator *only* if the Aquastat R-W is made.

When Aquastat R-B is made by a drop in water temperature, it acts as a call for heat, pulling in relay 2K to turn on the burner. Circulator cannot operate.

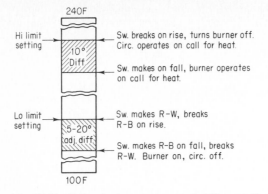

Fig. 17-10   Hot-water temperature control (Aquastat) switching for 8182A. (*Honeywell, Inc.*)

These combination controls (see Chap. 12, Primary Controls) provide the system operations described in this chapter.   Installation location should follow the control or boiler-burner unit manufacturer's specifications.

The control as shown in the wiring diagram (Fig. 17-9) includes the primary-control combustion detection and safety features, and a triple-function high-limit, low-water temperature control and circulator switching relay.   The switching operation features of the water-temperature controls are explained in Fig. 17-10.

SETTINGS R8182A

Because heating systems differ, the correct setting for one system may not be correct for another.   Follow the boiler manufacturer's recommendations for proper selection of settings.

1. All models: Set HIGH LIMIT indicator at desired shutoff temperature.   The burner is then turned off if the boiler water exceeds this setting.   The burner cannot operate until the water temperature falls at least 10°.
2. Set LOW LIMIT indicator at the minimum temperature recommended for a domestic hot-water supply.   This setting must be at least 20° below the high-limit setting to prevent one switch from locking out the other.
3. Set LOW LIMIT DIFFERENTIAL to the recommended number of degrees below the low-limit setting.   If the water temperature falls to this point, the burner automatically turns on; the circulator cannot operate until water is heated to the low-limit setting.

QUESTIONS

1. What are the two classifications of hot-water heating systems based on the method used to deliver water to the radiation?
2. What is the average setting of the high-limit control on a gravity system?
3. What circumstances may alter the setting that is the answer to question 2?
4. What is meant by a nonintegrated system? An integrated system?
5. Explain the sequence of operation of the system shown in Fig. 17-3.
6. Explain the sequence of operation of the system shown in Fig. 17-5; in Fig. 17-6(b).
7. What is the purpose of the reverse-acting limit control when a tankless heater is used?
8. What is the purpose of the switching relay?
9. What is the purpose of the high-limit control in Fig. 17-4? The low-limit control? The reverse-acting limit control?
10. How must the reverse-acting control always be set?
11. What is meant by "fixed differential"?
12. What are the advantages of the combination control shown in Fig. 17-9?
13. Explain the operation of the 8182A.
14. What controls are incorporated in the 8182A? The 8184 (Chap. 12)?
15. To what does the term "hydronic" refer?

CHAPTER 18

CONTROL SYSTEMS: WARM AIR

The application of automatic control systems for oil-fired warm-air units breaks down into almost the same types as for those used in hot-water heating. These two main groupings are gravity-warm-air heating systems and forced-warm-air heating systems, the essential difference being the introduction of the fan in the forced-warm-air system.

The control systems used for forced-warm-air heating can be divided, as was the case with hot-water heating, into integrated and nonintegrated systems. Integrated control systems are those in which we have simultaneous control of the fan and burner by the thermostat. Nonintegrated control systems are those in which the thermostat controls the operation of the burner alone, and the fan responds through a fan control to various temperature changes in the bonnet.

GRAVITY WARM-AIR CONTROL SYSTEMS

Figure 18-1 demonstrates the connection diagram and the controls that are used with a gravity-fed warm-air system. This system is almost the same as that used with the ordinary steam system or gravity-fed hot-

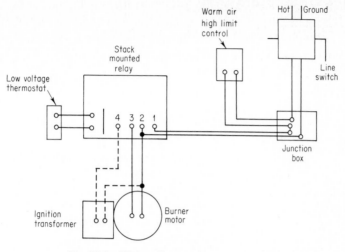

Fig. 18-1   Wiring diagram for a gravity warm-air system.

water system, except that in this case the warm-air, high-limit temperature control is used instead of the pressure control or hot-water temperature control. The operation of this control system is comparatively simple and occurs in the following manner.

When the thermostat calls for heat, it energizes the primary control and the burner begins to operate. The burner will not continue to operate to furnish heat until one of two conditions is met. Either the thermostat will be satisfied, in which case the burner relay will be deenergized and the unit will cease operation, or the setting on the warm-air, high-limit control will be reached, in which case the burner will cease operating even though the thermostat may still be calling for heat.

The high-limit control has as its purpose the prevention of too high a bonnet temperature. The setting on this warm-air, high-limit control will depend to a great degree upon the characteristics of the actual system. The setting of this limit control, depending on whether the gravity system is average size, oversized, or too small, can be found in the limit-control-setting table in Chap. 14.

In general, it should be noted that if a system is too small, a higher limit control setting will be necessary than if it is average or oversized. This is due to the fact that a system which is designed improperly and has not an ample capacity for good circulation will require a much higher bonnet temperature in order to achieve adequate heating.

The undersizing of the system results in poor circulation and a consequent higher drop in the temperature of the air moving through the ducts because of this sluggish circulation. Moderately oversized units with good circulation can have their high-limit controls set from 100 to 150° lower than is the case with inadequately sized systems. This differential in limit control settings demonstrates quickly the necessity for good circulation if economical oil heating is to be achieved through the gravity warm-air medium.

FORCED-WARM-AIR SYSTEMS

The wiring diagram shown in Fig. 18-2 gives us a standard nonintegrated forced-warm-air control system. In this case, the thermostat controls the oil burner only, and the operation of the fan depends upon various temperature levels in the bonnet. The control used to operate the fan also incorporates the limit control, and it is referred to jointly as a combination fan and limit control. In function, it is essentially two separate controls in a single casing.

With this system, the following operational steps occur: When the thermostat calls for heat, it will energize the relay and bring the burner on. The burner will now proceed to bring the bonnet temperature up, and when this temperature reaches the high setting on the fan side of

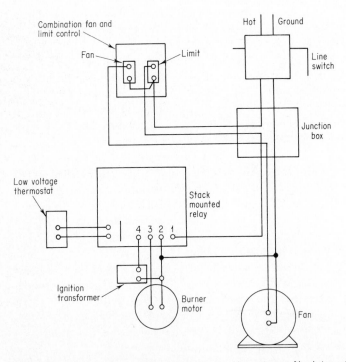

Fig. 18-2 Wiring diagram for a forced-warm-air system. Nonintegrated thermostat controls oil burner only.

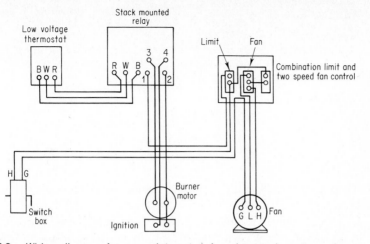

Fig. 18-3 Wiring diagram for a nonintegrated forced-warm-air system where thermostat controls oil burner only but combination control operates fan at two speeds. This can also be done with series 80 thermostat and primary control. (*Honeywell, Inc.*)

the combination control, the fan will then come on and provide forced-warm-air circulation.

The entire unit is now operating normally and we find that the fan control has somewhat the same function as the reverse hot-water temperature control in a hot-water heating system. It serves to hold the fan in the OFF position until the air in the bonnet is warm enough to furnish the required amount of heat and thereby prevents the fan from circulating cold air through the rooms.

With the entire unit now operating, either one of two things may occur. The air in the bonnet can rise in temperature until the setting on the limit control is reached, in which case the burner will be shut down but the fan will continue to operate, or the thermostat may be satisfied and shut down the burner, in which case the fan will continue to operate until the low setting on the fan side of the combination control has been reached.

Thus it can be seen that the only control over the fan furnished by this type of system is by the bonnet temperature; and even after the thermostat has been satisfied, the fan will continue to operate to dispel the residual heat of the furnace.

Although this may be a definite advantage to the furnace, especially in the case of steel furnaces, it may result in an override in the room temperature, and the thermostat differential must be adjusted to provide for this.

Figure 18-3 shows another nonintegrated forced-warm-air control system, but in this case the combination fan and limit control is capable

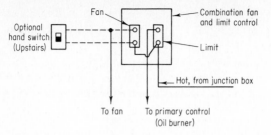

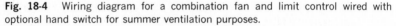

Fig. 18-4   Wiring diagram for a combination fan and limit control wired with optional hand switch for summer ventilation purposes.

of operating the fan at two speeds. Otherwise its sequence of operation is exactly the same as that of the system shown in Fig. 18-2.

In the event that the furnace blower fan is desired for ventilating purposes during the summer, the only thing that is necessary is to place a switch wired between the two terminals of the fan side of the combination fan and limit control. This connection diagram is shown in Fig. 18-4. With this hand switch placed upstairs in the kitchen or at the head of the cellar stairs for convenient access, immediate forced ventilation is available at all times merely by flicking the switch.

The combination limit and two-speed fan control provides for low- and high-speed fan operation, as well as limit protection against excessive bonnet temperature.

With a control of this sort, we can have the fan start as quickly as possible at a fairly low bonnet temperature, as low as 115 to 120° operating at low speed. The setting for the fan to go into high speed should be between 135 and 145°. The fan OFF setting should be 100°. In this case when the bonnet temperature reaches 115° the fan will begin operating at low speed and furnish heat.

On extremely warm days, it is highly possible that the fan may furnish enough heat at this low-speed setting to satisfy the thermostat and shut the unit down before the higher bonnet temperature is reached that would shift the fan to the higher speed.

For an average system, the limit side of this combination control should be set at 200°. One of the big advantages of a control that can operate a fan at two speeds is that it enables the fan to be kept running for as long a period as possible without circulating cold air into the rooms.

The ideal warm-air system fired by oil would be one in which we could modulate the size of the fire and keep the fan operating continuously. This would provide a constant input of heat to balance the heat losses in proportion to the temperature outside and thus enable the maintenance of close temperature control. The closer we can approach continuous operation of the fan in an oil-fired system, the more level will be the house temperature.

An integrated system which provides simultaneous thermostat control of the burner and fan is shown in Fig. 18-5.   In this case a combination limit and two-speed fan control can be substituted for the combination single-speed fan and limit control shown in the diagram.

In order to integrate the operation of the fan and burner with the demands of the thermostat, it is necessary to use an additional switching relay.   Sometimes a relay of this type is called a "wall" relay because it is often mounted on the wall.

In this system the closing of the thermostat contacts energizes the switching relay, which, in turn, sends current to the burner relay via the limit side of the combination control and to the fan via the fan side of the limit control.   Thus the burner will come on immediately, but the fan will remain off until the bonnet temperature reaches the fan-on setting of the fan control at which time the fan will begin operation. The unit is now in normal operation.

In the event that the bonnet temperature becomes excessive, the limit side of the combination control will interrupt the operation of the oil burner, but the fan will continue to operate.   Once the bonnet temperature has dropped to the low-side setting of the limit control, the burner will resume operation.   What is different in this case, however, from all the foregoing systems is that once the thermostat is satisfied, the switching relay will be deenergized and the *fan* and burner will stop simultaneously.   This completely eliminates any override due to continued action of the fan that prevails in the foregoing systems.

On the thermostat OFF cycle this system will not dispel the residual

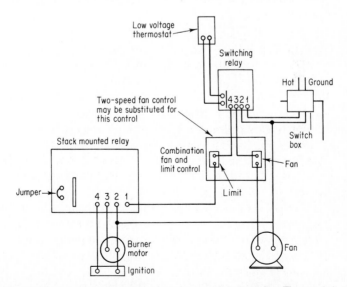

Fig. 18-5 Wiring diagram of a forced-warm-air system (integrated). Thermostat control of fan and burner eliminates fan override. (*General Controls ITT*)

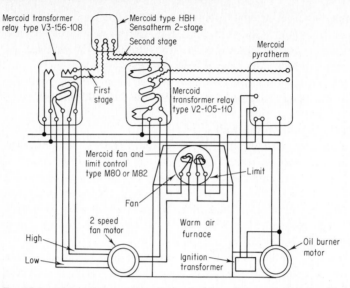

Fig. 18-6 Wiring diagram of an integrated forced-warm-air system with two-stage thermostat. The thermostat not only controls burner and fan but also operates fan at two speeds. (*Mercoid Corp.*)

heat left in the furnace as quickly as one that has a fan override will.

With this control system, as illustrated in Fig. 18-5, there can be substituted, as mentioned previously, a two-speed combination fan and limit control for the single-speed combination control. The two-speed operation will be achieved by changes in the *bonnet air temperatures.*

Figure 18-6 illustrates a control system whereby there is two-speed operation of the fan, *but it is achieved by regulation from the thermostat.* In such cases a two-stage thermostat is used. The operation of a two-stage thermostat is as follows:

Upon a slight drop in temperature, approximately $\frac{1}{2}°$, the second stage of a two-stage thermostat will close. Upon a further drop in temperature, about $1°$, the first stage will close. This means that the second stage can furnish a small amount of heat to the rooms, and if this is enough, it will be satisfied and the equipment will stop operating.

If this small amount of heat is not enough, the temperature will continue to drop and the first stage will close its contacts, bringing on the heat in full quantity. With this in mind, we can determine the consecutive steps of operation of the system shown in Fig. 18-6. On a slight drop in room temperature, the second stage of the thermostat closes. This starts the oil burner and operates the fan at low speed once the proper bonnet temperature is reached to enable the fan control to close its circuit.

If the weather is mild, the fan operating at low speed will be able to maintain the room temperature. If, however, the weather is cold and the heat demand is normal, this low-speed operation will not be able to make up the heat loss. As a result, the room temperature will continue to drop and the first stage of the thermostat will close.

The fan will now operate at high speed. When the temperature rises, the first stage of the thermostat will open and the fan motor will be returned to operation at low speed. The burner will now continue to operate until either excessive bonnet temperature causes the limit control to shut it off or the room temperature, continuing to rise, satisfies the second stage of the thermostat, simultaneously stopping both the burner and the fan.

This system, because of the two-stage thermostat, can come extremely close to providing a fairly continuous operation of the fan and is also able to increase the speed of the fan if the heat demands are not met in the rooms upstairs.

An important point to note about this system is that the two-speed operation of the fan is *controlled by temperature differentials in the actual living quarters* rather than, as in the case with the system in Fig. 18-5, by temperature changes in the bonnet.

The achievement of level temperature control with forced warm-air heating systems depends to a great extent upon the proper nozzle sizing

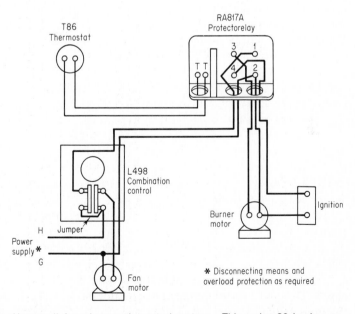

Fig. 18-7   Honeywell forced-warm-air control system. This series 80 hookup replaces the former series 10 system shown in Fig. 18-3. Both systems operate the same.

of oil burners used with modern warm-air furnaces. A warm-air unit should never be overfired, as this will lead to a "hill and valley" type of temperature fluctuation, which will be exceedingly uncomfortable for the occupants.

Since most heating surveys are based on a 0° to 70°F temperature change, that is, a 70° design temperature difference, the assumption is that the average winter temperature is zero. This is far from the truth in the greater majority of localities where automatic central heating is installed.

Units, however, are fired against the Btu losses calculated upon this temperature difference. This results in an overfiring and overriding that are reflected in uneven room temperatures with forced-warm-air units.

This too causes the intermittent operation of the fan, which further aggravates the cold 70° situation. Thus, it may be much wiser to underfire the average warm-air unit to such an extent that the heat input is balanced fairly accurately against the heat losses based on an average winter temperature that applies to the locality rather than on the arbitrarily accepted zero temperature used in most cases.

Such a method would mean smaller nozzle sizes with a smaller Btu input which will be unable to push the temperatures up so sharply that the fan operation would be intermittent. Undersizing the nozzle by the percentage of difference between the actual average winter temperature and the accepted zero base can result in a continual operation of the burner and a continual operation of the fan at a lower bonnet temperature that will be reflected in accurate temperature control and greater operating economy due to the higher CO_2 that can be attained from constant operation.

Experiments have shown that even with soft insulating firebrick at least 5 min of operation is required by a $1\frac{1}{2}$-gph nozzle to approach normal efficient combustion. This time will increase as the nozzle sizes get smaller and is a valid argument against the short-burst type of operation that may reduce operating efficiencies.

It may be more economical to undersize the nozzle in proportion to *actual* winter temperatures. The lower nozzle sizes that will result from such a method can well be reflected in greater comfort and more extensive combustion efficiency with its consequent fuel-oil savings.

QUESTIONS

1. Explain the operation of a forced-warm-air heating system; a gravity warm-air system.
2. What factors influence the limit control setting on a gravity warm-air system?

3. What is the difference between an integrated and a nonintegrated force-warm-air heating system?
4. Explain the sequence of operation of the system shown in Fig. 18-5.
5. What is a combination fan and limit control?
6. How may a forced-warm-air system be used for summer ventilation purposes?
7. Sketch the wiring diagrams of three different types of warm-air control systems.
8. What is the advantage of continuous fan operation?
9. Explain how a warm-air system operates with two-speed fan control.
10. Explain the sequence of operation of the system shown in Fig. 18-6.

CHAPTER 19
CONTROL SYSTEMS
FOR VAPORIZING BURNERS

The application of automatic electrical controls to the operation of vaporizing pot-type oil burners varies considerably from that of power-driven gun-type burners. The difference lies, not only in the type of controls, some of which may be similar, but also in the application of a group of the controls as a specific system. This is due to the fact that mechanical methods of preparing the fuel for combustion are not utilized by vaporizing burners.

The only method used by vaporizing pot-type burners to prepare the fuel for combustion is the application of heat. A fuller description of the principles of operation of vaporizing pot-type burners can be found in Chap. 6.

The individual controls used to govern the operation of vaporizing burners are similar to those of power-driven burners in the case of temperature and limit control.

When it comes to controls with a function other than the regulation of temperature or the control of limits, we find that there is a considerable difference. For instance, with vaporizing burners we do not use a stack-mounted primary control at all and substitute for it a combination oil-flow control valve and motor-speed controller. This control has as its purpose the regulation of the flow of oil and also the regulation of the speed of the fan.

In power-driven burners the regulation of the quantity of oil delivered is not the function of the electrical controls, but rather of the design of the burner itself. With vaporizing pot-type burners, we find that the regulation of fire size, which depends upon the quantity of oil delivered, can be a function of electrical control.

The main purpose of the electrical controls in vaporizing burners is to regulate the oil flow in accord with the temperature demands and to control the amount of fan air delivered so that the proper amount of air will be given to the variable flame sizes.

As far as oil delivery is concerned, this regulation can be translated into the term "high-low fire," which means that we have two stages of control over the fire. *High fire* refers to the full operation by which the unit is operating for heating purposes, and *low fire* to the operation in which the flame is reduced in size and operating for pilot fire (ignition purposes) only.

Figure 19-1 shows a typical method of providing high-fire and pilot-fire control for vaporizing burners. A float-operated constant-leveling device controls the rate of flow to the burner regardless of the amount of oil in the tank or the static head pressure exerted by this oil.

Upon a call for heat, the thermostat closes its circuit on the low-voltage side of the step-down transformer and passes current to the

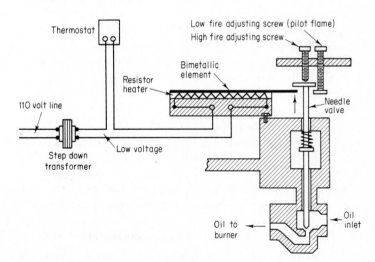

Fig. 19-1 Typical method of providing high-fire and pilot-fire control for vaporizing burners. Valve is lifted by bimetallic element.

resistor heater underneath or wrapped around the bimetallic element, as shown in the illustration. The bimetallic element proceeds to heat and warp, lifting up the needle valve and allowing an increased amount of oil flow to the burner, thereby enlarging the size of the flame.

The size of the flame is ultimately controlled by the height of the bottom of the high-fire adjusting screw from the head of the needle valve.

When the thermostat is satisfied, it will break its contact and the current will cease to flow to the resistor heater, which is adjacent to the bimetallic element. As a result, the element will cool and drop to its original position. The needle valve will now fall till it reaches the stop provided by the low-fire adjusting screw. At this point the needle is not in contact with the valve seat, and as a result a small amount of oil will continue to flow into the burner pot, where it will be vaporized and burned. However, as can be seen, the flame will be considerably diminished in size, having little heat-giving quality and existing only as a pilot fire.

FAN OPERATION

On some vaporizing burners, the fan will also operate at two speeds for this double-level fire, and on others it will operate at constant speed, furnishing the same amount of air for high and low fire. This difference is provided for in the burner design and also in the combination constant-level valve and motor controller.

In cases in which the fan operates continuously at a single speed, the constant-level valve will incorporate primarily the electrical control system shown in Fig. 19-1, with a float mechanism that provides a constant rate of oil flow. If the fan operates at multiple speed, then the wiring diagram will follow that shown in Fig. 19-4, in which the bimetallic-operated needle valve providing high-low fire control also incorporates a motor-speed controller that furnishes two-speed fan control.

On some vaporizing burners high-low fire control is furnished by a magnetic (solenoid) valve that may be either low-voltage or line-voltage operated, as in Fig. 19-2(a) and (b).

The use of this solenoid valve eliminates the bimetallic-operated high-low fire control. Such a solenoid valve will be used in conjunction with a simple constant-level valve.

This solenoid valve furnishes high-low fire by providing two stages of oil flow. When the thermostat calls for heat, the solenoid valve will be energized and snap open to the full ON position, allowing the maximum rate of oil flow to the burner. During the OFF position, at which time the thermostat is satisfied, this solenoid valve stem will fall and shut

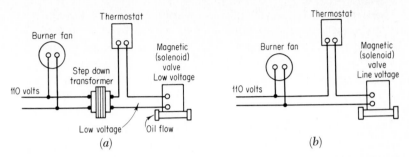

Fig. 19-2 (*a*) Low-voltage magnetic valve providing high-fire and pilot-fire control through thermostat. (*b*) Line-voltage magnetic valve providing high-fire and pilot-fire control through thermostat.

off the flow of oil to the burner.   At this point is utilized an adjustable bypass which can be regulated to govern the oil flow for the low pilot fire.   This bypass actually provides for the adjustment of any size of pilot fire.

THE SOLENOID VALVE

The application of a solenoid valve, such as the above, to a vaporizing burner gives a quicker cutoff than would be achieved by the bimetallic-operated valve.   Thus it is ideal for boilers that must have a rapid on-off cycle.   This is especially true when the limit control breaks its contact on a rise in pressure or temperature, whichever the case may be.

In such a situation as this, the gradual cutoff provided by a bimetallic-operated valve, as shown in Fig. 19-1, would usually result in the pressure rising higher than the cutoff setting on the limit control.   With the use of the solenoid, as shown in Figs. 19-2 and 19-3, a more rapid cutoff can be achieved, and for this reason it may be regarded as the preferred control when vaporizing burners are used for steam heating.

The general method of wiring either the bimetallic-operated high-low fire control or the solenoid-type high-low fire control, as shown in Figs. 19-1 and 19-2, should be followed.

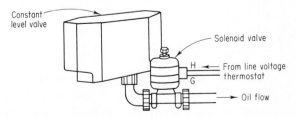

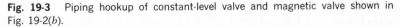

Fig. 19-3   Piping hookup of constant-level valve and magnetic valve shown in Fig. 19-2(*b*).

An unusual thing about vaporizing burners is that most manufacturers of this type of equipment avail themselves of special control systems for their specifically designed burner. A burner with a two-speed fan will have a different type of control system than will a burner with a continuously operating fan or an intermittent on-off fan operation.

Figure 19-10 shows the breakdown of vaporizing pot-type burner control systems based upon burner fan operation, and we will follow that breakdown in our explanation of these systems and in our wiring-connection diagrams for vaporizing burner control systems.

CONTROL SYSTEMS

A simple wiring diagram showing the connections for a high-low fire, two-speed fan operation type of vaporizing burner is shown in Fig. 19-4. Here we have low-voltage thermostat control and low-voltage limit control.

The bimetallic-operated constant-leveling valve has built into it a motor-speed controller. In this case, when the thermostat calls for heat, it completes a low-voltage circuit provided by the built-in transformer within the control. This energizes the resistor heater which causes the bimetalic element, as shown in Fig. 19-1, to warp and lift the flow control valve.

At the same time this bimetallic element actuates a device which closes a contact, increasing the voltage to the fan motor and thereby resulting in its coming up to full speed. The burner is now in normal operation with full-size fire and full-quantity air flow. This on cycle in coming up to full fire usually takes about 1 to 2 min.

The flow of low-voltage current which maintains this circuit runs in series through the thermostat and limit control, so that either of them upon being satisfied can break the circuit and deenergize the resistor heater, thus warping the bimetallic element and thereby decreasing the oil flow.

However, upon such a closing cycle it would not be wise to reduce

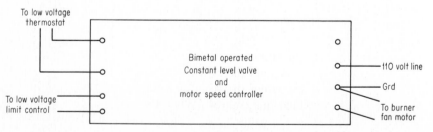

Fig. 19-4 Typical wiring diagram for thermostatically operated valve with low-voltage limit control and multiple-speed fan operation.

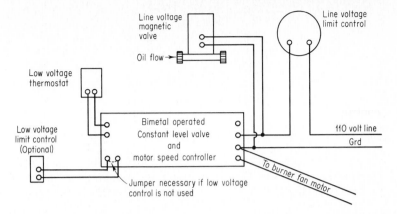

Fig. 19-5   Typical wiring diagram for low-voltage thermostat control of high-low fire with line-voltage limit control and intermittent multiple-speed fan operation.

the speed of the fan, as a considerable amount of oil would remain in the pot burner without sufficient air.   It is necessary, therefore, to have the fan operate at the higher speed in order to provide the required quantity of air for an additional 1 or 2 min.   During this time, the extra air delivered will result in the clean burning of the surplus fuel remaining in the burner pot.   The oil-flow rate and burner fan operation are now at the low or pilot level, and this completes the cycle of operation.

In the event that a limit control is not used, a jumper must be placed across the limit control wiring terminals at the constant-level valve if this system is to operate.

If a line-voltage limit control is required with the system just described, the hookup shown in Fig. 19-5, which includes a line-voltage-operated magnetic valve, must be used.   This is necessary because if at any time the line-voltage limit control breaks its contact, current ceases to flow to the combination bimetallic-operated constant-level valve and motor-speed controller.   As a result, the fan will cease to operate instantly.

Therefore, the positive cutoff of the oil flow provided by the solenoid valve is absolutely essential.   The slow cutoff furnished by the bimetallic-operated valve would allow a considerable amount of oil to flow into the pot and be consumed without the fan running.   Such a condition would result in large quantities of smoke and soot being deposited in the burner pot and throughout the furnace or boiler.

The operation of this system, shown in Fig. 19-5, except for the added feature of the line-voltage limit control and line-voltage magnetic valve, is the same as that shown in Fig. 19-4.

Any time the system in Fig. 19-5 is operating to fullfill the demands of the thermostat, it will be with the normal two-speed fan, high-low

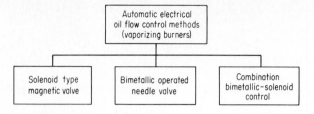

Fig. 19-6

fire operation, but at any time the line-voltage limit control interrupts the circuit, the fan will cease operation. We can, therefore, regard this system as having both multiple-speed and intermittent-fan operation.

CONTINUOUS FAN OPERATION

The next type of control system provides for continuous fan operation where the burner is at high or low fire. The use of this type of system eliminates the inclusion of the motor-speed controller in the constant-level valve.

The main control in this system is the bimetallic-actuated constant-level valve. The wiring diagram for such a system is shown in Fig. 19-7. It should be noted that the burner fan is connected directly to the line switch with a toggle switch in between.

The purpose of this toggle switch is to shut off the fan during such times as the operation of the burner is not required. This type of system utilizes a line-voltage limit control with a low-voltage thermostat.

The sequence of operation is as follows: A demand for heat results in the thermostat closing its contact and passing current to the resistor

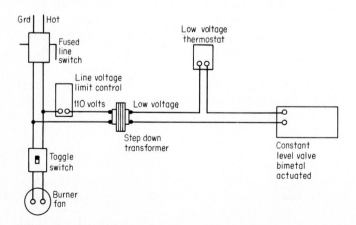

Fig. 19-7   Typical wiring diagram of thermostatic control of high-low fire with continuous single-speed fan operation.

heater which warps the bimetal in the constant-level valve and allows the burner to go to high fire.

The burner will now operate until either the thermostat is satisfied, at which time it will return to low fire, or the setting on the line-voltage limit control is reached. If this happens, all current is cut off to the step-down transformer and the bimetallic element cools and returns to the low-fire position.

It is well to emphasize at this point that in wiring a burner of this sort, the current to the fan does not pass through any control other than the toggle switch. Care should be taken to see that the burner fan motor in this case is always well lubricated, as its constant operation requires such attention.

COMPOUND SYSTEMS

Vaporizing burners with continuous fan operation can also be used with compound systems that require the addition of a hot-water circulator or warm-air circulating fan. Such hot-water control systems will be of the nonintegrated type. Wiring diagrams for both systems are shown in Figs. 19-8 and 19-9, respectively.

With the wiring diagram shown in Fig. 19-8, the water in the boiler is maintained at a constant temperature by the low-limit hot-water control, and any time the line-voltage thermostat calls for heat, bringing on the circulator, water is pumped to the radiators throughout the house.

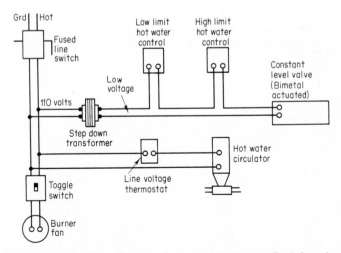

Fig. 19-8 Typical control wiring diagram of a vaporizing burner-fired forced-circulation hot-water system. Thermostat controls circulator only, and low-limit hot-water control operates burner. Single-speed continuous fan operation.

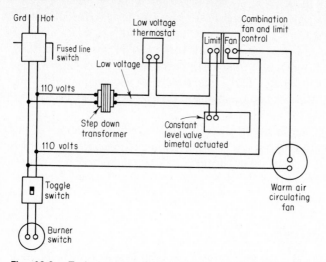

Fig. 19-9 Typical control wiring diagram of a vaporizing burner-fired forced-warm-air system. Single-speed continuous burner fan operation.

The low-limit hot-water control returns the burner to high or low fire in response to boiler water temperature demands.

The high-limit control functions only as a safety control in the event of a failure of the low-limit hot-water control to operate. Fan operation at single speed is continuous.

Figure 19-9 shows the wiring and connection diagram for a forced-circulation warm-air system, once again with continuous burner fan operation at single speed. A combination fan and limit control is utilized, the limit side being low voltage and the fan side line voltage. The closing of the thermostat contacts results in heating the bimetal

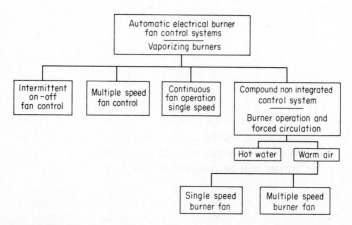

Fig. 19-10

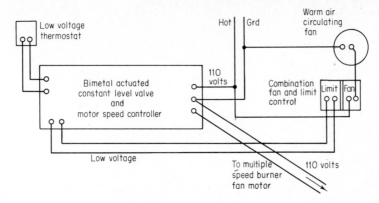

Fig. 19-11 Typical control wiring diagram of a vaporizing burner forced-circulation warm-air system. Multiple-speed burner fan operation.

in the constant-level valve, and the burner goes up to high fire. When the temperature setting on the fan control is reached, the warm-air circulating fan starts operating.

If either the limit control or the low-voltage thermostat is satisfied, the oil valve will reduce the oil flow to the low-fire level and the warm-air circulating fan will continue to operate until its low-level setting is reached, thereby dispelling the residual heat in the furnace.

Vaporizing burners with two-speed burner fan operation can be used with a warm-air circulating fan, as shown by the wiring and connection diagram in Fig. 19-11. In this case, however, the bimetal-actuated constant-level valve, unlike the type used with continuous single-speed fan operation burners, must incorporate a motor-speed controller.

The system shown in Fig. 19-11 utilizes a combination fan and limit control in the same manner as the system shown in Fig. 19-9. The limit side of the control is low voltage and the fan side of the control is line voltage. The thermostat is low voltage.

When the thermostat closes its contacts in response to a drop in room temperature, low-voltage current is passed through the limit control to the resistor heater adjacent to the bimetal strip. At the same time, the burner fan motor receives increased voltage and advances its speed. The burner is now in normal operation.

When the bonnet temperature in the furnace reaches the high setting on the fan control, the warm-air circulating fan will start. If the thermostat is satisfied or the setting on the limit control is reached, the low-voltage current flow is interrupted, and as a result the needle valve will fall and the burner will be returned to low fire.

The burner fan will continue to operate at higher speed for 1 or 2 min more in order to provide the necessary air to burn the residual oil in the pot. It will be reduced to low speed through a reduction in the voltage. The warm-air circulating fan will continue to operate

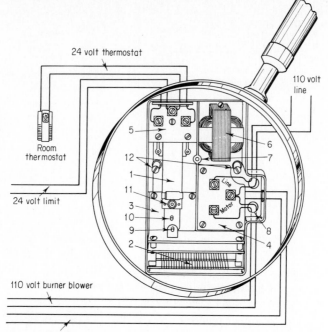

Fig. 19-12   View of the McCorkle control head for attachment to constant-level-flow control valve to provide thermostatic control of vaporizing burner.

until the bonnet temperature is reduced to its low setting.   At this point, the circulating fan will cease operation.

QUESTIONS

1. Why is a stack-mounted primary control not used with vaporizing burners?
2. Explain the sequence of operation with the control system shown in Fig. 19-5.
3. What is meant by high-low fire?
4. How is a solenoid valve used with vaporizing burners?
5. When is a solenoid valve especially useful with these burners?
6. What are the three electrical methods of controlling oil flow in vaporizing burners?
7. What are the different kinds of fan operation that may be found with vaporizing burners?
8. What are the functions of the bimetal-operated constant-level valve and motor-speed controller?

CHAPTER 20

ZONE CONTROL

Thermostatically controlled automatic oil heat often can result in uneven temperatures in two-story one- or two-family houses. This condition is also prevalent in split-level homes.

The condition is more noticeable in two-story and split-level houses than anywhere else. Usually, the lower floor contains the thermostat and receives the heat first, resulting in the thermostat being satisfied before the upper floor is properly heated. Of course, this situation could be aggravated if there were more than two stories.

Usually, moving the thermostat to the upper quarters, which are cooler because of the time lag occasioned by distribution of the heat, does not solve the problem. The result of such a change in position of the thermostat only relocates the trouble; for in this case, the lower floor becomes considerably overheated before the thermostat on the upper floor is satisfied.

In one- or two-family houses, steam-heated, this situation may be solved by the use of variable-vent valves on radiators. By adjusting the variable-venting orifice on the radiator valve, the radiators on the upper floors can be made to expel their air sooner and as a result heat more quickly. The radiators on the lower floor, whereon the thermostat is located, can be adjusted to vent slowly so that they will require a longer time to heat, and consequently the thermostat will take a longer period of time to be satisfied.

By some experimenting with a steam system equipped with adjustable air vent valves, the time-lag problem, with its consequent underheating of upper floors, can be solved. It is just a matter of regulating the rapidity with which the radiators become heated by controlling the rapidity with which the air in the radiators is vented. In this way, changes in location of the thermostat, which are usually unsatisfactory, are avoided.

Although this procedure solves the problem quite well for steam, it still remains for some steam installations of more than two stories and for warm-air and hot-water residential installations of multiple levels. The best solution for chronic problems of uneven temperature control that cannot otherwise be remedied is zone control.

Zone control means, simply, that there is a separate temperature control for each level or wing to be heated that could not be properly provided for by the normal action of a single thermostat. For instance, large, sprawling, ranch-type houses with multiple exposures—north, south, east, and west—require considerably less heat in the portion with southern exposure than with the sections having northern and eastern exposure.

Such is also the case with small apartment houses or multiple dwellings which run to two-, four-, five-, six-, or even eight-story levels. It is sometimes fairly difficult without multiple thermostatic control to achieve a proper and satisfactory distribution of heat.

The placing of separate thermostats on each of these levels or wings, which will henceforth be called zones, can offer a satisfactory and workable solution to this problem, which, over a period of years, will pay for the initial cost of additional installation equipment by savings in oil.

The amount of oil burned varies directly with the heat losses from a building. In a multiple-storied dwelling, there is some contradiction involved in furnishing a full quantity of heat (which is lost to the outside eventually) to every part of the house whether it requires it or not.

Such is the usual occurrence with single-thermostat operation, for if the room containing the thermostat cools below the level of the setting, the entire house is heated as a result of this action. It begins to lose this heat to the outside as soon as it is supplied, regardless of whether large portions of the dwelling require this heat. Thus, a good proportion of the Btu furnished by a gallon of oil as it burns may be furnished to a portion of the dwelling that does not need them. As a result, this section will overheat, and the rate of heat loss will increase because of the higher inside temperature due to the inability of the single thermostat to solve the distribution problem properly.

With a zone-control installation, those portions of the house requiring heat receive that heat, while those portions which do not require heat do not receive it, eliminating the added drain on the boiler or furnace output during its operation to fulfill the requirements of any single zone.

ADAPTABILITY OF ZONE CONTROL

Zone control is equally adaptable to *steam, hydronic,* or *warm-air* heat, but offers exceptionally close control in the case of steam and hot water (hydronic).

Figure 20-1 shows a typical piping diagram for the location of motorized steam valves. The action of these valves controls the flow of steam to each of the zones. The system shown in Fig. 20-1, with its accompanying wiring diagram shown in Fig. 20-2, offers fairly economical operation on a steam system, for the oil burner is brought into play only by the action of the thermostat.

If any thermostat in any zone calls for heat, it opens the valve. This valve is operated by low-voltage current through a step-down transformer and activates an accessory switch which starts the oil burner through the primary control, as shown in Fig. 20-2.

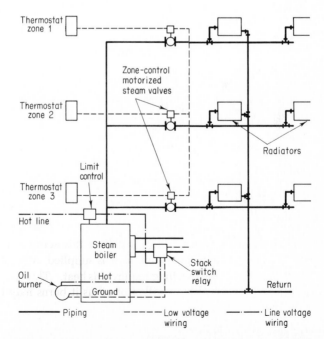

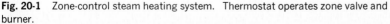

Fig. 20-1 Zone-control steam heating system. Thermostat operates zone valve and burner.

This is the type of control hookup that should be used in smaller dwellings where it is not necessary to maintain a head of steam pressure on the boiler. Thus in Figs. 20-1 and 20-2, the thermostat simultaneously operates the valve and burner, and the burner will run while any number of zone thermostats or any one zone thermostat is calling for heat. Series 20 thermostats are used in such cases. When the red arm touches the blue contact, the valve opens. When the thermostat is satisfied, the red arm has moved over the white contact and the valve is closed.

If very rapid heating is desired, a hot-water temperature control can be attached to the low-voltage terminals of the stack mounted relay and set for a temperature as high as $200°F$. In such a case the boiler water will remain at this constant temperature. If any zone thermostat then calls for heat, the burner will have only to push the water up $12°$ in order to make steam. This is less expensive an operation than maintaining constant steam pressure, as would be the case in Fig. 20-3.

The control hookup in Fig. 20-3 operates the burner constantly to maintain the desired pressure regulated by the pressure limit control. The thermostat in this case has no control over the burner, doing nothing but opening the valve to allow the steam to flow into the zone radiators. This type of system, however, may be necessary in a building of any height that has a large number of zones to which heat must be furnished constantly over long periods of time, like, for instance, an apartment house or a small office building.

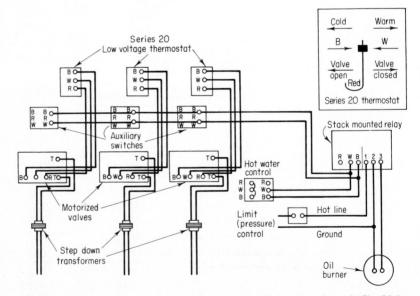

Fig. 20-2 Wiring diagram for zone-control steam heating system shown in Fig. 20-1. (*Honeywell, Inc.*)

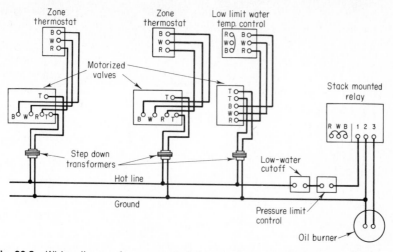

Fig. 20-3 Wiring diagram for zone-control steam system operating at constant pressure and equipped for domestic hot-water supply. Thermostat operates zone valve only. (*Honeywell, Inc.*)

In cases where constant steam pressure on the boiler is desirable because of high and constant demand, an additional zone can be added, as shown in Fig. 20-3, to provide faucet hot water. In such instances, a hot-water temperature control is inserted into the water generator or storage tank which opens and closes a valve in response to water temperature and allows steam to flow through the generator, thereby providing hot water.

In Fig. 20-2, the addition of a hot-water temperature control, as described previously, can furnish domestic hot water if a generator is attached to or installed in the boiler. In Fig. 20-3, steam from the boiler enters the generator by way of the motorized valve. This is the usual industrial commercial application, while the one in Fig. 20-2 is usually the domestic application.

HYDRONIC (HOT-WATER) HEATING

In larger dwellings with two or three zones, which are heated by hot water, a multiple-circulator installation which eliminates the necessity for motorized valves can be made. Figure 20-4 shows the wiring diagram for this system. Each circulator is controlled by a separate relay which, in turn, is operated by the zone thermostat.

A line-voltage stack-mounted relay operates the burner by means of a low-limit line-voltage hot-water temperature control. This maintains the water in the boiler at constant temperature at all times, and the thermostats merely operate the circulators which furnish the water

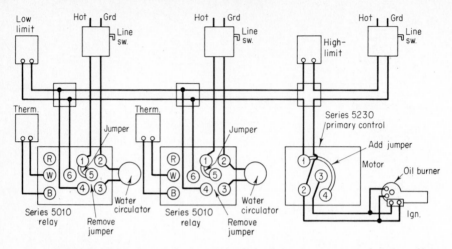

Fig. 20-4 Wiring diagram for forced-circulation hot water zone-control system. Note line-voltage primary control. Thermostat operates circulator only. Boiler water temperature is constant. (*General Controls ITT*)

to the various zones. This system is ideally adapted to large-size, two-family houses and gives adequate, accurate control at considerable savings in operating costs as compared with single-thermostat, single-circulator-type operation.

For smaller buildings, forced-circulation hot-water heating systems can utilize motorized valves with a single circulator. In this case, the thermostat, as shown in Figs. 20-5 and 20-6, operates the circulator and

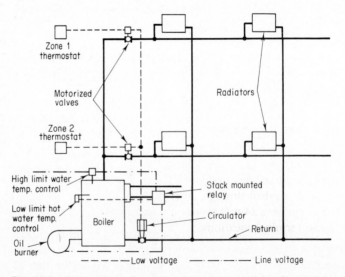

Fig. 20-5 Forced-circulation hot water zone-control heating system. Thermostat controls zone valve and circulator with boiler water at constant temperature.

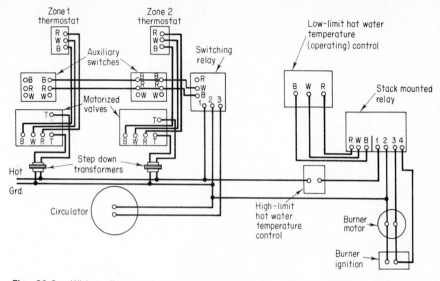

Fig. 20-6   Wiring diagram for system shown in Fig. 20-5.   (*Honeywell, Inc.*)

the motorized valves simultaneously, while the low-voltage, low-limit, hot-water temperature control operates the boiler to maintain constant boiler water temperature.   As is the case with the multiple-circulator installation in Fig. 20-4, the system in Fig. 20-6 has no thermostatic control of the burner, this being provided by the low-limit hot-water temperature control.

As far as zone control goes, hot-water heating will give accurate temperature control regardless of whether delivery is controlled by multiple circulators or single-circulator multiple-valve operation.

HYDRONIC ZONE CONTROL WITH COMBINATION CONTROL

The application of zone control has been somewhat simplified in installation and wiring as a result of combination controls.   The R8182A combination Protectorelay and hydronic heating control is an example. (For further information on the application of this type control for uses other than zone control, see the sections on primary controls and installation of limit controls, Chaps. 12, 14, and 15.

Model A of the R8182 has auxiliary ZC and ZR terminals that may be used to provide control through an R845A switching relay.   Each additional zone requires a 24-volt thermostat and an 845A relay.   Figure 20-7 shows these terminal locations.

Operation Sequence

See Fig. 17-9 for the schematic diagram of this control, as well as Fig. 17-10.   Chapter 17 discusses this control and the required setting and switching actions.   See Fig. 20-8 also.

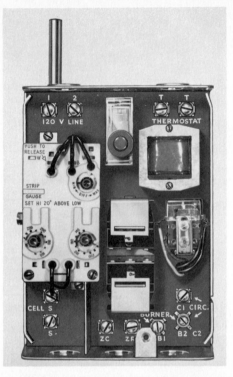

Fig. 20-7   The Honeywell R8182-R3 model of the combination Protectorelay and hydronic heating control shows at lower center the ZC and ZR terminals.   These terminals provide zone control through an 845A switching relay.   Each additional zone requires a 24-volt thermostat and an 845A relay.

1. The thermostat calls for heat.   Relays 1K and 2K turn on the burner.   The safety switch starts to heat.
2. The burner ignites within 70 sec; the cad cell sees flame, and relay 3K pulls in and shunts out safety switch heater.
3. The burner continues to operate until the call for heat is satisfied.
4. The circulator will operate when relay 1K makes contact if Aquastat R and W contact is closed.
5. When R8182A is used for zone control with zone circulators, the R845A relay and thermostat for each succeeding zone will control the zone circulator *only* if the Aquastat R and W contact is closed.
6. When Aquastat R and B contact is closed as a result of a drop in boiler water temperature, it will act the same as a call for heat.
7. Relay 2K will pull in, starting the burner; however, the circulator will not operate (see Fig. 17-9).

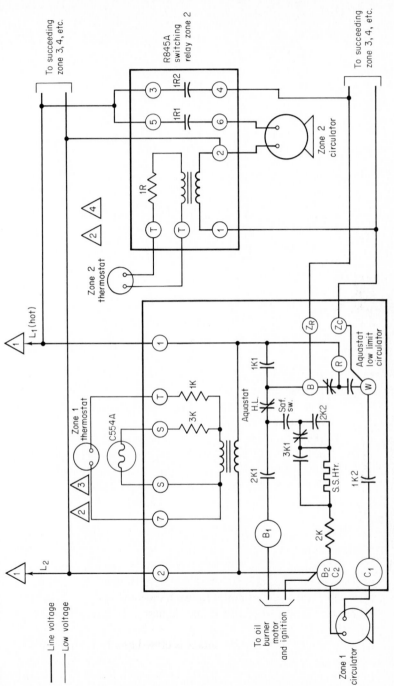

Fig. 20-8 Internal schematics for R8182A and R845A and typical connections for multiple circulator zoning. ⚠1 power supply, 120 volts ac. Provide disconnect means and overload protection as required. ⚠2 control wires can be run with line-voltage wires in conduit but then must have NEC class I insulation. ⚠3 Thermostat heater setting, 0.3 amp for R8182A. ⚠4 thermostat heater setting, 0.4 amp for R845A; and each succeeding zone using zone the R845A.

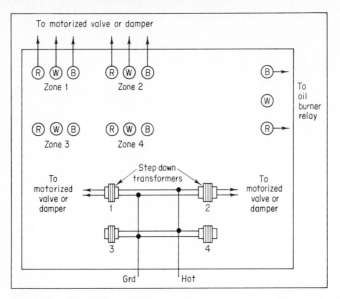

Fig. 20-9   Power box showing connections and transformers for four zones. (*Honeywell, Inc.*)

WARM AIR

By placing dampers in the ducts and having separate thermostats operate the damper motors, a fairly good application of zone control can be made to warm-air heating systems. Figures 20-10 and 20-11 show a warm-air zone-control system and its wiring diagram.

A call for heat from any zone brings on the burner and opens the damper to that zone. As soon as the setting on the fan side of the fan and limit control is reached, the fan will begin to operate and furnish heat to that zone. Upon satisfaction of the thermostat, the damper will close and the burner will cease operation, as will the fan.

The low-voltage terminals on the stack relay are connected by a jumper, as shown in Fig. 20-11, and the burner is controlled by a line current furnished to it by the switching relay connected through the limit control side of the combination fan and limit control. Thus, whenever a thermostat calls heat and opens the damper, this switching relay will be energized and the burner will operate.

Figures 20-10 and 20-11 show the inclusion of a relief zone which is provided for many times with hot-water heating and warm-air heating zone-control systems fired with solid fuels. It is nothing more than a zone which has an extra control on it that will open the damper to that zone even though that zone thermostat is satisfied.

The purpose of this control is to dispel any excessive boiler or bonnet

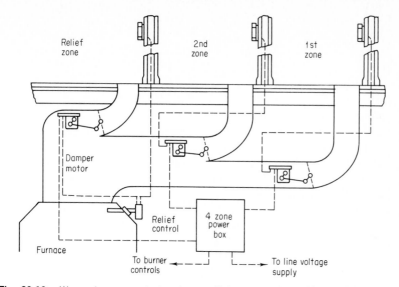

Fig. 20-10 Warm-air-zone-control system, utilizing power box. Note relief zone.

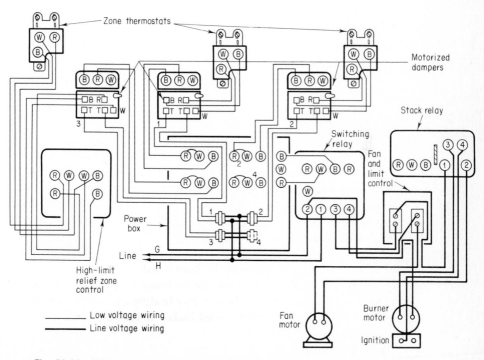

Fig. 20-11 Wiring diagram for warm-air control system shown in Fig. 20-10.

temperature that may build up in the event that all the dampers or motorized valves controlling the zones should close at the same time. If such a condition occurs, it results in a rapid rise in bonnet temperature. In such a case, this additional control, known as the *relief zone control*, will open the damper or valve to the relief zone and dispel the excessive rise in temperature. The setting of this control should always be higher than that of the limit control.

A *relief zone* may be necessary with warm-air systems if the furnace is of any capacity. This is due to the fact that a large-size furnace will require a combustion chamber of proportionate size.

If heavy firebrick is used and the unit is run for any length of time because of continuous zone demands, the combustion chamber heats to maximum temperature. The sudden satisfying of the zone thermostats will shut off the burner, but it will also close the duct dampers and air circulation will cease.

The glowing hot combustion chamber will continue for a considerable period of time, if constructed of standard firebrick, to give off heat to the furnace. This leads to a rapid and excessive rise in furnace temperature that requires the action of a relief zone.

Of course, when the relief zone damper opens, even though the zone thermostat is satisfied, there will be a considerable override in that zone. In order to control this condition and prevent this temperature override in the relief zone from being excessive, warm-air furnaces used in conjunction with zone operation should always be equipped with combustion chambers of insulating firebrick. This type of brick will not hold the large quantity of heat characteristic of ordinary firebrick, and the operation of the relief zone, therefore, if demanded, will occur for a considerably shorter period of time, contributing thereby to the comfort factor.

In any system, regardless of the type of heating that may be used, where zone control is applied and oil is being used for fuel, the use of lightweight firebrick will seriously diminish any override that might result from simultaneous closing or approximately simultaneous closing of all the zone controls. This desirable feature is in addition to the ability of insulating firebrick to aid in establishing balanced combustion conditions, as explained in Chaps. 9 and 10.

QUESTIONS

1. What sometimes occurs when small buildings are more than one story high and are equipped with automatic heating?
2. How can variable-vent valves help this trouble?
3. What is meant by zone control?

4. What are some of the advantages of zone control?
5. Explain the difference between the zone control system shown in Fig. 20-3 and that shown in Fig. 20-2.
6. Give the sequence of operation of the system shown in Fig. 20-4.
7. How is zone control achieved with a warm-air system?
8. What is the purpose of a relief zone?
9. Explain the function of a combination hydronic control as discussed in this chapter.
10. What are the advantages of such a combination control?
11. Can such a control be used with zone control? How?
12. What is the function of the switching relay?
13. Explain the operation sequence of the control shown in Figs. 20-7 and 20-8.

PART THREE

SERVICE
AND
MAINTENANCE

CHAPTER 21

ADJUSTING FOR
HIGHER COMBUSTION EFFICIENCY:
CO_2 AND STACK TEMPERATURE

Today the use of CO_2 analysis and stack-temperature measurements is fully accepted by the domestic oil-burner industry as a whole. This has been due to a gradual increase in education about, and publicity given to, the necessity for taking these tests, plus regulations by the Federal government agencies and local community or State requirements. The fact that excellent results have been achieved by the use and understanding of these tests has also been a great factor in their universal acceptance by the industry. Flue-gas analysis and stack-temperature readings as well as smoke readings are the only real scientifically accurate methods that can be employed on the average domestic job, and for this reason alone, every oil-burner dealer and mechanic has an obligation to understand what they mean and how they are made.

Many adjustments can be made by eye, but they are in truth just judgments affected by all the factors playing on the individual who makes them. This is not so with instrument tests. Such tests are not influenced by anything but the chemical and physical reactions being measured and therefore given accurate results not affected by all the things that influence human judgments. Many a flame which is concluded to be all right by a serviceman will be found, if subjected to a CO_2 test, to be capable of being increased in combustion efficiency by as much as 20 per cent, the human eye being incapable of picking up the slight changes in flame appearance that mean increased savings in fuel-oil consumption.

Actually there are two conditions which we must measure. These are (1) the efficiency of the combustion process which produces and releases the heat in the oil as expressed by the flame, and (2) the utilization or absorption of the heat. The release of the heat through the combustion process is the job of the oil burner; the absorption of the heat is the job of the furnace or boiler. We can measure both by instruments and thereby get an accurate picture of the job being done by the burner and the boiler.

The measurement of how well the oil burner is doing in mixing the oil and air for the purpose of burning it and how much of that air is excess or not necessary is indicated by CO_2 analysis. The greater the amount of CO_2, the better may be the fire and combustion process and the less the excess air (provided that the fire is not smoking). Let us see why this is so.

Roughly, fuel oil is composed of 15 per cent hydrogen and 85 per cent carbon. It is a hydrocarbon compound. There are also tiny amounts of sulfur, oxygen, and nitrogen, but they are small enough to be ignored. To burn this oil, we must unite it with the air. Air is composed of approximately 21 per cent oxygen and 79 per cent nitrogen. When the fuel oil is atomized and begins to burn as it unites with the air being pushed down the blast tube, the flame is the physical evidence that combustion is in progress. Our job is to burn to completion the full amount of the carbon and hydrogen in the oil.

From this process we get carbon dioxide and water vapor. The carbon in the oil unites with the oxygen in the air, and the hydrogen in the oil does the same thing. Thus we get carbon dioxide ($C + O_2 = CO_2$) and water ($2H_2 + O_2 = 2H_2O$). The more carbon dioxide we get, the more carbon is uniting with the oxygen in the air and the less excess air is being used. In all this process the nitrogen does nothing but use up a lot of the heat as it gains in temperature and goes up the flue. But as it makes up 79 per cent of the air, and as we must have air to get the oxygen to burn the oil, we can do nothing about it. It is a necessary evil, absorbing and wasting our heat. The less we have of it, the better, and from this we can see that the oil burner's job is *to burn the maximum amount of oil with the minimum amount of air without smoking.*

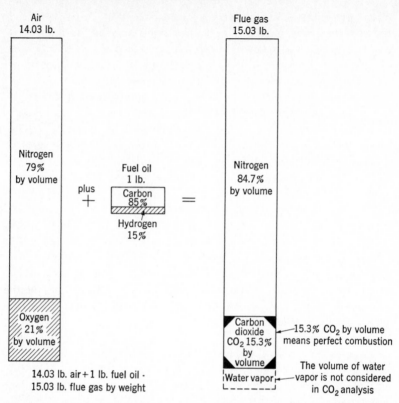

Fig. 21-1 Amount by weight and volume of air required and flue gas produced when 1 lb of fuel oil is burned.

EXCESS AIR

We want no *excess air* to absorb heat and waste it through the flue. The less air we consume while still achieving good combustion, the less waste we will have. The heat will be radiated to the boiler instead of being absorbed by the useless nitrogen of the excess air. Even the oxygen not used up in the combustion process is an enemy, for it too absorbs the heat and helps waste it. Therefore, as mentioned above, only the actual amount of air necessary to carry out the combustion process without smoking should be used. Since the CO_2 reading tells us the actual amount of air that is excess, we can have an excellent index of how much heat is being wasted because of that extra air (Table 21-1).

DETERMINING THE AMOUNT OF EXCESS AIR

Let us examine how CO_2 readings give us the exact amount of excess air that is wasting heat. The CO_2 reading gives (in per cent) just what

Table 21-1   Per Cent Excess Air for Various CO$_2$ Readings

	Per cent CO$_2$	Per cent excess air
	3	400
	4	280
	5	200
A low CO$_2$	6	155
	7	120
	8	86
A fair CO$_2$	9	66
A good operating CO$_2$	10	51
	11	37
A high CO$_2$	12	26
	13	17
An excellent but critical CO$_2$	14	9
	15	0

part of the total volume of the flue gases the CO$_2$ represents. A 10 per cent CO$_2$ reading means that 10 per cent of the volume of the flue gases is CO$_2$ (after the water vapor has been deducted). If the CO$_2$ reading drops to 8 per cent, then it means that only 8 per cent of the volume of flue gases is carbon dioxide or there has been an increase of extra air in the flue gases which naturally lowers the per cent of the volume represented by the CO$_2$. The greater the proportion of excess or unnecessary air, the lower part of the volume will be the CO$_2$. The less excess air, the greater will be the CO$_2$ in per cent of volume.

Chemical calculations show that 15.4 per cent CO$_2$ is about the highest reading we can get with the average light fuel oil. Thus, with a 15 per cent CO$_2$ reading there is no excess air and the CO$_2$ is taking up its full part as 15 per cent of the total volume of the flue gases. As it drops down it means that excess air is increasing and consequently lowering the proportion in per cent of the volume that CO$_2$ represents.

This excess air absorbs heat that should go to the boiler; wastes the heat by carrying it up the flue; cools the fire so that it is lower in temperature and slows down the combustion process by this cooling, which decreases the radiance of the flame and thereby seriously impedes the intensity with which the heat is transferred to the boiler. Because of this, we must take CO$_2$ readings in order to gauge how much excess air is present and from there make the necessary corrections so that we may raise the CO$_2$.

Excess air is one of the main causes of high fuel-oil consumption or, to put it conversely, low CO$_2$ readings are one of the main causes of high fuel-oil consumption. It must be remembered that CO$_2$ readings must be obtained without smoke. By curtailing the amount of air we may be able to raise the CO$_2$, but it must never be curtailed to the point where the oxygen supply is so limited that the carbon instead of forming CO_2 will have to deposit out as soot or smoke because there is not enough air to furnish the oxygen to carry the reaction to its conclusion. In such cases high CO_2 with smoke means that the combustion is not complete and the carbon in the oil is appearing as soot or incompletely burning to carbon monoxide (CO) because of the shortage of air.

TESTING FOR EXCESS AIR

The CO_2 test should be taken at the breeching as close to the boiler as possible on the boiler side of the draft control. A small hole is punched in the smoke pipe and the tube inserted at that point and the gas sample pumped into the analyzer. There are simple, inexpensive, and accurate CO_2 analyzers on the market that do an excellent job and are very easy to operate. A CO_2 reading can also be made over the fire, usually through a small hole in the fire door. Any noticeable drop in CO_2 between the firedoor reading and the reading at the smoke pipe means that air is getting in somewhere through the boiler sections, between the fire-door area and the breeching, or else around the base. A CO_2 reading of 10 per cent over the fire and 8 per cent at the breeching means that 40 per cent excess air has leaked into the boiler between the two points, a condition that could easily decrease the combustion efficiency by 5 per cent or more.

Up to fairly recent times the average burner was designed to deliver 40 per cent excess air or more, and for this reason it was almost impossible to get a CO_2 reading of more than 10 per cent. Now, a burner must perform with a minimum 10 per cent CO_2 reading even in gallonages as low as 0.75 gph in order to get Commercial Standards Label CS 75-56 that will permit the burner to be used in any home financed through a Federal agency. The addition of new air delivery devices such as combustion heads, turbulators, and diffusers, which do an excellent job in turbulating the air and mixing it with the oil, has increased CO_2's so that 11 to 12 per cent CO_2's are now quite ordinary. The better the mixing devices, the less necessity for delivering extra air to provide for contingencies, and consequently the higher the CO_2. Burners of newer design with special types of combustion heads today deliver no more than 20 per cent excess air, and this can be cut down to a smaller percentage by manipulating the air control devices at the nozzle.

Some circumstances make it necessary to deliver some excess air over the actual theoretical amount necessary, for no mechanical device or means has yet been designed to utilize completely all the oxygen in the air. Some escapes the oil spray and fire completely owing to mechanical deficiencies, inability of firebox design to meet all requirements, draft

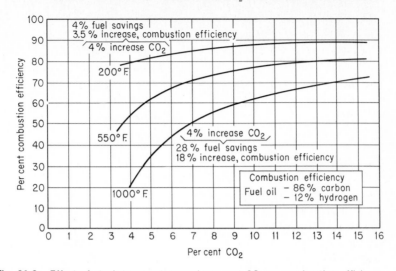

Fig. 21-2 Effect of stack temperature and per cent CO_2 on combustion efficiency and fuel savings.

conditions, and an apparent actual chemical necessity for some extra oxygen in order to carry the chemical reactions to their conclusion properly.

AIR REQUIREMENTS

Theoretically, about 1,540 cu ft of air is needed for the combustion of 1 gal of fuel oil, but actually from 1,900 to 2,000 cu ft is delivered, in a burner with good air delivery and proper turbulence, which is about 25 per cent in excess of the need. Regulation of the fan control shutter can reduce this considerably. The simple formula, gph × 1,540 × 1.25 = cubic feet of air necessary to burn a definite amount of oil *per hour* (gph = gallon per hour capacity of the nozzle) is all that is necessary to get an approximate figure on basic air requirements. The same formula divided by 60 gives the cubic feet of air necessary per minute.

$$\frac{\text{gph} \times 1,540 \times 1.25}{60} = \text{cu ft of air per min needed to burn a definite amount of oil}$$

These formulas allow for 25 per cent excess air, which can be cut down by mechanical air adjustments.

The causes of low CO_2 can be seen from Fig. 21-3. The chapters that follow this will discuss some of the main causes and remedies. The foregoing should demonstrate the absolute necessity for taking CO_2

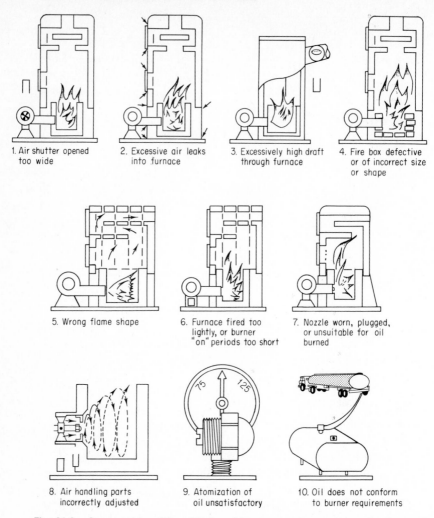

1. Air shutter opened too wide

2. Excessive air leaks into furnace

3. Excessively high draft through furnace

4. Fire box defective or of incorrect size or shape

5. Wrong flame shape

6. Furnace fired too lightly, or burner "on" periods too short

7. Nozzle worn, plugged, or unsuitable for oil burned

8. Air handling parts incorrectly adjusted

9. Atomization of oil unsatisfactory

10. Oil does not conform to burner requirements

Fig. 21-3   Causes of low CO_2.   (*Bacharach Instrument Div., American Bosch Arma Corp.*)

readings in order to determine combustion efficiencies and the amount of excess air.   Any increase in CO_2 without smoke will mean less excess air, finer combustion, lower fuel consumption, and *lower stack temperature.*

STACK TEMPERATURE

This now brings us to a discussion of the heat-absorbing ability of the boiler or furnace and how CO_2 readings are capable of affecting this quality of the boiler, as well as a number of other conditions that can affect stack temperature. There is little or no mystery implied in the term "stack temperature," as there is in the term "CO_2 percentage." Stack temperature means just what it says—the temperature at the stack of the flue gases. We take the reading at exactly the same place where we take the CO_2 sample, at the breeching, as close to the boiler as possible and *on the boiler side of the draft control.* The only instrument needed is a high-temperature stack thermometer that reads up to 1000° F. The unit should be run for 15 or 20 min and then the stack thermometer should be inserted and a reading taken when it stops rising. When this balance is achieved, the CO_2 reading should be taken.

We have a fairly accurate starting point from which to consider stack temperature when we know approximately the flame temperature. If the flame temperature is fairly constant, then we will have an idea by taking the stack temperature of how much the heat intensity has been reduced by the boiler. If a flame temperature is 1700° F, and we take a stack temperature reading and get 500° F, the absorption of heat by the boiler or furnace has reduced the temperature of the products of combustion by 1200°. If suddenly for some reason the stack temperature reading should rise to 700°, the heat being absorbed would be reduced and an additional 200° would be going up the stack instead of being picked up by the boiler. We would be able to cut down on the fuel consumption and restore the previous efficiency if we could reduce the stack temperature to the original 500° F. We strive for lower stack temperatures because they are evidence that the boiler is absorbing more heat. To put it more technically, the stack temperature is a comparative index of the boiler's heat-absorption efficiency. The higher the stack temperature, the more heat is going up the chimney and the less is being absorbed by the boiler or furnace.

It must be remembered that the stack temperature in degrees Fahrenheit is a measurement of the intensity of the heat absorption of the boiler, but it is not a measurement of the quantity of heat absorbed. Degrees are a measurement of *heat intensity;* Btu are the measurement of the *heat quantity.* To get a mathematically accurate determination of the total quantity of heat absorbed by a boiler we would have to make an evaporation test, which is very involved and can be done only in a properly equipped laboratory.

However, the use of the stack thermometer can give us a comparative guide or index that is easy to understand and easy to obtain and that furnishes a fairly accurate means of measuring performance. Many local communities have ordinances that limit the stack temperature before a permit will be granted to operate the unit.

Stack-temperature readings are lower in oil-burning boilers than in coal-burning boilers converted to oil. A round coal-burning boiler fired by oil with a 600° F stack temperature might be considered as doing a good heat-absorbing job, but the same stack temperature on an oil-burning boiler could be poor in comparison. Boiler-efficiency rating directly concerns stack temperature. A 70 per cent efficient boiler burning a gallon of oil per hour might have a 350° stack temperature, which would be considered good, while a 60 per cent efficient boiler at the same rate with a 480° stack temperature would be considered all right. The lower the efficiency of the boiler as regards oil firing, the greater will have to be the measures we take to hold down the stack temperature and thereby decrease fuel-oil consumption.

Restricted flue passages, a large amount of heat-receiving surface, and controlled draft all mean lower stack temperatures, and these are what we get in a boiler or furnace properly designed to handle the large volume of gases that is the result of oil combustion.

REDUCING STACK TEMPERATURES

Normally, cleaning the flue passages, installing baffles, reducing draft, firing at the proper rate, or building a properly designed combustion chamber will all result in a decline in stack temperature and a consequent increase in efficiency (see Chap. 29).

However if the high stack temperature results from excess air car-

1 - Excessively high draft

2 - Heating surfaces dirty

3 - Baffling needed

4 - Furnace undersize

5 - Poor combustion chamber

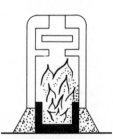
6 - Burning equipment needs expert tuning

Fig. 21-4   Causes of high stack temperature. (*Bacharach Instrument Div., American Bosch Arma Corp.*)

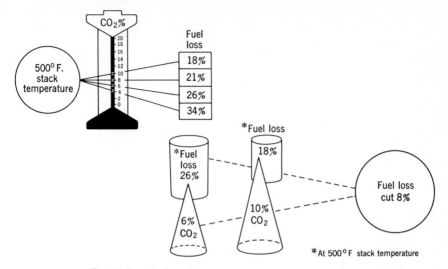

Fig. 21-5   (*Bacharach Instrument Div., American Bosch Arma Corp.*)

rying a large amount of heat wastefully through the boiler and cooling the fire, we must attack the stack temperature problem from the CO_2 angle.   An increase in CO_2 will result in a decrease in excess air (Table 21-1) and a consequent drop in stack temperature.   We can see from this that usually an increase in CO_2 will result in a decline in stack temperature, but this does not hold true 100 per cent of the time for various reasons.   Draft is an important factor that directly concerns the CO_2 percentage and the stack temperature, and its influence will be discussed at length in Chaps. 22 and 23.

The relationship of CO_2 and stack temperature is very close.   By good hot combustion we get the maximum quantity of heat from our fuel; any excess air as evidenced by a drop in CO_2 percentage decreases that combustion efficiency and reduces the intensity with which the heat is released.   Once the heat is released, the stack temperature gains in importance because the important thing then is how much of that released heat is being picked up by the boiler.   A direct relationship is established when excess air is causing the stack temperature to rise, for any increase in CO_2 will bring a corresponding decrease in excess air and stack temperature.

The causes and effects of low CO_2's and high stack temperatures are shown in Table 21-1 and Figs. 21-3, 21-4, and 21-7.   The correction of these defects can be easily made.   The effect that these measures have can be readily ascertained by referring to Table 21-2.   For instance, if we have a unit running with a 6 per cent CO_2 and a 700° stack temperature, by sealing up the air leaks and installing baffles we raise

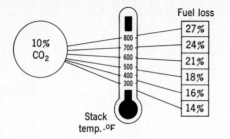

Fig. 21-6 (*Bacharach Instrument Div., American Bosch Arma Corp.*)

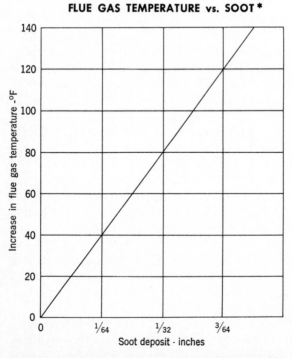

Fig. 21-7 Flue-gas temperature vs. soot. It is estimated by some authorities that a coating of soot ⅛ in. thick on the heating surfaces can cause an increase of fuel consumption of as much as 25 per cent. (*Bacharach Instrument Div., American Bosch Arma Corp.*)

Table 21-2 Per Cent Loss of Combustion Efficiency for Various CO_2 and
Stack-temperature Readings (*Shell Oil Co.*)

Carbon dioxide (CO_2), per cent	Stack temperature, °F							
	300	400	500	600	700	800	900	1000
	Loss of combustion efficiency, per cent							
15.0	10.7	12.7	14.8	16.8	18.8	20.8	22.8	24.8
14.5	10.9	12.9	15.0	17.1	19.2	21.2	23.3	25.2
14.0	11.0	13.1	15.3	17.4	19.5	21.6	23.8	25.7
13.5	11.1	13.4	15.6	17.7	20.0	22.0	24.3	26.4
13.0	11.3	13.5	15.8	18.1	20.5	22.5	24.9	27.0
12.5	11.5	13.8	16.2	18.4	20.7	23.1	25.5	27.8
12.0	11.6	14.0	16.5	18.8	21.4	23.7	26.2	28.6
11.5	11.8	14.4	16.8	19.3	22.0	24.3	26.9	29.5
11.0	12.1	14.7	17.3	19.8	22.6	25.1	27.8	30.5
10.5	12.4	15.0	17.8	20.5	23.3	25.8	28.8	31.5
10.0	12.6	15.4	18.3	21.2	24.0	26.8	29.7	32.6
9.5	12.9	15.7	18.8	21.8	24.8	27.8	30.8	33.8
9.0	13.3	16.3	19.4	22.6	25.8	28.8	32.0	35.2
8.5	13.6	16.8	20.1	23.5	26.8	30.0	33.5	36.8
8.0	14.0	17.5	20.9	24.5	28.0	31.5	35.0	38.5
7.5	14.5	18.3	21.8	25.5	29.3	33.0	36.8	40.5
7.0	15.1	18.9	22.9	26.8	30.8	34.8	38.8	42.5
6.5	15.7	19.8	24.0	28.2	32.3	36.7	41.0	45.0
6.0	16.5	20.8	25.5	29.8	34.3	39.0	43.4	47.9
5.5	17.3	22.2	27.0	32.0	36.7	41.5	46.5	51.3
5.0	18.3	23.6	29.0	34.3	38.6	45.0	50.2	55.4
4.5	19.5	25.5	31.4	37.3	43.2	49.0	54.8	60.3
4.0	21.1	27.6	34.2	40.7	47.4	53.7	60.5	67.0

the CO_2 to 10 per cent and lower the stack temperature to 550°F; we
will reduce the loss in per cent from 34.3 to 19.5 or a reduction of 14.8
per cent, an excellent reward for our efforts to increase CO_2 and decrease
stack temperature whenever possible.

SMOKE READINGS

As mentioned previously, the CO_2 adjustment has to be made in relation
to the amount of smoke produced. A customarily high CO_2 and a high
smoke reading will have a tendency to cancel each other out as far as
efficiency is concerned.

Fuel loss caused by excessive smoke is due to two factors: (1) the
fuel has not been burned completely; and (2) dirty combustion, deposit-

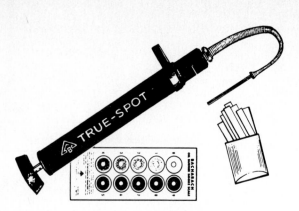

Fig. 21-8 A smoke-measuring instrument.

Fig. 21-9 Smoke scale. (*Bacharach Instrument Div., American Bosch Arma Corp.*)

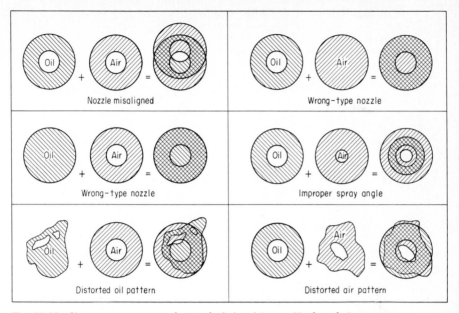

Fig. 21-10 Six common causes of poor fuel-air mixture. (*Bacharach Instrument Div., American Bosch Arma Corp.*)

ing soot on the heat exchanger or boiler surfaces, increases the rate of heat loss.

The smoke density as measured by the instrument shown in Figs. 21-8 and 21-9 is an important reading. The higher the smoke-density reading, the greater will be the eventual heat loss due to the deposit of soot and unburned fuel passing up the chimney in the form of vapor.

Figure 21-9, which shows the various smoke densities represented that can be obtained by readings with the smoke test meter, will not for any single reading affect all fuel-burning units in the same way.

This means that a No. 4 smoke reading with one type of unit will decrease in efficiency more than the same smoke reading with another type of unit, or vice versa. Depending upon the construction of the heat exchanger or boiler, some units will accumulate soot rapidly at a No. 4 smoke density, while the accumulation of soot as mentioned above on another unit can be relatively slower.

In any event, the safest practice to follow is not to allow any unit to operate with a smoke density in excess of a No. 3 on the scale and, if at all possible to obtain a smoke reading, not over a No. 2 on the scale.

There are many times in combustion testing when a service technician will be unable to obtain a high CO$_2$ with a low smoke reading. There are four basic conditions that can cause this:

Table 21-3   Effect of Smoke on Burner Performance

Bacharach-Shell smoke scale no.	Rating	Sooting produced
1	Excellent	Extremely light if at all
2	Good	Slight sooting which will not increase stack temperature appreciably
3	Fair	May be some sooting but will rarely require cleaning more than once a year
4	Poor	Borderline condition; some units will require cleaning more than once a year
5	Very poor	Soot rapidly and heavily

1. A nonuniform mixture of fuel and air. In this case sections of the flame will be starved for oxygen. These parts will have a very high CO_2 and a high smoke reading. Conversely, other parts of the flame will have more air than is required. These parts will have a low CO_2 percentage and a low smoke reading. The conditions may be caused by clogged nozzles, poorly placed nozzles, nozzles not in line with respect to air cone, spray deflected by electrodes, improper oil pressure, etc.

2. Improperly shaped or sized combustion chamber. The chamber that is too large for the firing rate may never reach the temperature equilibrium required for clean combustion.

3. Flame impingement on cold surfaces. This factor results from the improperly sized combustion chamber or oversized nozzle. Flame hits the side of the chamber on the start, and carbon is formed.

4. Air leakage into fuel burning unit. This is excess air that leaks into the unit but does not reach the combustion area. It reduces the CO_2. In adjusting to reduce the air supply for combustion to raise the CO_2 as a result of the dilution mentioned directly above, a dirty, sooty fire can result.

QUESTIONS

1. What are the advantages of taking instrument tests when adjusting an oil burner?
2. What are the two conditions that must be measured with these instruments?
3. What is the purpose of the combustion process?
4. The CO_2 reading gives an accurate indication of what?
5. What elements compose fuel oil?
6. What is the oil burner's job from the efficiency standpoint?
7. Explain the function of smoke measurement.

CHAPTER 22

ADJUSTING FOR
HIGHER COMBUSTION EFFICIENCY:
DRAFT

Before the application can be made of the information about CO_2, stack temperature, and smoke readings as discussed in the previous chapter, the part that draft plays in affecting them must be considered. After draft is understood, it will be comparatively easy to apply practical methods for raising CO_2 readings and lowering stack temperature.

A body of air when heated will become lighter and thus begin to rise. The higher the temperature to which the gas or air is heated, the faster it will rise. If we heat this air in a confined space, as in a tube or chimney, the result will be the same. As the gas is heated it will rise, and as a result an upward flow through the chimney is established.

A cubic foot of air entering a furnace at cellar temperature of about $60°F$ weighs about 0.07 lb; at $600°$ it weighs about 0.037 lb or slightly more than half its original weight. This difference in weight between the same initial volume of air graphically shows why it will rise to the top of the column or chimney. It is this established upward flow, provided by the low-pressure area created within the chimney, that causes the gases to move continually upward; this phenomenon is popularly known as "draft."

If the draft causes the gases to move up the chimney (which is what we want), it is called *negative draft* or, more popularly, *updraft.* If for some reason the air and gases do not move freely up the chimney but remain relatively static because of high pressure existing within the chimney, or if cold air pours down the chimney because of various conditions to be discussed, we call this condition *positive draft, downdraft,* or *back pressure.*

Whatever may be the term to denote this presence of pressure in the chimney or furnace, it is something that we definitely do not want and must prevent at all costs if we are going to get any good operating efficiency out of our heat-producing unit.

This updraft or downdraft we refer to by the term *draft intensity.* If we have an updraft and the gases are moving through the chimney freely, we have a *negative draft intensity.* If there is a backdraft, we have a *positive draft intensity.*

Thus we can see that *draft intensity* is the term we use to denote the condition concerning the free flow of the gases through the chimney. Specifically it is *negative draft intensity* that is desired.

Draft volume is the term used to specify the amount or volume of gases that a chimney may handle. Draft volume is measured in cubic feet.

We are mainly concerned in oil firing with draft intensity, for the greater the updraft, the less we are dependent on the diameter or width of our chimney, although the smallest brick oil-burning chimney should be at least 8 in. in diameter, and this even at heights of 30 ft would be good only up to about 1.75 gal of oil per hr unless the unit utilizes forced draft.

Our main concern, draft intensity, is directly proportionate to the *height* of the chimney, and while the draft volume is in proportion to the *diameter* of the chimney, we can utilize chimneys of smaller width *if our height and draft intensity* are adequate.

We can see from this that having chimneys of the proper height is one of our main considerations in creating the proper draft intensity.

This *upward flow, pull,* or *negative draft*—whichever we may choose to call it—can be created naturally in two ways. These are by heat and by outside air currents.

When we heat the gases and create the upward flow by lightening the gases, we have *thermal draft.* If the flow of gases upward is helped by proper air or wind currents across the chimney that create a pulling effect, we can call it *currential draft.* If we have a fan that is pulling or pushing the gases through the furnace and chimney, we have *induced* or *forced mechanical draft,* respectively. Almost all domestic oil burners burning No. 2 or heavier oil depend on *thermal* draft as well as *mechanical* draft; and if wind conditions are right, on all three.

The term "draft" as used from here on will refer to draft intensity that is *negative* or better known as *updraft*. If draft volume or down-draft is to be considered, each will be referred to specifically.

MEASURING DRAFT

We measure draft quite accurately by means of a simple device known as a *U tube*. The pull or suction exerted by the gases going up the chimney, if transferred to the U tube by a piece of tubing, will displace the column of water that is level in both arms of the U.

We can measure this displacement with a ruler, and in the case of domestic units we will find it will have been drawn or displaced a distance so small that it is measured in *hundredths of an inch.*

In large industrial plants with tall chimneys the water in the tube will be pulled out of place to measurements in inches or tenths of an inch, but that is not the case with domestic chimneys. Of course, we do not bother using the U tube and a ruler since inexpensive, effective instruments do the job for us with little trouble. Draft-measuring instruments are shown in Figs. 22-1 and 22-6.

Needless to say we must always have an updraft or free flow of the gases through the furnace and chimney. Draft is measured at two places: at the breeching and over the fire. The reading at the breeching must always be made on the furnace side of the draft control, that is, between

Fig. 22-1   Bacharach pocket draft gauge.

Fig. 22-2 Taking the draft reading.

the furnace and the draft control, as shown in Fig. 22-2. The draft reading on an oil-burning installation with a restricted flue passage type of oil-burning boiler should be about 0.07 in. of water at the breeching. Draft over the fire, taken through a small hole in the fire door, should be 0.01 to 0.02 in. The draft drop through an oil-burning boiler, because of the usual type of restricted flue passage, can be considerable.

If a boiler's restrictions cause a draft drop of 0.05 in. through the boiler and we have only 0.04 in. at the breeching to start with, then we obviously will have a positive pressure over the fire.

The smoke, soot, odor, and pulsations that occur can be properly remedied only by increasing the draft at the breeching so that draft drop

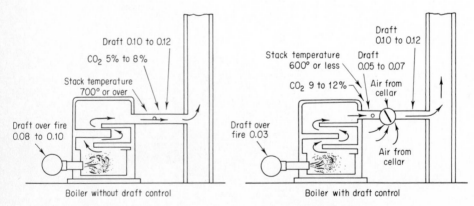

Fig. 22-3 Draft controls can increase operating efficiency.

through the boiler will not result in leaving us with no free flow of gases over the fire and through the initial flue passages of the boiler or furnace. With boilers which have a wide flue travel, the draft at the breeching can be as low as 0.03 and we will still have an updraft over the fire.

Remember, though, that the restricted flue passages of some boilers are the reason for their low stack temperatures and high heat-absorption efficiency even though they are somewhat sensitive to poor draft conditions.

A good rule to remember is that the greater the resistance to the uninterrupted flow of the hot gases in passing through the restricted flue passage of the boiler, the greater will be its heat-absorbing rate, but the greater will its draft have to be at the breeching if we are going to have trouble-free operation. This is especially true in cases where the firing rate is less than 3 gph.

It is always a good idea to check on the chimney recommendations made by the boiler manufacturer and compare them with the existing chimney before making the installation. This might also be the time when we find the chimney too large for the small amount of heat and flue products entering the chimney and a liner of double-wall construction, mentioned earlier in this chapter, would be in order. For example, a boiler or furnace with a 6-in. outlet (an area of 28 sq in.) going into an 8 × 10 chimney (an area of 63 sq in.) means we have to heat up an area almost $2\frac{1}{2}$ times larger than we really need, plus the heat required to heat up the chimney walls.

There must never be a draft pressure over the fire. Anything less than 0.01 in. over the fire can too easily cause a back pressure over the fire if for any reason the draft at the chimney decreases.

For instance, if we had a draft at the breeching of 0.05 in. water and over the fire of 0.01 in. water, the draft drop through the boiler would be the difference between the two figures, or 0.04 in. If for any

Fig. 22-4   Field standard type-M draft control.

reason the draft at the breeching dropped below 0.05 in., we would have no draft over the fire. This would result in trouble because of the pressure created.

The common results of such a condition are (1) smoke, (2) soot, (3) odor, (4) vibrations and pulsations, (5) hot nozzles, and (6) carbonized electrodes, resulting in ignition trouble. Conditions (1), (2), (3), and (4) are especially noticeable at the start.

The common causes of poor draft are as follows:

1. Improper size of chimney; usually chimney lacks height; interior should be round.

2. Leakage of air into the chimney through holes; open seams; clean-out door not properly sealed; breeching not tightly connected; air leaks through boiler sections not properly sealed; improper adjustment of draft control.

3. Interference of air flow over chimney because of high surrounding buildings, deflecting gables, etc.

4. Chimney clogged by some obstruction; its effective area may be considerably reduced by accumulations of soot. Chimneys should be kept clean.

5. Breeching with many 90-deg turns; turns in the breeching should be avoided as much as possible, but if they are absolutely necessary,

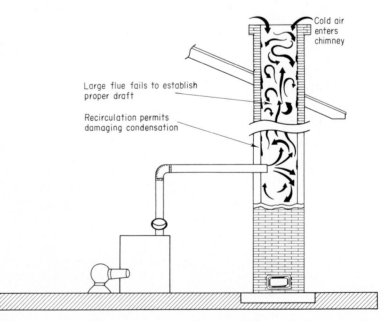

Fig. 22-5 The chimney is too large, causing poor draft.

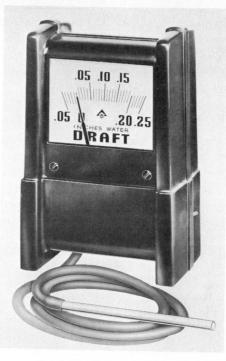

Fig. 22-6   Bacharach MZF draft gauge.

the turns should be achieved by 45- or 60-deg-angle smoke-pipe elbows.

6. Flue gases not hot enough.   The lower the temperature of the flue gases, the less will be the draft.   In spite of the greater efficiency involved, the flue-gas temperature should not go below 300°.   Temperatures below this will give erratic performance as the outside temperature gets lower.   If a chimney lacks insulating quality, flue gases may lose enough heat to slow their rise considerably and thereby seriously affect draft.

7. Fireplaces connecting with the oil-burner flue not kept closed to prevent cooler room air from being drawn into the flue, thereby reducing the draft on the oil-burner unit.

8. Boiler passages too restricted or too well baffled.

9. Furnace or boiler overfired, creating a volume of gases beyond the chimney's ability to handle it.

10. Draft control improperly adjusted.   The draft control should be adjusted to give 0.01 in. of water draft over the fire on days when there are no air currents evident on the outside and when weather

conditions are adversely affecting draft, that is, on windless, damp, or humid days. If the draft control is adjusted on a clear cold day when there is considerable air movement that improves draft, it will be found that when atmospheric conditions affecting draft are bad, soot, smoke, and odor will be noticed, especially on cold starts.

DRAFT AND ITS RELATION TO CO_2 AND STACK TEMPERATURE

On the other side at the opposite extreme, we have the problem of excess draft. It can be caused by a chimney too high or one excessively large in area, as well as by excessive stack temperatures. Excessive draft will affect the efficiency of oil-burner operation by lowering the CO_2. If the draft is excessive, it will cause a greater suction or pull through the boiler and breeching. As a result, a considerable amount of excess air will be drawn into the boiler. This excess air immediately lowers our CO_2 reading and increases our stack temperature.

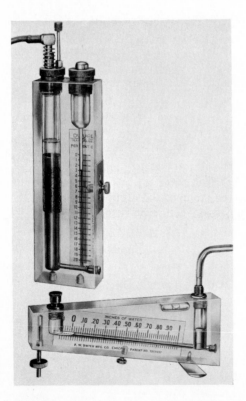

Fig. 22-7   Dwyer draft gauge with tapered connection and CO_2 analyzer shown above.

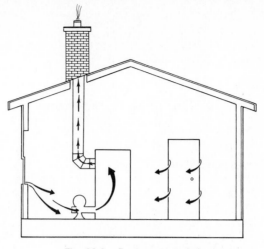

Fig. 22-8   Replacement air is necessary.

When CO_2 readings and stack temperature readings are taken, a stable draft condition must first be established over the fire. Fluctuations in draft will affect the amount of air delivered by the blower and from those spots, which cannot be detected, whereby air leaks into the boiler. As this increase of air from an increase in draft immediately lowers our CO_2, the necessity for a stable draft condition is obvious.

When we adjust for high CO_2's, that is, 10 per cent or over, draft over the fire should be from 0.01 to 0.02 in. This will give a safe margin. We obtain as high a CO_2 as possible with this draft setting by adjusting the air damper at the burner or by inserting devices in the blast tube that will increase the twisting turbulent motion of the air.

An increase in CO_2 percentage can be obtained by finer atomization. There should be no hesitation, therefore, in raising pump operating pressures 10 or 20 lb to achieve this. High atomizing pressures (100 lb or over) result in greater efficiency as reflected in a higher CO_2.

Cool fires, that is, those fires burning in a combustion chamber of improper size or design, will result in low CO_2's. This was discussed at length in an earlier chapter.

The taking of the CO_2 test is a simple procedure, as shown in Fig. 22-10. It is taken at the same opening as are the draft readings and stack temperature reading.

DRAFT READING OVER THE FIRE

The most important draft reading is the one that we take over the fire. This can usually be obtained by drilling a small hole in the fire door of the boiler and inserting the draft gauge tube at that point.

Fig. 22-9 A complete combustion testing kit containing Fyrite CO^2 analyzer, stack thermometer, smoke tester, and draft gauge.

Afterward the hole should be sealed with some compound such as furnace cement which can easily be removed should the necessity of taking a future reading arise.

The draft reading over the fire should always show an updraft. This means that we have a negative pressure area over the fire and the incoming air is finding its way to the fire without any pressure resistance while the hot gases from the fire are moving freely through the furnace and up the chimney.

Many dealers prefer to punch two holes in the breeching to be able to observe simultaneously the effect of the raised CO_2 readings on stack temperature and also to observe simultaneously the effect of fluctuating draft and the CO_2 readings. As the draft decreases, the CO_2 should rise; and as the CO_2 rises, the stack temperature will normally decrease.

It must be remembered that a negative pressure over the fire is the first necessity for trouble-free combustion. After that condition is ascertained, the stack temperature reading should be taken. After the stack thermometer has stopped rising and the unit is hot, the CO_2 readings should be taken with the 10 per cent or higher figure in mind. Never reduce the draft to an absolute minimum (0 over the fire) to obtain a higher CO_2. It is much more sensible practice to reduce the CO_2 1 or 2 per cent and retain the draft over the fire. The troubles that can result from no draft over the fire were mentioned in an earlier section of this chapter (see also Chaps. 27 and 28).

A drop in draft over the fire to the point where there is a positive pressure over the fire immediately retards the flow of air, disturbs and slows down the mixing of the oil and air, and interferes with the combustion process.   As a result soot forms.

The depositing of the soot on the boiler flue passages insulates them. As a result, the boiler does not absorb the heat as readily from the passing flue gases.   The result of this is to drive the stack temperature up and cause a greater heat loss through the stack.   Thus the drop in draft does not cause the stack temperature rise directly but, by affecting the air supply to the fire, can cause soot; and the soot's insulating qualities on the boiler surfaces does the rest.

Stack temperatures for oil-burning boilers that are being fired at the proper rate should not exceed $500°F$, but in the case of coal-fired boilers using oil, the figure $700°$ would be excessive.

From the foregoing, we can see that draft is an all-important condition.   It is necessary to provide the basis for trouble-free combustion; and from the trouble-free combustion provided by proper draft, we can adjust for high CO_2's and low stack temperatures that make for economical operation of the domestic heating plant.

The greatest single factor that will stabilize draft conditions and enable us to obtain the proper CO_2's is the installation of a draft control. No oil-burner installation should be made without this draft control. The device is merely a swinging panel or door that bypasses air from the cellar or surrounding area directly into the smoke pipe, thereby lowering the draft pull on the boiler itself.   The size of the opening

Fig. 22-10   Taking the CO_2 reading.   (*Bacharach Instrument Div., American Bosch Arma Corp.*)

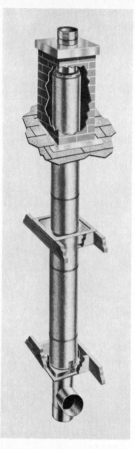

Fig. 22-11 An "all fuel" prefabricated flue (chimney) that can be used with coal, oil, gas, or wood. This factory-built chimney is 38 sq in. (*Metalbestos Div., Wallace-Murray Corp.*)

provided by the draft control in its maximum open position should be equivalent to the diameter of the smoke pipe.

The draft control should be installed as close to the boiler as possible for most efficient operation. Sufficient room should be left, however, for the stack control to be installed between the draft stabilizer and the boiler. The draft stabilizer in being installed as close to the boiler as possible should also precede any elbows or turns. This means that it normally should be on the straight run of pipe from the furnace or boiler prior to the first "el."

If this is not possible, every attempt should be made to keep it close to the boiler. Sometimes draft controls must, of necessity, be installed in the chimney proper, but this is not too good a practice.

It should be remembered that the purpose of the draft control is to regulate draft conditions in the boiler and thereby aid in producing high CO_2's by cutting down the amount of excess air caused by excess draft through the boiler. It follows from this, therefore, that it should be as close to the boiler as possible so that its changing adjustment may affect the boiler directly and with the greatest intensity.

The draft control should be adjusted as recommended in a previous part of this chapter. Care should be taken to see that its hinged door always swings open freely and that soot does not collect on the back of this swinging panel. Such accumulations will disturb the balanced adjustment and result in improper draft conditions.

The installation of the draft control in every oil-burner installation should be regarded as a must, for it is an important factor in maintaining high CO_2's and the proper flow of air in relation to intensity and quantity through the boiler or furnace. Furthermore, it stabilizes the draft effect

Fig. 22-12 A type-L vent pipe. This comes in 3- and 4-in diameters and is used with low-temperature flue-gas oil-fired units. Stack-gas temperatures with this vent do not exceed 500°F. Units utilizing the flue vent are known as "Low Temperature Oil Burning Appliances" and also as "Forced or Induced Draft" (FID). (*Metalbestos Div., Wallace-Murray Corp.*)

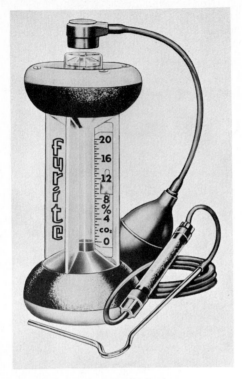

Fig. 22-13 Bacharach CO$_2$ Analyzer.

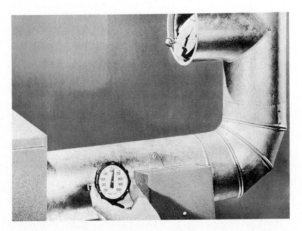

Fig. 22-14 Taking the stack temperature.

that changing barometric conditions will have upon the unit inasmuch as it equalizes the draft intensity through the boiler regardless of what atmospheric conditions may be outside.

This stabilization is extremely necessary if we are to maintain the operating CO_2 which we have adjusted for. Without a draft adjuster there is little chance of maintaining CO_2's at any set rate, since there would be no stabilized draft condition through the boiler and consequently fluctuating volumes of excess air would be disturbing and changing the CO_2 reading.

QUESTIONS

1. Explain how draft is created.
2. What are the different types of draft from the viewpoint of the manner by which they are produced?
3. How is draft measured? In what units?
4. What is meant by negative draft intensity? Positive draft intensity?
5. Where are the two locations at which draft should be measured?
6. Why is draft over the fire important?
7. What is the result of back pressure over the fire?
8. What are the common causes of poor draft?
9. How does draft affect CO_2 readings?
10. How do draft and CO_2 affect stack temperature?
11. How does the draft control work?
12. Why is draft control necessary?
13. Explain the value of a smoke reading when taking a CO_2 reading.
14. What is a type L vent?
15. Explain what is meant by "all-fuel" chimney?
16. What is meant by "replacement air"?
17. Why is "replacement air" necessary?
18. Give five advantages of the prefabricated chimney?

CHAPTER 23
FIRING THE
NEW OIL BURNER

The trouble-free, efficient operation of a newly installed domestic oil burner depends to a large extent upon its installation. The oil burner installed in accord with good engineering principles, properly sized, with a well-designed combustion chamber, and provided with sufficient draft and the necessary controls should operate for long periods of time with little service.

Aside from the proper installation, however, a thoroughgoing procedure for starting the new burner will help prevent excessive service at first when it is most likely to make an impression upon the homeowner.

In order to be sure that the oil burner will operate with little or no service at the start, a systematic method should be employed whereby all the points that may cause trouble will be thoroughly inspected and adjusted at the beginning.

The purpose of this chapter is to *provide a systematic, practical procedure consisting of a series of steps which will cover all the important points necessary to ensure the correct starting of a new oil burner.*

With reference to Fig. 23-1, it can be seen that there are 14 separate points to which careful attention should be given upon the firing of every new burner. These points are as follows:

1. Upon entering the cellar, somewhere adjacent to the meter box and main fuse block one will find the fused line switch, which has been installed as the master switch controlling burner operation. The first thing that should be checked by the serviceman is this fused line switch. The cover of this box should be opened and a 15-amp fuse inserted. This will give adequate protection.

Do not insert the fuse until the switch has been placed in the OFF position. Once the fuse has been screwed into place, use a test lamp to be sure that line current is passing through the box.

2. Leave the fused line switch in the OFF position for a moment and proceed to the burner switch (2). Put the burner switch in the OFF position. It will now be safe to turn on the fused line switch (1).

Control of the operation of the oil burner has now been passed to the burner switch, which normally should be placed on the inside or outside of the furnace or boiler jacket.

Sometimes this burner switch is also placed at the top of the cellar stairs, although there is some argument about whether or not this

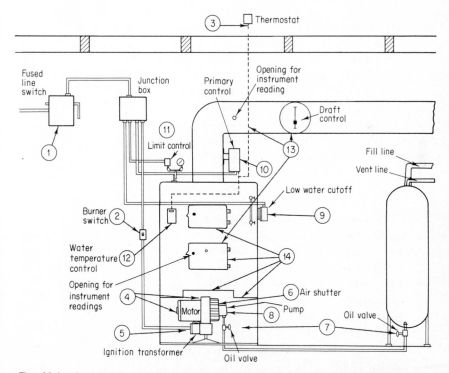

Fig. 23-1 Important points to be checked when starting the new oil burner.

is good practice. For better *service procedure,* the burner switch should be as close to the burner as possible, and preferably should be of the toggle type.

3. The next step to be checked is the thermostat upstairs. The cover should be removed gently with as little handling as possible. The thermostat should then be turned to the ON position, that is, until its contacts are making.

Move the dial that closes the thermostat contacts very slowly until they barely touch. Check this with the thermometer reading on the thermostat cover. They should be within 1° of each other. For instance, if the thermometer on the thermostat cover reads 70°, the dial setting at which the contacts are making should be no higher than 71°. Any substantial variation between these two will result in the homeowner receiving the impression that the thermostat is not accurate.

In most cases, the thermostat is accurately calibrated as it leaves the factory, and the fault is in the little thermometer contained in the thermostat cover. A little care at the start in seeing that the dial setting and the thermometer settings are fairly close, as explained above, will result in eliminating nuisance calls.

When a new system is installed, the homeowner is extremely interested in what is going on, and the thermostat which is upstairs in the living quarters will receive considerable attention. For this reason, if for no other, any considerable variation between the thermometer reading on the cover and the dial setting on the thermostat is bound to result in service calls.

This is a wise time to check the location of the thermostat and see that it is in the proper position. With the thermostat in the ON position, return to the cellar.

4. A good grade of SAE No. 20 motor oil should be used for lubrication at the ports on the motor. Four or five drops of oil are sufficient. Usually there will be two ports, one at the flange end of the motor where it joins the fan housing, and the other at the end of the motor bell somewhere close to the bearing. Be sure that these points are lubricated before proceeding.

Oil-burner motors are not to be lubricated more than several times a year. Overlubrication ruins more motors than underlubrication. It should be remembered, however, that the homeowner should be instructed to lubricate this motor about every 3 months.

5. The entire nozzle assembly is now removed from the burner. Check the size of the nozzle and tighten all fittings, especially the nozzle and nozzle adapter, and the point where the flare fittings join the nozzle oil line. At this point, it would be wise to inspect the

small strainer at the rear of the nozzle to see that it has been firmly tightened.

While the nozzle assembly is out, make certain that the electrodes are properly placed. The electrodes should be $\frac{1}{2}$ in. above the center line of the nozzle, and the points of the electrodes should be from $\frac{5}{16}$ to $\frac{1}{2}$ in. in front of the nozzle. The gap between the electrodes should be $\frac{3}{16}$ in. or whatever spacing the burner manufacturer recommends. Chapter 25 discusses ignition setting dimensions at length.

In the event that an extremely narrow angle of spray is used (30 or 45 deg), it is well to lower the electrodes toward the center of the nozzle so that the distance from the tip of the electrodes to the nozzle center will not be more than $\frac{3}{8}$ in.

It can be noted from this that in angles of spray above 45 deg, the distance between nozzle center and electrode tips is $\frac{1}{2}$ in. as compared with $\frac{3}{8}$ in. when the angle of spray is narrow. The important point is that there must always be $\frac{1}{4}$-in. clearance between the electrodes and any metal parts.

Ceramic insulators should be fastened firmly in the holder and should be held tightly enough to prevent their moving in the event of jarring or vibration.

The entire nozzle assembly should now be reinserted into the blast tube and the flare or compression fitting to the pump reconnected.

Replace the plate securely at the back end of the burner blast tube. This back plate should meet the rear of the blast tube securely, so that air cannot leak through any openings between it and the burner housing. If it does not sit securely, fill in the crack with furnace cement to prevent any air leaks. The terminals of the ignition transformer should be checked to be sure that they are clean and that the high-tension leads are firmly connected thereto.

6. Open the air shutter to its full opening, and if possible remove the adjusting band completely. Through the openings thus provided, check the coupling to see that it is fastened securely to both the motor shaft and the pump shaft. The usual coupling will be of the flexible type and have an Allen setscrew at each end to fasten it securely to the shaft.

Using the proper size of Allen key, tighten these setscrews as far as they will go. The metal air-adjusting band should then be replaced. The air shutter should now be adjusted so that it will be $\frac{1}{8}$ in. open, thereby rendering improbable the admission of too much air when the burner is first started. This initial air adjustment will be covered in a later step.

7. Check the oil tank to be sure that it contains a sufficient quantity of oil. Both the oil valve at the tank and the oil valve at the burner pump should now be opened. Open the fire door on the boiler or furnace and leave it in a half-opened position. Then proceed to open the cellar windows or doors to make sure that any fumes that may develop because of improper initial firing will be vented to the outside rather than through the house.

8. Attach a pressure gauge which reads to at least 150 psi to the pressure side of the pump, and if it is an underground tank, with a two-pipe system, attach a vacuum gauge to the vacuum side of the pump.

No vacuum gauge is necessary on a gravity-fed system. The burner switch (2) should not be put in the on position and the burner should begin operating if the controls are properly set. Once the oil is ignited, close the boiler or furnace door.

If it is a one-pipe system, it will be necessary to vent the air from the pump. This can be done by unscrewing or loosening the pressure gauge until oil begins to be expelled at the loosened fitting. A can or container should be placed below the pump so that this oil will not stain the cellar floor.

When air bubbles cease to come through at the loosened pressure gauge, the pump will have been thoroughly vented of the air, and at this time the burner will begin to fire. Tighten the pressure gauge quickly. The oil pressure should now be adjusted. Remove the cap screw from the pressure regulating valve and insert a screw driver or proper instrument and turn slowly in a clockwise direction to increase pressure, and counterclockwise to decrease the pressure.

On some pumps, this adjustment must be made with an Allen key. The pump pressure should be adjusted to read 100 psi. This is the standard setting, although, as will be seen later, it may be necessary to raise the pressure.

At this point it would be well to note that a two-pipe system will normally vent itself, and it will be unnecessary to loosen the pressure gauge to expel the air. However, if, because of the long horizontal or vertical pull, the pump is unable to pick up its own prime on a two-pipe system, open the suction side and fill with oil by hand. The pump should now pick up the prime and start to deliver oil with little or no trouble.

Check the vacuum gauge on a two-pipe system. If, after the line has been primed, it pulls no vacuum, then either the pump is not operating or, more probably, there are bad leaks in the suction line due to careless installation.

A pump hookup for a two-pipe system should be capable of pulling the oil with no more than 12 in. of vacuum showing on the vacuum gauge. If the vacuum gauge reading goes much higher than this, check the oil valves to make sure that they are completely opened, and check the oil line wherever possible to be sure that it is not kinked or obstructed.

With the burner now firing, check the flame for smoke by opening the boiler or furnace door quickly and then closing it. Do not attempt to adjust the flame with the boiler or furnace door open, as the influx of air through the door will change the normal flame characteristics. Observe the flame by quickly opening and closing the door.

The air shutter, which at this point is $\frac{1}{8}$ in. open, should now slowly be opened until the flame has ceased giving off any smoke. The fire should be clear.

9. The burner is now firing normally, and this is the time to check the low-water cutoff. Open the petcock at the bottom of the boiler and slowly drain the water until it is below the level line mark on the low-water cutoff housing. Keep draining until the float trips the mercury-tube switch and shuts off the burner. The low-water cutoff should stop the burner before all the water has disappeared from the gauge glass.

Usually the low-water cutoff is installed at a point where it breaks the circuit when there is still about $\frac{1}{2}$ to $\frac{3}{4}$ in. of water showing in the gauge glass. Refill the boiler till the low-water cutoff returns the burner to the ON position.

It may be that the low-water cutoff will restore the circuit to the burner before the primary control (10) has recycled. If this is the case, it may be necessary to wait a few minutes longer until the control has recycled to the starting position.

10. As the burner resumes operation, start and stop it several times, in order to find out if the ignition is working properly. There should be no delay in the appearance of the flame, and absolutely no visible evidence of white smokelike fumes in the firebox or upper portion of the boiler. These fumes demonstrate that the ignition is coming on late. This is commonly referred to by the term "delayed ignition."

After you have checked the ignition several times while observing the rapidity with which the flame appears, the primary control or stack mounted relay should be checked to determine the amount of time it will take this control to go into safety. Allow the burner to operate for a few minutes after checking the ignition and then shut it down by closing the burner switch (2).

Remove the wire from the No. 3 terminal on the primary control. Attach to this terminal one of the leads from a test lamp and ground the other lead to the relay frame or conduit leading into the relay. The lamp will represent the burner motor. Turn the burner switch on. The relay clapper will now pull in. The test lamp will light and the ignition transformer will furnish a spark at the electrodes. However, because no flame will appear due to the fact that the motor lead has been disconnected, the stack element of the relay will not shunt out the safety switch. As a result, the relay will go into safety.

With a watch, check the amount of time it takes for the test lamp to go out. When this lamp is extinguished, the primary control will have gone into safety. The bulk should not glow for more than 90 sec. This is ample safety time.

It should be remembered that the length of time that this bulb stays lit represents the number of seconds the burner would operate, in the event of ignition or oil failure, before it was shut down by the safety mechanism in the primary control. The location of the relay should be checked at this time to make certain that it is securely mounted and that the helix element is in the path of the hot free-flowing gases.

Also, check the high- and low-voltage terminals to see that all the leads are securely fastened. Disconnect the test lamp and return the motor lead to the No. 3 terminal. Next press the safety button; the burner should now resume normal operation.

11. The next step is to check the limit control. If it is a steam or hot-water system, close off all the radiators upstairs after adjusting the limit control to the proper setting. When the high setting on the limit control has been reached, it should break its contacts and shut the burner off.

Upon the adjusted drop in steam or water temperature, the limit control will resume its contact and start the burner.

If it is a warm-air system, close all the duct dampers and adjust the combination fan and limit control in accord with the furnace manufacturer's specifications. Drill a small hole adjacent to the bimetallic element and insert an ordinary stack thermometer so that its mercury bulb will be as close as possible to the limit control element.

The use of the stack thermometer in this fashion will serve as a check upon the calibration of the limit control and its rapidity in responding to the air temperature changes in the duct. The control should operate closely to the differential prescribed by the manufacturer. After observing the operation of this control several times, remove the stack thermometer and seal the small hole in the duct with a sheet-metal screw.

12. If there is a water temperature control on the system for the purpose of regulating domestic faucet hot water, adjust its setting

so that the water coming from the tap will be about 130 to 140°F. This, of course, will mean that the setting on the low-limit water temperature control mounted in the boiler or generator will have to be higher.

What this setting will actually be, however, depends upon the size of the generator, the capacity of the boiler, and the heat loss from the storage tank or lines carrying the water to the faucets upstairs.

13 and 14. The burner has now been operating for a considerable period of time. The new combustion chamber is hot and the final adjustment by instruments should now take place. Insert the stack thermometer in an opening drilled for it in the smoke pipe between the furnace and the draft control, leaving the stack thermometer in the smoke pipe until it ceases to rise.

With an oil-burning boiler, this stack temperature should not be above 500°F, and with a conversion installation, 700°F is excessive.

Once the stack thermometer has stopped rising, take a CO_2 test at the smoke pipe. It should read at least 10 per cent. If the CO_2 reading is considerably lower than this, it may be due to air leaks around the boiler base, fire door, or upper flue passage door (14). Seal these up with furnace cement. Also seal around the area where the smoke pipe joins the furnace or boiler.

This should help raise the CO_2 to the 10 per cent mark. If it does not, raise the oil pressure 10 to 15 psi and, if necessary, 20 psi. Reduce the air slightly, but not to the point where smoking ensues.

If a smoke test is made at this time, it should be made at the opening in the smoke pipe, and not read above the No. 3 disk for a gun-type burner.

Usually, if the air has been reduced to the point where any further reduction will result in the formation of smoke, and there are no air leaks, the CO_2 can usually be raised by increasing the oil pressure. Such an increase in pressure provides finer atomization and results in better oil-air mixture, giving a more thorough and complete combustion process.

The CO_2 also can be increased to the required point by adjusting the draft control. Cutting down on the draft by opening the draft control will result in less air being drawn through the boiler and a higher CO_2.

The adjustment of the draft control should be made preferably on a warm, humid day when natural draft conditions are at their worst. Adjust the draft control opening under such weather conditions so that it cannot be opened beyond a point where the draft reading *at the fire door* will be less than 0.01 in. of water. This means that there should always be 0.01 in. of draft over the fire, and the draft control should be adjusted so as to provide this minimum under all operating conditions.

Take a draft reading at the smoke pipe. The difference between the draft reading at the smoke pipe and the draft reading over the fire is the draft loss through the boiler.

It can be seen from this that the draft reading at the smoke pipe should always be high enough to take care of this draft drop through the boiler and still leave 0.01 in. of draft over the fire.

A good way to check on the extent of air leaks into the boiler or furnace is to take a CO_2 reading at the smoke pipe and one at the fire door (over the fire). If there is any considerable drop in CO_2 between the point over the fire and the point at the smoke pipe, it means that air is leaking into the boiler. The places at which these leaks occur should be found and sealed.

With a proper stack temperature not exceeding 500°F for an oil-burning boiler, adjusted for an operating CO_2 of 10 per cent and a draft of at least 0.01 in. over the fire, there will be a constant, service-free, efficient operation of the burner from the standpoint of lack of noise, smoke, soot, or odor.

The unit should now be ready to undertake its job of providing heat and comfort to the homeowner.

Post in the cellar, where it can be readily seen, the *instruction sheet* provided by the burner manufacturer for the homeowner. Also, post at the burner switch (2) a small sign or notice denoting it as *the remote-control switch.* The proper firing procedure for the new burner has now been completed.

QUESTIONS

1. What is the first thing to be checked when a new burner is being fired?
2. How should the thermostat be checked?
3. Give the 14 important points to be checked when starting a new burner.
4. When preferably should the draft control be adjusted? Why?
5. What should always be posted in the cellar? Why?
6. What should be the maximum smoke disk reading for a gun-type burner?

CHAPTER 24

SERVICING
NOZZLE PROBLEMS

The high-pressure gun-type oil-burner nozzle is one of the most precisely made parts of the ordinary burner. With orifices at the center of the nozzle as small as ten thousandths of an inch (0.010) and slots in the distributor insert as small as five thousandths of an inch (0.005), it must be handled with some care and understanding if it is to do properly the job for which it was designed. The nozzle not only breaks down the oil into particles small enough to mix with air and support combustion, but also meters the amount of oil to be burned per hour. For this reason, it is a *precision* instrument and should be respected as such.

The delicate tolerances essential to such a device require a certain amount of protection. Nozzles should never be carried around loosely in the pocket or in a container unless they are covered by the small, cardboard, cylindrical container in which they are shipped.

The purpose of this protection is to prevent dirt from entering the nozzle. Small particles of dust, dirt, rust, or lint can work their way into a nozzle and necessitate additional service that will not be discovered until it has been installed and operating under oil pressure.

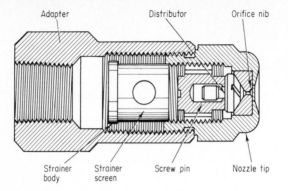

Adapter   Distributor   Orifice nib

Strainer   Strainer   Screw pin   Nozzle tip
body   screen

Fig. 24-1   Cutaway view of high-pressure nozzle.

Many service mechanics carefully remove the insert (distributor) from a new nozzle and check the slots to be sure that they are clean.

The orifice of the nozzle itself can be checked by holding it up to the light or by drawing air through it.   When the new nozzle has thus been inspected, it can be installed with some assurance of doing its job properly.

When nozzles below 1.50 gph are used, there should always be a filter installed in the line to make certain that dirt will not get through. This filter is in addition to the strainer in the pump and the small strainer at the nozzle.   With nozzles as small as 0.75 and 1 gph, a very fine filter should be used.   These nozzles give more trouble because of their very fine slots and orifices.

A 0.75-gph nozzle may have slots as small as 0.005 in. and therefore have to be well protected.   This filter should be of the replaceable-cartridge type, and extreme care must be taken when changing the dirty cartridge.   The oil line should be opened between pump and nozzle.

After the cartridge has been changed, the burner should run before the oil line is connected, and the oil should be caught in a bucket. This should continue until several quarts have been collected.   Then the oil line from pump to nozzle should be reconnected.

The reason for this procedure is to make sure that the sediment stirred up by removing the cartridge does not work through to the nozzle. Often the cleaning of pump strainers and the cleaning or changing of filter cartridges result in a number of "dirty nozzle" service calls immediately afterwards.

The purging of the oil into a container as mentioned above will prevent this stirred-up dirt and sediment from getting to the nozzle.

IMPORTANCE OF THE STRAINER

The strainer at the rear of the nozzle is an important device.   For a 1-gph nozzle or less, it should have a 200-mesh nozzle strainer or a porous bronze filter. For 1.50 down to 1 gph, a 120 mesh will do. Anything above 1.50 gph will get by with a 100-mesh nozzle strainer.

A nozzle should *never* be installed *without* this strainer. As the gph rates increase, a larger strainer will be required to give adequate area for the unhindered flow of oil through the nozzle. Strainers of extra length are available for such larger gallonages and should be used when the rating goes above 4 gph.

Service calls occasioned by dirty or worn nozzles are easily recognized by the service mechanic. Figure 24-2 shows four common symptoms of the dirty nozzle. Of course, the nozzle may be so clogged that there will be no flame at all and the unit will continue to go into safety each time the primary control reset button is pressed. Any irregularity in the shape of the flame usually points to dirt in the nozzle. If, however, the flame is normal and the service call has resulted from another cause, it is *not* necessary to clean the nozzle. Disturbing a nozzle that is functioning properly only invites trouble.

Servicing a dirty nozzle requires *care*. The nozzle must never be removed by a Stillson wrench, gas pliers, or water pump pliers. The teeth in these tools will only chew up and destroy the hexagonal head of the nozzle and adapter. Use a nozzle wrench or box wrench, and if these are not available open-end wrenches will do. Keep the nozzle off the dirty floor when removing it.

Avoid spilling the oil from the tube by plugging the end of the nozzle assembly that joins the pump with a small cork carried for that purpose.

Spilling the oil from the tube will allow air to enter. When the burner is reassembled and put into operation, this air in the line will cause erratic flame performance. With small nozzles (1.35 and less), it will remain in the tube for long periods of time instead of being purged through the nozzle.

While the burner is operating and the oil is at 100 psi pressure or more, this air in the oil tube will be compressed. After the burner has shut down, it will expand and force oil through the nozzle orifice, thereby creating an afterdrip or afterfire with all its consequent troubles.

 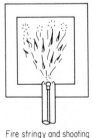  

Fire burns to one side   Fire stringy and shooting sparks   Fire very small and bright – Acrid fumes and odor coming from fire box   Fire floats away from nozzle and burns off back wall of fire box

Fig. 24-2   Flame formations resulting from dirty nozzles.

(1) Air bubbles trapped in oil line and compressed while oil is under pressure during firing period

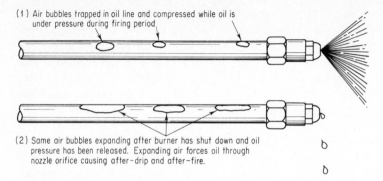

(2) Same air bubbles expanding after burner has shut down and oil pressure has been released. Expanding air forces oil through nozzle orifice causing after-drip and after-fire.

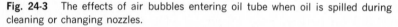

Fig. 24-3   The effects of air bubbles entering oil tube when oil is spilled during cleaning or changing nozzles.

The expansion of this air is increased by residual heat from the firebox, warming the oil tube after the burner has gone off (see Fig. 24-3). This air in the nozzle and oil line is a real troublemaker. With small nozzles, avoid it by taking care not to spill oil when the nozzle is being cleaned or changed. If it is necessary to remove considerable quantities of oil from the nozzle assembly, fill it up with oil from an outside source before putting the oil tube back into the burner.

When the nozzle has been removed from the adapter, use clean tools in taking it apart. Remove the nozzle strainer with a screw driver and, if it is dirty, wash it or soak it in a good solvent, such as carbon tetrachloride, naphtha, benzine, or even gasoline. A small toothbrush can be used to brush over the mesh and help remove the dirt. If the strainer is at all damaged or contains any perforations or loose threads of unraveled wire, replace it with a new one.

CLEANING THE NOZZLE

After the strainer has been removed and cleaned, unscrew the insert and examine the slots under strong illumination. See if the base of the slot has a layer of sludge or gum on it. If so, it will have to be soaked in one of the solvents mentioned above.

The slots should be run through with the edge of a stiff piece of paper or cardboard of the heaviness of an ordinary business card. A fine toothpick may also be used. Wipe the insert with a clean piece of rag that has been dipped in a good solvent.

Next, examine the head of the nozzle containing the orifice. If there are any gum or sludge deposits inside or out, it too should be soaked in naphtha or carbon tet. Use a toothpick to push out any specks of dirt in the opening. Use a lint-free clean cloth to wipe the nozzle head.

Never use anything other than the toothpick or a wooden probe in cleaning the slots and orifice. The use of metal prongs or brushes will damage the slots and orifice, resulting in a defective spray.

All parts of the nozzle should now be wiped *dry* with a *lint-free cloth.* Reassemble the nozzle by placing the head in a box wrench and inserting the distributor. Use a screw driver to seat the insert (distributor) firmly *but do not force it after it is once seated* by using all the strength available. This will only damage the slots.

Next replace the strainer by screwing it in tightly with a screw driver. Now screw the nozzle tightly into the adapter, using box or open-end wrenches. This must be a tight fit to prevent oil leaking from between the machined surfaces of the nozzle and adapter. Fill the nozzle tube with oil to replace any that spilled, and reconnect the oil line to the pump. The unit is now ready to fire.

The nozzle tube when replaced in the burner should have some support to hold it on a horizontal straight line. Usually this support is provided by the four-bladed air swirler, but as this device is commonly not a close fit within the blast tube, the nozzle may be slightly cocked. The use of an additional rigid support, as shown in Fig. 24-4, will help prevent this condition from happening either initially or later on from vibration.

Sometimes oil deposits inside the blast tube furnish a clue that the nozzle is not straight but cocked. The oil spray hits the side of the air cone and drips back into the tube. Such an oil puddle may also result from a leak at the oil tube where it joins the adapter or at the adapter where it joins the nozzle. This oil puddle may burn after the burner has gone off, causing the oil in the nozzle to crack and deposit hard, varnishlike gum inside the head or distributor slots. An oil-puddle fire of this kind can cause serious ignition troubles, which will be discussed in another chapter.

Check with a flame mirror to see that the nozzle sits level and avoid the aforementioned trouble. After the burner has been fired, check again

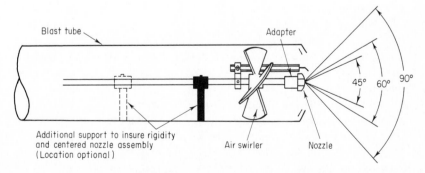

Fig. 24-4   Additional supports lend rigidity to oil tube.

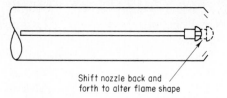

Shift nozzle back and
forth to alter flame shape

Fig. 24-5 Location of nozzle helps in adjusting for clean, compact fire.

with the flame mirror to see how close the flame is to the nozzle. The fire ought to be about 1 in. away from the nozzle to prevent it from overheating.

Move the nozzle back and forth, as shown in Fig. 24-5. This will alter the flame shape and also make the fire cleaner. Adjust until a clean fire with a 10 per cent CO_2 is attained. If there is not enough play to move the nozzle assembly back and forth, add a loop of copper tubing to the nozzle line, which will give the necessary play.

If the 10 per cent CO_2 cannot be obtained, try using the next *lower* size of nozzle and increase the pressure over the usual 100 psi. This will give a higher CO_2 because of the finer atomization furnished by the smaller nozzle at higher pressure.

MAJOR CAUSES OF NOZZLE TROUBLE

Of course, the major cause of nozzle trouble is dirt. The best way to control this is to adhere to the directions for filters and the proper size of nozzle strainers. The best way to avoid the dirty nozzle is to keep the dirt from reaching it. Use a good, replaceable cartridge-type filter.

Poor grades of oil often contain foreign matter, and a high sulfur content is detrimental to the nozzle, resulting in excessive wear because of certain chemical changes caused by the sulfur. The homeowner should be instructed to buy oil from a reputable dealer.

Overheating of nozzles causes the oil within the swirl chamber and in the slots to break down and form a varnishlike black substance that is often mistaken for carbon. It is important, therefore, that nozzles do not overheat.

Major causes of overheating and gum formation are (1) fire burning too close to the nozzle; (2) firebox too small; (3) nozzle too far forward; (4) inadequate air-handling parts on burner; and (5) burner being over-fired.

If the fire burns too close to the nozzle, narrow the blast-tube opening so that the air will increase in velocity as it leaves the gun. This will help move the flame away from the nozzle. The increase in air velocity can be achieved by installing a larger-diameter fan or, as mentioned above, by narrowing the blast tube by placing an air cone at the front of it.

Increasing the pressure will also increase the velocity of the droplets of oil leaving the nozzle orifice and help overcome this troublesome condition.

Figure 24-6 shows another common cause of clogged nozzles—that of reflected heat from a firebox playing back upon a nozzle that is too far forward after the burner has shut down. Nozzles in this position will always run hot and clog from the gum formation caused by the cracking oil. Draw the nozzle back into the blast tube by shortening the oil line or by using a stubby (short) adapter.

A fire box that is too small and consequently overheats will have the same effect on a nozzle that is in its proper place in the blast tube. In such a problem as this, rebuild the combustion chamber to the proper size. The burner in this instance is all right, but the firebox is too small.

However, there may be the reverse condition where the firebox is ample, but the burner is being fired beyond its maximum capacity. The deficiency of air in this circumstance may result in the nozzle overheating because the quantity is not sufficient to keep it cool. A new burner or a larger fan, if possible, should be installed to remedy this problem.

Any leakage of oil from any cause whatsoever after the burner has gone off will result in carbon formation and clogging of the nozzle. Do not allow an afterdrip or afterfire to go unchecked. There may be an oil leak, air in the line, or a defective cutoff valve causing it. Find out which and remedy the condition.

Attention to these five causes of trouble will eliminate most of the service difficulties arising from dirty nozzles.

Proper selection of the nozzle gph rate and angle of spray, along with the correct firebox, is extremely important. Refer to Chaps. 7, 8, and 9.

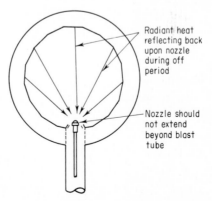

Fig. 24-6   Radiant heat from firebox walls overheats nozzle and cracks oil, causing gum formation within nozzle after burner goes off and cooling action of fan air ceases.

When gph rates go over 5 gph, double adapters should be used. These provide for two nozzles to be used with the one oil tube. Two 3-gph nozzles will do a much finer job with the average burner than one 6-gph nozzle. A cleaner fire, less smoke, higher CO_2, and all-round better operating efficiency will be obtained.

Finer atomization and a more compact flame can be obtained by multiple nozzles. Over 10 gph, use a triple adapter. Thus with a 15-gph rating, three 5-gph nozzles with a triple adapter should be used. The service mechanic should not be afraid to experiment with multiple nozzles in a large gph installation.

Many oil-burner experts believe that nozzles should be changed every year. However, this can be an inaccurate yardstick, as two jobs with the same size nozzle will burn vastly different quantities of oil in the space of 1 year. It is better to make nozzle changes in terms of thousands of gallons used. Many nozzles operate efficiently and accurately for long periods of time after having atomized exceedingly large quantities of oil.

NOZZLE APPLICATION FIELD TEST PROCEDURE

After the correct nozzle firing rate has been determined, the nozzle application test can then be made in the field. Instruments required for this are a draft gauge, a CO_2 analyzer, and a smoke tester.

Now proceed as follows:

1. Set draft at breeching for 0.02 in. The draft control should hold the draft constant.
2. Install an 80-deg hollow spray nozzle; adjust the air shutter on burner until a No. 1 smoke is obtained. Take the CO_2 reading and assume a 7 per cent reading.
3. Install an 80-deg solid spray nozzle. Adjust the air until a No. 1 smoke is obtained. Take a CO_2 reading and assume an 8.5 per cent reading.

The test at this point is half done, for it has been determined that solid spray on this burner is better, since a higher CO_2 was obtained with the same angle, using a solid spray. Now find which angle of solid spray is best.

° 4. Next install a 60-deg solid spray nozzle, set the smoke for No. 1, and take a CO_2 reading. Assume that the CO_2 reading goes to 10 per cent. One more nozzle should now be tried.

° If The CO_2 reading had been less than that obtained with the 80-deg solid spray nozzle, then a 90-deg solid spray could be tried to see whether the CO_2 performance was better.

5. Install a 45-deg solid spray nozzle, set the smoke for No. 1.   If CO_2 goes up to 11.5 per cent, the test is completed.   If the 45-deg nozzle gave a lower CO_2 than the 60 deg, then the 60 deg would be best.

This is an example of the procedure that should be followed to test a burner already installed.   It generally takes an average of 45 min to run an accurate nozzle-application test.

Once a nozzle-application test has been made on a burner, a record should be made of the make and model of the burner.   This will eliminate additional tests for this make and model.   The only exception to this would be in cases where a poorly designed and improperly sized chamber was installed.   In such cases a correct chamber should be installed or a new test made, as chamber size, shape, and height influence the air-oil mixture.

NOTE   After utilizing a nozzle for checking the proper type to use, it should be cleaned in carbon tetrachloride or some equivalent cleaning fluid before going back into stock.   Otherwise the fuel oil in the nozzle will dry out, leaving a film on the inside of the tip. This will alter the spray characteristics when next used.

QUESTIONS

1. Why can the oil-burner nozzle be regarded as a precision instrument?
2. How should a nozzle be carried?   Why?
3. Why is it a good practice to install a filter in the suction line?
4. What practice should be observed when a pump strainer is cleaned or a filter cartridge changed?   Why?
5. What precaution should be taken to prevent spillage of the oil from the nozzle assembly tube?   Why?
6. What happens when air is trapped in the nozzle line?
7. How should a nozzle be cleaned?
8. What is one method of altering flame shape?
9. What are the five major causes of gum or "varnish" formations in a nozzle?
10. Why are multiple nozzles preferable on higher gph installations?
11. What is the nozzle application test?
12. Where is the proper location for such a test?
13. Explain the procedure for such a test.
14. What occurs when fuel oil is left in the nozzle?
15. Does a poorly designed combustion chamber affect the nozzle application test?   How?

CHAPTER 25
SERVICING
IGNITION PROBLEMS

Of all the phases of oil-burner servicing, *ignition problems* are among the easiest to recognize and solve. Much ignition service consists of merely making the proper spark gap adjustment, cleaning the electrodes, and making secure all connections. Yet, no part of oil-burner servicing is more important, for defective ignition or delayed ignition is the prime reason for the *puffback*. The puffback is the most dangerous of all burner troubles.

As the secondary of the transformer of the average gun-type burner is 10,000 volts, the flow of current is extremely intense and active. Without exercising care in adjusting the electrodes, there is a great possibility that the spark will jump to some intervening metal surface to ground itself. The space between the electrodes must be the shortest metal-to-metal distance throughout the entire ignition system.

If, at a point along the line, the current is carried by an exposed metal part and the distance between this metal part and an adjoining metal surface is less than the spark gap, the high-tension current will follow the path of least resistance and ground itself at that convenient point. This will result in the spark being produced at a place where it is not wanted, usually within the blast tube itself. This is a dangerous condition and can result in a bad puffback.

The best way to prevent ignition from being delayed, or from not appearing at all, is to start right at the beginning by adjusting the spark gap to the proper dimension. Observe Figs. 25-1 and 25-2. There are three dimensions to be checked. In order of importance they are (1) the gap between the electrodes; (2) the height of the electrodes above the center of the nozzle; and (3) the distance of the electrode tip forward from the nozzle center.

In addition, no part of the electrodes should be closer than $\frac{1}{4}$ in. to any metal part of the burner.

The spark gap between the electrodes, as shown by dimension A in Fig. 25-1, is fairly standard today for all gun-type burners. Adjust this gap to the $\frac{3}{16}$ in., as shown, unless the manufacturer specifically states otherwise.

In dimension B the distance between the electrode tips and the center of the nozzle is $\frac{1}{2}$ in., as shown for nozzles with an angle of spray over 45 deg. For angles of spray of 45 or 30 deg, *reduce* this $\frac{1}{16}$ in. for the 45 deg and $\frac{2}{16}$ in. for the 30 deg. Otherwise, this $\frac{1}{2}$-in. dimension will hold pretty well through all other angles and for gph rates of up to 8 gal. For nozzles of 8 gph or higher, increase dimension B to $\frac{5}{8}$ in.

The distance of the electrode tip forward of the nozzle center (dimension C, Fig. 25-2) will vary according to nozzle size. The variation, however, is not very great. For nozzles of 1 gal or less, $\frac{5}{16}$ in. will be sufficient. For 1.35- to 5-gph nozzles, $\frac{3}{8}$ in. will be all right. With nozzles of over 5 gph, this space should be $\frac{1}{2}$ in.

These dimensions (A, B, and C), as set down above, can be used with some confidence. If, however, the burner has a special combustion head

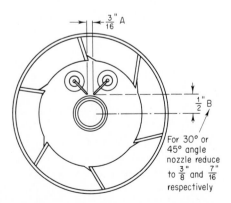

Fig. 25-1 Electrode setting, medium-angle nozzles.

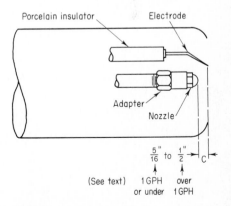

Fig. 25-2 Electrode setting, forward of the nozzle.

or specific unique air-handling parts, then the burner manufacturer's spark dimension specifications should be followed.

The air delivery parts of a burner can seriously alter the shape and size of the spark, as well as provide large extra areas of exposed metal surface close to the electrodes. This furnishes opportunities for misplaced ignition if extreme care and attention are not given to the manufacturer's directions.

At no time must the tips of the electrodes be in the path of the oil spray. This is a dangerous condition that results in a bridge of hard carbon being built across the gap, shorting out the electrodes and killing the spark. They should be slightly in back of the spray. The air from the fan will blow the spark into the path of the oil spray. Check this with the flame mirror by disconnecting the transformer at the No. 4 terminal on the relay and turning on the burner *for only a few seconds,* observing the position of the electrode tips in relation to the oil spray.

If this observation *cannot* be made with a flame mirror, remove the nozzle assembly from the burner and while pointing it into a bucket or other container (the transformer is disconnected as explained above), switch on the burner for a few seconds to see whether the tips are clear of the spray. Do not spray oil out into the open cellar, as its odor will permeate the house.

Once the spark gap has been adjusted and the entire assembly replaced, the timing of the spark, if it is intermittent ignition, should be checked. Attach a small 3-watt test lamp to the primary control, as shown in Fig. 25-8. Throw on the remote-control switch and check the time the bulb stays on.

The bulb, as shown, is hooked up parallel to the ignition transformer and will be on while the transformer is receiving current, thus providing a convenient way to check ignition timing. The ignition should remain

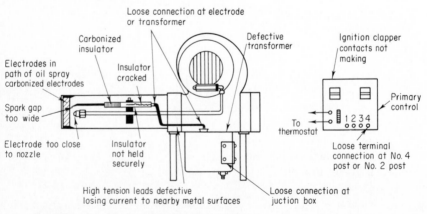

Fig. 25-3   Common causes of ignition troubles.

on for about 1 min. This period furnishes a good safety margin, but is not an absolute condition. Keep the boiler door open while making this check.

COMMON IGNITION PROBLEMS

The most common ignition troubles are usually caused by

1. Improper spacing of the electrodes
2. Carbon forming on tips of the electrodes
3. Carbonized or cracked ceramic insulators
4. Defective high-tension leads
5. Loose terminal connections
6. Defective transformer
7. Line-voltage drop

The *formation of carbon on the electrodes* can be a serious condition. Oil wetting the electrodes receives heat from the fire and cracks, forming hard crystals of carbon. After the burner has gone off, this carbon-forming process continues, owing to reflected heat from the firebox. In time the gap is completely breeched and no spark occurs at all. The chief cause of this trouble lies in the fact that oil is hitting the electrodes. Readjust them according to the foregoing directions and eliminate this troublesome condition.

If the nozzle assembly is not straight, oil may be hitting the air cone and falling back into the blast tube. This oil may burn after the burner has gone off. As a result, the entire front of the burner will be covered with deposited carbon. Of course, such carbon will eventually settle on the electrodes and short them out. The nozzle assembly should be set straight and this condition avoided.

A poor smoky fire created by lack of draft or air or any of the multitude of conditions that will cause an oil flame not to burn cleanly may result in this type of service. Clean up the fire to prevent it from recurring. The depositing of soot is always a condition that can result in ignition problems.

Just as *smoke, soot, and oil deposits* are detrimental to electrode performance, so also will they have a *serious effect upon the ceramic insulators.* The insulator will become impregnated with dry carbon or an oily film of soot and lose its ability to serve its purpose. Instead, it will become a conductor (Fig. 25-4).

The carbon conducts the electricity to the adjacent metal surfaces, where it shorts off in a number of weak sparks. Sometimes the spark will dance back and forth along the carbonized insulator. While the spark is behaving in this manner, it will also be burning off the carbon. When enough of the carbon film has been destroyed by the burning

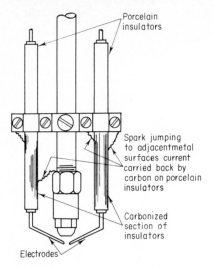

Fig. 25-4   Carbonized insulators will prevent spark at electrodes by short-circuiting current to closer metal surfaces.

action of the spark, there will be an insufficient amount of carbonized surface to conduct the current.   The spark will then appear at the conventional gap where it should be.

While this has been taking place, the oil from the nozzle will be filling the combustion chamber.   With the reappearance of the spark, this oil spray at the nozzle is ignited, and from there all the oil fumes in the combustion chamber and boiler flare up.   This usually blows open the furnace or boiler doors, knocks down the smoke pipe, blasts out the draft control, and liberally showers the adjoining area with soot.   The unit has "puffed back," and delayed ignition was the cause.

A serviceman checking this condition will find that everything appears normal as the spark will be functioning all right because of the burning away of the carbon on the porcelain insulator by the initial spark.   In time, this condition will repeat itself, leaving little or no trace of the actual cause of the trouble.

Whenever there has been a puffback or when sooty, smoky conditions are encountered, the *entire ignition assembly should be removed, inspected, adjusted, and cleaned.*

Examine the insulators carefully by wiping them clean with a cloth dipped in a good solvent.   If they remain a blackish, gray color after repeated cleanings, it is evident that they are filled with carbon throughout their porous surfaces.   Replace them with a new set.

The insulators can easily be tested by removing one of the high-tension leads and holding it close to the discolored portion of the other insulator which is still connected to its lead.   Throw the burner switch

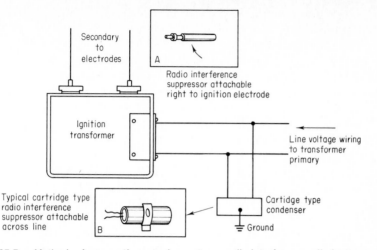

Fig. 25-5   Method of connecting condenser-type radio-interference eliminator.

on (but first remove the No. 3 wire from its terminal at the relay to disconnect the motor) and see if any spark jumps from the high-tension lead to the discolored surface.   If it does, however small it may be, it is an indication that the insulator is now a conductor.   Discard it and replace it with a new one.   Always replace cracked insulators.

High-tension leads that connect the electrodes with the transformer often have their insulation damaged by rubbing against the fan or by careless handling when the burner is serviced.

When nozzle assemblies are replaced, the leads should be clear of the fan, not kinked or stretched, but held in a nonconductor type of clamp so that they do not lie loosely in the blast tube.   The insulation on these multiple-strand wires should be kept free of oil, as it destroys the rubber.   In time, this insulation dries out and current escapes right through it.

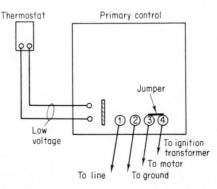

Fig. 25-6   Connect jumper between terminals 3 and 4 to change from intermittent to constant ignition.

Hold a neon test lamp about $\frac{1}{4}$ in. above the leads after the spark gap has been widened to the point where it cannot provide a path for the current. The neon test lamp should not glow. If it does, no matter how slightly, the leads are losing too much current by leakage to the atmosphere. This leaking will increase on damp and humid days. Install new high-tension leads in this case.

Check the connections all through the ignition assembly; at the transformer; at the electrodes; at the No. 4 terminal of the relay, if intermittent ignition; at the No. 3 terminal, if constant; and also at the transformer junction box (Fig. 25-9) if necessary. These connections must be secure and tight if the spark is to be fat and hot enough to raise the tiny droplets of oil to the 700°F required to ignite them.

Many modern burners no longer employ high-tension insulated leads and use instead bare metal bars or prongs that come to rest against the transformer terminals. These bars are rigidly connected to the electrode. If such is the case, see that there is enough tension present to seat them, with some force, squarely against the transformer terminals. If necessary, use a pair of pliers to bend them so that they will press firmly against the terminals.

A weak transformer is fairly easy to spot. Remove the nozzle assembly and connect the No. 4 wire to the No. 1 terminal of the relay after disconnecting the burner motor at the No. 3 terminal. This will provide continuous current to the transformer without operating the burner.

The spark should jump across the gap with a persistent buzz. Blow strongly at the spark; it should extend itself at least an inch and crackle loudly. It should not blow off the electrodes. This is a simple test.

Another method of testing the spark to see if it is hot enough is to place a small piece of newspaper, one sheet thick, in the spark (no air blowing on it). It should ignite in 3 to 5 sec. Any longer time means that the spark is weak.

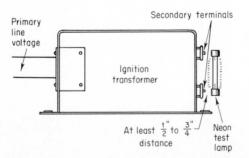

Fig. 25-7 Method of testing ignition transformer secondary with neon test lamp. Note that test lamp does not have to touch secondary terminals.

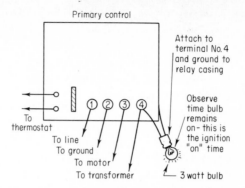

Primary control

Attach to
terminal No. 4
and ground to
relay casing

To
thermostat

To line
To ground
To motor
To transformer

Observe
time bulb
remains
on— this is
the ignition
"on" time

3 watt bulb

Fig. 25-8 Method of checking the length of the ignition "on" period.

A further test can be made by placing the ends of the high-tension leads about $\frac{1}{4}$ in. apart and letting the spark jump between them. Separate them slowly. The spark should still be jumping the gap when they are 1 in. apart. This is common with a good transformer.

A neon test lamp can also be used to check an ignition transformer. Observe Fig. 25-7. It is not necessary to touch the terminals of the transformer with the "cartridge fuse" type testing lamp. When held at a distance of $\frac{1}{2}$ to $\frac{3}{4}$ in., the lamp should glow strongly. If it does not, the transformer is weak or defective.

When, after these tests, the transformer is found to be inadequate, replace it with a new one. There is little or nothing that a service mechanic can do to repair a defective ignition transformer, as such repairs require special shop equipment.

Sometimes a drop in the line voltage to the transformer can cause a weak spark. This may be due to the source of supply (powerhouse difficulties); a loose terminal connection at the relay; the relay clapper not making a good contact; or the burner motor drawing too high a starting current. If it is the relay clapper, examine the contacts and see if they are pitted or arc excessively when the burner goes on. If so, replace them with new contacts and be sure that the relay clapper makes a good contact. Tighten the terminal connections at the relay wiring panel.

Check the starting inrush amperage of the motor and compare it with the manufacturer's rating. If it is too high, it may result in the transformer receiving too little current to furnish a good spark. The motor may also be defective, misaligned, or in need of lubrication or a new starting winding.

Whenever there is any doubt about the quality or the ignition characteristic of the oil, put the burner on constant ignition to prevent flame failure. This should also be done if there is water in the oil. To do this, place a jumper across the Nos. 3 and 4 terminals of the relay, as shown in Fig. 25-6. Many times a smoky fire can be considerably cleaned up by doing this.

The use of constant ignition will sometimes quiet a noisy installation when the noise is due to combustion pulsations or vibrations.

On many large jobs that are over 4 gph, the burner should *always* be on constant ignition to provide added assurance against puffbacks. The large quantity of oil vapor entering the firebox in installations above 4 gph brooks no delay in firing.

Ignition must be instantaneous and constant to provide adequate protection under faulty operating conditions. When the gph rating goes over 10 gal, it is wise to use twin ignition with two transformers, as shown in Fig. 25-10. The employment of two complete ignition assemblies gives about as much protection against ignition failure as can be had. Adjust electrode settings as shown in Fig. 25-10.

RADIO INTERFERENCE

Radio interference from the ignition transformer has been almost eliminated by the double-terminal, mid-point-grounded transformer that is in general use today. When these transformers are equipped with a built-in condenser across the line, as shown in Fig. 25-9, little trouble will be encountered in the form of radio interference.

In the event that the transformer is not equipped with a radio interference eliminator and is suspected of causing this type of trouble, it is simple to test and find out whether this is the case.

Simply disconnect all electrically operated devices throughout the house, such as fans, refrigerators, washing machines, etc. Place the burner on constant ignition, if it is not so already, and turn it on while the radio is playing. If the burner is causing the interference, it will now show up.

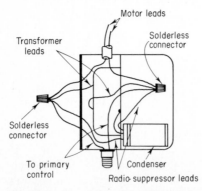

Fig. 25-9 Connection at transformer junction box. Note "built-in" condenser for suppression of radio interference.

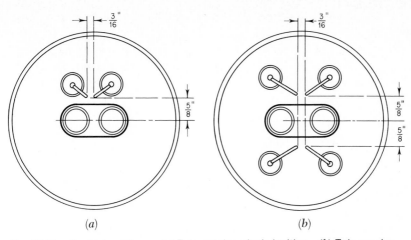

Fig. 25-10 Electrode settings. (*a*) Twin nozzles, single ignition. (*b*) Twin nozzles, twin ignition.

Once the burner is ignited and firing normally, disconnect the transformer lead at the No. 4 post on the relay. If the interference now ceases, the ignition system is causing the trouble by feeding back through the line leads to the house circuit and from there to the radio set.

To remedy this condition, install a *suppressor,* in either of the two ways shown in Fig. 25-5, across the line or attached directly to the ignition electrode.

In ninety-nine cases out of a hundred, this will solve the problem. If it does not, then it will be necessary to ground the burner itself in addition to using the suppressor. Ground the burner by soldering to its frame or base at some convenient place a piece of sheet metal or copper about 4 to 6 in. square. Solder a wire lead to this metal plate and attach this lead firmly and securely to a *water pipe* for grounding. Do not attach it to a piece of conduit or to the boiler. This further grounding of the burner housing should eliminate the trouble.

If it is difficult to find a place on which to solder the plate, then increase its size and set the entire burner on it so that the piece of sheet metal is interposed between the burner and the concrete floor. Then ground it to a water pipe, as explained above. This should eliminate the most stubborn cases of radio interference caused by the ignition system.

QUESTIONS

1. What are the characteristics of the type of current obtained from the secondary of an ignition transformer?

2. Why is it dangerous to have any part of the electrodes closer than ¼ in. to any metal part of the burner?
3. How do changes in the angle of spray affect electrode setting?
4. How can the air delivery of the burner alter the shape of the spark?
5. Why is it bad to have any oil impinge upon the electrodes?

CHAPTER 26

SERVICING PUMPS AND
PRESSURE REGULATING VALVES

The modern domestic oil-burner fuel-pump unit is in reality a threefold device, consisting of a strainer or filter, a gear pump, and a pressure regulating valve. The combination of these three devices in a single housing makes a compact unit that is easy to adjust and service if it is properly understood.

Most of the difficulties in pump servicing depend upon the proper diagnosis of the cause of trouble. By recognizing certain things—*symptoms*, they might be called—the serviceman can quickly locate and solve the problem.

Installation procedures affecting one and two stage pumps and one- and two-pipe systems were covered at length in Chap. 11.

Some points worth emphasizing in the installation of pumps and oil piping are that the suction and return lines, as they meet the pump, should have several coils of tubing (pigtails) in the line where these lines join the burner oil valve; and also that there should always be a valve where the tubing meets the pump and where it enters the cellar from a buried tank.

The addition of these loops of tubing will provide ample additional

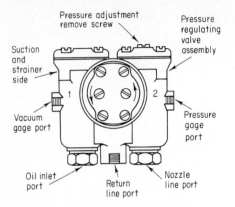

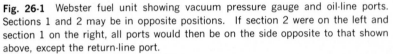

Fig. 26-1 Webster fuel unit showing vacuum pressure gauge and oil-line ports. Sections 1 and 2 may be in opposite positions. If section 2 were on the left and section 1 on the right, all ports would then be on the side opposite to that shown above, except the return-line port.

length and flexibility when the unit has to be serviced. There is nothing more aggravating than to have to make up a new flare at the tubing where it joins the valve before entering the pump, only to find that the tubing is not long enough. This means cutting the line and adding a piece to do the job, which requires three flaring operations and three additional fittings, as well as providing extra locations for possible leaks.

It can be avoided by using the tubing loops when making the installation. These loops also serve another purpose, as shall be seen later on.

In the event that an installation requires several burners to be fed from the same buried tank, it is best practice to use separate suction lines for each burner. Then if suction-line trouble develops, the other burners will not be affected. A single return line of sufficient size to carry the oil returned from all the burners is all that is required.

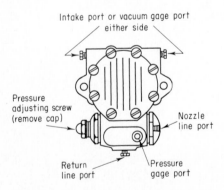

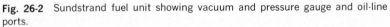

Fig. 26-2 Sundstrand fuel unit showing vacuum and pressure gauge and oil-line ports.

If, however, it is not possible to use separate suction lines for each burner and a single feed line must be used instead, a check valve should be installed as close to the pump of each burner as is possible. This will prevent the pump of a burner that is running from drawing the oil out of a pump of a burner that is not. It should be emphasized, however, that the best practice is to use multiple suction lines (see Fig. 26-3).

Whenever the installation is of the two-pipe type with a tank below the level of the burner and the pump is of the bypass plug design (Sundstrand), this plug must be inserted into the port within the pump housing, in order to close off the internal bypass. This forces the oil to pass out through the return-port opening and back to the tank, rather than bypass through the pump.

With a single-line, gravity-fed pump, the bypass plug must be removed so that the internal bypass channel through the pump is open.

In the event that a new burner is installed with a one-pipe gravity-fed oil system and this plug is left in place (as though it were a two-pipe system), the pressure will build up excessively when it is started, usually producing an abnormally large flame. In a few moments this will blow out the pump seal and cause it to leak seriously. The pump will have to be returned to a shop where the seal can be replaced.

With a two-pipe system, the same excessive pressure condition with

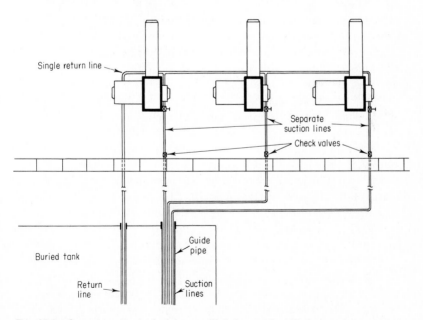

Fig. 26-3 Correct method of piping multiple-burner installations using separate suction lines.

its damaging effect upon the seal can occur if the return line is seriously restricted.   Always check the return line of a two-pipe system for any such clogging or restriction before starting the new burner.

PRESSURE ADJUSTMENTS

All pressure adjustments on a fuel unit should be made by gauge readings.   Do not, if possible, adjust the pressure by guesswork or by merely observing the flame.   Attach the pressure gauge at the port provided, as shown in Figs. 26-1 and 26-2.

Set the burner in operation and adjust the pressure.   Normally set it at 100 psi or at the pressure setting specified by the manufacturer. Sometimes increasing the pressure from 10 to 20 psi so improves the atomization that the CO_2 reading will increase 2 per cent or more.

A good procedure is to set the pressure at 110 psi and let the burner operate until the chamber is hot or until the stack temperature ceases to rise.   This takes about 10 min.   Now increase the pressure to 120 psi and wait a few minutes.   Take a CO_2 reading after the air has been adjusted for a clean fire.   Then reduce the pressure to the average 100 psi and after waiting a few moments take another CO_2 reading.   Compare it with the reading at the higher pressure.   If it is the same, leave the pump at the low pressure setting.

However, if the CO_2 has dropped considerably, the burner, because of inefficient air-handling parts, is extremely sensitive to atomizing pressures and the pump should be left at a higher setting.   Many maintenance mechanics are not conscious of the fact that the oil pressure adjustment can be the key to much higher operating efficiencies through its effect upon the CO_2 reading.

Servicemen will find that a little time spent in judging pressure adjustments by the change in CO_2 can result in oil savings to the consumer.

While adjusting the pressure, *start* and *stop* the burner several times and watch the dial on the pressure gauge to see how quickly the pressure builds up.   The pump should be at its operating pressure before the motor is up to speed, usually at about 1,150 rpm.   Causes of delay in building pressure will be discussed further on in this chapter.

When a two-pipe system is being adjusted for pressure, the vacuum pull of the pump should be checked at the same time.   This gives a picture of how hard the pump has to work to pull the oil from the tank. Attach the vacuum gauge at the vacuum port of the pump or at a tee in the suction line, as close to the fuel unit as possible.

The vacuum reading should not exceed 12 in. when the burner is in operation.   If it does, it indicates a restriction, kinking, or clogging in the suction line; oil too heavy; check or foot valve stuck; a dirty line

Table 26-1 Suction-line Sizes for No. 2 Oil

Suction-line length, ft	10–40	40–100	100–200
Size of iron pipe, in.	⅜	⅜–½	½–¾
Size of tubing OD, in.	⅜	⅜–½	½

Vertical lift should not exceed 10 ft if possible.
Size suction line to avoid pulling over 12 in. vacuum.

filter or strainers; a tank too far away or too far below the unit; or a suction line that has too small an inside diameter (see Table 26-1).

The causes of delay or failure in building up to the adjusted oil pressure are specific and not too varied.   When the unit starts, the dial of the pressure gauge should move quickly and steadily up to the required setting.

By observing its motion, one can determine whether or not the pressure is building up smoothly, as it should.   If there is any delay in building the pressure, it will be caused by the following: (1) air-bound pump, (2) leaking pump seal, (3) dirty, clogged strainer, (4) restriction on the suction side of the pump, (5) sticky pressure regulating valve, (6) worn pump gears, (7) suction lift too high, (8) suction line too small.

1. In the event that the pump is air-bound, it will be necessary to vent it.   Place a container under the pump, loosen the gauge port plug, and turn on the burner.   The oil will be discharged along with

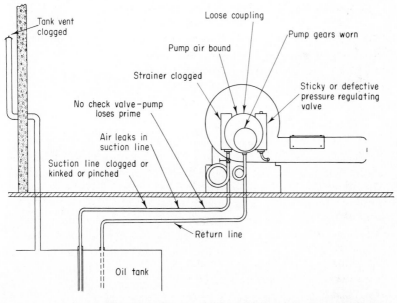

Fig. 26-4 Causes of delay or failure in building oil pressure.

the troublesome air in a bubbly, foamy mixture. Continue this until about a pint of oil is discharged and the fuel is flowing from the port in a solid stream. Then replace the plug and the pump will operate normally.

Single-line systems have to be vented in this manner. It is not absolutely necessary to vent a two-line hookup this way, as such a system will purge itself of air. However, the removal of the plug to vent a two-line system will certainly hasten the process. The fact that a pump is air-bound indicates that either the tank ran dry of oil or air entered the system. This will be discussed further on in this chapter.

2. In the event that a pump has a leaking seal, it may be difficult to build pressure, as the oil may be escaping in considerable quantities as the pressure attempts to rise. Air may also get into a pump with a leaky seal when the burner is not running. Check the seal and housing pump shaft by wiping with a clean dry rag. There should be no oil on the cloth. If it is stained with oil, there is evidence of a leak at the seal. Do not attempt to repair a leaking pump seal in the field. It is a shop job. Replace the pump in this case.

3. Dirty or clogged strainers will prevent a pump from building pressure quickly. This condition is easily recognized as it is accompanied by a rhythmical grunting noise from the pump as it labors to pull up the oil. Remove the strainers and clean them by vigorously scrubbing the mesh with a toothbrush, meanwhile immersing the strainer in a good *solvent* such as carbon tetrachloride, naphtha, or even hot water.

Inspect the strainer by holding it up to the light. Light should be clearly visible through all parts of the mesh.

4. A restriction on the suction side of the pump will delay the pressure build-up. Usually a clogged suction line can cause this. Check by using a vacuum gauge. No more than 12 in. of vacuum should be required to lift the oil.

Try blowing out the suction line with air pressure if possible. Also disconnect it at the pump and fill it with a good solvent. If gum or sludge is causing the restriction, the solvent may turn the trick. Other causes of such a restriction may be a defective foot valve, check valve, or antisiphon valve.

Never run a suction line under the furnace or too close to a hot surface. The oil in the line will crack from the heat and build up deposits of hard carbon that are almost impossible to remove. In this circumstance, the only cure is to run a new suction line. Connect the return line to the suction side of the pump and use it as a feed line in such emergencies.

5. A sticky pressure regulating valve will cause pressure difficulties by preventing pressure build-up. Oil cracking in a pump that is receiving heat may cause this by depositing a gumlike varnish on the valve plunger or piston.

Disassemble the valve and clean the needle and seat thoroughly. If it is the piston type, rotate constantly (after brushing with oil) in the cylinder until it moves smoothly and freely in all positions. If it is the bellows type, clean it with a good solvent and hold it up to the light to see if there are any perforations in it, however small. Compress the bellows and hold the palms of the hands tightly across the top and bottom to form an airtight seal; the bellows should not expand freely. If it does, it is defective and should be replaced.

Sealing one end of the bellows with the hand and blowing through the other with also demonstrate if it is leaking.

6. In the event that the pump gears are badly worn, there is nothing that can be done by the serviceman. The only remedy is to replace the pump.

7 and 8. If the suction lift is too high or the suction line too small, difficulties may arise in raising pressure. The vertical lift should not exceed 10 ft whenever possible, and the suction line should be sized according to the length of the run. Table 26-1 gives the proper sizes for various lengths of run.

LOSS OF PUMP PRIME

Many times pumps will lose their prime for what appears to be no apparent reason. This is prevalent in two-pipe systems. No two-pipe system should be installed without running the return line to the bottom of the tank, and, secondly, every two-pipe system should have a check valve on the suction line just before it leaves the cellar. This is to be certain that the check valve is in an accessible location. The running of the return line to within 3 or 4 in. of the bottom of the tank provides an excellent seal against air entering the line and getting to the pump when the oil is low in the tank.

Sometimes upon starting in the morning, after having been off for a considerable time, the primary control will go into *safety*. When the homeowner presses the safety button, after this usual morning occurrence, the burner will start for the second time. It will run for approximately 30 sec or more and ignite, operating from thereon normally. The occupant will complain that he has to do this every morning.

With a buried tank installation, this is a common symptom of a pump dropping its prime during the long off period occasioned by the night setback of the thermostat.

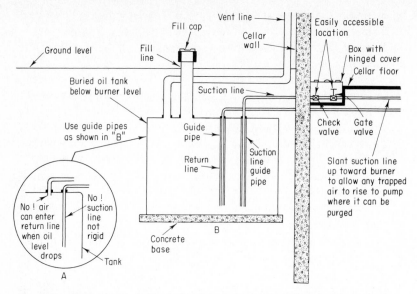

Fig. 26-5. Return line to bottom of tank and check valve will prevent loss of prime.

When the burner comes on in the morning, the pump begins to move the oil up the line, but the relay goes into safety before the pump accomplishes its task. When the owner presses the safety button, the pump gets the oil to the nozzle on the second try and the unit operates normally.

Whenever a unit goes into safety after a long shutdown period and it is a buried tank installation, this is usually the cause of the trouble. Install a check valve as far away from the burner as possible. If a check valve already is installed on the job, remove it and clean thoroughly. If it does not work freely after cleaning, install a new check valve.

If the trouble persists after this, there is an air leak in the suction line. It will then become necessary to put a pressure test on the suction line, using air for this after exposing the entire suction line in order that the location of the leaks may be detected. If there is a valve on the suction line where it enters the cellar, as shown in Fig. 26-5, the line can be tested in sections by closing this valve.

If the leak shows up in the suction line within the cellar, it more than likely would not be necessary to uncover the entire line.

Always disconnect the suction line at the pump when such a test is being made so that the pressure will not damage the pump seal.

If it is necessary to operate the burner while this test is going on, simply run a short return and suction line from the pump into a 5- or 10-gal container of oil and furnish the fuel this way, refilling the emergency container when necessary. As stated above, the return line may be switched to the suction port of the pump in such a contingency and used as a suction line.

If, on a gravity-feed system, the pump continuously becomes air-bound even though the tank has not run dry, the oil feed line has developed air leaks. Close the valve at the oil tank and insert a vacuum gauge in the proper port at the pump. Run the unit until it reads 12-in. of vacuum; then shut it off. The gauge should show the 12-in. vacuum reading for at least 10 min. If it falls off sooner than this, then there is evidence of an air leak. Tighten all fittings at the pump and tank and try again.

If it continues to lose the vacuum too quickly, run a new suction line. *Do not try to test a two-pipe system in this manner.* With the oil valve *at the burner* closed, any pump should produce 25 in. of vacuum. If it does not, then it is defective or worn.

PUMP NOISES

The most prevalent of the noises caused by the fuel-pumping unit on an oil burner is known as *tank hum.* It is generally agreed that it is caused by a pulsation in the delivery of oil by the gears as they mesh or by the fact that the oil does not completely fill the space between the gears. In any event, it sets up an harmonic sequence which is plainly audible and which is amplified by the tank into a pronounced hum.

It is usually remedied by installing an antihum valve or needle valve in the line close to the pump. Either of these valves sets up an adjustable restriction in the line so that a vacuum must be maintained by the pump to get the oil through.

Always adjust these valves with a vacuum gauge on the pump in order to be certain that over 12 in. of vacuum is not being pulled. At higher vacuum, the oil may vaporize in the pump and line and cause vapor lock, which necessitates venting the pump.

Tank hum will usually occur when the oil level is higher than the burner or whenever a head of oil rests on the suction side of the pump. The use of any type of an air cushion in the suction line as near to the pump as possible will usually prevent this hum. Sometimes just closing the oil-line valve at the burner, part way, will eliminate this trouble.

As any pump vibrations can be passed along the suction or return lines back to the tank and there be amplified, it is wise to bury these lines to muffle the sound. Always have two or three loops of tubing at the burner so that the vibration may pass off as motion through the flexible loops rather than as sound, as is liable to be the case when the oil line at the burner is rigid.

A rhythmic grunting or groaning noise gives evidence of straining or laboring on the part of the pump. This laboring demonstrates that

PUMP PRESSURE PROBLEMS AND THEIR CAUSES

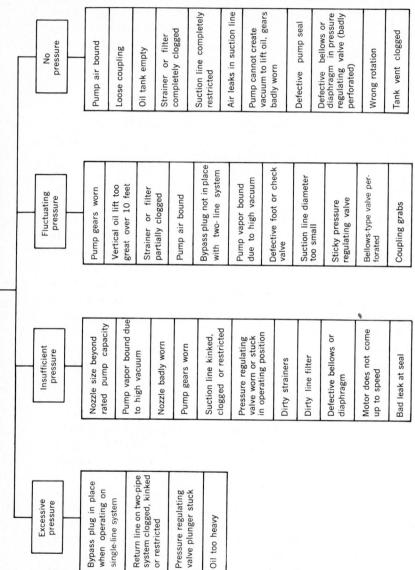

Excessive pressure
- Bypass plug in place when operating on single-line system
- Return line on two-pipe system clogged, kinked or restricted
- Pressure regulating valve plunger stuck
- Oil too heavy

Insufficient pressure
- Nozzle size beyond rated pump capacity
- Pump vapor bound due to high vacuum
- Nozzle badly worn
- Pump gears worn
- Suction line kinked, clogged or restricted
- Pressure regulating valve worn or stuck in operating position
- Dirty strainers
- Dirty line filter
- Defective bellows or diaphragm
- Motor does not come up to speed
- Bad leak at seal

Fluctuating pressure
- Pump gears worn
- Vertical oil lift too great over 10 feet
- Strainer or filter partially clogged
- Pump air bound
- Bypass plug not in place with two-line system
- Pump vapor bound due to high vacuum
- Defective foot or check valve
- Suction line diameter too small
- Sticky pressure regulating valve
- Bellows-type valve perforated
- Coupling grabs

No pressure
- Pump air bound
- Loose coupling
- Oil tank empty
- Strainer or filter completely clogged
- Suction line completely restricted
- Air leaks in suction line
- Pump cannot create vacuum to lift oil, gears badly worn
- Defective pump seal
- Defective bellows or diaphragm in pressure regulating valve (badly perforated)
- Wrong rotation
- Tank vent clogged

Fig. 26-6

the strainer or line filter is clogged with dirt. Clean it according to the directions set down previously.

Misalignment of the pump and motor shaft, as well as a loose pump mounting, may also be the cause of noise. If it is the former it will soon destroy the pump by causing excessive wear at the gears and by distorting the seal.

PRESSURE REGULATING VALVES

A sticky pressure regulating valve can be diagnosed by watching the pressure gauge. Its rise and fall should be constant. Any jerky action indicates that the valve may be sticking and is in need of cleaning, provided that all other conditions (strainer, suction line, etc.) are all right.

The cutoff of the pressure regulating valve must be clean and sharp, as evidenced by instantaneous extinguishing of the flame. Many oil-burner authorities advocate the widening of the bypass slot to accomplish this. The widening of the slot causes the pressure to drop off more quickly on the shutdown. Any ordinary file may be used to do this.

Do not, however, widen the bypass slot so much that the pump cannot build up pressure because it is bypassing too much oil. Avoid widening this slot in pumps that are old and worn. In such cases, a quick cutoff is achieved at the cost of a lowered operating pressure or fluctuations in pressure while running.

Sometimes when a pump is being used at or near its rated capacity, the flame will build up and die off and then build up again. This is due to the bypass action of the pressure regulating valve when the pump is at its critical capacity.

As the bypass port opens, the amount of oil bypassed results in a sudden drop in pressure and the flame suffers. This can be remedied by using a small amount of solder to reduce the size of the bypass slot, thereby enabling the pump to hold its pressure. This practice can also be used to increase the life and pressure-producing quality of old or worn pumps.

Pressure regulating valves of the bellows and diaphragm type should be closely checked for perforations whenever they are serviced. Always avoid taking apart a diaphragm-operated valve unless absolutely neces-sary. The main parts to be checked on any of these valves are the valve needle, valve seat, and valve stem. These parts should be clean and free of any sludge or gum.

A pressure regulating valve that is in a position to receive heat will develop trouble because of the cracking of the oil within it. This leaves a varnishlike gum deposit that will cause its moving parts to stick. Clean this valve with alcohol or lacquer thinner before reassembling, and insulate, if possible, from the reflected heat of the unit by strapping a piece of asbestos between the pump and the boiler.

QUESTIONS

1. Why is a "pigtail" advisable where the tubing joins the pump?
2. Explain how to connect the oil lines on a multiple-burner installation.
3. What is done with the internal bypass plug on a two-pipe system? On a single-line system?
4. Explain how to make the pressure adjustments.
5. Explain the use of the vacuum gauge. Vacuum readings should not usually exceed what number of inches?
6. What are the causes of delay in building up oil pressure?
7. Why is it important never to run a suction line under the furnace or boiler or too close to a hot surface?
8. What difficulties are caused by a sticky pressure regulating valve?
9. How are tests for air leaks in the suction line made?
10. What is the cause of tank hum? How is it cured?
11. Of what importance is the cutoff?
12. What happens when the bypass port or slot is made smaller?

CHAPTER 27
COMBUSTION PROBLEMS:
SMOKE AND SOOT

High up on the list of common service complaints caused by disturbed or defective combustion conditions while oil-burning units are operating are those of smoking and sooting. Smoking can be of different intensities, varying all the way from an intermittent light-gray haze to large quantities of dense black smoke.

The depositing of carbon may take two forms, being either soft and flaky, in which case it settles out as smoke or soot, or hard and crystalline, in which case it appears as a very hard mass. The former arises from the oil being burned with a deficiency of air. The latter is caused by liquid oil impinging on a hot surface and a cracking action taking place that results in the hard carbon formation.

All such service troubles require that some attention be given to the combustion process and the environment in which it is occurring.

In order that the burning of fuel oil be complete, clean, and thorough, four basic conditions must be complied with. These are (1) the oil must be thoroughly divided into tiny particles (atomized); (2) it must receive the proper quantity of air; (3) this oil and air must be completely mixed (turbulence); (4) the mixture must be burned without surface contact in a correctly sized and shaped combustion chamber.

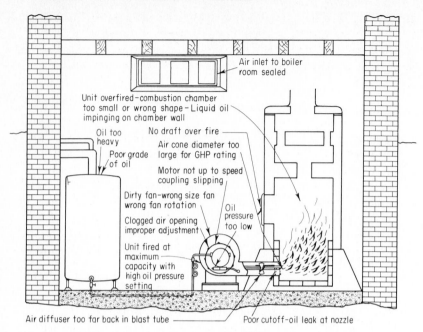

Fig. 27-1 Common causes of smoke, soot, or hard-carbon formation.

If an oil burner is producing smoke, soot, or hard carbon formations, it is because one or more of these four basic conditions are not being met by the burner while it is operating. It may be the fault of the burner itself or of the installer. Of course, it will be the job of the serviceman to find out which and correct it.

In answering any smoking or sooting complaint, the mechanic should observe the condition of the upper part of the chimney before entering the house. Such an observation can furnish an important clue as to how long the trouble has been going on.

If the outer surface of the chimney is streaked or black with soot, the condition has been going on for some time and has progressively got worse, until it now has forced the homeowner to call for service. This may point to faulty installation procedure.

The outer surfaces of the chimney should always be clean and free of soot. Neither should any smoke be issuing from it while the burner is operating. The ideal condition is to have a slightly brownish haze issuing from the chimney. It should be barely visible on a clear day. Observation of the color and density of the flue gases as they leave the chimney should be the final step in the servicing occasioned by a smoke and soot complaint.

The best way to find out the remedies for such burner troubles is to examine the basic causes of smoke, soot, and the formation of hard carbon.   These are (1) insufficient air; (2) poor mixture of oil and air; (3) bad nozzle operating conditions; (4) faulty pump operation; (5) overfired unit; (6) improper combustion-chamber size and shape; (7) inadequate draft; (8) miscellaneous mechanical defects; and (9) wrong grade of oil.

1. Insufficient air is a simple problem to solve.   The average oil burner is designed to deliver 25 to 40 per cent more air than is required.   This trouble, therefore, is not a burner design problem but rather an adjustment problem.   The correct method of making an air adjustment is to close the air shutter opening until about one-eighth the size of the fully opened shutter.   Start the unit and slowly open the shutter until the fire burns clearly.   Take a CO_2 reading and try to raise it to 10 per cent *without any visible smoking*.   A burner should be able to do this if it has been installed properly, if all air leaks are sealed, and if it has correct oil-air spray pattern.

If a 10 per cent CO_2 cannot be achieved after a short period of operation (about 10 to 15 min) without smoking and there are no bad air leaks in the furnace, something is wrong.   Examine the fan to see if it is clean.   A small deposit of dirt on the concave blades of the fan will seriously affect its ability to deliver the rated amount of air.   Remove the fan and clean it thoroughly.   Also clean the fan housing and blast tube so that deposits of dust and dirt will not hamper the air delivery.

Make certain that the fan is the proper size for the burner housing and the gph rate.   Check the manufacturer's specifications on this. If the fan is too small for the burner housing, it will not only fail to supply a sufficient quantity of air but also much of the air it does develop will be bypassed around the fan housing owing to the large

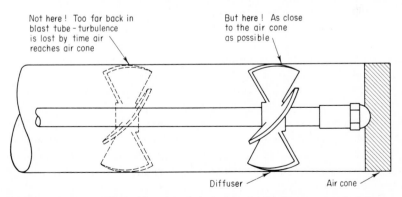

Fig. 27-2 Correct method of locating air turbulator to obtain necessary turbulence for thorough mixture of oil and air.

space between the fan and the fan scroll part of the casting. In this instance, it will be necessary to install a larger fan.

If a fan of the same diameter with wider blades is used, it will deliver more air at the same velocity as the old fan. But if a fan of larger diameter with the same width of blades is used, it will deliver more air with a higher velocity. If a fan of greater blade width and greater diameter is used, the delivery will have maximum velocity and volume.

On the other hand, if the fan is *too large*, the air velocity and quantity will be too great. The flame will be small and stringy with an acrid odor and a low CO_2. The flame may even be blown away from the front of the blast tube and flattened against the rear wall of the firebox.

In order to achieve more positive control, the air adjustment should be on the discharge side of the fan rather than on the intake side. More and more burner manufacturers are coming to realize this and incorporate such a feature into the design of their burner. This is the control principle (discharge control) involved in the use of such devices as the combustion heads that have come into such prominence in the last few years.

Service mechanics should always check on smoke and soot calls to see that the fan is of the correct size, clean, and rotating in the right direction. The air shutter openings must be clean, and enough draft should be available to move the gases through the boiler freely. These are basic conditions necessary for smoke-free combustion.

2. Poor mixing of the oil and air can be a result of improperly designed air-handling parts in the burner blast tube. All burners should have some type of vaned air cone at the mouth of the blast tube.

In addition, a stabilizer or diffuser, as shown in Fig. 27-2, should be used. This diffuser should be placed as far forward as possible in the blast tube. This brings it closer to the air cone at the mouth of the tube. In this way the spin and turbulence it gives to the air is not lost before it reaches the air cone as so often happens when it is placed too far back.

If possible, install one of the new types of combustion heads in the burner. These devices, by increasing the velocity of the air and directing it into the oil spray close to the nozzle, create the turbulence necessary to produce good, clean, smoke-free combustion.

The diameter of the opening of the blast tube is also important in obtaining a high CO_2 and avoiding smoke and soot. Do not use an air opening (air cone) of the same diameter through the full gph range of a burner. A smaller diameter opening for air is necessary at the end of the blast tube with smaller gph ratings.

Thus it is necessary to select narrower diameter air cones to obtain a good mixture when the gph rating goes below 1.50. These cones should get progressively smaller as the gph goes lower. A service mechanic should experiment to see which works best with various burners.

It makes little difference whether the vanes in the air cone turn in one direction or the other, as the spray issuing from the nozzle moves out in a straight line regardless of which way the slots in the insert are placed. There is absolutely nothing to the popular notion that the oil spray rotates in one direction and the air should spin in the other.

Sometimes a fire will appear to be distorted and smoky on one side. That is, it will burn cleanly on one side and with some smoke issuing from the other. This is especially prevalent in small burners. The cause of this is the swirling action given to the air by the average air cone. The air is directed downward on one side of the fire and upward on the other. This results in one side of the flame being slightly smoky. It does not, however, affect the heat-release quality of the fire. The flame is liberating as much heat on one side as on the other.

If this condition, however, is exaggerated and the fire is completely one-sided, it can be that the burner is not set straight; the nozzle line is cocked to one side; the nozzle is dirty or defective; or oil is hitting the electrodes.

Occasionally a one-sided fire may be caused by interference in the air delivery due to the ignition assembly. Rotate the assembly so that the electrodes are on the bottom of the blast tube instead

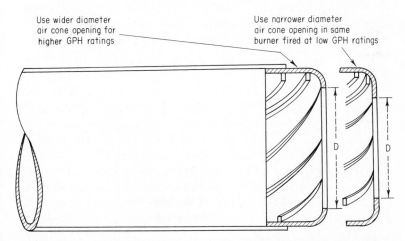

Use wider diameter air cone opening for higher GPH ratings

Use narrower diameter air cone opening in same burner fired at low GPH ratings

Fig. 27-3 Do not use the same diameter air-cone opening for entire gph range of burner.

of the top. This will usually remedy the condition. If it does not, try putting the burner on constant ignition. In many instances, constant ignition will clear up one-sided or smoky fires.

Smoking will also result from the oil being too coarsely atomized. The droplets are too large, and even though the air delivery is good, the oil particles are too coarse to mix thoroughly with the air. Readjust the pressure by increasing it. This will result in a finer spray and a better mixture of oil and air, which will provide a cleaner fire.

3 and 4. Nozzles or pumps that operate defectively are causes of smoke or soot. A dirty, defective, or worn nozzle will produce a bad or coarse spray or too large a quantity of oil for the existing air adjustment. Poor combustion will result. Likewise an old and worn pump will be unable to furnish the proper amount of pressure to do a good atomizing job.

If a burner is being fired at its *maximum capacity* and the pressure setting is too high, a quantity of oil too great for the fan capacity will be delivered. This will cause smoking.

A poor cutoff valve will result in a smoky fire after the burner has gone off, as will also any type of oil drip or leak at the nozzle. Recent tests have shown that a burner equipped with a special cutoff device will smoke 50 per cent less time after the burner has gone off than one that is not so equipped.

In the event that a nozzle is too far back in the blast tube or is cocked to one side, the oil spray will impinge upon the air cone, causing an uneven spray. The oil that drops down into the blast tube and burns produces large quantities of soot that foul up the air cone and the entire front of the burner. Such a job should be cleaned thoroughly and the nozzle straightened or moved forward far enough to prevent this deflection of the oil spray.

5. Overfiring a unit can readily cause smoke and soot. As a result of this there is usually impingement of the flame on the chamber walls and cooling of the flame tips when starting. Soot results from the cooling effect this produces. The large volume of gases created by overfiring also have a bad effect. They do not leave the boiler as fast as they are produced, as is the case when the firing rate is normal. The result of this is to blanket the flame and cut it off from the surrounding air. Without this surrounding supply of air, combustion is incomplete and large volumes of soot and smoke are formed. High stack temperature indicates overfiring.

6. Following closely upon overfiring as a cause of smoke and carbon formations is that of improperly designed and sized combustion chambers. This condition can be critical with gph ratings below 1.50 gal. The cool fires produced by small nozzles need a very

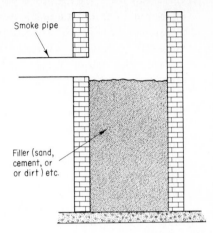

Smoke pipe

Filler (sand,
cement, or
or dirt) etc.

Fig. 27-4 Fill in unused portion of chimney base to provide better draft for cold starts.

well-designed chamber of light-weight insulating firebrick if they are to burn without smoking at the start.   Always use insulating firebrick with low gph rates.

The only time the use of heavy-weight standard firebrick is permissible is when there is a wet-base boiler.   Even in this case, only the floor of the chamber should be of heavy brick, and the walls and sides constructed of insulating brick.   The reason for the heavy firebrick floor with wet-base boilers is to allow heat to be transmitted to the water in the base.   With insulating brick floors, this water will remain cool and pocketed in the base, retarding circulation.

The insulating firebrick chamber holds the heat at the inner wall adjacent to the flame, thus increasing the flame temperature.   This means a shorter smoking period at the start.

Place a corbel or shelf at the front or rear of the chamber to force the gases back over the fire in order to completely consume any unburned oil particles that might otherwise travel up into the flue passages and settle out as an oily film of soot.

Avoid constructing a firebox with square corners.   Insert small triangular blocks of firebrick to fill the corners, or round off the rear walls of the combustion chamber by cutting pieces of insulating firebrick to fit.   These corners pocket the air and cause low-temperature areas in the chamber that cool the flame tips, creating a considerable amount of smoke before the firebox is hot enough to achieve balanced combustion.   Observe the shape of the flame produced by the burner and design the firebox around it.

Burners that are equipped with special air-handling parts, such as combustion heads, have a definite flame shape.   The installer should know this and build the chamber to fit it.

Burners with adjustable flame shapes controlled by air-handling parts have more flexibility and can be used with greater advantage in boilers with bases of varying shapes and sizes.

Any time and care given to the study of chambers and flame shapes and sizes will result in good clean combustion, with an absence of smoke and soot complaints. It can be said with some emphasis that the average domestic oil-burner installation is only as good as the combustion chamber.

Hard deposits of carbon building up on the floor or walls of the chamber show that liquid oil is impinging on the surface. This oil cracks and causes mounds of hard crustlike carbon to appear. Changing the angle of spray may help to avoid this. If it is a result of improper firebox size or shape, the chamber will have to be rebuilt, or the flame size and shape altered by new air-handling parts.

Many times a burner, upon starting in a cold firebox, will deposit a film of soot on the walls. Usually this is no problem, as it burns away when the chamber gets hot.

7. Draft conditions are important to quiet operation and strongly affect performance and the burner's ability to operate cleanly. Lack of draft over the fire will result in the blanketing of the flame with exhaust gases, as explained earlier, and cause smoking.

Always take a draft reading over the fire, that is, at the fire door or peep hole. It may be necessary to drill a hole to do this. *Always have 0.01 in. of draft over the fire.* This gives assurance that the firebox is a low-pressure area and that the gases will freely move through the boiler. If there is no draft over the fire, there is always danger of excessive smoking and other problems.

It is well to remember also that any decrease in firebox draft will also have an effect on the amount of air being delivered by the fan. Lack of draft over the fire makes it more difficult for the fan to deliver its air, as it must now push it against a pressure area. As a result, if the burner fan housing is not properly designed, the fan will begin to bypass some air around the scroll instead of delivering it through the blast tube.

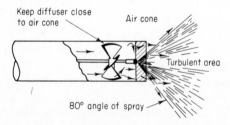

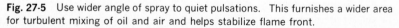

Fig. 27-5 Use wider angle of spray to quiet pulsations. This furnishes a wider area for turbulent mixing of oil and air and helps stabilize flame front.

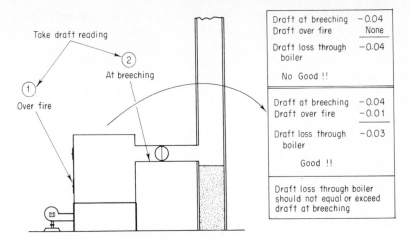

Fig. 27-6 Check on draft loss through boiler. Excessive draft loss through boiler or furnace means noisy flame pulsations.

A huge volume of air is required for combustion and chimney operation. It has been found that because of the tight construction practices, even furnaces or boilers located in an open basement are sometimes air-starved because the air cannot get into the basement in the first place. This usually occurs after the house has been closed up at night. The doors are not being opened and closed as they are during the daytime when sufficient replacement air can enter the building. After a no-heat call, the service technician cannot find anything wrong with the heating system. All controls check out because he has opened the door to enter the premises and allowed replacement air to enter. Often, there may be another no-heat call several hours after the first one. The unit has consumed the air let in after the first call. Air drawn from the building through the furnace must be replaced. Kitchen exhaust fans can intensify or cause this air-starved condition. This is true not only in residences but also in restaurants, which are notorious for this type of air starvation.

8 and 9. The mechanical defects that may cause smoking are limited in number. If the fan coupling is loose or grabs, it means that the fan will not be running at full speed and delivering the full quantity of air. The same condition will occur if the motor does not come up to its full speed. Check the rotation of the fan and motor to be sure that they are rotating in the right direction.

Another obscure cause of smoking is lack of ventilation in the cellar. The cellar or basement should not be sealed tight against the influx of outside air. This will result in the burner fan being unable to pick up enough air to support combustion. Always be certain to check that there is some air opening into the boiler room capable of furnishing all the air that is needed.

If the oil is of poor quality or too heavy for the burner nozzle to atomize thoroughly, smoking and sooting are bound to occur. Adjust for as much air and draft as possible, and step up the oil pressure. This will help overcome the smoking that is incidental to the use of such oils. The best assurance for the homeowner against a condition of this kind is to buy oil from a well-known, established, reputable dealer.

QUESTIONS

1. What are the two types of carbon that may be deposited? How does each originate?
2. What are the four basic conditions for clean and complete combustion?
3. What are the basic causes of smoke, soot, and hard carbon?
4. How can each condition in question 3 be corrected?
5. How does the diameter of the blast tube affect CO_2 readings?
6. What can cause a one-sided fire?
7. Explain how overfiring can cause smoke or soot.
8. Why are draft readings important when smoking and soot are resulting from burner operation?
9. Explain how lack of draft over the fire affects performance of the burner.
10. Explain how a building or dwelling can be "air-starved."
11. What results from this condition?
12. How can it be remedied?

CHAPTER 28

COMBUSTION PROBLEMS: VIBRATIONS AND PULSATIONS

The most annoying of all combustion problems are those of vibrations and pulsations. These usually occur with some sort of rhythm owing to either disturbed draft or faulty combustion conditions. If the pulsation of the flame, which is nothing more than a constant movement with contraction and expansion as it burns, is strong enough, it will result in vibration of the fire doors or any free-moving parts of the unit, such as the draft control, and add to the noises.

The noise caused by the pulsation of the flame, which is definitely a service problem of no small proportion, should not be confused with flame roar. *Flame roar* is a constant-combustion noise that does not take place with any sort of rhythm. It is caused by a blowtorch action of the flame, resulting from air being delivered at too great a velocity to an oil spray that is too narrow. The quieting of a flame roar is a simple problem compared to that of removing a pulsation.

To minimize flame roar, which is present in all power burners to some degree, the combustion chamber should always be built of insulat-

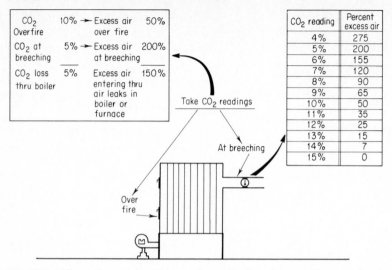

Fig. 28-1 CO_2 readings at breeching and over the fire often reveal cause of pulsations: excess air entering upper part of boiler cools flue gases, increases volume, and decreases draft.

ing firebrick. The porous construction of such brick acts as a sound absorber.

If the burner being used seems to produce an *exceptionally* noisy fire, build the chamber 3 or 4 in. higher than is normal and corbel it on the back and side walls. Then use a nozzle that will give a wider angle of spray and cut the draft back so that it is almost zero over the fire. This will usually quiet the most persistent flame roar. Do not, however, cut the draft down so far that it will result in a pulsation, for this will substitute a greater for a lesser evil.

If, after these remedial measures, the fire still roars, then it will be necessary to install a smaller diameter fan. Reducing the diameter of the fan will deliver less air at lower velocity. If the smaller diameter fan does not give enough air, then use one with wider blades, but do not increase the diameter. Remember that by increasing the width of the blades, the quantity but not the velocity of the air is increased. Increasing the diameter enlarges both velocity and quantity.

The main problem in flame roar is to reduce air velocity. This can also be accomplished by enlarging the air cone opening at the mouth of the blast tube. It is questionable though whether this is good practice, for such an increased opening may result in a poor mixture of oil and air and cause smoke and soot.

If the draft *over the fire* is in excess of 0.04 in., flame roar may occur owing to the large quantities of air that will readily flow into such a low-pressure area. Install a draft control; baffle the boiler or properly adjust an existing draft control to produce a maximum of 0.02 in. of draft over the fire.

On the other hand, the rhythmic flame pulsation which may vary in intensity from a barely audible fluctuation of the fire to one that is so great as to puff open the boiler doors presents a difficult service problem that often is not easily solved. These *pulsations* are of three types, namely, the *starting pulsation*, the *running pulsation*, and the *stopping pulsation*. The names imply when they occur. Pulsations can also be classified by their basic cause, and as such there are *combustion pulsations* and *draft pulsations*. This means that such service problems can be caused by either poor combustion or inadequate draft or a combination of both.

Perhaps the best method of approaching the service problem presented by pulsations is to discuss them in the order in which they may occur—at starting, while running, or at stopping.

STARTING PULSATIONS

The pulsation that occurs at starting is usually a draft problem. When the unit starts, the flame flutters and fluctuates violently, causing all loose parts of the boiler or furnace to vibrate. The cause of this is basic. As the unit begins to fire, there is no draft because everything is cold and the chimney may not be capable of producing any draft until the gases are hot enough to rise of themselves. As a result, when the unit starts, a pressure area is built up over the fire by the flue gases because they do not freely flow through the boiler.

Any restrictions in the boiler in the form of baffles, spirals, soot deposits, etc., will make the situation worse. This also applies to chimneys. The pressure area over the fire will cause the flame to gasp and flutter many times each second and the pulsation occurs.

The starting pulsation also has another contributing factor—the *lack of balance* between the quantities of oil and air at the start. The oil

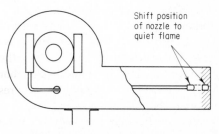

Shift position
of nozzle to
quiet flame

Fig. 28-2   Adjusting nozzle position a short distance will help eliminate pulsations.

spray reaches its maximum quantity before the fan can deliver the maximum amount of air. This means that the flame may smoke for a few seconds on starting and increase the pulsation.

It may be necessary to install a delayed-action oil valve before the pump if the gph rate is over 5 gal to remedy this condition. This delays the delivery of oil until the fan is furnishing its full quantity of air. This will also require a special primary control containing a delayed-action switch for the oil valve. Such a device, however, is not necessary on the small domestic unit with its low gph rate of oil consumption.

The best way to avoid the starting pulsation is to have adequate natural draft at the chimney. It may be necessary to lengthen the chimney to do this. If the smoke pipe enters the chimney well above the base, do not leave the intervening space between the chimney floor and the smoke pipe opening hollow. Fill it with sand, as this will help create the draft required for a smooth start.

If a chimney is in an exceptionally exposed area, it may have to be insulated from the cold, in order that the flue gases will not cool too quickly. By keeping the flue gases at a higher temperature in the chimney, the required thermal draft is more easily obtained.

The use of a wider spray angle will help minimize starting pulsation, as will a narrower diameter air cone at the front of the blast tube. Be sure that the burner has air-handling parts that will give good spin and turbulence to the air as it leaves the gun. This is an absolute must in helping prevent any kind of pulsation.

RUNNING PULSATIONS

If a unit develops a running pulsation, which occurs all through its operation, the flue gases are unable to leave the boiler freely. As a result, the pressure area over the fire is fluctuating constantly. This causes the flame to flutter, contract, and expand, and it pulsates, therefore, with a sort of rhythm. This in turn sets up vibrations of all loose parts throughout the unit.

The explanation of this is simple. If the gases do not leave the boiler as quickly as they are produced, they will cause a pressure to be built up around the flame. This pressure does two things: (1) It blankets the fire with flue gases, cutting off its supply of surrounding air; and (2) it makes the job of the fan difficult by forcing it to deliver the air against the pressure in the firebox.

The fan, therefore, will bypass air around the housing instead. The supply of air will now be further diminished. The flame with its supply of essential air considerably reduced decreases in size. When it does this, it also decreases the quantity of flue gases produced, as the rate of combustion is lowered. This momentarily causes a relief and the gases

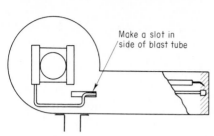

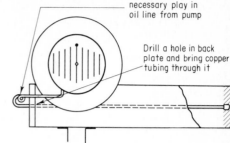

Make a slot in side of blast tube

Note loop to give necessary play in oil line from pump

Drill a hole in back plate and bring copper tubing through it

Fig. 28-3 Method of providing a means for adjusting nozzle toward or away from air cone.

Fig. 28-4 Additional method of providing for adjustment of nozzle position.

pass through the boiler, releasing the pressure over the fire. The flame now suddenly enlarges to normal size, increasing the quantity of flue gas liberated. Higher pressure ensues and the whole cycle, as explained above, repeats itself. This is the *pulsation*. This fluctuation of pressure area over the fire can occur many times per second, setting up the rhythmic pulsation from which the condition gets its name. The extent of the violence of the pulsation depends on how high the pressure of the gases over the fire develops.

The major cause of pulsations is lack of draft over the fire, and this condition in turn is usually caused by excessive draft drop through the boiler or furnace.

No oil burner can operate quietly and efficiently unless the flue gases being produced by the flame are moved quickly from the combustion area. This is the function of draft. *However, the draft or low-pressure area that assures the flow of the gases away from the combustion area is that draft which exists over the fire.*

It makes no difference how much draft there is at the chimney or breeching; it is the draft over the fire that counts. Often there may be adequate draft at the breeching while there is no draft at all over the fire. This is caused by the frictional resistance set up by the tubes or flue passages in the boiler or furnace.

The loss of draft in the boiler is called "draft drop through the boiler." For instance, if the draft at the breeching is 0.04 in. of water and it is 0.01 over the fire, then the draft drop or draft loss through that boiler is the difference between these two figures of 0.03 (see Fig. 27-6). This means simply that, owing to the restriction in the boiler, the draft dropped from 0.04 at the smoke pipe to 0.01 over the firebox. Usually, the more efficient a boiler is, the greater will be its draft drop.

Always check the draft over the fire with a draft gauge. It should be at least 0.01 and not below that. Adjust the draft control to furnish

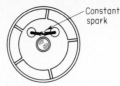
Constant spark

Fig. 28-5   Constant ignition may stabilize flame front and quiet pulsating flame.

this minimum draft at the fire.   The draft control may have to be sealed up in order to do this.

Take a reading at the breeching also, and be absolutely certain that the draft at that point is at least 0.01 in. greater than the draft loss through the boiler.   Some oilburner experts suggest adjusting the over-the-fire draft at zero.   However, if for any reason the draft at the breeching drops, this means there will be a pressure over the fire and pulsations will ensue.   Everything possible, from insulating the smoke pipe to keep the gases hot to lengthening the chimney, should be tried if there is difficulty in obtaining draft over the fire.   It may require the removal of baffles or spirals in the flues or tubes of the boiler or furnace to cut down the frictional resistance to the free flow of the gases. Cleaning the boiler, breeching, and chimney will also help.

Sometimes, because of air leaks through sections around the base, through the seams in the combustion chamber, or at the joints of the smoke pipe, the draft over the fire will be lowered.   The quantity of excess air leaking in at these points will increase the volume of gases moving through the boiler and can even decrease their temperature. This adversely affects the draft and actually increases the draft loss through the boiler.

With the jackets covering boilers as they do today, it is difficult to observe the places where there may be air leaks.   To ascertain whether such hidden air leaks exist, take a CO_2 test at the breeching and another one over the fire.   Any lowering of the CO_2 at the breeching as compared with the CO_2 over the fire shows excess air to be leaking into the boiler.   The exact amount of excess air can be calculated by referring to Fig. 28-1.   Remove the jacket and candle the boiler or furnace to find out where the leaks are and seal up the cracks or openings with furnace cement.

Be sure that the unit is not overfired.   Any heavily overfired oil unit will give one symptom of excessive air leaks, that is, abnormal draft loss through the boiler.   Check the rating of the boiler against the nozzle size to see if it is being fired at the correct gph rating.

If draft conditions are all right and pulsations still occur, then combustion conditions are faulty.   Usually, in this case, the flame is moving back and forth, toward and away from the nozzle.   At the same time, it may be irregular and constantly changing its shape.

To remedy this, use a nozzle with a wider angle of spray. This spreads the same quantity of oil over a larger area and provides better oil-air mixture. Increasing the oil pressure will also help. If this does not effect a cure, install a narrower air cone at the nozzle with a good diffuser in the blast tube, as close to the air cone as possible (see Figs. 27-3 and 28-6).

If there is a diffuser in the blast tube, try moving it forward toward the air cone. Next put the burner on constant ignition. This sometimes clears up stubborn cases of pulsations. Also, corbels on the chamber back and sides help.

Occasionally, it is necessary to rebuild a chamber completely if it is excessively small or large. New chamber dimensions may ensure quiet operation and good pulsation-free combustion.

One important factor that can do much to clear up a fire and end pulsation is the position of the nozzle in relation to the air cone at the front of the burner. Many times just moving a nozzle forward or backward $\frac{1}{4}$ to $\frac{1}{2}$ in. will provide a clean, quiet, stable fire entirely free of any pulsations. Provide for such an adjustment in a burner not so equipped by using one of the methods shown in Figs. 28-2 to 28-4.

All the defective combustion conditions covered in this chapter and Chap. 27 can also be the cause of obnoxious odors. If any condition causes soot, smoke, or pulsations, it can also cause odors if such soot and smoke leak out into the basement. Thus it is important that there be sufficient draft to draw off any smoke or gases.

Pressure (lack of draft) through the boiler or breeching will force smoke or partially burned oil fumes that cause unpleasant odors out into the boiler room. This makes it doubly important that the required draft exist all through the oil-fired heating unit. Sealing up air leaks around the burner gun, peephole, or fire doors, between sections of the boiler, and at smoke-pipe joints, or even sealing the draft control, may be needed to avoid this trouble. Large deposits of soot in the flue passages and chimney will also cause odor complaints.

If the boiler room is sealed so that there is no influx of fresh air, it will cause the burner to smoke. This occurs because of the fact that

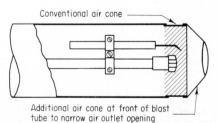

Conventional air cone

Additional air cone at front of blast tube to narrow air outlet opening

Fig. 28-6 Additional cone narrowing blast-tube mouth may stabilize and quiet the fire.

the entire boiler room has become a low-pressure area on account of the rapid exhaustion of the supply of air which cannot be replaced quickly enough because of lack of ventilation.

Oil leaks, however small, will cause odor complaints, especially if they are close to the boiler or furnace. Here, the heat vaporizes the leaking oil and the fumes spread all through the house. Oil-storage tanks should be kept tightly capped and the vent line should not have its opening too close to a window. Fumes from the vent can enter the house in this case.

Dirty nozzles will also cause acrid odors by producing peculiar combustion conditions resulting in the formation of evil-smelling compounds known as aldehydes. This comes from excessive chilling of the oil flame and consequent breaking down of the burning oil. These fumes are heavy, white, and misty and do not resemble smoke. Clean the nozzle to stop this. Occasionally if the air shutter is opened too wide and the burner is firing from a cold start, this condition will occur. Closing off the air shutter part way will cure it by providing a richer mixture at the start.

QUESTIONS

1. What is meant by "flame roar"?
2. How can flame roar be remedied?
3. How may pulsations be classified? Explain.
4. Explain what occurs when a pulsation takes place.
5. Give two causes of starting pulsations.
6. Give two methods of correcting starting pulsations.
7. What is a running pulsation?
8. What is the major cause of pulsations?
9. How can "draft drop" through the boiler be measured?
10. Why is "over-the-fire" draft so important?
11. Give three causes of combustion odors.
12. Why should all air leaks be thoroughly sealed?

CHAPTER 29
EXCESSIVE FUEL-OIL CONSUMPTION

High-oil-consumption complaints on the part of the homeowner deserve much more consideration than they really get. There is hardly a unit in the field which, after operating through a winter season, should not be checked over and adjusted. The accumulation of soot, changes in draft conditions, nozzle wear, mechanical defects, differences in the oil, and condition of the boiler water all have a decided effect upon the quantity of oil being consumed.

At the beginning of each winter, a little care in checking on the performance of a unit and the conditions under which it has to operate can result in substantial fuel-oil savings.

The use of combustion testing instruments is necessary in the servicing of high oil consumption complaints. The CO_2 analyzer gives an exact indication of how much excess air is passing through the unit and carrying with it, to the chimney, heat that should be going to the furnace or boiler. The draft gauge helps in adjusting for less excess air and in obtaining quiet, smoke-free, efficient combustion.

The stack thermometer gives a good indication of the intensity with which the boiler or furnace is absorbing heat. A high stack temperature

437

shows the boiler to be falling down on the job, whether through its own inadequacy or because it is being asked to do a job that it was not designed to perform. Conversely, a low or normal stack temperature, if the unit is being fired at the proper gph rate, indicates that it is performing efficiently.

Oil-fired heating systems that are using too much oil for the quantity of heat they are producing usually show one or more of the following symptoms: high stack temperature, long periods of constant operation, low CO_2 readings, high draft readings, insufficient heat.

If a high-stack-temperature condition exists, it may be due either to the boiler or furnace being overfired or to the inefficiency of the boiler or furnace in absorbing the heat being furnished to it.

Check the capacity of the boiler in Btu or square feet of radiation against the gph rating of the nozzle. A gallon of No. 2 fuel oil contains 140,000 Btu. One foot of steam radiation equals 240 Btu, while a foot of hot-water radiation may vary between 150 and 200 Btu. An oil-burning boiler or furnace converts about 70 per cent of the Btu in a gallon of oil to actual room heat. A converted coal boiler utilizes about 50 or 60 per cent of the oil's Btu in the form of room heat.

Thus an oil-fired boiler should produce about 400 ft of radiation per gal of oil, and the average conversion job should produce between 300 and 350 ft per gal. These figures give a serviceman an approximate basis upon which to determine whether a unit is being underfired or overfired. Both these conditions cause waste of large quantities of fuel.

CAUSES OF FUEL WASTE

When a unit is underfired, it is not getting enough oil to do the job efficiently. Consequently, the stack temperature will be low, but the unit will have to run for much longer periods of time to furnish the required amount of heat. This will result in a severe waste of oil.

Any oil-fired heating plant that is adequately sized should furnish heat to all parts of a residence on a cold morning after a maximum run of 45 min. It should not have to run for 1 or 2 hr or even longer to bring up heat. If it does, the unit is being underfired; the boiler or furnace is too small, or the standing radiation or ducts are inadequate. Excessively long periods of operation (an hour or more) are indications that the heat input is inadequate among other things.

If the boiler and burner gph rate are adequate, then it may be necessary to make a room-by-room heat-loss survey of the house to determine if the radiation is sufficient.

Sometimes long running periods may be caused by a defective or dirty nozzle that decreases the amount of oil being delivered, furnishing a flame too small in size to do the job. Clean or replace with a new nozzle to remedy this.

CAUSES OF HIGH OIL CONSUMPTION

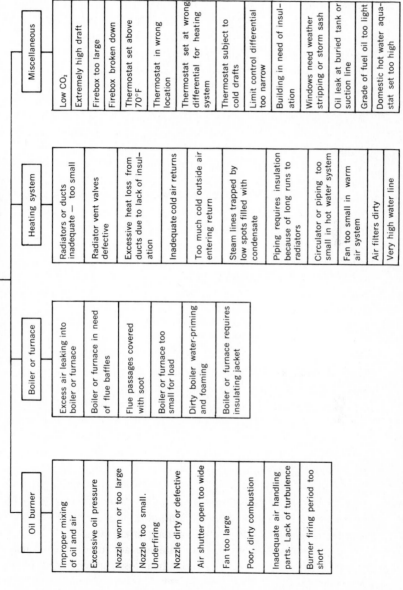

Oil burner	Boiler or furnace	Heating system	Miscellaneous
Improper mixing of oil and air	Excess air leaking into boiler or furnace	Radiators or ducts inadequate — too small	Low CO_2
Excessive oil pressure	Boiler or furnace in need of flue baffles	Radiator vent valves defective	Extremely high draft
Nozzle worn or too large	Flue passages covered with soot	Excessive heat loss from ducts due to lack of insulation	Firebox too large
Nozzle too small. Underfiring	Boiler or furnace too small for load	Inadequate cold air returns	Firebox broken down
Nozzle dirty or defective	Dirty boiler water-priming and foaming	Too much cold outside air entering return	Thermostat set above 70°F
Air shutter open too wide	Boiler or furnace requires insulating jacket	Steam lines trapped by low spots filled with condensate	Thermostat in wrong location
Fan too large		Piping requires insulation because of long runs to radiators	Thermostat set at wrong differential for heating system
Poor, dirty combustion		Circulator or piping too small in hot water system	Thermostat subject to cold drafts
Inadequate air handling parts. Lack of turbulence		Fan too small in warm air system	Limit control differential too narrow
Burner firing period too short		Air filters dirty	Building in need of insulation
		Very high water line	Windows need weather stripping or storm sash
			Oil leak at buried tank or suction line
			Grade of fuel oil too light
			Domestic hot water aquastat set too high

Fig. 29-1

The location of the thermostat may have a great deal to do with long wasteful ON periods. Should this control be in a cold location it will be affected. Keep it away from drafts, outside walls, halls, doorways, air shafts, etc. Placing the thermostat in a spot affected by temperatures cooler than that of the room only means that it will take a long time to satisfy it. The burner then runs longer than it should; parts of the building are overheated; and much fuel is wasted. For the proper location of this all-important control, see Chap. 13.

The differential setting on the thermostat is also important, for it will help determine the length of the ON period of the burner. Adapt the differential setting to the characteristics of the heating system and provide the proper adjustment by observing the directions of the thermostat manufacturer. In general, to decrease the ON period, the differential should be decreased.

Another cause of fuel waste due to longer ON periods than are necessary is *bad boiler water conditions*. The presence of dirt, grease, cutting oils, soap, etc., in the boiler causes either *priming or foaming*. *Priming* is the surging of water in the boiler resulting in an unsteady water line and lack of steam. *Foaming* is the formation of a foam or froth on the boiler water that makes it difficult to form steam. The steam is trapped in the foam and condenses before it breaks free. With water in this condition, a domestic boiler may run for hours without making steam, and if the oil or grease combines with certain elements in the rust and forms soap, it will be almost impossible to get sufficient quantities of heat. Blowing down or draining the boiler will not solve this problem permanently.

A good boiler cleaning compound of the *flocculent* type should be used in the manner directed on the container. After treatment with a good boiler cleaning compound, the water level as shown in the gauge glass should be steady and fluctuate no more than a total $\frac{1}{2}$ in. while the unit is in operation, which means about $\frac{1}{4}$ in. above and below the water-line level. Avoid the use of washing soda (sal soda or sodium carbonate) or vinegar (acetic acid) in domestic boilers. These compounds only aggravate the trouble and may harm the boiler.

All the foregoing service-making conditions concern those units which are running with a low or normal stack temperature but wasting oil by operating for excessively long periods of time. The opposite condition, that is, running for a normal period of time with excessive stack temperature, is a much more prevalent indication of high oil consumption.

The average boiler or furnace designed for oil firing should run with a stack temperature not above 550°F. It it is a converted coal-fired boiler furnace, a 700°F stack temperature is excessive. Stack readings higher than these indicate that fuel is being wasted in the form of heat going up the chimney.

CAUSES OF HIGH STACK HEAT LOSS

High stack temperature can be caused by the following conditions: (1) dirty, soot-covered flue passages, (2) flue passages too large and unrestricted, (3) excess air, (4) overfiring, and (5) inadequate boiler or furnace capacity for attached load.

The accumulation of soot in the tubes or flue passages of a domestic boiler will drive up the stack temperature because of the insulating quality such soot has. A deposit of soot should never be allowed to accumulate over $\frac{1}{16}$ in. on furnace or boiler surfaces. A soot deposit of $\frac{1}{16}$ in. will cause a 4 to 6 per cent decrease in boiler efficiency.

Remove the soot with a brush, or vacuum-clean the entire unit. For small soot deposits, chemical soot removers in the form of powders which cause the soot to burn off can be used. Once the soot remover has begun to burn the soot, be sure to shut off the burner. Otherwise, there may be a chimney fire if there is any appreciable quantity of soot in the stack. Adjusting for proper draft over the fire to produce smoke-free combustion will help eliminate the formation of smoke and soot.

Large or unrestricted flue passages result in slow, lazy movements of the flue gases through the boiler. This causes stratification of the flue gases and much waste of heat. The center of the flue passage contains the hottest and most turbulent gases, which in an unrestricted flue passage never touch the surface of the boiler.

It is necessary for efficient operation to force the flue gases against the sides of the flue or tube where they will give up their heat. *This is the purpose of baffling a boiler.*

THE USE OF BAFFLES

The use of flue baffles is by far the most effective method of cutting down fuel consumption and one of the most neglected. The baffle, if properly applied, forces the gases to change direction, thereby increasing the turbulence that is so necessary to get effective heat transfer to the flue surface and thence to the water or air on the other side.

Secondly, it directs the gases against the flue surface with *greater velocity*, minimizing the quantity that will pass through the boiler never touching anything. Because of this, a baffle should *never* lie on the surface of the flue passage, as it will then defeat its purpose by *preventing* the flue gas from coming in contact with that surface upon which it rests. The baffle should have as its purpose the blocking off of large open areas so that the flue gases will be forced against the sides of the boiler or furnace.

Round, pancake-type boilers or warm-air furnaces should have a stool or hanging baffle (Fig. 29-5). This type of boiler or furnace can usually be baffled heavily as the draft loss through it is very small.

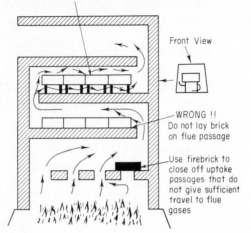

RIGHT !!
Raise brick off flue passage by resting
it on section of split brick – Then flue gas
can reach all surfaces of flue sections

Front View

WRONG !!
Do not lay brick
on flue passage

Use firebrick to
close off uptake
passages that do
not give sufficient
travel to flue
gases

Fig. 29-2   Correct method of using firebrick for baffles.

If, however, a boiler has a large draft loss through it, then care will have to be exercised. The use of baffles *increases* the draft loss through the boiler and it should never be decreased to the point at which it is less than 0.01 over the fire. After baffling, a draft reading should be taken at the fire door to ascertain whether this minimum draft requirement exists. If it does not, then the baffles must be rearranged or part of them removed.

The draft gauge is an important instrument and should be used to obtain readings before and after baffling. Boilers or furnaces that have an excessive draft drop should be adjusted for maximum draft at the breeching by closing the draft control and even sealing it if necessary. Then the boiler should be baffled with one eye on the draft over the fire. In a case like this, it is good practice not to allow the over-fire draft to fall below 0.02. This gives protection on those days when atmospheric or temperature conditions adversely affect the chimney's ability to produce draft.

With rectangular cast-iron boilers, whether designed for coal or oil firing, baffles can be used advantageously in the form of firebrick or lengths of capped sheet-metal pipe. This type of boiler has little draft loss and presents an ideal surface for baffling.

If brick is used, it should not rest squarely, whether on the wide or narrow side, against the flue surface. Instead, it should be raised by setting it on small rectangular sections of split brick that have been cut uniformly for that purpose. Each end of the brick should be supported by these pieces, as shown in Fig. 29-2. This allows the gases to touch all sides of the flue and effectively blocks the central passage wherein the gases travel, touching nothing (Fig. 29-2).

The supports for the brick should be from 1 to $1\frac{1}{2}$ in. in height. They aid by giving increased turbulence and twisting to the flue gas as it passes around them, as shown in the illustration.

The lower portion of Fig. 29-2 shows the manner in which the upsweep flue passages above the crown sheet or first section level can be blocked off to give a *longer* travel to the flue gases coming off the fire. Using a brick in this fashion has somewhat the same effect as a corbel on the back wall of a combustion chamber.

Ordinary gutter piping capped on each end with a vent hole somewhere in the pipe can also be very effectively used as a baffle in cast-iron boilers. Supporting legs, as shown in Fig. 29-4, can be attached to lift the pipe off the floor of the flue passage.

Be careful about using solder to attach supports, as the temperature of the flue gasses in the first passes of the boiler may be high enough to melt the solder. Gases at this point may run over 1000°F in temperature. A flap can be used to attach the leg by putting a nut and bolt through it to fasten it to the pipe.

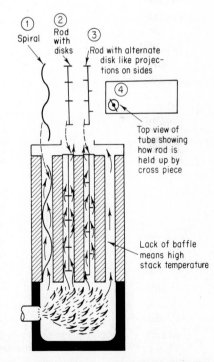

Fig. 29-3 Baffling a vertical firetube boiler.

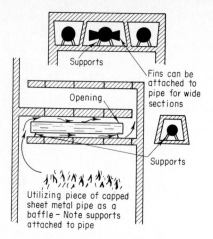

Fig. 29-4 Capped conductor pipe (gutter pipe) used as a baffle.

If the center section is very wide, larger diameter pipe may be used or fins attached, spaced about 6 to 8 in. apart through the length of the pipe.   When fins are attached, do not make them so large as to cause a pulsation.

The size of the pipe or fins is a matter of trial and error and if there are any doubts, try several sizes, checking with the draft gauge to be sure of the 0.01-in. draft over the fire at all times.

A cast-iron boiler that is running with an excessive stack temperature should always be checked to see if it was assembled properly.   Many times, sections are not pulled up in the proper sequence and whole lengths of flue passage in the boiler are never touched by the hot gases. The waste of oil and heat, as well as the sluggish circulation caused by

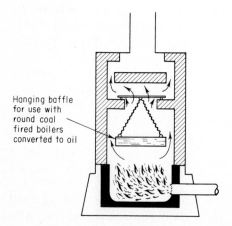

Fig. 29-5 Baffling a round boiler.

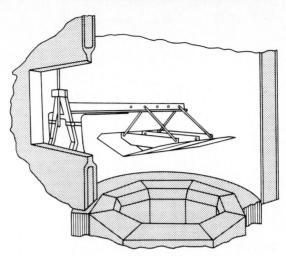

Fig. 29-6 A steel hanging baffle suspended over the firebox. (*Boston Machine Works*)

such short circuiting of the gases, is obvious and requires no comment.

Hanging baffles made of chrome steel are effective when hung over the combustion chamber as shown in Fig. 29-6. These steel baffles are adjustable to many sizes. They have a small mass and are light in weight. Consequently they absorb and hold little heat. This cuts down on temperature override after the burner shuts down. Such a baffle as this is best located about 10 in. above the combustion chamber. In this location, it gives maximum return in radiant heat.

BAFFLING TUBULAR BOILERS

Vertical or horizontal firetube steel boilers can be baffled in the various ways shown in Fig. 29-3. The spiral baffle is the most popular type in these boilers. A metal rod through the center of disks about 8 in. apart can also be used. The disks can be welded to the rod at the point where it passes through their centers. Be careful *not* to have the diameter of the disk more than *two-thirds* the diameter of the firetube. If the whole disk causes too great a draft loss, as well it might, the boiler can still be baffled by using method 3 in Fig. 29-3. Here, only half disks are welded to the rod about 8 in. apart on alternate sides. This cuts the stack temperature without too large a reduction in draft, as may occur with methods 1 and 2. The rod is held up by a crosspiece welded to its top as shown in method 4.

As the horizontal steel firetube boiler is usually the most restricted because of its high efficiency, draft and pulsation troubles are commonly encountered when it is baffled. If draft at the breeching is low (less

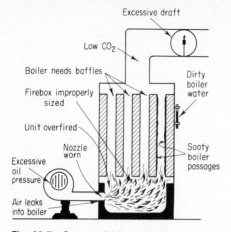

Fig. 29-7   Causes of high stack temperature.

than 0.04), it may be impossible to use any baffles. Then it will be very important that the flues be as clean as possible with an operating CO_2 no higher than 10 per cent. Seal the draft control in the *closed* position in a problem such as this.

Excess air entering the furnace or boiler at the base, through sections, through the casing at the burner, results in heat being carried up the chimney that should be going to the boiler. Take a CO_2 reading over the fire and one at the breeching. Any drop in the CO_2 at the breeching as compared with the CO_2 at the fire shows excess air to be leaking into the boiler.

Remove the jacket, if the unit has one, and candle all seams and cracks at doors to locate the leaks. Seal them with furnace cement and watch the stack temperature drop. After all leaks are sealed, adjust the oil burner to run with a 10 per cent CO_2 *without smoke.*

Overfiring usually results on those installations which were converted from coal to oil where the boiler or furnace was not adequate. In cases such as this, the homeowner many times will resist all attempts to sell him a new boiler. As a result, he pays in wasted fuel for the boiler many times over. If a unit cannot furnish enough heat without over-firing, then the boiler or furnace is too small and the real solution is a new one of adequate size.

The overloaded unit is the most aggravating of all service makers. The best advice is to adjust for the cleanest combustion possible and to clean the flue passages several times, even once a month during the winter season. To achieve this clean combustion under these conditions, use a nozzle about 15 to 20 per cent smaller than is needed, and adjust for higher pressure to give the added quantity of required fuel.

If the unit is the proper size and is suspected of being overfired, check with the boiler manufacturer for his specifications on the correct rate for the unit. Baffling the boiler may result in being able to use a much smaller nozzle and end overfiring.

Remember to check the combustion-chamber size. Although the gph rate for the boiler is all right, the chamber may be overfired because it is too small. This means wasted oil. Build a properly sized and shaped combustion chamber. It will pay for itself in one season.

Insulating the outer surfaces of a boiler will increase its efficiency. Avoid using asbestos laid on with a trowel and instead use one of the more efficient insulating materials of the "air-cell" type such as mineral wool or magnesia block. With cold cellars, this practice can save considerable oil, for many times as much as 20 per cent of the total heat in the oil passes into a basement where it is not wanted or needed.

Another cause of high oil "consumption" that occurs without any warning is oil leaking from a tank or suction line below ground. Any unwarranted increase in fuel consumption without any abnormal rise in stack temperature, decline in CO_2, or increase in smoke or soot will give a clue to this defect. Clocking the exact number of hours a unit runs in a day by using an operations recorder and multiplying this ON time in hours by the nozzle rate will give, with fair accuracy, the quantity of oil consumed in 24 hr. Check the oil content in the tank before and after the clocked running period and compare the decrease without the amount consumed by the burner. Do this several days. If there is an increase of over 5 per cent beyond that which the burner consumes, as compared with that which is left in the tank, the difference is probably being caused by an underground leak. A new suction line or tank may have to be installed.

QUESTIONS

1. What instrument gives a good indication of the intensity with which the boiler or furnace is absorbing heat?
2. How does underfiring waste fuel?
3. What is meant by "bad boiler water conditions"?
4. How should the problem in question 3 be taken care of?
5. Give five causes of high stack heat loss.
6. Explain the purpose of a baffle.
7. Explain the proper method of using firebrick for baffles.
8. Name and describe four different types of baffles.
9. How does the use of baffles affect draft drop through the boiler? Why?
10. What effect does combustion-chamber size have on fuel-oil consumption?
11. What are the advantages of a hanging steel baffle?
12. How should it be located?

CHAPTER 30

SERVICING VAPORIZING POT-TYPE BURNERS AND LOW-PRESSURE GUN-TYPE BURNERS

Because vaporizing pot-type burners do not employ mechanical means such as pumps and nozzles to prepare fuel oil for combustion, they are relatively simple from a mechanical viewpoint. The method used by pot-type burners to achieve the breakdown of the oil into particles small enough to mix with air and support combustion is that of *vaporization by means of heat.*

Actually, the heat from the oil flame itself heats the oil until it passes off as a vapor, mingles with air, and burns. The air to support combustion may be furnished either by natural draft or by mechanical draft obtained from a fan.

The fact that heat is the only medium employed to prepare the oil for combustion means that such burners have certain limitations on the grade of oil they may burn. The fuel must be volatile, that is, capable of being evaporated easily. Therefore, care has to be taken to see that a light grade of oil is being used. Check the pot-type burner manufacturer's specifications on this point.

Any use of oil that is too heavy will result in a smoky, sooty fire that will burn down in the pot instead of above it. Such an improperly located flame means that the metal parts of the pot will be overheated and warp out of shape. Constant use of the wrong grade of oil will eventually plug all the air holes in the pot walls with carbon. This means aggravated smoking and soot conditions due to lack of air. The ultimate result is no fire at all, and a completely ruined pot that will have to be replaced.

Natural-draft vaporizing pot-type burners are usually used with kerosene and No. 1 oil, and on some larger models No. 2 fuel oil may be utilized. Vaporizing burners should not use oil over the No. 2 grade.

To be able to service this type of burner properly, it is a good thing to understand the difference between "vaporizing" and "cracking." Heat will do either of these to a fuel oil. The thing to avoid is the "cracking" action without the proper quantity of air, for when oil cracks in a deficiency of air, it deposits carbon in the form of smoke and soot. The latter closes up the air holes in the pot, cutting off the air supply to the fire, and can even close off entirely the flow of fuel from the line opening.

However, *all* cracking is not detrimental. When it occurs at the proper temperature and with the necessary quantity of air being present, it forms compounds that will vaporize more readily and at lower temperatures. Remember that any time an insufficient quantity of air is present, cracking action caused by the heat will form hard carbon or smoke and soot. The other condition that governs the extent of cracking is the temperature of the fuel in the pot. It should not go above $650°F$.

If it does, and there is a shortage of air, smoke and soot will occur with a straight-run distillate and hard carbon will be formed with the newer catalytic fuel oils. As far as service is concerned, it comes to this:

1. A deficiency of air in the pot will cause the oil to crack out to carbon and soot. This cracking will be prevented if sufficient quantities of air are always present to mingle with the oil vapors.

2. The oil in the pot should not be heated above $650°F$, for above this temperature *extensive* cracking occurs. Below $650°F$ little cracking takes place that will form soot or carbon, even if the air is deficient.

3. Catalytic oils heated for vaporizing purposes in an oxygen-deficient atmosphere result in the formation of compounds that are difficult to burn and deposit a hard crystal-like carbon or coke that is quite different from the smoke and soft soot formed under the same circumstances from straight-run distillates.

VAPORIZING POT-TYPE BURNERS

Smoke and soot	Flame goes out	Burner won't ignite	Excess fuel consumption
Insufficient draft	Pilot or low fire too small — increase oil flow rate	Oil tank empty	Low or pilot fire setting too high
Oil flow excessive	Not enough air caused by insufficient draft, dirty or loose fan, clogged air holes in pot	Oil line plugged	Excessive or inadequate draft
Oil too heavy	Air lock in oil line	Air lock in oil line	High fire flame setting too high
Air holes plugged	Oil level too high — safety float "locks out"	Pot excessively carbonized	Burner operates continuously at high fire
Pot carbonized	Valve opening clogged with dirt	Strainer clogged	Improper ratio of oil and air
Fan dirty or not up to speed	Valve strainer clogged with dirt	Safety lever in "OFF" position	Thermostat in cold location
Pilot or low fire set too high	No ventilation in room with burner	Oil too heavy	Excessive heat loss from house
Chimney or flue passages clogged with soot	Water in the oil	Ignition fire out	Inferior oil
Leaky float in flow control valve	Bad down draft	Flooded pot	Oil too light in grade
Dirty valve seat in flow control valve	Fan motor not up to speed	Water in the oil	Unknown oil leaks
Fire burning down in pot — not enough oil		Flow control valve is defective	
Pot not level		Continual cold down drafts	
Down drafts		Pot not level	
Draft control locked in "ON" position			

Fig. 30-1

All this means that not only must the oil get enough air, but it must be shielded from the intense heat radiated to it from the flame above.

This is accomplished by certain manufacturers by providing a shield over the oil inlet to protect the oil from excess radiant heat from the flame. The ring or baffle found in many vapor pots serves this purpose, as well as that of providing a means of getting greater turbulence to mix the oil and air. *These shields and baffle rings should never be removed from the pot except for cleaning.* Removing them just means that the fire will burn down in the pot or too close to it, thereby destroying the pot, while creating large quantities of soot and smoke in the process.

DRAFT

The next condition that must be given serious consideration in servicing pot-type burners for clean, smokeless fires is that of draft. The amount of draft existing in a vaporizing unit will determine how much air that burner is receiving, even though it is supplied air by a fan. Check on the draft specification deemed necessary by the manufacturer and never operate below this minimum.

This means that if a manufacturer specifies 0.05 in. of draft for a certain oil-flow rate, e.g., 1 gph, and the draft is actually only 0.04, then

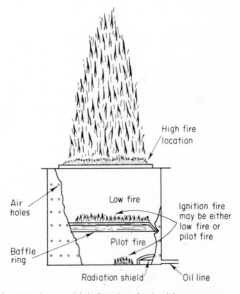

Fig. 30-2 All vaporizing pot-type burners have a high fire, but for ignition purposes they have either a low-fire position which burns above the ring or a pilot fire which burns on the floor of the pot.

the quantity of oil will have to be decreased correspondingly. The rate of decrease in oil flow should be 10 per cent for each 0.01 in. of draft below the required amount.

After any draft adjustment has been made (with the draft gauge, of course), check to see if the fire is clean by opening the draft control for an instant, with a flashlight playing on the opening. If any smoke is passing up the flue, it will be immediately visible in the flashlight's rays. This must be done quickly, for opening the draft regulator immediately cuts down the air, and smoking will begin to increase rapidly if it is held open for any length of time.

If the fire roars or is too high off the pot or the stack temperature is excessively high, it indicates that the draft is too great. Sometimes this high draft will result in the entire heater becoming so hot as to glow red. The latter condition will be aggravated if the oil-flow rate is in excess of what it should be.

If the draft cannot be cut down within normal limits by the draft control, it may be necessary to install a second draft regulator. This one should be installed as close to the unit as possible.

In order to obtain the proper oil-flow rate, a vaporizing burner must be calibrated to be sure that it is receiving the correct amount of oil per minute from the flow control valve. Any increase over the right amount means smoke and soot, with a pulsating, gasping flame. Too little oil means a bright, white fire burning down inside the pot with a blowtorch effect.

CALIBRATING THE VAPORIZING BURNER

To calibrate a pot-type burner, all that is necessary is a 200-cc beaker and a 100-cc graduate. Open the tee where the oil line meets the pot and allow the oil to flow into the beaker for 3 min. Pour this oil into the 100-cc graduate and note the number of cubic centimeters. Divide this by 3 and the resulting figure will be the cubic centimeter flow rate per minute.

This calibration should be made for high-fire and pilot- or low-fire rates. Compare these with the manufacturer's rate and adjust the burner so that the flow rate on both high and ignition fire will be 10 per cent below the rate prescribed. Such a cutback will give protection against smoking if the draft falls off, the fan becomes dirty, or a grade of oil is delivered that is too heavy.

HIGH FIRE

When a pot-type burner is at high fire, the flame should be clear of the pot with a blue base and yellow-white tongues. A *low-fire* position will be an orange-yellow flame burning off *the ring inside the pot*. If

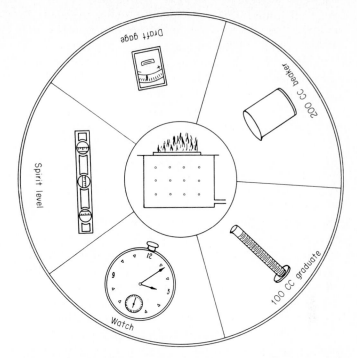

Fig. 30-3 Articles of service equipment essential to the correct adjustment of air and oil in vaporizing pot-type burners.

it has a *pilot-fire* position, the flame will be dull and slightly smoky and burn down *on the floor of the pot.*

All pot-type burners have a high-fire position, but when maintaining the ignition flame will have *either* a low fire or pilot fire—never both.

A low-fire type of burner should always have its ignition flame burning off the inside ring. A pilot-fire type of burner will always have its ignition fire burning on the pot floor. Be certain that the ignition fire is in the right place. If a low fire is on the floor instead of up on the ring, the oil is too heavy or the burner is not receiving enough fuel. If a pilot fire is burning up in the pot instead of on the floor, it is receiving too much oil or the oil is too light or the draft is excessive.

Any continual smoking and sooting with the proper grade of oil after adjusting for correct oil flow and draft means that the air-hole perforations in the inner pot wall are clogged with carbon. Remove the pot, take out the baffle ring, and scrub the sides of the retort with a stiff wire brush. If necessary use a good solvent such as naphtha or carbon tetrachloride. A prong, preferably of wood, should be used to punch out any carbon that has baked into the air holes. *Do not bore or punch new holes into the pot wall.*

If the fire is one-sided, erratic, or not level, it means that the retort is tilted or some carbon may be blocking the proper distribution of oil on the floor of the pot. A vaporizing pot-type burner should always be leveled *at the pot* and *at the flow control valve*. Placing a level on the outer casing and having the bubble centered *does not* mean that the pot and valve are level. A proper fire cannot be obtained from a pot-type burner that is tilted. It must be level to give a correctly placed, properly shaped, and clean fire.

FEATURES OF A LOW-PRESSURE GUN-TYPE BURNER

Low-pressure gun-type burners present a different sort of problem to the maintenance mechanic because of the unique construction of each brand. No two manufacturers of low-pressure burners have an identical mechanical method of achieving low-pressure atomization. In this respect, they differ radically from the standardized high-pressure gun-type burner. This section deals with the Williams Oil-O-Matic and will attempt to give a picture of what service on this burner entails *including* the Fifty-Ten.

Figure 30-4 shows the flow diagram of the primary air and oil in this burner. Air pressure is used to force the oil from the sump stabilizer (float-assembly chamber) to the nozzle. The solid stream of oil is broken up at the nozzle by the impact of a stream of air that meets it. This air at low pressure (1 to 4 psi) pulverizes the oil into small particles as it leaves the nozzle. The air moves down to the nozzle through an outer concentric tube *Y*, as shown in the diagram.

Three main adjustments

There are three main adjustments on this burner: the *rate of oil flow,* the *pressure,* and the *fan* (secondary) *air.*

The fan air adjustment is accomplished by a rotating shutter, as in the conventional high-pressure gun-type burner.

The air pressure (atomizing pressure) is adjusted at the pressure adjusting screw [(1) in Fig. 30-4], and it merely opens or closes the bypass, thereby decreasing or increasing the amount of pressure exerted on the float chamber and the bellows- or diaphragm-operated oil valve. The increasing of this pressure will often result in making the flame noisy, and decreasing it will have the opposite effect.

Do not adjust the operating pressure on this burner below 1 psi or over 4 psi. If adjusted below 1 psi, the burner will continue to run, but will not start again after stopping. This happens because at least 1 psi of pressure is required to open the bellows-operated oil valve that allows the oil to flow to the metering pump.

The second adjustment, shown at (2) on Fig. 30-4, is the oil-flow rate

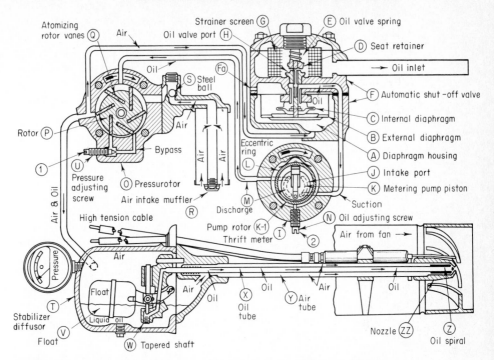

Fig. 30-4 Diagram showing internal view of operating parts of older-model Williams Oil-O-Matic low-pressure burner.

control. The turning of this screw lengthens or shortens the stroke of the metering piston and thereby increases or decreases the amount of oil being delivered.

Adjustments on this burner do not give an immediate response, as is the case with high-pressure burners. Several minutes will elapse before the results of changes in the pressure or oil-flow rate will be apparent in the flame. For this reason, no serviceman should adjust such a burner and leave immediately. Instead, he should wait a few minutes to see the actual results of his adjustments on the flame. This is important.

When this burner is started, the flame will not appear instantly. When these burners are installed, there is a 3-deg pitch to the blast tube from the burner to the nozzle. Upon shutting off, the oil in the nozzle spiral (Z in Fig. 30-4) and oil tube flows back by gravity into the float chamber. The lapse between the instant the burner goes on and the moment when the flame appears is the time it takes to force the oil up from the float chamber to the nozzle outlet.

In the event that the flame pulsates and fluctuates, it is evidence that either the quantity of oil being delivered is not constant or the

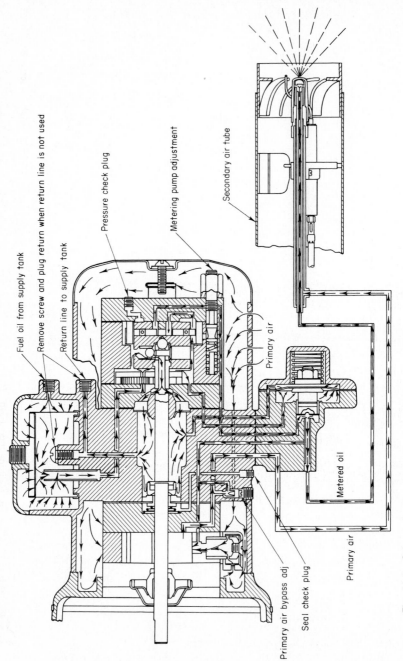

Fuel oil from supply tank

Remove screw and plug return when return line is not used

Return line to supply tank

Pressure check plug

Metering pump adjustment

Secondary air tube

Primary air

Metered oil

Primary air

Primary air bypass adj

Seal check plug

Fig. 30-5 Schematic flow diagram, model Fifty-Ten. (*Williams Oil-O-Matic*)

456

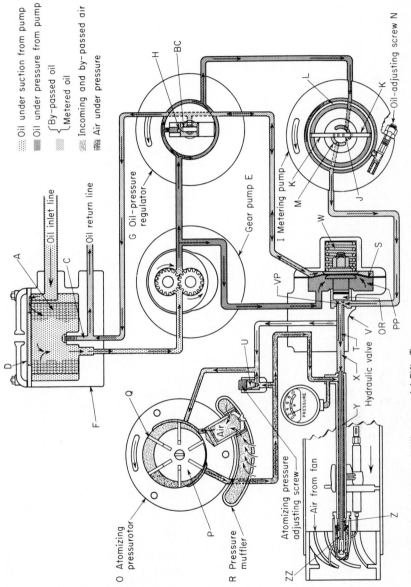

Oil under suction from pump
Oil under pressure from pump
By-passed oil
Metered oil
Incoming and by-passed air
Air under pressure

A

C

D

F

Oil inlet line

Oil return line

G Oil-pressure regulator

Gear pump E

I Metering pump

H

BC

L

K

Oil-adjusting screw N

M

K

J

VP

W

S

OR

PP

V

T

X

Y

Hydraulic valve

Q

U

O Atomizing pressurotor

P

R Pressure muffler

Air

PRESSURE

Atomizing pressure adjusting screw

Air from fan

Z

ZZ

Fig. 30-6 Flow diagram, Williams model Fifty-Ten.

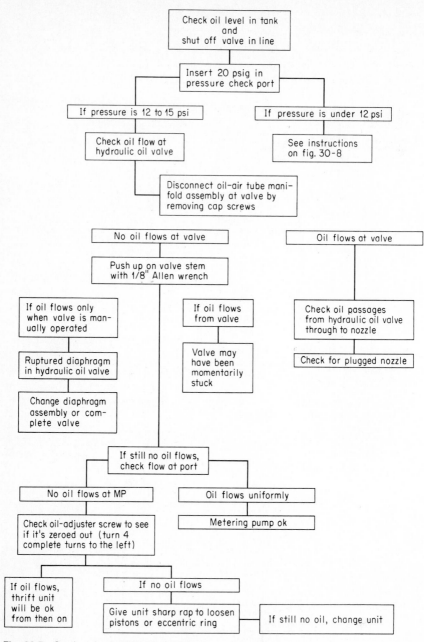

Fig. 30-7 Service chart, Williams Oil-O-Matic model Fifty-Ten.

pressure is not being constantly maintained. The cause of this can be in either the metering pump or the pressurotor.

If it is the former, it may be a sticky piston or a broken metering pump spring. If it is the pressurotor, then it will be sticky vanes preventing the pressure from being built up and maintained constantly (Q, Fig. 30-4).

Sometimes a large, smoky, fluctuating fire is encountered even though the secondary air adjustment (fan shutter) is adequate. This is caused by the float (V, Fig. 30-4) being partly filled with oil. As a result it will not be buoyant and will rise slowly. This means that the oil level

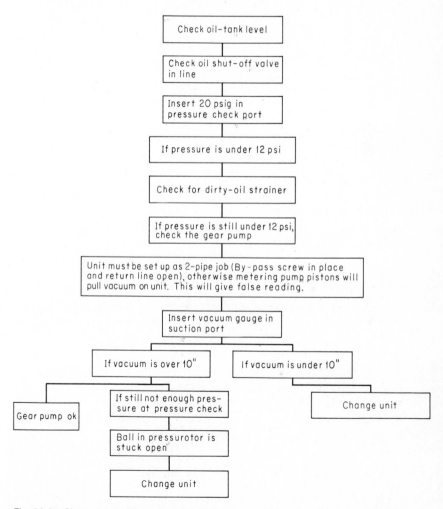

Fig. 30-8   Chart showing procedure for checking out Williams model Fifty-Ten "thrift unit."

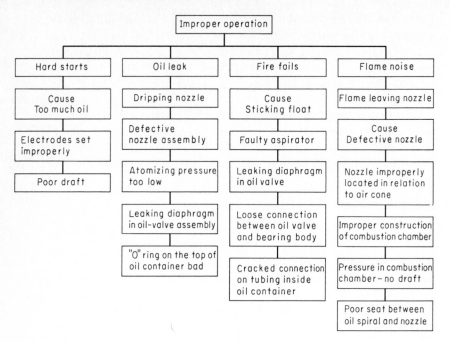

Fig. 30-9 Service chart for Williams model R160 low-pressure burner.

in the float chamber will be too high. Oil can then pass into the air tube Y and cut off part of the primary air supply. Smoke and flame fluctuations then ensure. A sticky needle valve causes similar trouble. The float should be replaced or the perforations soldered up with as little solder as possible. The same condition as described above will occur if there are any leaks from the oil tube X into the air tube Y.

If for any reason this burner has been off for a long period of time, it will have an abnormally large fire that will pulsate on starting. In a short period of time, the fire will decrease and burn smoothly at the proper rate. This is caused by seepage of oil passing the needle valve W and raising the level in the stabilizer chamber above the normal point. After the burner has run a short time, the oil will resume the normal level and the fire decrease to proper size.

Clogging of the air intake muffler will prevent air pressure from building up. As a result, the bellows or diaphragm valve will not open and the burner will not start. Remove the air intake muffler R by removing the bolt at the bottom, and clean it thoroughly.

In the event that a service call on one of these burners requires disassembling of the metering pump or pressurotor, extreme care must be exercised in replacing the gaskets. The gaskets must be of proper thickness. Improperly sized gaskets between the atomizer Q and metering pump will mean loss of pressure if they are too thick and increase in pressure if they are too thin. It is necessary to check on the manufacturer's specifications as to thickness before replacing gaskets on this burner.

Aside from their specific, unique parts, which require a knowledge of their operation, the standard parts of these burners such as the transformer, motor, and fan are serviced in the same manner as they are on high-pressure gun-type burners. Successful servicing of the characteristic parts on various low-pressure burners depends upon a thorough knowledge of their operating principles and methods.

SERVICING MODEL FIFTY-TEN WILLIAMS OIL-O-MATIC BURNER

See Figs. 30-5 to 30-8.

SERVICING MODEL R160 WILLIAMS OIL-O-MATIC BURNER

See Figs. 3-12 and 30-9.

QUESTIONS

1. What type of oil should be used with vaporizing burners?
2. What temperature limit should be observed as a top limit for the oil in the pot?
3. If draft is below that specified by the manufacturer, what adjustment should be made in the oil-flow rate?
4. Explain how to calibrate a vaporizing burner.
5. What is the difference between pilot and low fire?
6. What respectively are the positions of high, low, and pilot fire with regard to the pot?

CHAPTER 31

SERVICING THE COMMERCIAL LOW-PRESSURE GUN-TYPE BURNER

Using Nos. 4 and 5 Oil

The maintenance and service of the commercial low-pressure gun-type burner as shown in Fig. 31-1 is illustrated in Figs. 31-2 to 31-4. The basic factors involved in the service of this burner are (1) the motor, (2) the ignition, (3) the oil flow, and (4) the flame-sensing element. See Fig. 31-2 for these major check points.

MOTOR SERVICING
See Fig. 31-3, section 1.

TRANSFORMER
See Fig. 31-3, section 2.

OIL-CIRCULATING PUMP
See Fig. 31-3, section 3.

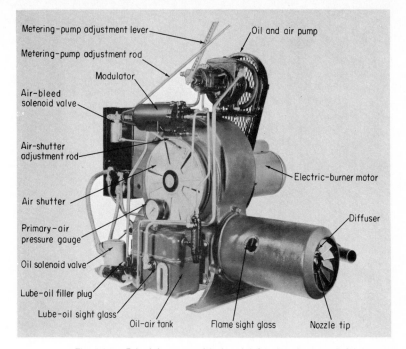

Metering–pump adjustment lever

Metering–pump adjustment rod

Modulator

Air–bleed solenoid valve

Air–shutter adjustment rod

Air shutter

Primary–air pressure gauge

Oil solenoid valve

Lube–oil filler plug

Lube–oil sight glass

Oil–air tank

Oil and air pump

Electric–burner motor

Diffuser

Flame sight glass

Nozzle tip

Fig. 31-1 Principle parts of Industrial Combustion Hev-E-Oil burner.

OIL-METERING PUMP

See Fig. 31-3, section 4.

PRIMARY-AIR PUMP

See Fig. 31-3, section 5.

OIL NOZZLES

The successful operation of the burner depends on the use of proper-style nozzle tip and on keeping the nozzle orifice clean.   The standard nozzle tips furnished with burner units are of a special emulsifying type which deliver a solid cone spray of extreme fineness and at such an angle as to ensure proper mixing with the air stream through the burner. Unsatisfactory burner performance and loss of efficiency may follow the use of nonstandard tips.

If the burner flame becomes stringy or lazy, it is possible that the nozzle spring is not in place or the nozzle is clogged; an abnormally high reading on the air-pressure gauge is usually a definite indication of this trouble.   To remove and clean the nozzle tip and swirler, unscrew the nozzle tip from the nozzle body, being careful not to distort the

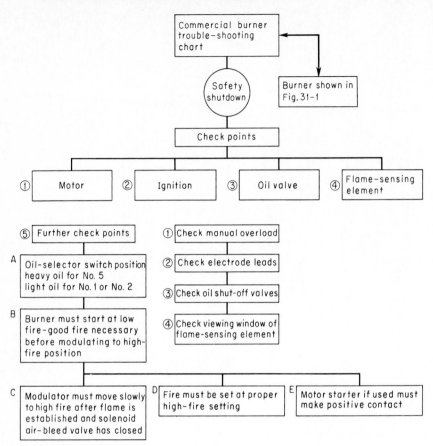

Fig. 31-2

heater tube. Either hold the nozzle body in a vise or use two end wrenches, one applied to the body and one to the tip. Disassemble tips by removing the internal portion.

Carefully clean all parts in a solvent. Never use wire or sharp metallic tools, since they can destroy the orifice and render the nozzle unfit for further use. Instead, use a sharp-pointed piece of soft wood. In reassembling the nozzle tips, the internal portion must be screwed in tightly to ensure proper atomization of oil. Make certain that the swirler seating spring is in the nozzle and holds the swirler tight against it. The swirler should be turned a few times to make sure that it fits snugly in the nozzle and to assure that the spring presses the swirler against the nozzle.

Brush off all carbon and soot deposits from electrodes and diffuser plate at this time.

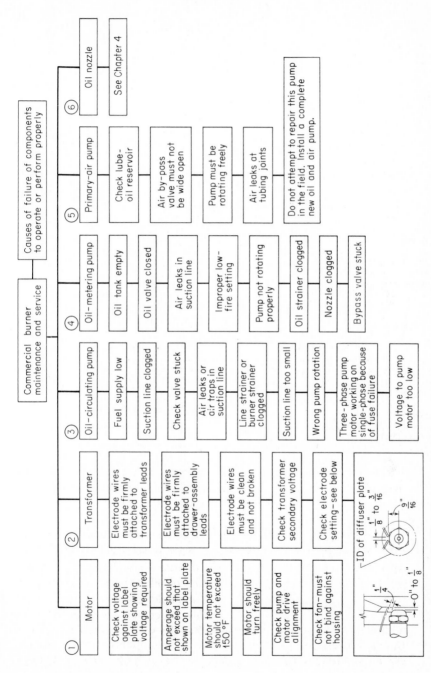

Fig. 31-3 Service chart for component parts of Hev-E-Oil burner.

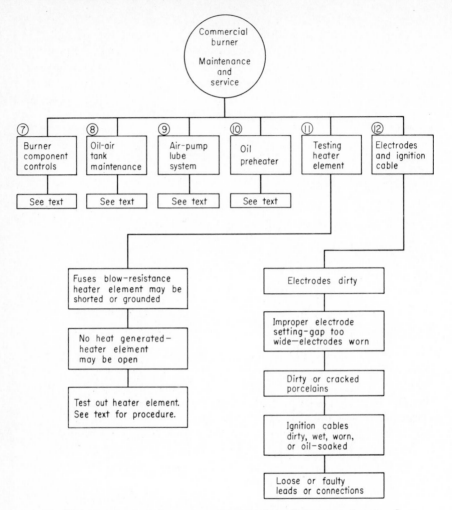

Fig. 31-4   Service chart for component parts of Hev-E-Oil burner (*continued*).

It is wise to thoroughly inspect the burner and its controls once (or oftener if required) every week.   At such times, remove the drawer assembly.

BURNER COMPONENT CONTROLS

Temperature or pressure controls may be used to control the action of the modulator.   Air lines and air-bleed solenoid are connected so that the air pressure within the cylinder of the air motor can be relieved when the electrical contacts of the controls open the air-bleed solenoid. These temperature or pressure controls work within a set range of temperature or pressure variations. The air-bleed solenoid, being a normally open valve, automatically allows bleed-off of air pressure within the cylinder of the modulator through a small orifice in the pipe plug at one end. This is done at a gradual rate, so that the variation of pressure permits the spring tension to force the piston in the air motor to a set point in its stroke. Therefore, on pressure rise in the boiler (or shutdown), the burner will always return to low-fire position. Reverse procedure of controls closes the air-bleed solenoid, allowing air-pressure rise. This changes the burner to high fire.

OIL-AIR TANK MAINTENANCE

Once a year the oil-air tank should be removed from the burner, drained of oil, and thoroughly flushed with kerosene. At the same time the two inserts of bronze wool should be removed and cleaned with kerosene. One layer of bronze wool can be removed through the plug on the right side of the tank; the other is removed through the oil-and-air-tube connection at the center front section of the tank.

AIR-PUMP LUBE SYSTEM

Experience has shown that an air pump is no better than its lubricating system. Therefore an automatic pressure-lubricating system is provided. The air-oil tank serves as a lubricating-oil reservoir; air pressure supplied by the primary-air pump forces the oil through a tube submerged in this reservoir and into the pump by way of the pipeline, thus lubricating it. The oil vapor in the discharge from the pump is separated by bronze wool as well as a baffle in the upper section of the air-oil tank.

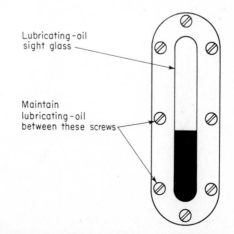

Lubricating-oil sight glass

Maintain lubricating-oil between these screws

Fig. 31-5 Oil-level indicator, Hev-E-Oil burner. (*Industrial Combustion*)

OIL PREHEATER

This heater requires no service except a check to ensure tight connections to the oil-supply line. In case of trouble, the entire preheater can be withdrawn after removing the mounting screws that secure the preheater head to the back plate of the drawer assembly. The oil preheater is a nickel-chromium resistance wire embedded in insulating material which is encased in a metal tube and so designed that the fuel oil is evenly heated throughout its entire length.

No attempt should be made to repair this heater. If trouble develops, the entire heater should be replaced.

TESTING HEATER ELEMENT

A 100-watt lamp may be used to test the preheater element by the following method (see Fig. 31-6).

Connect the lamp in series with the hot lead from a 110/220-volt power line. When the prods are together, the full-circuit voltage is applied to the lamp, causing it to glow with full brilliance. Next apply the prods to the two prongs indicated on the heater plug. The lamp should glow dimly if the heater element is good; if the heater circuit is open, the lamp will not light; if the heater is shorted, the lamp will glow brightly.

To check for a "ground" in the heater, touch the ground-line test prod to the metal rim on the heater plug or outer casing of the heater and the other prod to one prong of the heater plug, then to the other. If the lamp fails to light in either case, no ground is present; but if the lamp lights, a ground is present and the heater is defective.

ELECTRODES AND IGNITION CABLE

See Fig. 31-4, section 12.

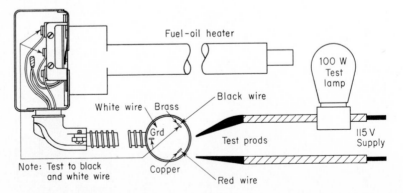

Fig. 31-6 Lamp-test diagram.

QUESTIONS

1. Discuss the major service procedure for the following: motor, transformer, oil-circulating pump, oil-metering pump, primary-air pump, oil nozzle.
2. Discuss oil-air-tank maintenance.
3. What is involved in servicing the oil preheater?

CHAPTER 32

SERVICING
VERTICAL ROTARY
WALL-FLAME BURNERS

The vertical rotary wall-flame burner depends to a large extent upon oil that is fairly volatile in order to achieve proper combustion. This burner, as noted in a previous chapter, uses centrifugal force to throw the oil on a ring, which is the outer circumference of a specially built hearth, where it is vaporized and burns. For this reason, it is important that the manufacturer's specifications on the type and grade of oil that should be utilized by this burner be adhered to closely. Oil which is too heavy either will not ignite or will burn with a smoky panting fire.

Burners should be installed in full accord with the manufacturer's specifications, and every effort should be made to be certain that the burner is level, that the hearth is constructed of the proper material, and that it has the correct shape and dimensions for the burner being installed.

An automatic draft regulator is a very necessary part of every vertical rotary wall-flame burner installation. This control, of course, compensates for the changes in draft intensity so that a constant draft pull is exerted at the fire. This is necessary if the fire is to burn at the proper

VERTICAL ROTARY WALL FLAME BURNER – CAUSES OF SERVICE TROUBLES

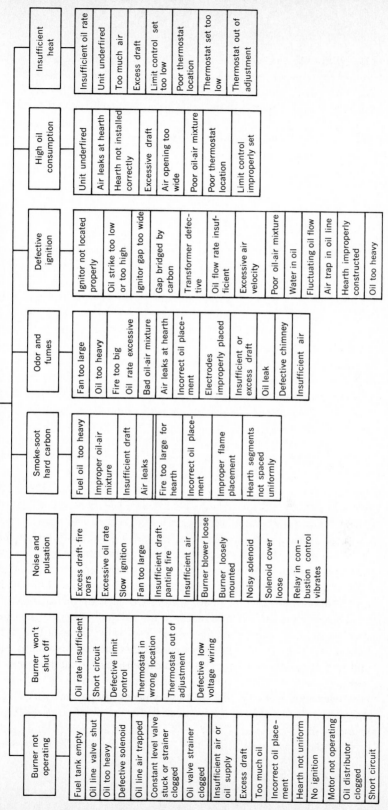

Burner not operating	Burner won't shut off	Noise and pulsation	Smoke-soot hard carbon	Odor and fumes	Defective ignition	High oil consumption	Insufficient heat
Fuel tank empty	Oil rate insufficient	Excess draft-fire roars	Fuel oil too heavy	Fan too large	Ignitor not located properly	Unit underfired	Insufficient oil rate
Oil line valve shut	Short circuit	Excessive oil rate	Improper oil-air mixture	Oil too heavy	Oil strike too low or too high	Air leaks at hearth	Unit underfired
Oil too heavy	Defective limit control	Slow ignition	Insufficient draft	Fire too big	Ignitor gap too wide	Hearth not installed correctly	Too much air
Defective solenoid	Thermostat in wrong location	Fan too large	Air leaks	Oil rate excessive	Gap bridged by carbon	Excessive draft	Excess draft
Oil line air trapped	Thermostat out of adjustment	Insufficient draft-panting fire	Fire too large for hearth	Bad oil-air mixture	Transformer defective	Air opening too wide	Limit control set too low
Constant level valve stuck or strainer clogged	Defective low voltage wiring	Insufficient air	Incorrect oil placement	Air leaks at hearth	Oil flow rate insufficient	Poor oil-air mixture	Poor thermostat location
Oil valve strainer clogged		Burner blower loose	Improper flame placement	Incorrect oil placement	Excessive air velocity	Poor thermostat location	Thermostat set too low
Insufficient air or oil supply		Burner loosely mounted	Hearth segments not spaced uniformly	Electrodes improperly placed	Poor oil-air mixture	Limit control improperly set	Thermostat out of adjustment
Excess draft		Noisy solenoid		Insufficient or excess draft	Water in oil		
Too much oil		Solenoid cover loose		Oil leak	Fluctuating oil flow		
Incorrect oil placement		Relay in combustion control vibrates		Defective chimney	Air trap in oil line		
Hearth not uniform				Insufficient air	Hearth improperly constructed		
No ignition					Oil too heavy		
Motor not operating							
Oil distributor clogged							
Short circuit							

Fig. 32-1

location on the ring and also as quietly as possible. Usually the draft regulator should be adjusted so that the draft will be between 0.025 and 0.03 in. over the fire during such times as the chimney is hot.

In the event that a catalytic fuel is being utilized, the draft regulation becomes increasingly important. A decided increase in draft will cause an increase in the amount of carbon deposited on the flame ring, as well as alter the coloring of the fire. The fire will increase in yellow coloring and decrease in blue. With extremely strong draft caused by oversized chimneys it may be necessary to install two draft controls.

OIL-FLOW RATE

A constant rate of oil feed must be maintained; and as the oil usually is fed by gravity, a control of the oil level from a fixed height from the point of flow will be necessary. Usually the standard burner installation will include a 275-gal oil-storage tank, with the bottom of the tank not less than 30 in. above the floor. At this tank outlet there should be installed a constant-level valve which will maintain a constant level of oil in its float chamber.

As can be seen from this, the rate of flow of oil to the burner is determined by the height of this constant-level valve above the outlet of the burner fuel tube and the opening that is adjusted at the metering valve of the magnetic oil valve on the control stand. Usually the height of the oil-level line on the constant-level valve should not be less than 10 in. above the outlet of the fuel tube on the burner. Actually, a greater height should be achieved. In any event, the manufacturer's direction on this should be followed.

The hearth plate should always be sealed tightly, since any small leak of air through the hearth would have a bad effect on the fire, causing it to become distorted and uneven at the points of air leakage. Actually, if the air leakage is really excessive, there is a great possibility that the fire will drop back upon the ring, and under this condition the ring will burn out because of the constant direct impingement of the flame.

Any adjustment of the fire must of necessity involve a proportioning of the oil-and-air mixture. The oil rates specified by the manufacturer should be adhered to. For satisfactory and efficient operation, however, the serviceman should check this rate of flow. This can be accomplished by disconnecting the oil line on the discharge side of the magnetic valve and extending a tube upward to the height of the burner fuel tube and bending the end over. Now the burner can be turned on and the oil flow measured by allowing it to pour from the gooseneck into a cubic centimeter (cc) graduate. Now check the time it takes for this quantity of oil to flow.

The next step is to divide the 100 cc by the time in minutes, and the result will be the cubic centimeter per minute rate of flow. Dividing this by 63.1 will give the gph rate:

$$\frac{100 \text{ cc}}{1.5 \text{ min}} = 66.6$$

$$66.6 \div 63.1 = 1.05 \text{ gph}$$

FLAME PLACEMENT

The typical vertical rotary wall-flame burner is one in which a lifted fire burning out of the oil ring extends from the top of the hearth flame segments to approximately midway up the burner or furnace walls. This fire should be stable, appear blue at the base and through most of the body, and have yellow tongues. It should show no tendency to float above or away from the ring but should maintain itself positively from the top of the flame segment adjacent to the boiler wall.

With thermally cracked No. 2 fuel oil, the fire should have a blue base, extending well above the flame segments, with slight streaks of yellow interjected through the base. From this height it should shade off to a white or pale yellow, with the uppermost tips a dark red. When catalytically cracked No. 2 fuel oil is used, the flame will also appear with a blue base, but there will be a larger amount of yellow coloring,

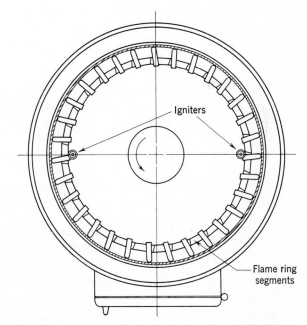

Fig. 32-2 Top view of hearth showing flame ring and igniters. (*Fluid Heat*)

shading off into a real, deep yellow with the tongues usually longer than those that occur with thermally cracked oil.

One of the problems encountered in adjusting for the proper flame color and placement on vertical rotary burners is caused by the fact that upon opening of the fire door an immediate change occurs in the flame. The admission of large amounts of additional air through the opened fire door causes this alteration in the physical characteristics of the fire. Therefore, it is necessary when observing the position and color of the flame in a burner of this type to open the door, take a quick look, and close it very rapidly before the inrush of additional air has a chance to alter the physical aspects of the flame. It is wise to provide a small peephole in the furnace door so that this problem can be eliminated.

The position of the oil strike is also important and should be checked by servicemen. A target test can be made. The target can be laid on the segment and the igniter disconnected. Now observe the oil spray strike, which must be done while the fuel is actually striking the target. This strike should be gauged after the first second the burner starts. Usually the main body of the spray should strike the proper location approximately $\frac{1}{4}$ in. before the air-deflecting face (Fluid Heat). This would be the solid portion of the spray. Usually the fine fringe or bottom of the oil spray will strike the face in the area of the spark.

If the oil strike is too low, the electrodes will carbonize and there will be ignition failure. If the oil strike is too high, considerable overshooting of the spray will result in a continuous afterfire after the burner has shut down. This can also cause delayed ignition.

AIR ADJUSTMENT

The air adjustment is extremely important because it affects the economy, quietness, and efficiency of operation, as well as the general cleanliness of the combustion process. Furthermore, the stability and placement of the flame will be directly affected by the quantity of air delivered. Any insufficiency of air will make the fire rise or float away from its correct position at the top of the flame segments. It will also dilate or enlarge the fire, causing it to burn with considerably more blue coloring.

The introduction of excess air will result in making the fire harsh and noisy and may even cause it to roar. The tips of the fire will become a dull yellow. Excess air will also cause the fire to burn within the oil groove completely. If the excess air is limited in amount, the flame will intermittently flash or move down into the groove.

The proper air-oil adjustment will produce a full-bodied, intensely hot fire, always burning in the proper location at the top of the flame segments.   The base will be blue from the top of the grille, and orange-colored or yellow-colored tongues will lick up along the heater combustion-chamber wall.

Draft over the fire will have a definite effect on the air delivery. Adequate draft, which results in a low-pressure area over the fire, will facilitate the introduction of air provided by the fan to the flame. Inadequate draft will result in a soft, blue, unstable, moving fire, while excessive draft tends to create a harsh, yellow, uneven, noisy, and even roaring flame.   Draft adjustments should be made according to the specification of the manufacturer of the burner, or as set down above.

GENERAL SERVICE

Referring to Fig. 32-1, we can see the general causes of service for the various types of trouble that may arise in vertical rotary wall-flame burners.   The chart confines itself primarily to service caused by difficulties with the burner and does not go into heating system or general control problems that may also cause such service.

In the event that the burner is not operating, the flow of the fuel should be thoroughly checked.   First, be certain that there is oil; then check to see if it is of the proper grade; and finally trace the flow through the oil line, the constant-level valve, the oil-line valve, and the solenoid valve.   Examine the strainers on the constant-level valve and also on the solenoid valve to be certain that they are not clogged.   See that the oil placement is correct, and if necessary make a target test.   Check

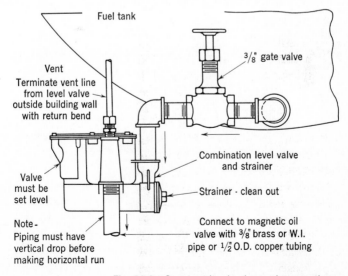

Fig. 32-3   Constant-level valve and connections.

the ignition and motor to see that both the transformer and motor are performing properly. The oil distributor may be clogged. If so, remove it and clean out the distributor tubes, using a good solvent with a small, stiff brush.

Excess draft will make it difficult to ignite the burner, first by disturbing the pattern of the strike, and second by making it difficult to reach the kindling temperature of the fuel oil.

Noise and pulsations in burners of this type can have a number of causes. Pulsating noises can be caused by excessive draft, which will result in a noisy, unstable, and even roaring fire. An excess oil-flow rate will also cause an enlargement of the fire and consequently make it noisy. Slow ignition may lead to puffing at the start. If the fan is too large, a noisy fire will be the likely result. Insufficient draft or insufficient air will lead to a panting, pulsating fire. This is due to gradual diminishing and enlarging of the fire taking place many times in a short interval of time. Mechanical noises may be caused by a loose fan, a loosely mounted burner, a noisy solenoid (hum), or a solenoid with the cover loose. Sometimes the relay in the combustion control may vibrate or hum loudly enough to be noticeable.

Incomplete combustion can express itself either in the formation of smoke or soot (soft carbon) or in the formation of stalactites of hard carbon. Soft carbon is usually caused by fuel oil being too heavy, improper oil-and-air mixture, insufficient draft, or air leaks. Hard carbon may be formed as a result of a fire too large for the hearth, incorrect oil placement, improper flame placement, or the hearth segments not being uniformly spaced.

Many times there may be a condition of defective ignition, which has nothing to do with the transformer, it being in good condition. These burners are sensitive to the proper location of the spark and oil strike. Therefore, it is essential for proper ignition that the igniter be

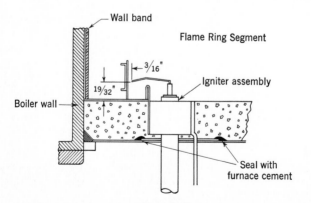

Fig. 32-4 Location of igniter. (*Fluid Heat*)

located properly, as specified by the manufacturer—the same condition holding for the oil strike. Check, too, the width of the gap at the igniter, and be certain that carbon does not form at the ignited tip, which will result in the gap being completely bridged and no spark appearing at all. If the oil-flow rate is insufficient or the air has excessive velocity, or if there is a very poor mixture of oil and air, ignition trouble will appear. This means that the air must be properly adjusted, that there is no fluctuation in the oil flow, and that the proper oil-flow rate for the diametric dimension of hearth must be closely adhered to; in addition, the general construction of the hearth must be in accord with all the directions set down in the manufacturer's installation manual. Miscellaneous causes of defective ignition can be water in the oil, air traps in the oil line, or a grade of oil too heavy for proper utilization by the burner.

QUESTIONS

1. How does the vertical wall-flame rotary prepare the fuel for combustion?
2. What will be the result if the oil is too heavy?
3. Why is a draft regulator necessary when a vertical wall-flame rotary is operated?
4. What is the average draft reading over the fire with this type of burner when the chimney is hot?
5. Why is it necessary to seal the hearth plate tightly?
6. Explain the procedure for checking the flow rate.
7. Describe the characteristics and location of a correctly sized and placed fire.
8. Give two results of an oil strike that is too low.
9. Give the causes of a noisy, pulsating fire.

CHAPTER 33

WATER-LEVEL PROBLEMS AND CONDITIONS

Steam and hot-water (hydronic) heating systems, of course, use water as the medium for transferring the heat produced by the burner. By the movement of steam or hot water through the piping, the heat is carried from the boiler to the rooms or areas where it is required. In like manner, a warm-air system utilizes heated air to carry the warmth from the furnace to the areas to be heated. Instead of pipes or tubing, a warm-air system uses ducts to carry the heated air.

With steam and hot-water systems, the use of water as the transfer medium requires some attention to the water level. In a steam system, the boiler is kept partially filled and the steam collects as it is generated in the space above. Water must be added from time to time to keep the boiler at the proper level for the most efficient production of steam and to make up for evaporation and other losses.

In a closed hot-water system, the entire heating system is filled with water and is under pressure all the time. As the system is heated, the water expands and the pressure increases. An air-cushion chamber (expansion tank) filled with air provides additional area or space in the system for the mass of heated water to expand. Residential, domestic hot-water heating systems are designed for a maximum operating pressure of 30 psi.

The employment of water either as steam or water to transfer the heat, as is the case with steam or hot-water heating systems, provides two conditions that have to be guarded against. These are:

1. Excess pressure
2. Low water level

Another condition in a steam system which has to be prevented or eliminated is a surging, fluctuating, or unsteady water line. This problem occurs when the water in a steam boiler is contaminated with grease, dirt, or impurities. In this case, the boiler can be blown down and the dirty water removed. The boiler is then treated and flushed with the proper boiler compound to clean it, and fresh, clean water is added. This procedure usually takes care of water-level fluctuations due to dirty boiler water.

Excess pressure conditions in a steam system are guarded against by a blow-off or pop valve, a safety valve that will release steam if the pressure is excessive. This is actually a pressure-relief valve set to relieve at a certain fixed pressure.

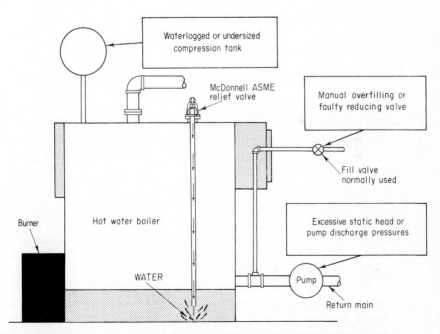

Fig. 33-1 Reasons why a relief valve is called upon to open and discharge water from a hot water heating system are depicted above. (*McDonnell & Miller, Inc.*)

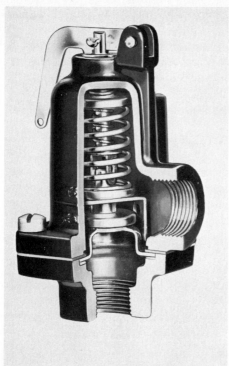

Fig. 33-2   A McDonnell 230 pressure relief valve for hot-water space-heating boilers. These valves conform to the ASME Boiler Code and are Btu rated so that their selection can match the heat output of the boiler. Independent-action test levers cannot interfere with automatic operation of the valve even if tied down.

RELIEF VALVES

The reasons for the use of an ASME pressure-relief valve on hot-water space-heating boilers are obvious. Pressures for various reasons, as shown in Fig. 33-1, can build up. In a residential heating boiler, when these pressures exceed 30 psi or even less, they should be relieved. This is the function of the relief valve and is an important and necessary safety feature, as boiler pressures must be kept within the designed working limits (Fig. 33-2). Moreover, such valves must operate under the two dissimilar conditions of hydronic heating—hot-water systems and steam systems.

Relieving pressure encountered in hot-water heating systems is considered to be normal operation. A closed hot-water heating system filled with water will naturally encounter expansion as the water in the closed system is heated.

The need for relief of pressure in a steam system is something else again, however, and is the result of some abnormal operating condition. It is evidence of an emergency. A comparison of the volume occupied by water and by steam demonstrates the different situations.

A pound of water occupies about 277 cu in., a pound of steam at atmospheric pressure occupies about 26.8 cu ft. This demonstrates that a pound of water when converted to steam increases in volume more than 1,600 times. No wonder protecting against water and steam pressures presents different problems.

Now, what causes a relief valve to open in a hot-water heating system?

(The average hot-water boiler is constructed for a maximum working pressure of 30 psi. The relief valve is set to open at the same pressure. Therefore any circumstance which will elevate the boiler pressure to 30 psi will cause the relief valve to open, except where more than one valve is used to match boiler capacity; then one valve is set at 30 psi and the secondary valve or valves within 20 per cent higher.)

These causes are:

1. Hand filling the boiler and system and allowing the full city water-supply pressure to act against a full system.
2. Hydrostatic testing a system with pressures in excess of 30 psi.
3. Waterlogged compression tanks which eliminate space required for thermal expansion of water in the system.
4. Undersized compression tanks not adequate for thermal expansion in the system.
5. Excessive static head or pump discharge pressures.

In these instances the relief valve discharges water to the drain, as the boiler water temperature is normally below 212°F. The most critical demand is placed on a relief valve during the "emergency" stage, when it must discharge both high-temperature water and steam. Basically, the "emergency" stage is caused by an overfiring of the burner. The heating system cannot dissipate the heat energy as fast as it is developed in the boiler, and temperatures and pressures continue to rise.

Overfiring may be caused by the following:

1. Failure of a limit control to stop the burner.
2. Mechanical failure of a fuel valve.
3. Burner considerably oversized in relation to boiler and system. In these instances, the relief valve discharges steam.

NOTE Without make-up water replacing the loss through the relief

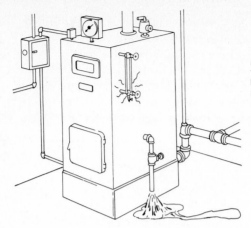

Carelessness or Inattention

Not watching water glass
Leaving blow-off valves open
Drawing hot water from boiler
Draining without stopping firing

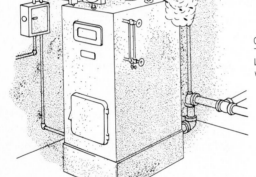

Overfiring of boiler

Loss of water through safety
valve discharge

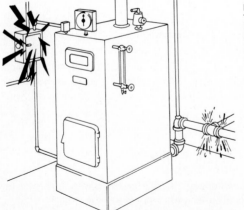

Defects in system

Leaking air valves
Pump stoppage
Leaky supply or return
Condensate held up in system
Faulty check valves
Foaming or priming
Returns not pitched properly
Boiler leaks
Automatic control failure
Process use of steam; no
    condensate returned

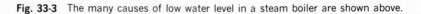

Fig. 33-3 The many causes of low water level in a steam boiler are shown above.

valve, a hazardous low-water condition can result. For this reason, the ASME Boiler Code recommends the use of a low-water-cutoff on hot-water heating boilers.

In a steam system, the causes (emergency) that make the relief valve open and discharge steam are:

1. Failure of a limit control to stop the burner.
2. Mechanical failure of fuel valve—a valve held in the open position.
3. Placing the automatic burner on manual operation.
4. Closing of zone controls isolating the boiler from the system, with residual heat in boiler.
5. Overfiring the boiler in relation to the capacity of the boiler and system.

For the relief valve to give good performance in discharging water, it must open at the pressure setting of the valve, discharge only the amount of water necessary to relieve the pressure (thereby minimizing wasteful blowdown), and then close off drip-tight. This requires only a small capacity, but with steam it is a far different story. It is necessary that the valve have a very large capacity—not dependent on variable factors—and the ability to close off tightly after each operation.

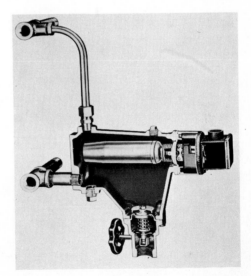

Fig. 33-4 No. 67 McDonnell low water cutoff. For boilers of any size, operating at pressures up to 20 psi. The twin-switch feature of this control provides an extra switch independent of burner cutoff, for use with a low water alarm or an electric water feeder.

WATER-LEVEL CONTROLS

The two water-level controls involved with residential heating systems are (1) the low-water-cutoff, (2) the automatic water feeder, or (3) a combination of (1) and (2).

Simply, the low-water-cutoff is a float-actuated mechanism that trips a switch which shuts off power to the burner when the water level is low and consequently unsafe (see Fig. 33-7).

The automatic water feeder is just what its name implies. When the water level is low, it automatically feeds water into the system to bring it back to normal level. This action is shown in Fig. 33-8.

WATER-FEEDER TEST PROCEDURE: BROKEN-UNION TEST

Automatic feeder operation maintains the proper boiler water level. If the boiler water level is wrong, it is not necessarily the feeder's fault. Therefore, it is necessary in servicing such a condition to go through a test procedure. This is as follows (refer to Fig. 33-9):

Condition 1 Boiler gets too much water.

Test Having made sure that boiler water level is above the closing level of the feeder, close the feed valve with the float. Consequently if water trickles out of the broken union, the feed valve is not closing properly. This would explain an excessively high water level in the boiler.

Manually open and close the water-feeder valve several times with

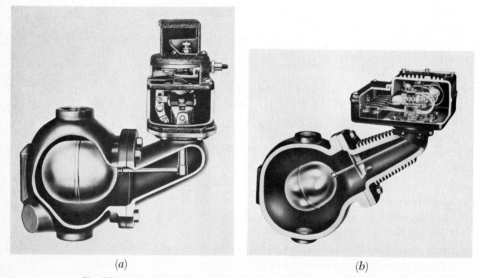

(a)   (b)

Fig. 33-5 (a) Model 63 and (b) model 150 low-water fuel cutoffs. Model No. 63 is used with boilers up to maximum of 50 psi and Model No. 150 with up to 150 psi.

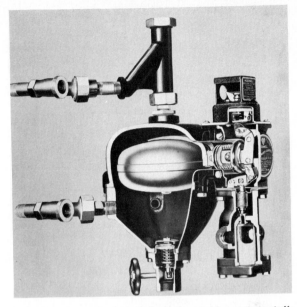

Fig. 33-6 McDonnell No. 47-2 combination automatic feeder and low-water-cutoff. Maximum protection is given to the low-pressure steam boiler by combining a mechanical boiler water feeder and an electrical low-water-cutoff.

screw driver. Figure 33-10 shows how to do this. This should remove any obstruction from the valve seat. It should now close drip-tight. If manual operation of the feeder valve fails to stop leaking, the valve should be replaced.

However, if no water shows up at broken union, the feeder is not the cause of flooding. The next cause can be a partially plugged feed line to the boiler. Lime deposits build up where the cold city water supply meets the hot return. If the feed line is partially plugged, back pressure is created whenever the boiler calls for water and the feed valve is open. This holds up the feed valve, and it continues to supply water after normal boiler level is restored.

Test Open valve B (broken-union test) with the union still broken. A tricklelike flow will prove partial plugging.

Remedy Take down the piping and thoroughly clean it or replace it with new pipe.

Another cause of flooding is a leaky hand-bypass valve.

Test Break union (D) with the bypass valve closed. Water leaking out shows that the hand-bypass valve is defective.

Remedy Install a new globe valve.

Faulty installation can be a cause of flooding. The closing level of the feeder on heating boilers should be set 2 to $2\frac{1}{2}$ in. below the normal boiler water line.

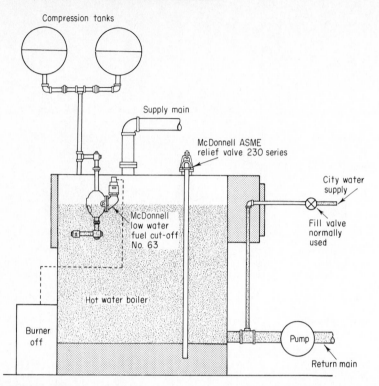

Fig. 33-7 This shows the action of the low-water-cutoff when an emergency condition arises. The lowering of the boiler water level and the simultaneous lowering of the water level in the float chamber causes the float to drop, thus opening the electrical circuit and stopping the automatic burner. Here is a means of stopping the automatic firing device if the water in the boiler drops below the minimum safe level.

Some other causes of flooding are:

1. Dirty water.
2. Faulty swing check valve in the return header.
3. Leaking hot-water coil in the boiler.
4. Overfilling by the hand valve.
5. Difference between level of dry return and boiler water level too small.
6. Equalizing pipe connection plugged.
7. City water pressure over 150 psi. Pressure reducing valve in feed line required.
8. Return pump not operating properly.

Condition 2 Boiler is getting too little water.

Test Test the feeder by breaking union (C). When the valve is manually operated, a full stream of water should flow from the broken

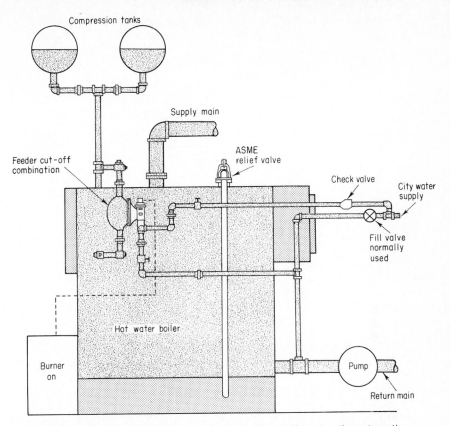

Fig. 33-8 If we could rely absolutely on the low-water-cutoff to stop the automatic burner each time a low-water condition developed, then the problem would be solved completely. However, experience has shown that under certain circumstances the low-water-cutoff does not function properly.

A more complete measure of safety is provided by using a combination boiler water feeder and low-water-cutoff. This provides (1) mechanical operation of feeding water to the boiler as fast as it is discharged through the relief valve, and (2) electrical operation that stops the burner when low-water conditions occur. (*McDonnell & Miller, Inc.*)

union each time valve is lifted. If the valve cannot be easily lifted, this is an indication that the float is being held up by sediment in the float chamber. To verify this, open the blow-off valve under float chamber. If, with the blow-off open, little or no water flows from the broken union, it can be assumed that the float chamber is loaded with mud or sediment.

Remedy   Open up the float housing and clean out all foreign matter. Then operate the valve manually as before and the feeder should feed full stream.

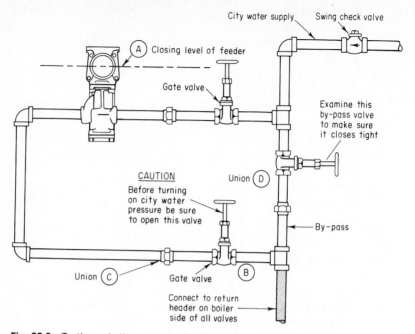

Fig. 33-9 Testing a boiler water feeder (broken-union test). (1) Make sure water level in boiler is above closing level of feeder (*A*). (2) Close valve (*B*) in feed pipe running from feeder to boiler. (3) Break union (*C*) between feeder and valve (*B*).

If the foregoing test shows the feeder to be in operating condition but still fails to supply water to the boiler, the feed line may be fully plugged, usually right where the connection is made into the return header or bottom of the boiler.

Other causes for too little water are:

1. A plugged strainer; this should be removed, cleaned, or replaced.
2. Priming, foaming, and surging due to dirty boiler water.
3. City water pressure less than boiler pressure.
4. Faulty swing check valve in return header. This allows water to be pushed out into return.
5. Operation of boiler feed pumps faulty.
6. Condensate hung up in system.

FEEDER AND CUTOFF SWITCH PROBLEMS

Burned-out switches show that something is wrong. Although such switches are conservatively rated and, when utilized in accordance with Underwriters listed ratings, should last for years, there are conditions under which they will burn out. Some of these causes are as follows:

1. Burner motor having greater power requirements than shown on manufacturer's nameplate.
2. Motor, having a dead spot, may stall and heat, causing overloading of switch.
3. Grounding of wiring in control circuit.
4. Switch submerged in water.
5. Lightning striking electrical service to building, causing tremendous overload. (This actually did occur rather recently.)
6. Overloaded circuit in building, resulting in low voltage conditions, which in turn causes too heavy amperage draw and consequent switch burnout.
7. Other limiting devices, like pressure controls, relays, and thermostats, may short circuit, overloading all switches on the line.

These are merely some of the causes of burnouts in properly applied switches. As previously stated, the most common cause of switch overload is incorrect application. Check the electrical ratings against the ratings of equipment controlled.

Some additional factors important to water-feeder operation are finally worth mentioning. Three basic rules should always be observed.

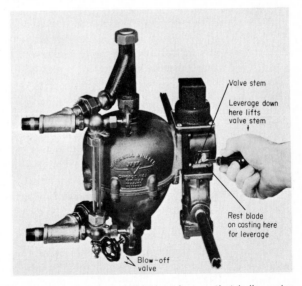

Fig. 33-10 A step in the broken-union test. Having made sure that boiler water level is above the closing level of the feeder, the feed valve should be closed by the float. Consequently, if water trickles out of broken union, the feed valve is not closing properly—this would explain an excessive high-water level in the boiler.

Now proceed as follows: (1) Manually open and close feed valve several times with screw driver as shown. This should remove any obstruction from the valve seat, and the valve should drive itself to a drip-tight closure. (2) If manual operation fails to stop leaking, the valve assembly must be replaced.

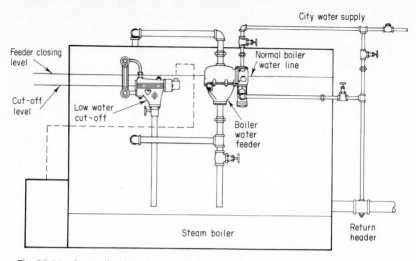

Fig. 33-11 An application where a separate feeder and separate cutoff are employed with a closed heating system. The feeder is added later.

In many cases, where boilers are installed with only a low water cutoff, the advantages of using a boiler water feeder are recognized soon after installation. In such a case the preferred addition should be a mechanical boiler water feeder as illustrated. Wherever the boiler openings and space facilities allow a mechanical feeder to be installed, this practice should be followed.

1. Always make certain that the feeder is supplied with *cold* water. Feeders are usually designed to operate "cool." This prevents water at the valve from reaching the critical temperature at which lime and scale can form.
2. A common cause of feeder and low-water-cutoff troubles is failure to periodically blow down the control. The systematic blowing down of the control prevents sediment from forming, which in turn hampers or prevents operation of these important safety controls.
3. Use complete replacement mechanisms when replacements or repairs have to be made.

In most cases these replacement heads represent the best way to repair controls in the field, since they (1) save much labor and expense required for disassembly and reassembly, (2) eliminate risk of disturbing critical factory adjustment, and (3) include all latest refinements in design and materials.

QUESTIONS

1. What is the difference between hydronic and warm-air heating systems?

2. Explain the difference between a steam and a hot-water heating system?
3. What two conditions must be guarded against in steam and hot-water systems?
4. What is a pressure-relief valve? How does it work?
5. Give four reasons why a pressure-relief valve will open in a hot-water heating system; in a steam heating system.
6. Give several causes of overfiring.
7. What is a low-water cutoff? An automatic feeder?
8. Explain the purpose and procedure of the "broken-union test."
9. Give six causes of boiler flooding.
10. What is meant when a feeder is said to operate "cool?"
11. Why are feeders designed to have cold-water feed?
12. Give four causes of switch burnouts in feeders or water-level controls.

CHAPTER 34

SERVICING CAD-CELL AND OTHER PRIMARY CONTROLS

HONEYWELL R8184 AND R8185 AND R4184 PROTECTORELAYS

Figs. 34-1 and 34-2; see also primary controls, Chaps. 12 and 15

Tools and equipment required   (1) Screwdriver; (2) 0- to 150-volt (or 0- to 300-volt if needed) a-c voltmeter with probes; (3) Honeywell #117004 Tattlelite or equivalent low-voltage, very low-amperage test lamp (or 240-volt lamp if needed); (4) insulated jumper wires; (6) small piece of pasteboard, such as a business or index card, for cleaning contacts. *Do not* use a file or abrasive material.

CHECKOUT (ALL MODELS)

A. *Starting Procedure*

1. Check combustion chamber to be certain that the combustion chamber is free of oil and vapor.

2. Push the red reset safety lever to the right or "up" on the R8182 and release.

3. Open the oil-line supply valve if such is not electrically inter-locked with the burner ignition.

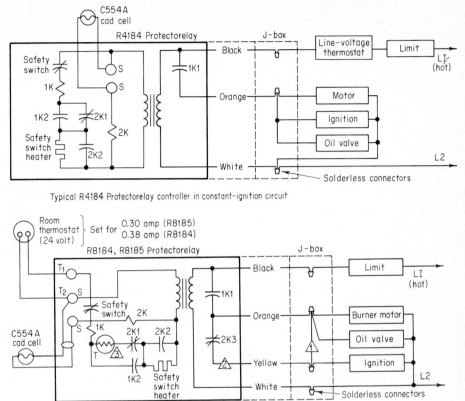

Typical R4184 Protectorelay controller in constant-ignition circuit

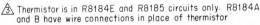

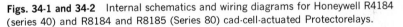

Typical R8184 and R8185 Protectorelay controller circuit

Figs. 34-1 and 34-2   Internal schematics and wiring diagrams for Honeywell R4184 (series 40) and R8184 and R8185 (Series 80) cad-cell-actuated Protectorelays.

4. Close the line switch to the power burner.

5. Set the limit control(s) and thermostat to call for heat.

The burner should now start.

B. Normal Cycle   If all is normal, the burner will run until the room thermostat or hot-water temperature control (aquastat) is satisfied. If the burner starts and then locks out on safety, see the "Flame Detector Check" further on in this chapter.

C. Safety Switch Timing

1. Let the burner operate for 5 min, then disconnect one of the C554A flame detection leadwires at the Protectorelay. After ap-

proximately 70 sec (60 sec on R8182D-E and -F models) the control control should lock out on safety. The burner will then stop.

2. Open the line voltage switch.

3. Reconnect the leadwire from the (C554A) flame detector.

4. After waiting about 3 min for the safety-switch heater to cool, operate the red manual reset lever to reposition the Protectorelay for starting.

D. High Limit and Thermostat

1. Close the line switch; set the thermostat high enough to call for heat.

2. Adjust the high-limit controller to its lowest setting. The burner should stop (unless the furnace or water temperature is below the minimum of high-limit controller). On the R8182A-B, -D and -E combination-type controllers, the circulator operates when the thermostat contacts are made—even when the high-limit contacts are broken. (See Chaps. 12, 15, and 17.)

3. Reset the high-limit controller to an appropriate setting. The burner should start.

The R8182C and -F controls switch the circulator according to the water temperature sensed by the aquastat and can operate the circulator even though neither the thermostat contacts nor the high-limit contacts are made.

4. While the burner is operating, adjust the space thermostat to its lowest setting. Unless the space temperature is actually below this setting, the burner should stop.

In systems using the R8182A and -D controls supplying hot water for domestic use, the burner will operate, but the circulator cannot operate whenever the low-limit aquastat switch calls for heat. When the low-limit controller is satisfied, the circulator operates whenever the space thermostat calls for heat.

5. Set the space thermostat to its original setting.

E. Low Limit and Circulator

E. Low Limit and Circulator   On the R8182A and -D models, the low-limit control acts to maintain a minimum water temperature (for domestic hot-water service) independent of the space thermostat. The SPDT contacts of the low-limit switch also open the circuit to prevent the circulation of water until it has been heated to the low-limit setting plus the differential (adjustable from 5° to 20°F).

1. Set the low-limit Aquastat switch to its lowest setting to simulate the low-water temperature condition, such as might be brought on by a heavy call for domestic hot water. The burner should start, but the circulator should not run.

2. Reset the low-limit switch to its normal or required setting. The burner should stop when the water temperature is above the low-limit setting.

To check circulator operation: Set the space thermostat high enough to call for heat. The circulator should run (if the system's water temperature is above the low-limit setting on the Aquastat as described above).

F. Flame Detector Check Equipment required: a 1,500-ohm resistor (any wattage). If the burner starts normally but the safety switch locks out after approximately 70 sec (60 sec on R8182D, -E, -F models), use the following procedure to determine where the trouble lies.

G. Basic Cautions Be sure to remove the 1,500-ohm resistor from the SS terminals after testing. The Protectorelay controller will not operate the burner on call for heat with the terminals SS jumpered.

1. Open the line switch, wait 3 min, and then operate the red manual reset lever.

2. Remove the leadwires from the SS terminals on the primary controller.

3. Push *one* leadwire of the 1,500-ohm resistor into one of the SS terminals and close the line switch to start the burner. As soon as the flame has been established, push the other resistor lead into place on the other SS terminal. Note that this must be done before the safety switch can lock out (approximately 70 sec, 60 sec on R8182D, -E, -F models).

4. If the primary controller locks out with the resistor across the SS terminals, the primary controller should be replaced. If necessary, repeat this check after a period of 10 min to verify the result.

H. Cad-cell Service Causes If the Protectorelay (primary) controller does *not* lock out with the 1,500-ohm resistor across the SS terminals, the C554A cad cell is dirty, defective, or improperly positioned (*not* sighting the flame properly).

Checkout Procedure

1. Stop the burner by opening the line switch, and remove the 1,500-ohm resistor. Reconnect the C554A flame detector leads (cad cell) at terminals SS.

2. *Unplug* the cad cell from its socket (just pull it out). If the surface of the cell has an accumulation of dust or soot, clean it carefully with a soft cloth and replace it in the socket assembly.

3. Restart burner. If it continues to operate (does not lock out), then a dirty cad cell was the trouble.

4. If the cad cell is found to be clean (or if the Protectorelay locked out on safety in Step 3), replace the cad cell with a new one.

5. Restart the burner. If it continues to operate (does not lock out), then the old cell was defective.

6. If the Protectorelay controller still locks out on safety, then check the positioning of the C554A flame detector. It must view the oil flame directly. Also, check to see that the flame shape and burner input are normal. A fouled nozzle could alter the flame pattern.

The only other possibility is an open circuit in the leadwires to the cad cell socket assembly or poor contact at the pins (prongs) in the socket.

THE CAD CELL (C554A)

The cadmium sulfide cell—commonly called *cad cell*—is the most suitable flame detector for many heating applications. The cad cell is actually a resistor which changes its characteristics of conductivity in direct proportion to the amount of light striking it.

In darkness, the cad cell has a very high resistance to the passage of electrical current. In the presence of light its resistance becomes very low and permits current to pass. This characteristic behavior permits its use as a switch to open or close a circuit in relation to a sensed condition.

The C554A cad cell is particularly sensitive to light from an oil flame. Its fast response in supervising the operating of an oil burner eliminates the lags found in stack-mounted, bimetal sensors to give safer and more efficient cycling.

PROCEDURE FOR PROPER PLACEMENT

Application   The location of the C554A flame detector and its proper mounting depends upon the furnace or boiler being used. However, some general instructions for the most efficient use of the detector apply to all installations.

1. *The burner flame must be viewed directly*   Mount the C554A at the rear of the burner, positioning it to have an unobstructed view of the oil flame. Never use the light reflected from the walls of the fire box for detector operation. Manufacturers often blacken the housing on new equipment to simulate actual working conditions at the time the cell is installed (see Fig. 34-3).

2. *Light must be adequate for sensing*   Avoid locating the flame detector too far back in the blower housing where light rays from the oil flame may be too scattered to permit proper operation. Be sure that the light falls uniformly over the entire surface of the cell and is not concentrated on a small area.

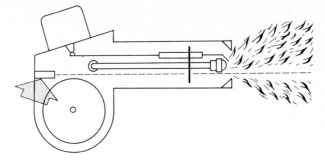

Fig. 34-3 Proper positioning of the flame detection cad cell is shown by the shaded arrow.

3. *Temperature threshold must be correct* In placing the cell select a location in which the ambient temperature normally does not exceed 140°F at the surface of the cell.

4. *Clearance must be adequate* Be sure to allow adequate clearance so that metal surfaces near the cell will not affect it by movement, shielding, or radiation.

Cleaning and Replacing Cell Under normal operating conditions the C554A cad cell does not require cleaning. Small accumulations on the surface of the cell will not affect its operation. However, if a badly adjusted burner has caused a heavy accumulation of soot, the surface should be wiped carefully to remove all opaque substances and restore full view of the oil flame.

If the cell should ever be damaged, it may be removed easily by simply unplugging it from the socket assembly. Be careful that the positioning of the socket assembly is not disturbed.

WHITE-RODGERS KWIK-SENSOR
OIL-BURNER PRIMARY CONTROLS
Figs. 34-4 and 34-5

General Basic Good Practices Refer to the wiring diagrams shown for Kwik-Sensor primary controls in this chapter. Instructions on specific installations provided by the manufacturer should always be strictly followed.

After each Kwik-Sensor installation, follow the procedure for the appropriate control checks as listed in "Checkout Procedure" below.

All wiring should be performed according to local and national electrical codes and ordinances. The following general wiring practices are recommended:

1. If *line-* and *low*-voltage wires are run in the same conduit, the

insulation of the low-voltage wire must be equal to the maximum of any wire in the conduit.

2. Do not use smaller than No. 14 wire for line-voltage wiring.

3. Do not use smaller than No. 18 wire for low-voltage wiring.

4. All terminal connections should be tight and carefully made.

5. When making splices, either solder and tape the splice, or use an approved solderless connector. Splices should be made only at a junction box, and not in conduit runs.

6. The last few feet of connections to the primary control should be flexible to permit control removal for servicing.

7. Always connect the high limit control in the "hot" side of line to either terminal 1 or to black lead of primary control.

CHECKOUT PROCEDURE (ALL KWIK-SENSOR MODELS)

A. Preliminary Checks The following control checks should be made after each Kwik-Sensor installation to insure that the controls are correctly wired and functioning properly. (These control checks apply equally well for all series Kwik-Sensor combination oil-burner–hydronic controls.)

1. Open the main line switch.

2. Adjust the thermostat or operating control to call for heat.

3. Operate the red manual reset lever.

4. Make certain that the high-limit control is set at the correct temperature.

5. Open the hand valve in the oil line. The system is now ready for the following tests.

B. Normal Cycle Close the line switch. The burner should start and continue to run normally. (If the burner starts, establishing flame, but then locks out on safety, refer to the "Flame Detector Check" further on in this chapter.)

C. Safety Timing
1. Let the burner run for about 5 min. Then remove one of the flame detector leads from the low-voltage FD-FD terminals. After a time period corresponding to the safety timing has elapsed, the primary control should lock out on safety, stopping the burner.

2. Open the line switch.

3. Replace the flame detector lead removed in Step 1.

4. Wait about 3 min. Then operate the red manual reset lever.

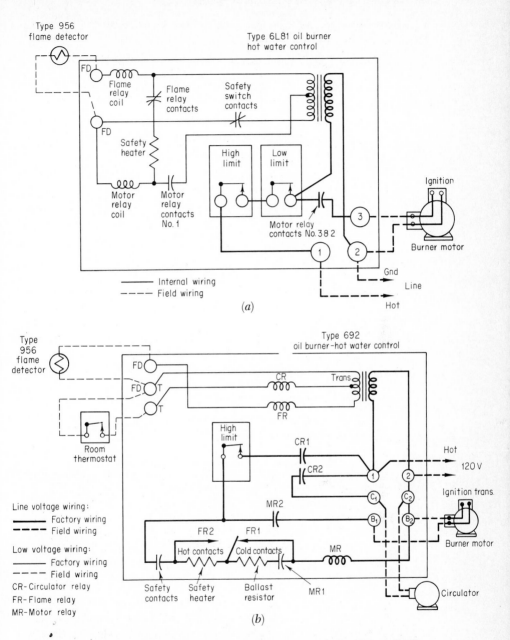

Fig. 34-4 Internal schematics and wiring diagrams for White-Rodgers cad-cell-actuated (Kwik-Sensor) combination oil-burner primary and hydronic controls for hot-water heating systems. (*a*) Type 6L81 Kwik-Sensor primary control, combination oil-burner–hydronic control; line voltage, constant ignition, non-recycling. (*b*) Type 692 Kwik-Sensor primary control, combination oil burner–hydronic control; low voltage, constant ignition, non-recycling.

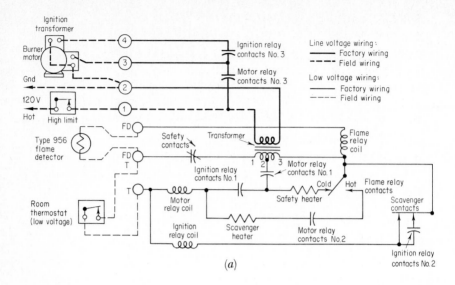

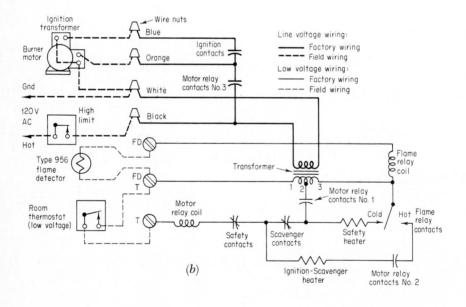

Fig. 34-5 Internal schematic and wiring diagrams for White-Rodgers cad-cell-actuated (Kwik-Sensor) combination oil-burner primary controls. (*a*) Type 663-1 and 663-3 Kwik-Sensors; low-voltage, intermittent-ignition, recycling type. (*b*) Type 669 Kwik Sensor; low-voltage, intermittent-ignition, recycling type.

D. *High Limit and Thermostat Check*

1. Close the line switch to start the burner.

2. Lower the setting of the high-limit control to its lowest setting. This should stop the burner, unless furnace or boiler temperature is below the minimum setting of high limit. (On type 682 and 683 Kwik-Sensor combinations, the SPDT high limit should also start the circulator if it is not already running.)

3. Return high-limit control to its proper setting.

4. With the burner running, turn the thermostat to its lowest setting. This should stop the burner, unless actual room temperature is below the lowest setting of the thermostat.

(**NOTE**   On systems supplying domestic hot water, the burner will continue to run if low-limit control is not satisfied.)

    E. Ignition Timing (For Types 663 and 669 Only)   Start the burner. The length of time from the start of flame to ignition cutoff is the ignition time and should be about 45 sec.

    F. Scavenger Timing (For Types 660, 663, 664, 666, and 669)

1. Start the burner and let it run for about 3 min.

2. Open and then immediately reclose the line switch. This should stop the burner. (If it does not, replace the primary control.)

3. Note the length of time from reclosing of the line switch to the time when the burner restarts. This is the scavenger time and should be about 1 min.

FLAME DETECTOR CHECK

(To determine whether the primary control or the flame detector is faulty)

    A. Burner Starts But Then Locks Out   If burner starts but then locks out on safety, determine whether the trouble is at the primary control or the flame detector as follows:

1. *Check of primary control*
   (a) Open the line switch. Operate the red manual reset lever.
   (b) Remove the flame detector leads from FD-FD terminals.
   (c) Attach one lead of a 2,000-ohm resistor (any wattage) to one of the FD terminals. Close the line switch and start the burner. As soon as the flame is established, immediately attach the other lead of the 2,000-ohm resistor to the other FD terminal.

       NOTE   The resistor must be connected within a time period less than the safety timing or the safety heater will perform its normal function of locking out on safety because of open FD-FD terminals.

(d) If the primary control locks out on safety with the 2,000-ohm resistor across the FD-FD terminals, the primary control should be replaced.

NOTE If any doubt exists about having had the 2,000-ohm resistor connected soon enough in Step (c), wait 10 min and then repeat Step (c) before placing the primary control.

2. *Check of flame detector* If the primary control did *not* lock out in Step 1 above, the flame detector is at fault. To determine whether the flame detector is dirty, defective, or improperly positioned, proceed as follows:

(a) Stop the burner. Remove the 2000-ohm resistor and reconnect the flame detector leads to FD-FD terminals.

(b) Remove the cad cell from the socket assembly of the flame detector (grasp end of cell, push in, and turn counterclockwise). If the cad cell has soot accumulation on its face, wipe clean with a soft cloth and put the cell back into the socket assembly. Then start the burner. If it continues to run normally (no lockout), then the cad cell was only dirty.

(c) If the face of the cad cell is clean [or if primary control is locked out on safety in Step (b)], replace the cad cell with a new one. Start the burner. If it continues to run normally (no lockout), then the original cell was defective.

(d) If the primary control still locks out on safety, then the flame detector is not properly positioned. (The only other possibility is an open circuit between contacts of the cad cell and socket assembly, or in the leads of the socket assembly.) Refer to the burner manufacturer's instructions and recommendations for correct flame-detector location.

NOTE Be sure to remove the 2,000-ohm resistor after completing the tests. The primary control will not allow the burner to start on call for heat if the FD-FD terminals are jumpered.

B. Burner Will Not Start If the burner will not start, the flame detector leads (or cell) may be shorted, or there may be false light. Make a check as follows:

1. Remove one of the flame detector leads from the FD-FD terminals.

2. Close the line switch. If the burner now starts, the trouble lies with the flame detector.°

3. If the burner does not start, see Chapters 35–37 on basic service causes for other possible reasons.

SERVICE PREVENTION PRECAUTIONS

Application procedures

The proper location, mounting, and application is determined by the furnace, boiler, and/or burner manufacturer, and the factors that are the basis for such location are important. Every service technician should know these. They are:

1. *Direct view of burner flame* The flame detector must have a direct view of the burner flame. In some instances, it may be necessary to drill holes in static discs, etc., in order to provide the flame detector with a clear view of the burner flame.

The flame detector should not depend upon reflected light for its operation since the amount of reflection changes after the burner has been in service for a short time. When making an application on new burner units, some manufacturers blacken the inside of the housing in order to simulate actual field conditions.

2. *Cool location* The flame detector must be located so that the temperature of its face never exceeds 140°F.

° **Trouble at 956 flame detector**

Causes:
1. Flame-detector leads shorted.
2. Short circuit in cad cell of 956 flame detector.
3. Flame detector exposed to false source of light. (The flame detector must be "seeing" darkness when the thermostat calls for heat or it will not allow burner to start.)

Remedies:
1. Separate the leads.
2. Replace the cad cell. If no change, install the old again.
3. Correct the false-light condition.

B. Burner starts but primary control locks out on safety
Causes:
1. Soot on face of cad cell.
2. Open circuit in cad cell. (See "Flame Detector Check.")
3. Defective location of flame detector. (See "Flame Detector Check.")
Remedies:
1. Clean face and correct cause of soot.
2. Replace cad cell. If no change, install old cell again.
3. Refer to burner manufacturer's instructions for proper location. Replace socket assembly if necessary.

3. *Insufficient light* If the flame detector is located too far back in the housing, the light rays from the oil flame might be too widely scattered to allow the flame detector to function properly.

4. *Avoid focus concentration* The flame detector should not be located too close to a hole used for viewing the oil flame. Light rays from the flame should be spread uniformly over the face of the Flame Detector.

5. *Maintain proper clearances* Proper clearances must be maintained between the flame detector and any exposed live metal parts of the burner. Sufficient clearances should also be allowed between the flame detector and any moving parts of the burner.

Cleaning face of 956 flame detector

Normal accumulations of dust and soot on the face of the flame detector will not affect its operation. If a badly adjusted burner or extremely dirty atmosphere should have caused an excessive accumulation on its face, simply wipe the face clean.

Replacing flame detection cad cell

If ever damaged, the cad cell of the 956 flame detector can be easily removed from its socket assembly. Simply grasp the end of cell, push in, and turn the cell counterclockwise as if removing an auto light. Take the following precautions when replacing a cad cell:

1. Do not disturb the position of socket assembly.

2. Do not use tools to grasp end of cell, and do not scratch the face of the cell.

3. Be sure that the replacement cell has the same part number as the old cell.

QUESTIONS

1. What tools and equipment are required to service cad cell primary controls?
2. Give the starting procedure for the Honeywell cad cell primary controls, including the normal cycle, safety switch timing, high limit and thermostat, low limit and circulator.
3. Explain the procedure for a "Flame Detection Check."
4. Explain the check-out procedure for determining the causes of cad cell service.
5. What is meant by proper placement of the cad cell?

6. How is the cad cell cleaned?
7. Give seven basic good practices when installing a primary control.
8. List the preliminary checks for Kwik-Sensor primary controls.
9. What is a cad cell?
10. How does it operate?

CHAPTER 35

BASIC OIL-BURNER
SERVICE METHODS:
NO HEAT

One of the most important factors in properly servicing domestic oil burners is to have a *definite service procedure* that can always be followed and thereby facilitate the solution of the problem. The use of a definite method eliminates hit-or-miss solutions that may result in starting the burner but not solving the real cause of trouble. This type of service usually means repeat calls that are time and money wasters, as well as a personal discredit to the service mechanic.

For these reasons the adoption of a specific system in approaching all service calls is of great value to both the mechanic and his employer. Further, the use of a basic service procedure that incorporates certain safety precautions will result in eliminating certain approaches to service that have in them an element of trouble or danger.

Newcomers to the service mechanics field with a method of approach consisting of a few simple operations taught to them by their employer will be more certain and safe in their new work and less likely to do things that may result in later nuisance calls.

All oil-burner service complaints can be divided into three main types. These types of complaints are

1. "No heat" calls
2. "Too much, or not enough, heat" calls
3. "Defective operation" calls (vibrations, odor, smoke, etc.)

This chapter will deal with the system of approaching "no heat" calls, and the following chapter will cover the complaints mentioned in call types 2 and 3.

The fact that oil-burner service complaints are so standardized as to fall into any one of these three categories gives us an opportunity to illustrate graphically the correct method of operation and approach. This means that the major causes of trouble plus the systematic approach to diagnosing that trouble can be set down with comparative ease.

As mentioned previously, the first and most important complaint, which comprises approximately 60 per cent of all service calls, is the "no heat" call. In this case we have the *main* service complaint, for the oil burner is not operating at all and the customer is deprived of the necessary heat.

In steam and hot-water systems this call may appear during the summertime as a "no hot water" call, but the most important thing to remember is that both of these calls, the "no heat" in the winter and the "no hot water" in the summer, are calls that give evidence that the heating unit has ceased operating completely.

Figure 35-1 shows the eight basic steps that should be observed in approaching the "no heat" service call. Starting from Step 1 and progressing clockwise around the chart, we find the following eight steps should be observed.

Step 1   Upon entering the house, the main source of power—the house fuse and switch box—should be examined to see that the line fuses are not blown and that the switch is in the ON position. There is little use in approaching the oil-burner fuse and switch box if there is no power in the house at all.

Step 2   Check the oil-burner fuse to be sure that it has not blown.

Step 3   Now check the remote-control switch, which may be found at the head of the stairs leading into the cellar or may be located directly within the boiler or furnace jacket. See that this remote-control switch is in the ON position. If it is, then proceed to Step 4. If it is not in the ON position, but instead is in the OFF position, leave it that way until the boiler or furnace is checked to see that it is not full of oil fumes.

Open the boiler or furnace door and check for oil saturation. Do not attempt to start the unit if the boiler is saturated or full of oil fumes

Fig. 35-1

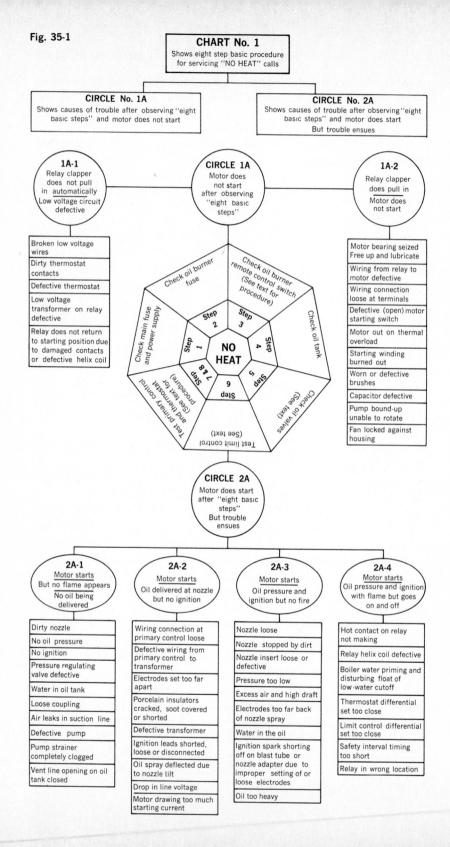

CHART No. 1
Shows eight step basic procedure
for servicing "NO HEAT" calls

CIRCLE No. 1A
Shows causes of trouble after observing "eight
basic steps" and motor does not start

CIRCLE No. 2A
Shows causes of trouble after observing "eight
basic steps" and motor does start
But trouble ensues

1A-1
Relay clapper
does not pull
in automatically
Low voltage circuit
defective

CIRCLE 1A
Motor does
not start
after observing
"eight basic
steps"

1A-2
Relay clapper
does pull in
Motor does
not start

Broken low voltage wires

Dirty thermostat contacts

Defective thermostat

Low voltage transformer on relay defective

Relay does not return to starting position due to damaged contacts or defective helix coil

Check oil burner fuse

Check oil burner remote control switch (See text for procedure)

Check main fuse and power supply

Check oil tank

Step 2
Step 3
Step 1
NO HEAT
Step 4
Step 7 & 8
Step 6
Step 5

Test primary control and thermostat (See text for procedure)

Test limit control (See text)

Check oil valves (See text)

Motor bearing seized Free up and lubricate

Wiring from relay to motor defective

Wiring connection loose at terminals

Defective (open) motor starting switch

Motor out on thermal overload

Starting winding burned out

Worn or defective brushes

Capacitor defective

Pump bound-up unable to rotate

Fan locked against housing

CIRCLE 2A
Motor does start
after "eight basic
steps"
But trouble
ensues

2A-1
Motor starts
But no flame appears
No oil being
delivered

2A-2
Motor starts
Oil delivered at nozzle
but no ignition

2A-3
Motor starts
Oil pressure and
ignition but no fire

2A-4
Motor starts
Oil pressure and ignition
with flame but goes
on and off

Dirty nozzle

No oil pressure

No ignition

Pressure regulating valve defective

Water in oil tank

Loose coupling

Air leaks in suction line

Defective pump

Pump strainer completely clogged

Vent line opening on oil tank closed

Wiring connection at primary control loose

Defective wiring from primary control to transformer

Electrodes set too far apart

Porcelain insulators cracked, soot covered or shorted

Defective transformer

Ignition leads shorted, loose or disconnected

Oil spray deflected due to nozzle tilt

Drop in line voltage

Motor drawing too much starting current

Nozzle loose

Nozzle stopped by dirt

Nozzle insert loose or defective

Pressure too low

Excess air and high draft

Electrodes too far back of nozzle spray

Water in the oil

Ignition spark shorting off on blast tube or nozzle adapter due to improper setting of or loose electrodes

Oil too heavy

Hot contact on relay not making

Relay helix coil defective

Boiler water priming and disturbing float of low-water cutoff

Thermostat differential set too close

Limit control differential set too close

Safety interval timing too short

Relay in wrong location

as there may be danger of a serious puffback. To throw the remote-control switch indiscriminately to the ON position may ignite these vapors and cause the very puffback that we wish to avoid.

Once the mechanic has checked the boiler and furnace and they are not full of oil fumes or saturated with liquid oil, he should throw the switch to the ON position.

If the boiler is full of oil vapor, every effort should be made to wait until the fumes have been dispersed; and if the chamber is saturated with liquid oil, it may be necessary later to allow it to burn out with the burner not operating, by igniting the excess oil with a piece of burning newspaper or rag. Certain materials, such as powdered cement or any other good absorbent, can be sprinkled in the chamber and then cleaned out. These absorbent materials will pick up a considerable amount of the oil and leave less for the troublesome burning out.

Once it definitely has been determined that there are no fumes or liquid oil present, throw the switch to the ON position and proceed to Step 4.

Step 4 Now check the oil tank and make sure that it contains oil.

Step 5 Check the oil valves both at the tank and at the burner to be certain that they are open and oil can flow or be drawn to the pump.

Step 6 Now using the test lamp, proceed to the limit control or controls, and test to see that both the incoming and outgoing terminals are hot.

In a steam system, the limit control will be a *pressure* control and there may also be a *low-water-cutoff*. It will be a series hookup with the hot line running from the limit control to the low-water-cutoff or vice versa, and then to the No. 1 terminal on the relay.

In a hot-water heating system, the limit control will be a *line-voltage water-temperature control*, and from there the hot line will proceed to the relay.

In a warm-air system, the limit control will be a warm-air temperature control or may be contained in a *combination fan and limit control*. The important thing to remember is that the limit control merely breaks the hot line, and therefore both terminals—the incoming and outgoing—in a limit control should test hot if the limit control mechanism is in the ON position.

After ascertaining that current is passing through the limit control or controls, proceed to Steps 7 and 8.

Step 7 Since the limit control breaks the hot line to the No. 1 contact on the relay and we have ascertained in the previous step that current is flowing through the limit control, the No. 1 terminal on the relay should now test hot. If not, check the No. 2 terminal (ground), for the polarity could be reversed. If such is the case, the No. 2 terminal on the relay will test positive. Reverse the No. 1 and No. 2 wires. We now have current to the No. 1 terminal on the relay.

Step 8   At this point, with the boiler door *open,* trip the safety reset button. If the thermostat is in the ON position, the burner should start. If the thermostat is not in the ON position, put it in such position by turning it up above room temperature. The burner should start. If it does not, then refer to Circle 1A. If it does start, but trouble ensues, then refer to Circle 2A.

Circle 1A   If we find upon following the eight basic steps that the motor does not start, either one of two conditions has occurred.

Circle 1A-1   The relay clapper did not pull in automatically, which gives evidence of a defective low-voltage circuit, the causes of which can be observed by checking the box attached to Circle 1A-1. A good point to remember is that if the relay clapper does not pull in, we have some sort of electrical trouble. The average low-voltage circuit on oil-burner controls is anywhere from 20 to 32 volts. A low-voltage test light should be used to test this circuit.

Be sure that the starting contacts of the relay are making firmly. The relay must be in the "start" position or "cold" position before the clapper can pull in and shunt the line voltage to the burner.

Circle 1A-2   If the relay clapper does pull in, which shows that the low-voltage circuit is operating, but the burner motor does not start, then the causes of trouble can be ascertained by checking the box attached to Circle 1A-2. We find here that the great majority of troubles are in the motor and may be anything from a seized bearing or other mechanical defect to defective wiring.

It is wise to check the thermal overload switch on the motor, for in many cases the motor may not be able to operate because this device has shut off the flow of current to it by opening the circuit from the No. 3 terminal on the relay to the motor.

Actually, when the relay clapper closes, it shunts the current from the No. 1 terminal on the relay to the No. 3 terminal on the relay and from there to the burner motor. The line from No. 3 to the burner motor is intercepted by the thermal overload device on the motor or by a fusetron that can be placed in the line by the installer.

Check the No. 3 terminal on the relay when the clapper closes; it should test hot; if not, the relay is defective.

Occasionally, the pump may bind up and prevent the motor from turning. If there is a doubt in such a case, loosen the coupling at the pump and if the motor then turns freely, it is the pump itself that is bound. These points take care of the major causes of service if the motor does not start after observing the eight basic steps.

Of course, there can be a number of other causes not listed, but it is impossible because of space limitations to set down every minute cause that would prevent the motor from starting after observing all the conditions in Circle 1A. If the motor cannot be repaired, it should be replaced by another motor.

Circle 2A. The motor does start after the basic eight steps are ascertained, but trouble ensues.

Circle 2A-1 The motor starts, but no flame appears, as there is no oil being delivered. The main causes of this are set down in the box adjoining Circle 2A-1. In the event of a defective pump, the part should be changed and the oil pump rebuilt, unless it is a minor repair such as replacing the bellows in a pressure regulating valve.

In pump troubles, it is wise to use gauges, and a pressure gauge should be attached to the pump at the port provided to make sure that the proper operating oil pressure of at least 100 psi is being furnished.

If the pump is air-bound, vent it at the pressure-gauge port.

If proper pressure is being furnished, but no flame appears, *check the nozzle,* for it is undoubtedly clogged.

If a groaning or grinding noise is evident in the pump, it usually demonstrates that the *pump strainers are clogged and dirty.* They should be removed and cleaned in some good type of noninflammable solvent, such as carbon tetrachloride.

In the event of a sunken tank, a vacuum gauge should be used. A vacuum in excess of 12 in. usually is evidence of a clogged or restricted suction line, or could result from the remote case of the vent line opening on the oil tank being clogged.

Air leaks in the suction line will prevent the pump from drawing oil. Close the valve at the tank and if the vacuum in inches on the gauge does not increase, it is evidence that air is leaking into the line, or that the pump is so defective or worn as to be of no further use.

Look for a *loose coupling.* The motor will be operating in such case, but the pump will not rotate, and of course no pressure or vacuum readings will show on the gauges.

Circle 2A-2 This refers to cases where the motor starts and oil is delivered at the nozzle, but there is no ignition. Observe the causes in the box adjacent to Circle 2A-2. This is primarily electrical trouble due to a defective transformer or any of the causes listed. In the event of a defective transformer, there is nothing to do but to replace it.

In an intermittent ignition relay, current flows from the No. 4 terminal to the transformer. Be sure that when the ignition clapper is in, the No. 4 terminal is hot.

Circle 2A-3 The motor starts in this case; we have oil pressure and ignition, but there is no fire. The causes of this condition are diverse. Check to see that the nozzle and all its parts are tight and clean. A dirty nozzle is likely to cause trouble in this case.

Be sure that the oil pressure is at 100 psi. If oil pressure is too low, it may result in atomization so coarse that it will not start combustion.

Excess air or high draft will aggravate any defects in achieving initial combustion. See that the oil is not too heavy or does not contain a large portion of water.

Improper setting of electrodes so that the spark does not appear in the proper place or shorts off before reaching the electrodes can cause this trouble.

Circle 2A-4 In this case, the motor starts; we have oil pressure and ignition with a flame operating, but the burner jumps on and off. Here it may be that the hot contacts on the relay are not making. This may result in the burner going into safety if the stack-switch helix element cools quickly.

A defective helix coil, one that is dirty and covered with soot or mounted in the wrong location, can also cause this trouble.

Close differentials on thermostats and limit controls may also result in this trouble. On a steam system, the limit-control differential should be at least 3 psi and in a hot-water system, at least 15°; in a warm-air system, at least 40°.

Dirt, oil, grease, or other impurities in the boiler will result in an unsteady water line. The boiler water will surge and cause a fluctuating water level. This may disturb the float in the low-water-cutoff and cause constant on-and-off action. If such is the case, use a good boiler cleaning compound and the trouble should cease.

This concludes the breakdown on "no heat" calls. The following chapters contain Figs. 36-1 and 37-1, which, respectively, deal with the basic procedure for handling "too much" and "not enough heat" calls and "defective operation" calls (vibration, odor, smoke, etc.)

QUESTIONS

1. How may service calls be divided?
2. Give the eight basic steps in approaching a service call.
3. What two alternate conditions can occur after the eight basic steps are observed?
4. Give five causes of a defective low-voltage circuit.
5. What can be the trouble if the relay clapper does pull in but the motor does not start?
6. What can be the causes of trouble if the motor does start and oil is delivered but no ignition appears?
7. How can one tell if there is water in the oil?
8. What can be the cause of a groaning and grinding noise?
9. What may be the result of a close differential setting on a thermostat or limit control?
10. Explain how dirty boiler water may affect the operation of the burner.
11. What will happen if the hot contacts on the primary control do not "make"?

CHAPTER 36

BASIC OIL-BURNER
SERVICE METHODS:
UNDERHEATING AND OVERHEATING

The second of the three classifications into which all oil-burner service problems fall is the "insufficient or too much heat" calls.

Underheating and overheating service calls often present something more than just a service problem. In many cases the trouble is much more basic than any burner defect and can even be purely of a psychological nature.

Homeowners have been known to hang thermometers in various places on the walls of a room that underheats and be highly indignant if all of them vary much more than a couple of degrees. In any room there is bound to be a considerable difference in temperature between floor and ceiling, and 2° or 3° is not abnormal. The nature of warm air is to rise, and in such cases, some basic instruction on the nature of convection currents (air) rising is all that is needed to placate the irate consumer.

An important point in clearing up complaints of a psychological nature is to be sure that the thermometer in the thermostat cover is fairly accurate. A close agreement between the thermostat cover thermometer and the thermostat setting dial will convince many homeowners that their heating system is doing the proper job even though it may be short or over a couple of degrees.

No matter how well the heating plant is performing its task in heating the house evenly, however, there is the opportunity for a complaint if the thermostat setting is 72°F and the thermostat cover thermometer reads 69°F and at that point the burner goes off.

In this case if the heated radiators do not bring the room up to 72°F, there is likely to be a complaint of underheating. People observe this thermometer much more than is realized, and any wide divergence between it and the thermostat setting lever or dial will bring the inevitable "nuisance call."

However, the psychological underheating or overheating call presents but a small picture of the total causes of such service. In referring to Fig. 36-1 we can see that both *underheating* and *overheating* conditions are due to certain troubles or conditions that are peculiar either to the burner, the controls, or the system.

Circle 2A: Underheating   Observe Circle 2A, which deals with *underheating* and its causes. We find that causes of insufficient heat can be in the burner, the controls, the heating system, and in miscellaneous causes such as the combustion chamber, draft, or chimney conditions.

Burner defects that will cause insufficient heat express themselves by constantly altering the normal flame necessary to produce the required amount of heat or by not giving a flame large enough, although constant in size, that will furnish enough Btu per hour to heat the building.

One of the commonest causes of this trouble is the *nozzle*. Either it is too small (in which case it should be replaced) or it is worn, loose, or dirty and is not doing its job properly.

If it is the former, calculate the correct gph rate and put in the proper size of nozzle.

If it is the latter, clean the nozzle or replace it. Nozzles that have been in use for a long time should be replaced, for the constant wear diminishes their ability to atomize the oil properly. Such a nozzle change will probably result in an actual saving to the consumer.

In order for nozzles to atomize the oil properly the operating pressure furnished by the pump should be *at least* 100 psi. This is the pressure at which the nozzle was designed to do its job.

Do not hesitate to increase this to 110 or 120 psi if such an increase sharply increases the CO_2 reading. The finer atomization obtained by running at pressures over 100 psi more than compensates for the small increase in oil consumption by furnishing higher operating CO_2's that are reflected in actual oil savings.

Make certain that all parts of the nozzle are tight and that it is in the proper place in the blast tube and not too far forward or back of the mouth of the blast tube. Follow the burner manufacturer's specifications on this.

Next to be considered is the pump. Be certain that it is operating at the proper pressure and use a gauge to determine this. *Do not guess.* A loose coupling or motor failing to come up to speed means that the pump is not receiving sufficient rotary power to do its job. Be sure that the coupling holds the pump shaft securely.

Dirty strainers, defective pressure regulating valve, a sticky bypass valve, and air leaks in the suction line will all cause a fluctuating fire or a lack of pressure that will result in a fire too small to do the job.

If the pressure regulating valve is causing the trouble, replace the piston and valve seat if it is that type of valve, or replace the bellows if it is a bellows type. Always check the bellows to see if it has a hole in it. Replace it if it has.

In the event that excessively dirty strainers are impairing the performance of the pump, a grunting or groaning noise will give evidence of this condition. Clean the strainers with hot water or carbon tetrachloride.

Put a vacuum gauge on the pump at the port provided. Twelve inches should be the maximum vacuum needed. If it runs higher, there may be a partially clogged or kinked suction line, or the vent opening on the oil tank may be clogged. In the event that the pump is air-bound, no oil would be delivered at all. Vent the pump and it will operate. This occurs on one-pipe systems when the oil tank runs dry.

If the pump is leaking around the shaft, it means that the seal is defective and oil is getting through it. Replace with a new pump and have the old one rebuilt at the shop. It is not practical to do a job on replacing the seal in the field.

A hissing or spurting noise in the combustion chamber demonstrates that water is being flashed to steam by the fire and there is water in the oil. If water exists in appreciable quantities in the oil, the fire may go out and the possibility of a puffback becomes probable. In this case, the tank may have to be pumped out.

The next burner part that influences flame stability is the fan. The blades should be clean and it should be of sufficient size to furnish the necessary amount of air to provide clean, efficient combustion.

Be careful when increasing nozzle sizes that the fan has the capacity to take care of the increased gallonage. If not, a smoky, fluctuating fire will be the result. The burner should be equipped with air-handling parts that will enable it to mix oil and air in such a ratio as to provide a 9 to 10 per cent operating CO_2, at least, at all times. A loose coupling will affect fan performance in the same manner as it affects pump performance.

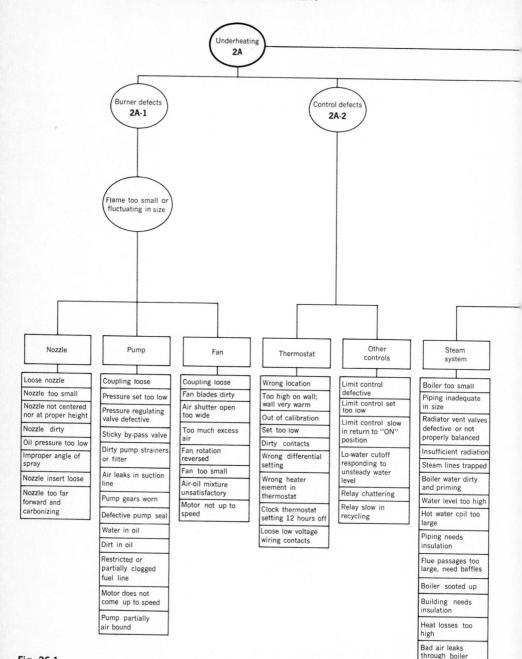

Fig. 36-1

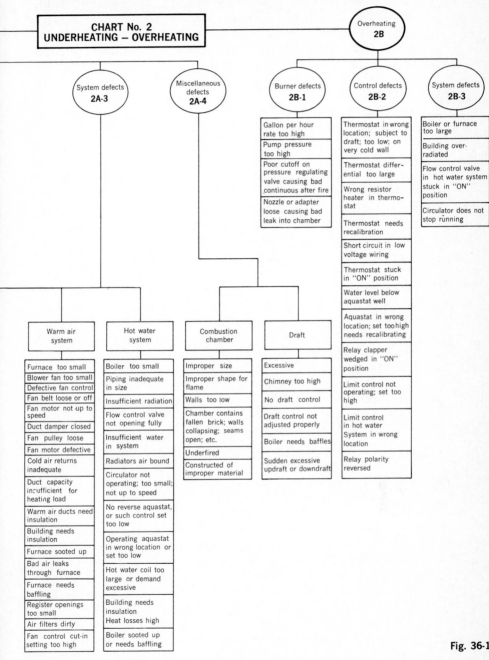

Fig. 36-1

Control defects   In cases of underheating, the key control is the thermostat.   In general it should never be located in the path of warm or cold air currents, adjacent to a window, or on an outside wall exposed to the north winds.   Neither should it be placed on a wall that backs on a kitchen or any really warm surface.   Such a wall (kitchen wall) is usually warm and will thus affect the thermostat.   It should be about $4\frac{1}{2}$ ft from the floor.   Thermostat contacts should be clean but do not use an abrasive substance to effect this.   An ordinary business card furnishes an edge stiff enough to scrape the dirt from the contact points.

Check the thermostat differential setting and see if it is the one recommended by the control manufacturer for that type of system. Increasing the differential setting increases the ON period of this burner.

If there is a complaint that the heat is excessive at night and insufficient in the day, the clock thermostat may be advanced 12 hr, reversing thereby the day and night settings.   Advance it another 12 hr and this situation will be corrected.

If the limit control, because it is defective, returns slowly to the ON position, the house may be cold or inadequately heated.   It may be that the bellows or bourdon tube is defective, or the *control is not level*. The latter is extremely important in controls that employ mercury-tube-type switches.

In a domestic installation, the limit control on a steam system can be set for 5 psi with a differential of at least 3 psi.

An unsteady water line will constantly disturb the float of the low-water-cutoff and thus cause the burner to jump on and off.   Such intermittent operation will result in an inadequate supply of heat.   Use a good boiler cleaning compound to obtain a steady water line.

Loose low-voltage wiring or reversed polarity will result in relay chattering that can remotely affect the heat supply.   A relay that is slow in recycling because of a defective helix can delay the burner in coming back on in response to thermostat demands, and a lag will result that can drop the house temperatures below the comfort point.

System defects   Whenever there are constant, chronic complaints that a system is not doing its job and the service mechanic is unable to remedy the matter, then it is time to check the system and see if the ducts or radiator and furnace or boiler are adequate in size.

Make a complete survey from room to room or in such rooms where the trouble is localized and see if the radiation is sufficient.   If not, add the additional radiation.

The installation of an oil burner cannot work a miracle, and if a system is too small there is little the burner can do to remedy it, regardless of the popular concept that an oil burner greatly increases the capacity of an old system.   Overfiring is no solution to such a problem; it is just an extremely wasteful method of applying heat.

In a steam and hot-water system there should be a balance between the capacity of the system and the hot-water generator. The larger the generator or coil, the greater the demand it makes upon the boiler; and if the heat and hot-water demands are simultaneous, as they usually are in the mornings, then one of the two will suffer. Follow the boiler manufacturer's recommendation as to what size of coil to use.

In a hot-water system, always install a reverse-acting hot-water temperature control to stop the circulator if the boiler water gets too low in temperature. This really gives precedence to the domestic hot water should that demand and the heat demand be made simultaneously.

In a steam boiler the water level should be such that the boiler is two-thirds to three-quarters full, and the boiler water must be clean if sufficient quantities of steam are to be generated at reasonable costs. Knocking in the pipes gives evidence that water is trapped in the lines or the boiler water is dirty. The pipes should be properly pitched to ensure an even flow of the condensate to the boiler.

In a warm-air system, the blower fan is important as it is the agent that delivers the heated medium. The fan blades should be clean, the fan of the proper size and rotating at the proper speed. Check the fan belt, pulley, and motor to ensure the speed factor being normal.

The fan control cut-in point should not be so high as to cause too great a time lag before the heat reaches the rooms. If this lag is too great, excessive cooling and the complaint of insufficient heat will occur.

Dirty air filters will result in an inadequate volume of heated air reaching the rooms, as will insufficiently sized air ducts.

The furnace should not run an excessive stack temperature if it is a conversion job, and if it does it should be baffled to prevent this heat loss from going up the chimney. The more heat going up the flue, the less there is to do the real job of heating.

A hot-water system has considerable flexibility, inasmuch as any increase in the temperature of the water entering the radiators in effect increases the size of the radiators. This should be taken advantage of in cases where the heat falls short of demands by raising the setting of the operating hot-water temperature control.

Check the flow-control valve to be sure that it opens fully. Foreign matter may prevent this valve from opening, and a strainer should always precede it. Its failure to open fully will radically cut down the amount of water flowing through the radiators. Radiators should be vented, as an air-bound radiator in a hot-water system will not heat properly. The consumer should be taught to vent these himself.

The circulator must be operating and up to speed to get adequate quantities of heat, and a reverse-acting control should be installed to prevent the circulator from pumping cool or lukewarm water through the system. This reverse control will help ensure an adequate supply of domestic hot water as mentioned previously.

The operating control should be set in the boiler about halfway down where it can receive the benefits of unobstructed convected circulation of the hot water.

Whether the system be steam, hot water, or warm air, the flue passages of the boiler or the surface of the furnace should be clean and not covered with soot. This is to ensure that the full supply of heat is transferred to the boiler or furnace and not to the chimney. Baffle the furnace and boiler whenever stack temperatures get up to or over 600°F.

Miscellaneous defects—combustion chambers and draft Although the bearing that combustion chambers or draft conditions may have on insufficient-heating complaints may be somewhat remote, nevertheless they are important. Both contribute heavily to successful operating efficiencies.

The combustion chamber should be of adequate size and design (see Chaps. 9 and 10) so that the maximum rate and quantity of heat transfer can be accomplished. It should be in good condition, free from obstructions, properly corbeled, constructed of the proper refractory material, and fired at the proper rate.

Draft should be adequate and not excessive (see Chap. 22). A draft control should be on every installation to take care of fluctuations and prevent them from being passed on to the fire. In the event of excessive draft besides the draft control, baffling the boiler or furnace will aid considerably. Sudden excessive updrafts or downdrafts may extinguish the fire. This condition can cause insufficient heating.

Circle 2B: Overheating The number of complaints that result from *overheating* are much less in volume than with *underheating*. The average homeowner when he finds his house overheated will lower the thermostat, shut off a radiator, or even open a window. As a result, *overheating* has to be consistent and fairly high to elicit a complaint.

The numbers of causes of *overheating* are not as many as with *underheating* and center mainly in control or electrical difficulties. The defects causing this condition can be narrowed down to the burner, the controls, or the system.

The burner defects that cause overheating are few in number and concern themselves with excess quantities of oil being burned or the burning continuing after the demand for heat has been satisfied. Excess quantities of oil will be burned and can furnish too much heat if the gph rate is too high, although this usually will result in high stack temperatures.

Any condition that will cause a considerable leakage of oil into the chamber after the burner has gone off causes a continued application of heat to the boiler and a rise in temperature. Bad, continuous afterfires caused by a poor cutoff on the part of the pressure regulating valve can result in this as can a bad leak due to a loose nozzle or leaking nozzle adaptor.

Operating with excessively high pump pressures remotely can cause a condition of overheating, as it increases the gph rate. This, however, would be a rare case and more likely to be felt in a warm-air system than with steam or hot water.

Control defects This once again centers on the thermostat. It should be about $4\frac{1}{2}$ ft from the floor, not on an excessively cold outside wall struck by north winds or close to a window or in a draft.

A large or wide differential setting will result in longer ON periods and can result in overheating. In such instances lower the differential.

The wrong type of resistor heater in a thermostat, or a damaged one, can result in the failure of it to accelerate the shutdown and an undesired rise in temperature will occur. Replace the heater.

A short circuit in the low-voltage wiring will keep the burner running constantly with only the limit control operating it. Such a condition will result in excessively high temperatures. A thermostat or operating control stuck in the ON position, as well as a relay clapper wedge in the contact-making position, can cause the same thing.

The water-temperature control must be below the water line so that the boiler water circulates freely over it and must be set at a temperature that is reasonable (below $200°F$) if it is not to furnish heat in a steam system. Both the water-temperature control and the thermostat must be in calibration. Follow the control manufacturer's specifications on this.

Limit controls should be properly calibrated, not set too high and with adequate differential (see note on Circle 2A-2). In a hot-water system the limit control must not be in a "trapped" or wrong location. It should be at the top of the boiler and in a spot that provides free circulation of the water over the element.

If the burner furnishes a good ground and the polarities of the No. 1 and No. 2 terminals on the relay are reversed, the burner may run continuously. Reverse the wiring and restore the proper polarity.

The system defects that cause overheating are few. The boiler or furnace should not be oversized and thus overfired and deliver too great a capacity. The building should not be overradiated as this causes continuous "overshooting" after the burner has gone off owing to the large amount of radiation still furnishing heat.

In a hot-water system, the circulator may be operating continuously due to some wiring defect, or the flow-control valve may be stuck in the "open" position, causing continuous gravitational circulation that will furnish additional heat when not wanted.

The next chapter will contain the final service chart, Fig. 37-1, and deal with faulty or defective burner operation as reflected by soot, smoke, noise, odor, puffbacks, high oil consumption, and inadequate domestic hot-water supply.

QUESTIONS

1. What are the four basic, general defects that cause underheating?
2. What are the three basic, general defects that cause overheating?
3. Explain each of the control defects that might cause underheating.
4. Explain each of the control defects that might cause overheating.
5. What are the defects in a steam system that could cause underheating? In a hot-water system? In a warm-air system?
6. Why is it sometimes necessary to make a heat-loss survey when a condition of underheating exists?

CHAPTER 37

BASIC OIL-BURNER
SERVICE METHODS:
DEFECTIVE BURNER OPERATION

The third and last general group into which all service calls can be divided is that of defective operation. In this case the heating system is usually doing its job of furnishing the proper quantity of heat, but in so doing is performing in a manner that shows it to be defective. This results in what is popularly termed "nuisance" calls. These nuisance calls can be generally grouped into three main types: *smoke, odor,* and *noise;* and three subsidiary types: *puffback, high oil consumption,* and *insufficient domestic hot water.*

An interesting thing about "defective operation" calls is their multiplicity of causes and in many cases the apparent slightness of the cause. "No heat" calls result from a definite defect usually of some gravity, but in "defective operation" calls any minute misadjustment can cause the trouble.

Oil-burning equipment is more susceptible to nuisance calls if not properly installed, as the opportunity for small misadjustments or poor operating conditions increases proportionately. A well-installed job, properly sized, with an efficient burner and good draft is not susceptible to many nuisance defects.

Observing Fig. 37-1 we can see that the first manifestation, and one of the most important, of *faulty operation* is soot and smoke, the causes of which are shown in Circle 3A.

Circle 3A: Smoke and Soot The prime cause of smoke and soot in oil-burner operation comes back to the basic mixing of oil and air by the burner. The delivery of air by the fan is not enough. The burner blast tube must contain devices that will give spin and direction to the air.

Within the blast tube itself some type of diffuser or bladed spinner should be inserted. This will impart some spinning or rotary motion to the air as it moves through the gun. At the end of the tube a cone or choke with spiraled blades should pick up this partially spinning air and increase its rotary motion.

The cone on the front of the blast tube should decrease the size of the tube opening, thereby increasing the velocity of the spinning air as it leaves the burner. The inner diffuser or bladed air spinner should be as close to the cone at the front of the burner as possible so that the turbulence it creates is not lost through the gun before it reaches the outer cone. Thus the air when it leaves the burner will have velocity and direction and upon meeting the oil will create a turbulent area in the chamber wherein the oil and air mix.

Without this turbulence, the oil and air *cannot mix properly* and a smoking fire is the likely result. The less turbulence we have, the more air will escape the oil completely and the greater will be the excess amount that will have to be furnished to achieve the proper oil-air ratio. This will lower the CO_2 reading and operating efficiency even if it does eliminate the smoking.

Conversely, if there is not enough air, the burner will smoke. The lack of air can be the result of a dirty fan, a fan that is too small, or an air shutter that is not open wide enough. Theoretically about 1,500 cu ft of air is needed per gallon of oil, but the average burner furnishes 25 to 40 per cent in excess of this theoretical requirement because of the losses due to the mechanical difficulties of mixing.

The oil also has a great bearing on the smoke and soot problem. If the grade of oil is too heavy or the atomizing pressure too low, smoking and deposits of soot on the boiler passages will occur.

Any accumulation of soot is evidence of an aggravation of the smoke condition. It is an indication that something is wrong. Cleaning the boiler or chimney every time it occurs (if it occurs frequently) is not enough. The cause of the trouble should be ascertained and corrected. It is not proper or normal for an oil burner to soot up a boiler continually.

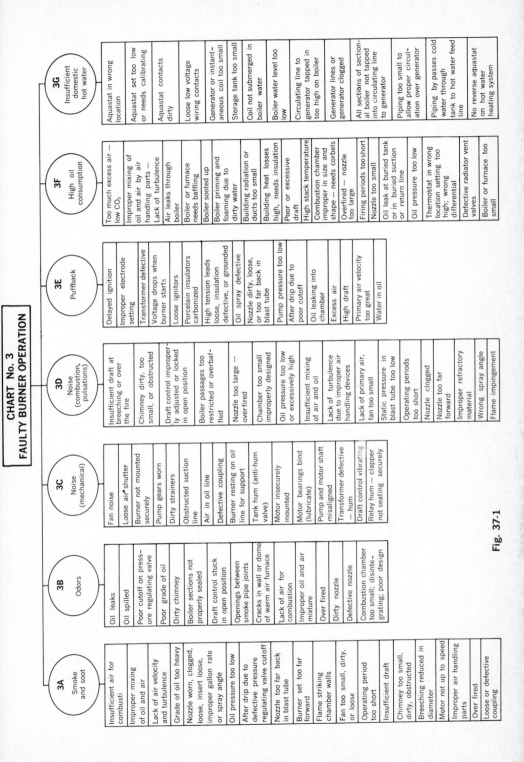

Fig. 37-1

The nozzle itself may be a cause of the smoke or soot. If too large in size or if the chamber is too small, impingement of the fire or oil on the sides of the chamber will occur. This causes smoke and soot deposits. A worn nozzle, clogged nozzle, loose nozzle, or an improper angle of spray can all cause the same trouble. *Nozzles should be changed* according to the number of hours of operation per heating season.

In the event of any oil leak into the chamber, whether due to an afterdrip or loose nozzle, it will cause smoking after the burner has gone off. The oil dripping into the hot chamber will burn in an oxygen-starved atmosphere, and as a result combustion will be incomplete and carbon will deposit as soot or pass off as smoke.

Any defective draft condition can cause smoking if it results in a lack of draft over the fire. There should always be 0.01 in. of draft over the fire or smoking will ensue if atmospheric or other conditions cause a reduction in draft at the breeching. Causes of reduced draft can be a chimney that is dirty or too small, a draft control improperly adjusted or locked in the open position, breeching between boiler and chimney too small in diameter, and boiler passages too restricted or too well baffled.

Remote causes of smoke and soot can be a loose coupling or motor not up to speed, in which case the pump speed would be reduced, resulting in lower pressures, coarser atomization, and incomplete combustion, occasioning thereby the smoke or soot.

Circle 3B: Odors   Odors can be easily divided into two groups: (1) oil odors and (2) combustion odors. Oil odors result from leaks in the line from which oil escapes and vaporizes, or from careless delivery of oil whereby oil is spilled. The fittings on the oil line should be *felt* occasionally to see if they are *sweating* oil. With flare and compression fittings, expansion and contraction of joints (not properly tightened) resulting from sharp changes in temperature may cause these slight leaks. They are noticed by a slight wetness at the flare nut. These tiny leaks may be the cause of oil odor.

The *causes* of combustion odors are the same as those of smoke and soot. The odor is evidence that the smoke is escaping into the basement or through the house.

The sections of the boiler should be *properly sealed with a good grade of furnace cement.* From time to time the *jacket should be removed* and the *sections checked* to make certain that the furnace cement has not dried out and fallen from between the sections. Such open spaces not only let fumes out into the house, but allow excess air into the boiler, thus raising the stack temperature and lowering the operating efficiency.

With an old warm-air furnace converted to oil, there may be cracks in the dome which should be sealed. A *periodic inspection* should be made in this case as with the previous case of the boiler sections.

Any opening in the joints of the smoke pipe or an improperly sealed junction of the same with the chimney wall will allow fumes to escape into the cellar. The same can occur with a draft control locked in the open position.

If complaints concerning odor show up on damp or humid days when atmospheric conditions result in reduced draft, it shows that there is a leak of the combustion gases into the house. The pressure created because of the insufficient draft is forcing the fumes through some crack or opening in the system. This leak should be found and sealed.

It should be remembered that the door is usually the indication of *poor combustion,* and smoking and sooting have progressed to some degree before this condition is so aggravated as to result in penetrating the house. Do not treat *odor complaints* lightly, for if they do not result from oil leaks then their causes are the same as smoke and soot complaints and are of a serious nature.

Circle 3C: Mechanical Noises Mechanical noises are not usually indicative of serious trouble and are easily located and remedied. Groaning or grunting noises in the pump are occasioned when it strains to pull oil through clogged strainers or an obstructed suction line. Vibration from the pump will sometimes pass along through the oil line where it will be amplified into a tank hum.

In such case, install an antihum valve or leave several loops (pigtail) of tubing from the pump connection to the suction line. The pigtail, not being rigid, absorbs the vibration instead of passing it on to the suction line and thence to the tank, where it is magnified. Avoid letting the burner rest on the oil line for support.

A knocking noise in the housing shows that the fan is loose. This noise, though harmless, is usually quite loud and insistent and frightens the homeowner considerably.

Check to see that the motor is securely mounted to the frame and that there is no misalignment between pump and motor shaft—a tolerance of 0.005 in. is all that is allowed. Any greater misalignment can result in noisy operation of the pump or motor, or both, and eventually will ruin the pump.

A hum in the relay usually is caused by either the low-voltage transformer, in which case there is no remedy but changing the relay, or by the clapper failing to seat securely. This can be caused by a low-voltage drop due to a partial short circuit, a defective relay coil, dirty relay contacts or thermostat contacts. Check the wiring terminals (low voltage) at the relay to see if the connections are secure.

A hum in the ignition transformer is an indication that its life is drawing to a close and that one of the secondary coils is defective. The only remedy is to *replace the transformer.*

Circle 3D: Combustion Noises   Combustion noises are usually known as *vibrations* or *pulsations* and are of three types: (1) the *starting* pulsation, where the rumble or vibration occurs only when the burner starts; (2) the *running* pulsation, where the rumble continues throughout the entire firing cycle; and (3) the *closing* pulsation, wherein the rumble occurs as the burner cuts off.

The over-all causes of *pulsations* are, to all extents and purposes, the same as those of *smoke, soot,* and *odor.*   Any adjustment that will tend to correct a smoke or odor condition will reduce the accompanying pulsation.   The pulsation is the registering of the combustion trouble on the sound level and is actually caused by fluctuations in the size, place, and shape of the flame.

The *starting* pulsation is primarily caused by poor draft and insufficient initial air volume.   Once the fan is up to speed and the volume of gases is heated and proceeds to rise, causing thermal draft, the pulsation ceases.

This demonstrates that the normal draft through the boiler is insufficient at the start even with the help of the fan, and pressures build up over the fire, altering its size and shape.   Once thermal draft conditions are established, the pulsation ceases.

This condition can be helped by building chambers of proper design, shape, and material and installing a draft control or increasing the draft at the breeching.

Running pulsations are a more serious condition, for they demonstrate that all through the entire firing cycle combustion is improper, incomplete, and inefficient.   Draft is the great requisite here.   Unless there is a constant low-pressure area over the fire all through the operating period (provided that the fire is efficient), there will be trouble with pulsations regardless of what efforts are made to increase the efficiency of the oil-air mixture.

Many boilers aggravate this condition because they are so restricted. They start out with excellent draft at the breeching, but by the time the firebox is reached, the draft is lost and there is a positive pressure over the fire.   In such a case as this, the baffles should be permanently removed from the boiler.

In checking the cause of pulsations under Circle 3D, it can be seen that the air-oil mixture follows draft in importance in preventing this condition.   These air-oil mixture conditions that cause pulsations follow those of Circle 3A closely.   This shows that the *pulsation problem* is an extension of the smoke and soot problem; any condition that can cause smoke and soot, left alone long enough, will cause a running pulsation.

The *closing* pulsation results from a condition called "poor cutoff," in which case the oil supply diminishes gradually, or in jerks, rather than instantaneously as the burner comes to a stop.

Once the oil pressure has dropped to about 70 psi, as the burner is stopping, no more oil should get through to the nozzle. Pressure below this point is insufficient to atomize the oil properly for combustion.

If the pressure regulating valve does not cut off instantaneously as it should, but instead closes sluggishly or in jerks, the resulting fluctuation in flame size as it diminishes and expands and diminishes again causes a vibration that lasts a few seconds—the closing pulsation. A new pressure regulating valve should be installed.

The installation of a *solenoid valve* will further eliminate this afterfire condition by providing a good, sharp, clean, instantaneous cutoff.

Much of the pulsation problem could be cleared up completely if initial draft conditions were checked and proper-sized fireboxes of insulating firebrick were used.

Circle 3E: The Puffback   The term "puffback" has been in use now for many years to describe a condition that is more or less of an explosion of varying degrees of intensity. Of all the conditions that the oil-burner maintenance mechanic can run into, the puffback is the one that can be most dangerous to the homeowner.

Essentially the puffback results from the oil vapor not igniting instantaneously as it leaves the nozzle when the burner starts. Once the pressure regulating valve has opened, the oil issues in a fine, highly inflammable spray from the nozzle in considerable volume. The ignition, of course, should be on at this time with the spark, but not the electrodes, directly in the path of the spray.

Any delay for any reason whatsoever in the igniting of this oil vapor results in a considerable volume of it collecting in the chamber and throughout the boiler passages. This, as can be seen, is highly dangerous. The greater the time delay in igniting the oil, the greater the danger, for the larger will be the amount of vapor that bursts into flame. *Delayed ignition*, therefore, is the basic cause of puffbacks; and the longer the delay, the greater the puff.

The *causes of delayed ignition* are several. The electrodes should be set according to the burner manufacturer's specifications. These specifications will provide for the electrodes themselves to be in back of the oil spray and the air from the fan will distort the spark so that it is in the path of the oil vapor. The improper setting of electrodes, loose electrodes, electrodes shorting off on adjacent metal surfaces all can cause the puff by delaying ignition. In such case, the chamber fills with oil vapors and these fumes work their way back eventually to the spark.

The electrodes should be firmly clamped and adjusted in place in the holder provided, so that they cannot be forced out of setting by any vibration resulting from the operation of the burner.

The ceramic insulators that hold the electrodes in place and insulate them from the metal holder are porous. With dirty, sooty operation, they become coated with soft carbon and are changed into conductors themselves, thereby shorting out the electrodes. The ignition spark, when this occurs, is far back in the blast tube; and if the relay does not go into safety in time, the fumes may work back and a *serious puff* occur. This carbon on the ceramic insulators can be burnt off by the spark and they may then suddenly assume their normal function. The spark then will appear on the electrodes and cause a puff.

Intermittent puffbacks occurring, and everything appearing normal when the mechanic arrives, may be caused by this intermittent carbonizing of the porcelain insulators. By the time the serviceman arrives, everything appears all right and there are no symptoms of displaced ignition. In time the insulators will carbonize again and the puffback will repeat. If there is any suspicion, however remote, that the insulators are not performing their job, *replace them.*

Occasionally a motor that draws too great a starting load of current will leave the transformer with a weak spark or practically none at all. If the transformer tests normal by itself but gives a weak spark with the motor running, this may be the cause of the trouble. Check the starting input load of current to the motor in amperes and see if it is excessive when compared with the motor manufacturer's specifications.

The position of the nozzle is also important in preventing puffbacks. The oil spray should be directed straight into the chamber. Any tilt or deflection of the nozzle may cause the spray to miss the spark initially and later cause a puff. Low oil pressure also may result in the fire coming on late with a sudden burst.

Excess air and high draft may move the oil spray so quickly that it cannot reach its kindling temperature. A dense white cloud of vapor on starting shows this to be occurring. Close the air shutter in such case and reduce the draft so that normal ignition may be attained.

Oil leaking into a hot chamber after the burner has gone off will instantly vaporize and flash into flame. The greater the quantity of the leak, the more intense the puff will be. This can be caused by a loose nozzle, a loose nozzle insert, a loose nozzle adaptor, or any loose oil-line fitting within the blast tube. A poor pressure regulating valve cutoff can also cause this condition.

Any quantity of water in the oil can do the same thing. The sudden passage of water through the nozzle extinguishes the flame and the chamber is red hot. As the oil replaces the water, the vapor ignites off the sides of the hot chamber and a slight or intense puff occurs, depending on how much oil has found its way into the hot firebox.

Circle 3F: High Oil Consumption   High oil consumption is a common complaint, especially during the winter season.   The validity of the complaint is easily ascertained by taking a CO_2 reading and stack temperature reading.   The CO_2 should be at least 10 per cent and the stack temperature not over 550°F if it is an oil-burning boiler.   If it is a conversion job, the CO_2 should not be below 9 per cent and a stack temperature of 700°F would be excessive.

The common cause of low CO_2 and high stack temperature, which means inefficient operation and high oil bills, is excess air.   Seal up all air leaks, see that the burner has proper air-handling parts, clean and baffle the boiler or furnace, properly design and install the correctly sized chamber of insulating firebrick, and *oil bills will take a decided drop.*

One of the little-suspected but nevertheless important causes of high oil consumption is the *condition of the boiler water.*   Boiler water that is dirty, containing oil or grease or other impurities, will not steam freely.   Instead it will throw slugs of water up with the steam or not make any steam at all, producing a foam on top of the water.   These conditions are *surging* and *priming,* respectively.

The water in the gauge glass should not fluctuate much over half an inch, and if it does there is an indication that priming and surging are occurring.   This means high oil bills, because considerably less steam is obtained per gallon of oil.   In such case a *good boiler cleaning compound* should be used and the directions followed.

If combustion is good, the boiler is steaming freely, and oil consumption is still high, then check the size of the boiler, furnace, radiators, or ducts; the job may be short radiation or the boiler or furnace may be too small.

Improper location of the thermostat is a common cause of high oil consumption.   If it is on a cold wall, in a cold draft, out of calibration, set too far down on the wall, or maintained at too high a setting (over 72°F), excessive oil will be consumed.

Poor or defective vent valves will prevent the air from purging from the radiators and the heat will be insufficient; longer periods of operation consuming more oil will be necessary.

Check building construction.   Insulation may be necessary because of severe exposure or high heat losses.

Check the nozzle.   A nozzle too small will result in longer operating periods and more oil consumed.   A smaller nozzle does not necessarily mean a saving.   A nozzle that is too large will result in high stack temperatures and consequent waste of oil.

If all the foregoing conditions are fulfilled and high oil consumption continues, then check for oil leaks.   This is especially important with underground tanks where leaks can continue unsuspected over long periods of time.

Circle 3G: Insufficient Domestic Hot Water   This complaint arises in the summertime primarily.   During the winter the homeowner has been getting larger quantities of hot water due to the higher temperature of the boiler water.   With a tankless coil, the mixing valve is open during the winter to bypass some cold water into the excessively hot domestic supply.

When the heat is off and control of the burner returned to the aquastat, this open mixing valve is now a liability, cooling the water too much.   The customer should be trained to *adjust the mixing valve on a tankless coil himself.*

If the hot-water temperature control is installed too high up on the boiler, or in a trapped location where there is no free circulation over it, an insufficient supply of hot water will result.   This will result, too, if the hot-water temperature control setting is too low, if it is out of calibration, or if its contacts are defective or dirty.

The generator may be dirty or the lines circulating to it partially clogged.   All sections of a cast-iron sectional boiler should be tapped into the circulating line to the generator to provide an adequate supply in sufficient quantity of heat-bearing generator water.

Check the size of the tank and coil to be sure they are adequate in size for the quantity of water demanded.

If hot water is difficult to obtain in a hot water heating system when the circulator is running, *install a reverse-acting hot-water temperature control.*   This will shut off the circulator when the hot water is being used in quantity and give definite precedence to the domestic hot-water demand over the heat demand.

Be sure at all times that the boiler water level is high enough to cover the hot-water generator or the instantaneous coil.

QUESTIONS

1. What is the basic cause of the formation of smoke and soot?
2. How can defective nozzles cause smoking?
3. Give 10 causes of combustion noises.
4. Give 15 causes for puffbacks.
5. Give 10 causes for an insufficient supply of domestic hot water.
6. What does a dense white cloud of vapor signify on starting?
7. What happens when an "afterdrip" occurs?
8. What is the purpose of the mixing valve?
9. What is the advantage of installing a reverse-acting hot-water temperature control?
10. If the vent valves on a radiator are defective, what will occur?
11. Give five causes of mechanical noises during the operation of the oil burner.
12. What are the causes of delayed ignition?

INDEX